HIKING THE PACIFIC CREST TRAIL

WASHINGTON

HIKING THE PACIFIC CREST TRAIL

WASHINGTON

SECTION HIKING FROM THE COLUMBIA RIVER TO MANNING PARK

TAMI ASARS

MOUNTAINEERS
BOOKS

Mountaineers Books is the publishing division of The Mountaineers, an organization founded in 1906 and dedicated to the exploration, preservation, and enjoyment of outdoor and wilderness areas.

1001 SW Klickitat Way, Suite 201, Seattle, WA 98134

800.553.4453, www.mountaineersbooks.org

Printed in China

Distributed in the United Kingdom by Cordee, www.cordee.co.uk

First edition: first printing 2016, second printing 2018

Copyeditor: Julie Van Pelt
Design and layout: Peggy Egerdahl
Cartographer: Pease Press
All photos by the author unless otherwise noted

Cover photograph: *The PCT near White Pass, Glacier Peak Wilderness (section 6)*
Frontispiece: *The PCT meanders through green, restful valleys near Chinook Pass, the boundary between sections 3 and 4.*

The background of the leg maps for this book were produced using the online map viewer CalTopo. For more information, visit caltopo.com.

Library of Congress Cataloging-in-Publication Data

Names: Asars, Tami, author.
Title: Hiking the Pacific Crest Trail, Washington : section hiking from the Columbia River to Manning Park / Tami Asars.
Description: Seattle, WA : Mountaineers Books, [2016] | Includes bibliographical references and index.
Identifiers: LCCN 2015051029 (print) | LCCN 2016024401 (ebook) | ISBN 9781594858741 (pbk.) | ISBN 9781594858758 (ebook)
Subjects: LCSH: Hiking—Washington—Guidebooks. | Hiking—Pacific Crest Trail—Guidebooks. | Washington—Guidebooks. | Pacific Crest Trail—Guidebooks.
Classification: LCC GV199.42.W2 P343 2016 (print) | LCC GV199.42.W2 (ebook) | DDC 796.5109797—dc23
LC record available at https://lccn.loc.gov/2015051029

A NOTE ABOUT SAFETY: Safety is an important concern in all outdoor activities. No guidebook can alert you to every hazard or anticipate the limitations of every reader. Therefore, the descriptions of roads, trails, routes, and natural features in this book are not representations that a particular place or excursion will be safe for your party. When you follow any of the routes described in this book, you assume responsibility for your own safety. Under normal conditions, such excursions require the usual attention to traffic, road and trail conditions, weather, terrain, the capabilities of your party, and other factors. Always check for current conditions, obey posted private property signs, and avoid confrontations with property owners or managers. Keeping informed on current conditions and exercising common sense are the keys to a safe, enjoyable outing. —*Mountaineers Books*

ISBN (paperback): 978-1-59485-874-1
ISBN (ebook): 978-1-59485-875-8

CONTENTS

The tranquil shores of Mig Lake (section 5) beckon PCT hikers to stop for a snapshot or perhaps the night.

ACKNOWLEDGMENTS

THERE ARE TIMES when the words "thank you" seem trivial compared with the gratitude one feels. I can't begin to express how thankful I am for all who helped me with countless data, various information, and resilient emotional support when I wanted to, occasionally, beat my head on my desk. From my endless phone calls to patient Forest Service and Park Service personnel, to my whining to friends and family when the task seemed overwhelming, the support of friends and colleagues got me through some challenging moments, and for that I'm tremendously grateful.

Special thanks to my husband, Vilnis, who not only hiked half of the miles for this book with me but also took care of our aging dog as I huffed and puffed up hills one whole summer, solo. For my dream of this book, he hiked nine of thirteen days in pouring rain and managed to smile as he sloshed through muddy trails and crossed rushing creeks. He was my rock, the center of my storm, and the ever-present voice of reason as I navigated the hinterlands and subsequently penned what I'd seen.

I'd also like to acknowledge the love and loyalty of my precious dog, Summit. While I was writing this guide, he fell ill and wasn't able to hike with me, yet when he saw me again, after time on the trail, he ran as fast as he could to greet me, in his doggie wheelchair with his ears back. It's that kind of love that made my heart swell and words flow freely for this guide. Rest in peace, Sweet Boy.

To my mom, Joani, and Uncle Randy, I can't thank you enough for your support as Trail Angels as I cruised over large stretches of the PCT. Seeing both of you waiting at a Forest Service road with resupplies, fried chicken, fizzy drinks, and a hug despite my sweaty shirt meant more than you'll ever know. You helped lighten my load both physically and metaphorically. To my extended family and friends who have become family, you too mean the world to me and I appreciate your shared excitement, enthusiasm, and support as I marinated in backcountry magic and lived my dreams.

To Lisa Petersen, thank you for being patient as I pointed my camera at you again and again!

Kate Rogers, Laura Shauger, Emily White, and so many others at Mountaineers Books, thank you for laughing with me at my verbose manuscripts, silly idioms, and wordy details. You guys are great!

I would be remiss not to thank Eli Boschetto, my partner on the Oregon section of this guidebook series. The time we spent brainstorming, venting, and hobnobbing brought life to this series. You believed in me from the start, and for that I'll always be grateful. To Philip Kramer and Shawnté Salabert, it has been an absolute pleasure working with you and collaborating on the dream.

Special thanks to Barry Danton, Canada Border Service Agent; Julie Rodriguez, Forest Service Administrator, Gifford Pinchot National Forest, Mount Adams Ranger District; Andrea Durham, Wilderness, Trails, and Developed Recreation Ranger, Gifford Pinchot National Forest, Cowlitz Valley Ranger District; Laurie Dowie, Special Uses, Mineral, and Wilderness Ranger, Okanogan-Wenatchee National Forest; and Douglas Anderson, Trout Lake Trail Angel Extraordinaire. You have all been patient enough to help with questions and ensure that the PCT is preserved for years to come.

Last but not least, thank you, readers. If you're reading this guide, you're likely looking for a place to rest your soul in the backcountry and have turned your eyes to these pages. Thank you for seeking solitude through the purity of trails and paths that lead to unfathomable beauty. It is in these places that we grow stronger, both emotionally and physically, and find the quietness we seek with each twist and turn. May all of your journeys be adventurous and safe. See you on the trail!

Opposite: *A hiker enjoys the ambiance near Cispus Basin (section 2).*

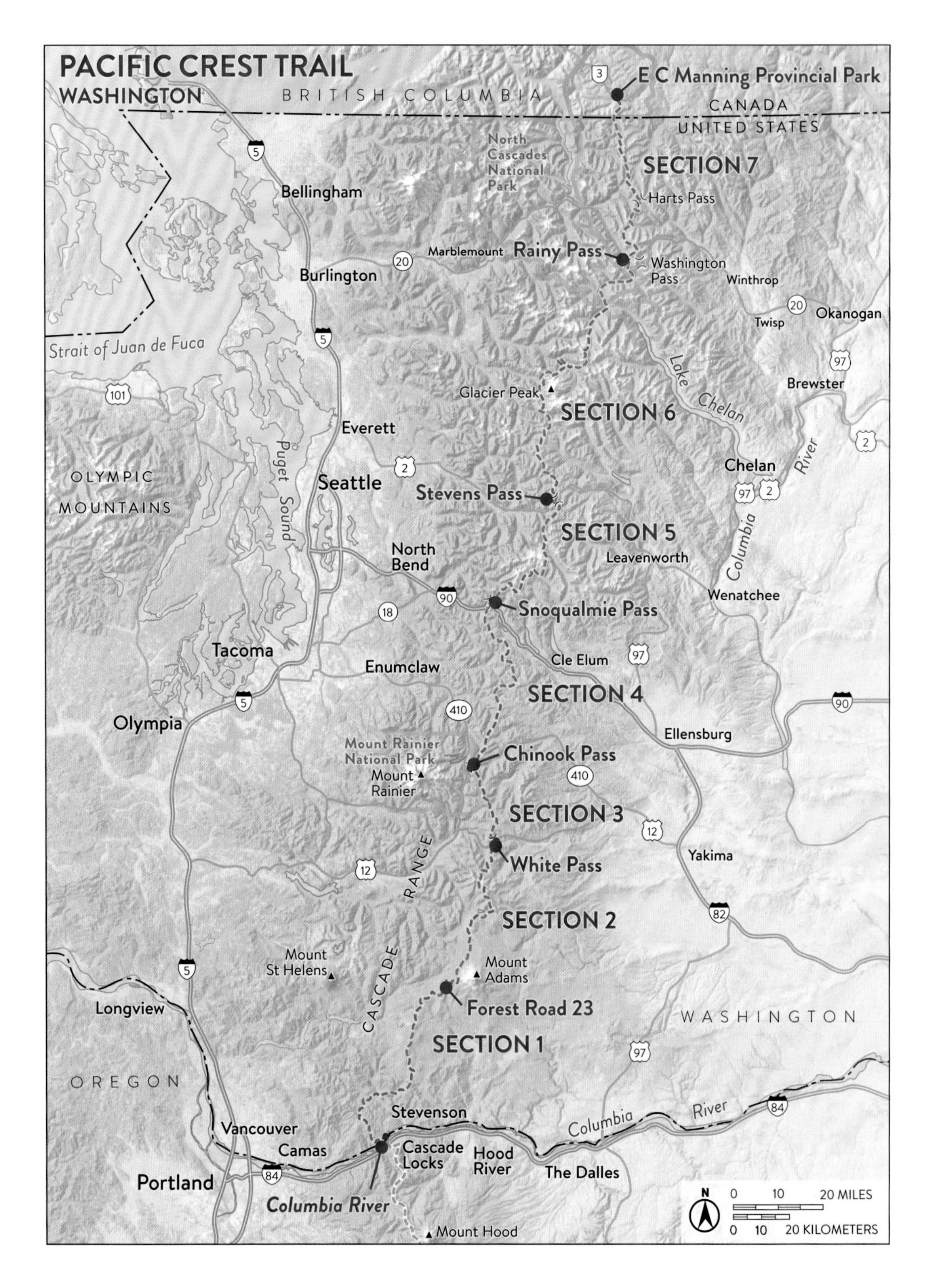
PACIFIC CREST TRAIL
WASHINGTON
BRITISH COLUMBIA
E C Manning Provincial Park
CANADA
UNITED STATES
North Cascades National Park
SECTION 7
Harts Pass
Bellingham
Marblemount
Rainy Pass
Washington Pass
Winthrop
Burlington
Twisp
Okanogan
Strait of Juan de Fuca
Lake Chelan
Brewster
Glacier Peak
SECTION 6
Everett
Puget Sound
OLYMPIC MOUNTAINS
Seattle
Stevens Pass
Chelan
Columbia River
SECTION 5
North Bend
Leavenworth
Wenatchee
Snoqualmie Pass
Tacoma
Cle Elum
Enumclaw
SECTION 4
Olympia
Ellensburg
Mount Rainier National Park
Chinook Pass
Mount Rainier
SECTION 3
White Pass
Yakima
CASCADE RANGE
SECTION 2
Mount St Helens
Mount Adams
Longview
Forest Road 23
WASHINGTON
SECTION 1
OREGON
Stevenson
Columbia River
Vancouver
Camas
Cascade Locks
Hood River
The Dalles
Portland
Columbia River
Mount Hood
0 10 20 MILES
0 10 20 KILOMETERS

INTRODUCTION

A PATH OF UNIMAGINABLE adventure, the Pacific Crest National Scenic Trail leads from the beating heart of California's hot southern desert to Washington's high, chilly subalpine and alpine terrain. The PCT, as it's known, is where you make memories, realize your dreams, and find out exactly what you're made of. It's as much a trail for backcountry exploring as it is for learning about yourself. It's a cocktail of annoying foot blisters, barely palatable backpacking meals, sweat, and dirt, served up with a twist of sweet freedom, spectacular crags, grazing wildlife, and powerful rivers.

This guidebook takes you from the Oregon-Washington border all the way to Canada. From quiet forests to the jagged ridgelines of the Goat Rocks Wilderness, Washington has something to entice everyone who steps on the trail. Where else can you marvel at sweeping volcanic views and in the same day drop into deep river valleys with giant mossy trees and raging white water? Washington has some of the best scenery on the entire PCT, all waiting for you to explore. Your next adventure is calling . . . loudly!

A BRIEF HISTORY OF THE PCT

No one knows exactly who first proposed a border-to-border trail through the western coastal states, but history favors a handful of people. Joseph T. Hazard, author and member of the Seattle-area Mountaineers, claimed that Catherine Montgomery, in Bellingham, proposed the idea to him in 1926. Meanwhile, Fredrick W. Cleator, an overseer with the Forest Service, designed the Oregon Skyline Trail in the 1920s, now encompassed by today's PCT. Finally, Clinton C. Clarke, chairman of the Mountain League of Los Angeles, organized the PCT System Conference in 1932 to market the trail idea, earning him the moniker "Father of the PCT."

The PCT System Conference was a group of outdoor clubs and nonprofits led by Clarke and dedicated to creating one trail system made up of new and old trails that would extend from Mexico to Canada, cresting the mountainous states. Clarke inspired and planned the YMCA PCT relays—forty teams of young hikers between the ages of fourteen and eighteen who were the first to scout routes for the trail. In 1935, the teams, under the guidance of an outdoorsman named Warren Rogers, left Campo on the Mexico border and meticulously noted their route and adventures. Each subsequent summer, the teams picked up where they had left off, until they reached what is now Monument 78 on the Canada border on August 5, 1938. Their journey proved that, through combining trails, open country, and existing roads, a person could get from Mexico to Canada along a scenic alpine route. Much of the PCT still follows that same route.

In the 1960s, backpacking and hiking gained popularity, and in early 1965 President Lyndon B. Johnson sent a special message to Congress stressing the importance of environmental conservation and the development and protection of trail systems. Not long after, Secretary of the Interior Stewart L. Udall instructed the Bureau of Outdoor Recreation to head up a nationwide trail study. This study led to the National Trail System Act, enacted by Congress on October 2, 1968. The new law facilitated the development and operation of National Scenic Trails and National Historic Trails. As a result, the Appalachian Trail and the Pacific Crest Trail were the nation's first scenic trails.

In 1970, the Pacific Crest National Scenic Trail Advisory Council was appointed, a mix of local recreationists, ranchers, tribal members, timber and mineral representatives, and members of conservation groups. At the council's second meeting, in 1971, it suggested a "Guide for Location, Design and Management," which was approved and published by the US secretary of agriculture.

In fall, the leaves of vine maples, such as this one near Snoqualmie Pass (the boundary between sections 4 and 5), turn brilliant colors.

This document is still the official management plan used by various agencies. In January 1973, the advisory council, in agreement with the Bureau of Land Management, Forest Service, and other participating agencies, published the official route of the PCT in the *Federal Register*, another big step in creating the trail. In 1988, two monuments were placed at the southern and northern terminuses of the PCT, although the trail wasn't officially complete until 1993. The trail is primarily managed and maintained thanks to the stewardship of volunteers and employees of the Pacific Crest Trail Association (PCTA). Founded in 1977 as the Pacific Crest Trail Conference, the PCTA is a very active nonprofit that coordinates with the Forest Service, private landowners, and other agencies. One of the group's primary goals is to help you, the backpacker, experience the magic of walking this scenic and historic trail.

PCTA: YOU CAN HELP!

The Pacific Crest Trail Association (PCTA) needs you! Volunteers can help with trail repairs, trail widening, drainage improvement, and other projects that keep the PCT passable and hikers safe. Become a member and help with critical trail needs, such as trail maintenance, protection, and promotion, by donating an annual, monthly, or one-time gift. The PCTA website (www.pcta.org) alone is worth a mint in the information it provides.

WASHINGTON'S PCT: AN OVERVIEW

Washington's portion of the PCT kicks off at the Bridge of the Gods that spans the Columbia River, the lowest-elevation point of the entire PCT and the border of Washington and Oregon. From there, the trail wanders amid peaks and valleys, climbing brushy hillsides and crossing healthy creeks, until it arrives at the spectacular Indian Heaven Wilderness, a relatively flat landscape dotted with lakes, meadows, and grazing deer.

Next up is the first of Washington's volcanoes, Mount Adams, with her lupine-covered flanks and behemoth glaciers. The trail ebbs and flows and then encounters the rugged ridgelines and peaks of Goat Rocks Wilderness, left over from an eroded stratovolcano. Wide-open wildflower meadows are everywhere you look, and you'll cross the impressive, picturesque Goat Rocks Spine, or Knife Edge, a narrow, shaley tightrope with 2000-plus-foot drop-offs on either side.

Mount Rainier comes into view as the PCT ducks into the William O. Douglas Wilderness, passing countless lakes before flirting with the outskirts of Mount Rainier National Park. Long stretches over peaks and through basins lead to Snoqualmie Pass at Interstate 90, the artery that leads to the major metropolitan area of Seattle. The next section's convenience and grandeur, from Snoqualmie Pass to Stevens Pass, make it the most popular PCT stretch among locals. Snowy buttes, swift rivers, and 70-plus miles of roadless wildness await!

North of Stevens Pass is Glacier Peak Wilderness, with its vast rugged stretches of trail tracing the perimeter of the mighty volcano. You'll find solitude and remoteness along with cheery, rainbow-colored wildflower fields and plenty of buzzing, hopping insects. The PCT then drops into the Suiattle River valley, climbing next to the eastern side of the Cascade Crest, a transition zone introducing new foliage such as ponderosa pine.

Lake Chelan National Recreation Area and North Cascades National Park show up just before you arrive at Stehekin Valley Road, at the north end of fjord-like Lake Chelan. A detour via shuttle bus to the tiny town of Stehekin allows you to pick up your cache at the post office, visit a bakery, or take a night off at one of several lodging options. Just beyond Stehekin, North Cascades National Park continues, where you'll need a permit for overnight stays. The trail reenters Forest Service land just before Rainy Pass and you're once again free to camp without prearranged paperwork.

From Rainy Pass, the PCT climbs to lofty Cutthroat Pass before traversing rocky mountain shoulders that overlook countless unnamed peaks. The elevation makes this stretch the perfect habitat for western larches, deciduous conifers whose leaves change to brilliant yellow in autumn. After the mountainous traverse, the trail drops into the forest before climbing back into the high country and cresting the saddle of Grasshopper Pass. Not far beyond is Harts Pass, a car-camping area frequently used by PCT hikers for staging. The last stretch into the Pasayten Wilderness and to the Canada border passes over the highest point of the PCT in Washington, at roughly 7100 feet near Lakeview Ridge. Once you reach the PCT's northern terminus at the border, at Monument 78, a little more than 8 miles of Canada trails take you to civilization, where a warm shower and real food await!

STATE MILEAGE AND ELEVATION GAIN AND LOSS

The PCT's total mileage in Washington (along with the final stretch in British Columbia) is 511.8 miles, give or take a few side trips or camp spur trails. Add a total elevation gain of 111,000 feet and a loss of 107,450 feet (rounded to the nearest 10), and Washington's PCT makes for a superb fitness challenge.

HOW TO USE THIS GUIDE

This guidebook is designed for those of us who, between work commitments and life's nutty schedules, hike sections of the PCT when we can, starting and ending at logical points. To that end, this book organizes the Washington PCT into seven sections, south to north, that range from about 30 to 125 miles each, so that a section is hikable within a vacation time frame, whether you have a few days or a few weeks. Each section consists of several shorter legs that

PCTA SECTION LETTER AND MILEAGE

The PCTA uses a widely recognized lettering system to identify PCT sections from the Mexico to Canada borders. This guidebook, aimed at section hikers, breaks the trail into manageable chunks and therefore doesn't link up exactly with the PCTA letters. But each section does include the corresponding PCTA letter for your reference.

The PCTA also counts overall PCT mileage from mile 0 at the Mexico border to mile 2668.98 at the Canada border. For hikers who are interested in such figures, or who are tackling multiple sections all at once, this guide gives cumulative *state* mileage for each section, starting from mile 0 at the Oregon-Washington border.

go from landmark to landmark. A leg doesn't necessarily have to be a full day on the trail; rather, the legs can help you plan your perfect itinerary.

Washington's PCT Sections

Each of the state's seven sections begins with trail facts. The **distance** is the overall mileage for that section, calculated using a GPS unit as I hiked the trail and later correlated with paper maps and mapping software. **State distance** tells you how far along the Washington PCT you've gone. **Elevation gain/loss** tallies the cumulative ups and downs over a section (rounded to the nearest 10 feet), so you'll know when you'll need to give your knees and your ticker a pep talk. Next comes the section's **high point** and **best time of year** to hike that particular span—in general, higher-elevation sections have a shorter optimal hiking season, opening up later in summer and getting first snowfall earlier in autumn. To help with your trip planning, each section also notes the corresponding **PCTA section letter**, as well as the **land managers** for the lands you'll be passing through and any **passes and permits** required. You'll find contact information for all agencies in the **appendixes** at the end of the book. Before you head out, always check with the relevant land managers to get the latest on trail conditions, bridge washouts, forest fires, detours, possible trailhead crime, and much

MAP SYMBOLS

Featured PCT leg or segment
Alternate PCT route
Adjacent PCT leg or segment
Connecting trail
Divided highway
Highway
Paved road
Unpaved road
Unpaved road (on profiles)
5 90 205 Interstate highway
2 12 101 US highway
4 20 123 State route
24 200 Forest road
3 BC highway

Start/end of leg or segment
Official trailhead
Trailhead
Point of interest
Peak
Frontcountry campground
Camp
ford Cautionary note
no fires Restricted area
Pass or gap
Lookout
Footbridge
Tunnel
Ski lift

Park or forest boundary
Boundary between forests
Wilderness boundary
State or county boundary
National boundary
River or creek
Fall
Water
Spring
Water source (on profiles)
N True north

MAPS AND APPS

These are the most commonly used PCT maps and apps in Washington:

Halfmile's maps (www.pctmap.net) are fantastic, free, up to date, and accurate. Halfmile, a hiker with an appropriate trail name and amazing generosity, has mapped the entire PCT using GPS, including key waypoints. As the trail changes or detours happen, he's quick to update. Also fantastic are **Halfmile's apps** and **Guthook's apps** (www.atlasguides.com) for both Android and iOS smartphones. The apps use your phone's GPS technology to pinpoint your location and calculate trail distances to landmarks. Thankfully, these apps don't need cell service to work, and they include a battery-conservation setting.

US Forest Service (USFS) PCT maps (www.fs.usda.gov/main/pct/maps-publications) are large, easy-to-read, full-color, waterproof topographic maps that include elevation profiles and historical notes. They're printed in conjunction with the PCTA and perhaps their best use is for planning, as they provide a great overview.

Green Trails publishes more than 140 topographical maps for recreational areas in Washington, Oregon, and parts of California. These maps include current road, trail, and access information and, because they're created by boots-on-the-ground research, they're detailed and frequently updated.

Google Maps and **Google Earth** offer online mapping that uses shaded relief. The Google Earth satellite views of the trail are great for assessing the terrain of your chosen section. What's more, the PCTA website (www.pcta.org) links to PCT overlays that you can layer on top of Google Earth views.

more. Next up is a list of the **maps and apps** that you'll find useful (see sidebar), and of that section's trip **legs** between major landmarks.

To entice you, each section briefly describes what you'll find—from huckleberries and flowers, to lakes, to lonely valleys and high peaks, to subalpine rambles. Washington truly has something for every hiker! Next, you'll find **access** directions to a section's starting and ending trailheads. **Notes** then give you a heads-up on what's coming. **Cities and services** close to trailheads can help you plan for resupplies or off-trail time. **Camping and other restrictions** explain where you'll have to skip putting your tent or building a campfire. Stretches of trail without **water** are listed, so you're forewarned and don't end up parched. Good water sources are called out in trail descriptions with the 💧 symbol; even if these water sources are seasonal, they're usually reliable in all but the driest summers. **Hazards** tell you about a section's challenging river crossings or other potential dangers so you can plan a safe trip within your comfort zone. Finally, each section's opening details end with **suggested itineraries** from camp to camp, including daily mileage.

Section Legs

The leg descriptions come next within each section, starting with the landmark-to-landmark **distance** followed by the cumulative **elevation gain and loss** for that leg and its **high point**. The list of **connecting trails and roads** tells you what major trails and roads you'll cross on that leg that could serve as alternate or emergency entry and exit points—this doesn't mean you'll be near a trailhead when you reach one of these connectors, but the route will eventually lead back toward civilization.

Next comes the best part: reading the detailed **trail descriptions** for each leg and choosing where to go. The trail descriptions cover every mile of the PCT in Washington. You'll find out what's around each bend—from water sources to camps—with enough left to your imagination so that your trip will be unique. **Maps** and **elevation profiles** for each section and each leg link up with the trail descriptions, so you can easily find a place that's mentioned and see how much up and down it'll take to get there. Each leg ends with a list of **camp-to-camp mileages**, so you can plan ahead or change your mind at the last minute, knowing that another snooze spot is just a mile or two ahead.

Camps

Pretty much anywhere flat along the PCT has likely been used as a camp. Some of these spots are suitable and sustainable Leave No Trace options, perhaps even named and signed, while others are sloped and laden with tree roots. It's impossible to list every place to camp along the PCT, but I've done my very best to include camps that are close to the PCT and in logical locations. I do not describe camps that are in fragile areas, such as meadows or wetlands, even though they exist. Practice good outdoor ethics and avoid such camps.

Numbered camps are one-offs or trailside pullouts, often useful for solo travelers or small groups. These camps are numbered sequentially over an entire section and are called out on that section's maps and elevation profiles. **Named camps** are destination locations, generally with multiple sites and more visitors. Shoot for the named camps if you have a larger group or want more scenic, established sites. Some of the named camps are actually **car campgrounds**, managed by national forests, national or provincial parks, or private entities. Such campgrounds usually show up near trailheads and can be handy for PCT hikers (and any friends you've sweet-talked into meeting you with your favorite treats!). Unlike backcountry camps, most campgrounds charge a fee, and that's noted in the trail description.

PLANNING AND PREPARATION

Before you step foot on the trail, you'll be deciding on daily distances, nightly camps, and dreaming of adventure—almost as much fun as seeing the trail in person! This guide, with drool-worthy photos and logistical details, will arm you with everything you need to fulfill your own personal PCT journey.

South to North or North to South?

Most section hikers opt to hike the PCT south to north, like their thru-hiking cousins. For the thru-hikers, this is because it's easier to start in the dry California desert in spring and end in Washington in late summer, after the snow has melted.

SEPTEMBER 2013: THE WORST WEATHER TANTRUM IN YEARS

In September 2013, Washington's Cascade Mountains pitched a fit and threw down thunder and lightning storms nearly every day. Hikers were forced to hunker down in camp and avoid high peaks to stay safe. One particular day, a large storm handed out more than six thousand lightning strikes. Later that month, a rare snowstorm blanketed the PCT, causing treacherous conditions and making routefinding difficult. Hikers woke up to find waist-deep snow on the ground and more falling from the sky.

Hikers trying to get to safety trudged over the snowy peaks, rationing what food they had. Those who made it to roads or civilization counted their blessings and described their harrowing experience as life-threatening, because most of them hadn't brought snowshoes or heavy winter clothing. Hikers from Mount Adams Wilderness to Glacier Peak Wilderness were unaccounted for, and rescue teams were sent in. Because of the inclement weather, the search teams were limited in their abilities. One by one, happy endings made the news and the state breathed a collective sigh of relief. While snow that early and that deep is rare, it's always best to be prepared for whatever weather you may encounter.

PCT PERMIT FOR THRU-HIKERS

If you intend to hike **500 or more miles continuously** along the PCT, you'll need to secure a permit from the PCTA. This free permit comes with permission from federal land-management agencies for travel and overnight stays along the PCT corridor. When requesting this permit, be sure to include your start and ending locations along the PCT proper instead of the nearest city, national park or forest, or wilderness area.

The PCTA begins processing long-distance permit requests in **early February** and will send your permit via US mail. Each hiker must secure his or her own. If you're **younger than eighteen**, you'll need a signed letter from your parent or guardian stating the dates and locations of your trip. Keep the letter with you at all times when you're on the PCT.

Southbounders will not be issued permits starting at the E. C. Manning Provincial Park trailhead in British Columbia, as it's illegal to cross into the United States from Canada on the PCT. The closest starting point is Harts Pass.

Note that if you intend to bring **pets or stock**, certain sensitive areas have restrictions. The PCT permit does not override any such restrictions.

Since the United States does not permit entry via the PCT from Canada, most southbounders must start in June at Harts Pass, often getting waylaid by a closed, snowy road or dangerous trail conditions. Another factor is water. Southbounders heading into Southern California late in the year will likely have trouble finding enough water.

I've hiked Washington State in both directions: both options are jaw-droppingly scenic and give your soul a rest and your quads a workout. True, some sections are definitely easier southbound if you prefer descent over climbing—take section 1, for example, where you'd end with a moderate descent to the Columbia River instead of starting out with a daunting uphill. But if you section hike northbound to the US-Canada border, you can cross into Canada, traipse on foreign soil, visit a mountain lodge, and arrange for transportation knowing you've completed the *entire* section.

To Everything There Is a Season

In Washington, summer is the most cooperative season for hiking the PCT, with August being the prime month. Wildflowers are at their peak, the weather pattern favors sunshine, and the trail is mostly snow free (in an average snow year). In late August through September, the huckleberries are so prolific that you could eat your way almost all the way through the state. Later in the season, after snowmelt ponds and such have dried up and cooler nighttime temperatures arrive, there are generally fewer insects, making for a more pleasant journey. Starting too early or too late can lead to serious hazards, such as icy conditions on narrow trails, adverse weather, and navigation risk.

That said, the PCT in Washington runs along the spine of the Cascade Mountains, a range famous for weather challenges. Even in the heart of summer, fickle mountain weather can throw you a curve ball. If you have the luxury of starting your trip with short notice, watch the forecast for a week or more of sunshine. Otherwise, you'll just have to gamble. Whatever the case, always be prepared for foul weather, especially rain, sleet, and snow.

Many of the nasty Northwest storms come from the west and make their way to the Cascades. As the storm moves inland, the air mass rises and quickly cools down, which raises the relative humidity. Clouds sitting over the west-slope mountains drop their moisture on the heads of unsuspecting hikers. Just the opposite happens on the eastern side of the Cascades. The looming clouds wring themselves out over the west, allowing the east to avoid much of the moisture. As you drop from one side of the Cascade Crest to the other, you'll notice the difference in flora and fauna—ponderosa pines prefer the dry, loamy soils of the eastern side, while Douglas-firs tend to stay to the west.

Permits and Passes

Section hikers do not need a PCT-specific permit. Instead, you'll need to follow the rules for permits and passes depending on what land-management agency is in charge of where you're walking. In Washington, that means the Forest Service and the Park Service, including regulations for wilderness areas. And for the wee bit in Canada, you'll first need to adhere to border-crossing requirements, and then you'll be under the purview of a provincial park.

Wilderness-Use and Camping Permits

Most Washington wilderness-area trailheads have a small wooden box containing a bundle of carbon-copy-style wilderness-use permits and, if you're lucky, a stubby golf pencil. (Do yourself a favor and keep a pen handy.) This permit is free, and you fill it out when you come to it—*each time* you come to it. Each wilderness area is its own jurisdiction, and the agency in charge relies on you to help keep track of who's using what when. The information helps agencies apply for trail-funding grants and also tells someone where you are, which is essential to getting you out safely in case of a natural disaster such as wildfire or landslide.

Fill in the name and address of the party leader, number of nights you intend to camp, trip beginning and end dates, points of entry and exit, and the number of people, stock, and dogs in your party. Then sign the form, stating that you agree to the laws, rules, and regulations of the area. (Most permits list the local wilderness regulations and guidelines.) Leave one copy in the box and attach the other copy to your pack.

In Canada's E. C. Manning Provincial Park, you must use designated wilderness camps, which charge a small fee and are first come, first served (see "Passes, Permits, Regulations" in appendix 1). You can pay later, once you're off the trail.

WILDERNESS AREA REGULATIONS

- **Maximum group size is twelve bodies,** which includes any combination of people or stock.
- **Motorized and mechanized use** of any kind is prohibited.
- **Camps must be 100 feet from lakes and the PCT.** This rule applies everywhere in wilderness areas, but especially in sensitive environments.
- **Pack-and-saddle stock must be 200 feet from lakes** when grazing, hitched, or hobbled.
- **Caching equipment, property, or supplies** for longer than forty-eight hours is prohibited.

Parking Permits

At the northern end of the PCT, E. C. Manning Provincial Park does not require a parking permit. But most designated trailhead parking areas in Washington do. Don't fret! Several passes are accepted.

The **Northwest Forest Pass** covers Forest Service and North Cascades National Park trailheads. An annual pass costs $30 and a day pass costs $5 (plus possible service fees if you buy from a retailer).

If you're a frequent visitor to US national forests and parks, consider buying an annual **Interagency Annual Pass** ($80), which covers trailhead parking on Forest Service lands as well as those managed by the Bureau of Land Management, US Army Corps of Engineers, US Bureau of Reclamation, and US Fish and Wildlife Service; this pass also pays for national park entrance fees. If you've reached the lucky age of sixty-two, you're eligible for the annual **Interagency Senior Pass** (a bargain at $10), which covers all of the above. Additionally, if you have a permanent disability, you may qualify for a free **Interagency Access Pass**.

All passes are sold at Forest Service offices in the Pacific Northwest and at some retail stores, as

A hoary marmot scurries about with a tasty treat near Lake Sally Ann (section 6).

well as online (see "Passes, Permits, Regulations" in appendix 1).

Crossing the US-Canada Border

It is illegal to cross from Canada into the United States on the PCT, but Canada allows hikers to enter from the United States! If you want to finish your hike in E. C. Manning Provincial Park, British Columbia, you'll need to obtain permission from the Canada Border Services Agency by submitting the "Application for Entry into Canada," found on the PCTA's website. Three months before your trip, submit your form—and then hang tight for the permit to be approved and mailed back to you (yes, the agency will do a background check). Once you have it, you must carry the permit with you at all times when you're in Canada.

For questions about the form, or any other Canada-entry details, contact the Canada Border Services Agency (1-866-496-3987; press "0" and ask for the Pacific Crest Trail Coordinator). For US-entry requirements, visit www.getyouhome.gov. Remember: it's illegal to cross into the United States from Canada on the PCT. You must use designated US-Canada border crossings.

Getting to and from Trailheads

Getting to the trailhead or getting picked up requires some forethought. This part of your plan can be challenging, especially if you aren't hiking out and back or if you need a ride at a remote Forest Service road.

If you're hiking in a group, you can always shuttle a car to your final trailhead. This can require several hours of driving before you start, but it means a guaranteed ride at the end of a long trip. Don't forget to pack your waiting vehicle's keys!

If you're relying on getting a ride to and from trailheads, research local online hiking forums and Facebook pages related to the PCT. This is a great way to meet friends who might give you a lift or even join you on your hike. In Washington, NW Hiker (www.nwhikers.net) is an active forum for hiking in general, and it's a good way to get acquainted with your fellow backpackers.

As for buses and trains, most public transit and private companies go to towns, not trailheads. But you can always take a cab or rent a car for your final hop to the trail. In Washington, Northwestern Trailways runs a bus that stops right at Stevens Pass on US Highway 2 (see appendix 3 for transportation options at trailheads). Of course, always check ahead to make sure that a bus schedule and route meet your needs—changes are frequent.

Resupplying Food and Other Supplies

As a section hiker, you can usually carry all that you need—but you don't have to! If you're hiking long distances or traveling through areas where caching is convenient, you can save yourself a little pack weight. Most backpackers need 1–2 pounds of food per day, which quickly add up, especially if you're out for more than a week.

For a resupply strategy, most PCT hikers do one of three things: mail a box (to a post office or designated resupply retailer or facility near the trail), buy as they hike (from stores at or near trailheads), or talk a friend into meeting them somewhere along the way with a food or supply cache. Appendix 3 lists cities and services near trailheads, including where you can send packages for later pickup.

Most places will hold your package for free, but some—especially private lodges—ask for a nominal fee. For longer trips, you might enlist a friend to mail your packages on agreed-upon dates. If you go this route, don't seal your packages before you leave—that way, you can ask your supply guru to add a thing or two you might be missing on the trail—or she can add a surprise treat! Some hikers mail a bounce box up the trail, from resupply facility to resupply facility, with things like extra batteries, phone and camera chargers, extra bug spray, sunscreen, and so on. Post office hours vary, so always check ahead. You may also have to show photo ID to pick up a package.

If you buy as you hike, you can end up with glorious fresh food, but it can also cost you time off the trail and some head scratching to figure out your nutritional needs for the coming stretch. You also may not find exactly what you're looking for. People with stringent dietary restrictions may find the mail-ahead strategy a better (and necessary) option.

At some places—like hostels, hotels, PCT host homes—you might find a hiker box of freebies for long-distance trail users. Oatmeal, ramen, sunscreen, extra plastic baggies, partially used fuel canisters, and the like are yours for the taking, and you can cast off your own extras that you don't need—very handy! But it's best to use these free boxes only as a backup.

Fueling the Beast of the Belly

Replenishing electrolytes and getting plenty of calories are important on the PCT, and food will account for a lot of weight in your pack. Most backpackers carry 1–2 pounds of food per day. Dehydrated and freeze-dried foods can help you consume more calories for less weight. But whether you purchase prepackaged food or prepare your own, it has to be something you like or you'll wilt like a falling leaf. Keeping your food simple is also good, but that doesn't mean it has to be boring!

Whether you cook your own or buy premade, a test run is a good idea: fire up a meal or two before

COME ON BABY, LIGHT MY STOVE

If you need to resupply stove fuel during your hike, follow these guidelines:

- Never mail flammable substances—ever.
- If you use white gas, research ahead where you can buy it along the way, typically at trailhead towns or resorts.
- If you use compressed fuels like isobutane, research ahead where you can buy new full canisters and/or carry extras with you.

HOW MUCH FUEL?

Some backpackers simply boil water, while others rival celebrity chefs like Emeril. Temperature, wind, elevation, and weight of the fuel bottle can all affect stove performance and efficiency.

If you want to be scientific about what you'll need, first weigh your fuel bottle or canister on a small scale. Next, cook one of the meals you intend to bring, using your camp stove. Then weigh your fuel container again and subtract the result from the before weight. Then multiply the difference by how many meals you'll prepare on the trail.

If you plan on cooking moderately elaborate meals, a loose requirement is 15 grams of fuel per person, per day. Spend some time doing calculations with your own stove.

your big trip to make sure everything agrees with your palate and the portion sizes are correct.

Once you're on the trail, make your trash tiny by stuffing folded baggies and performance bar wrappers inside the largest bag you've emptied. Squeeze all the air out and zip it closed. If you do this daily, you'll end up with a small, flat, and manageable trash bag to toss on your last day. It also may go without saying, but never cook in your tent. Aromas attract wildlife, and you risk fire and carbon monoxide poisoning. Cook outside and enjoy the beauty of nature, in your raingear if you have to, doing your best to ward off bugs.

GEAR AND CLOTHING: LIGHTEN UP!

When it comes to gear and clothing for the PCT, every ounce counts! Years ago, I used to giggle at the "ouncer" folks who cut off toothbrush handles and chopped extra webbing on pack buckles to lighten their load. But then I realized that if I could shave 8 ounces from my pack, that's half a pound. And if I pieced together the ounces, whole pounds could melt away.

As a rule of thumb, your pack weight should not exceed 25–30 percent of your optimal body weight, even for hikes of less than a week. To figure out what makes the cut, make two columns on a sheet of paper: "Must Haves" and "Wanna Haves." Be realistic and pragmatic. A tent is crucial for most people on most trips, but a fifth pair of socks is a wanna have. Ditch the wanna haves, or treat yourself to one luxury item.

Boots and Socks

Keeping your feet happy on the trail is paramount, and a lightweight sensibility applies here as well. It's been said that 1 pound on your feet equals an extra 5 on your back. Almost all thru-hikers and long-distance backpackers use trail-running shoes these days. These shoes are lightweight, have enough torsional rigidity to handle uneven surfaces, are extremely breathable, and have tread designed to handle a variety of trail conditions. Because your feet probably won't fatigue as quickly while wearing

PCT TRAIL NAMES

Odd trail nicknames are part of the PCT's unique subculture, even for section hikers. Your trail name becomes part of your persona.

Here's how it works. Other hikers, based on a story you tell or trait you exhibit, crown you with a nickname—Shoestring, Frost, Leg Bones, to list a few I've heard. You can choose whether or not to accept it, and those who bestow it should make an effort to avoid outright offense.

On one trip, my husband and I hiked with a thru-hiker named Happy who was just that—a joy to be around. Another time we hiked with Mr. Clean, who had meticulous trail hygiene. My trail name is Smile, because I'm constantly pointing cameras at people and requesting their joyful grin. Sometimes, you'll bond with other PCTers and never learn their real names, livelihoods, or histories, but none of that matters. Learning about a person through a trail name is like getting to know someone on fast-forward.

TIPS FOR LIGHTENING YOUR LOAD

- **Use tiny travel containers.** Never carry a full tube or can of anything.
- **Discard all pouches**—your pack's rain cover case, your camp mattress stuff sack, and so on. Let stuff wiggle around loose in your pack or use plastic baggies.
- **Pare down your first-aid kit** to the realistic "what-ifs" and those items you use most frequently.
- **Lighten up your potty paper.** Remove the cardboard core from your TP, or buy rolls at your outdoor retailer that come without.
- **Get creative with multipurposing.** You can use a piece of cord as a clothesline, backup shoelace, to make your tent taut, or secure a splint. A stuff sack filled with clothes can be your pillow, and a compass sighting mirror will serve as a personal mirror as well as emergency signaling device.
- **Wrap duct tape around a trekking pole** to use in case of emergency repairs.
- **Carry only the amount of water you need.** If you know water is plentiful, stop and drink, carrying only minimal water.
- **Ditch the hard-sided water bottles and opt for the grocery-store variety.** The water bottles found on your grocery shelves are surprisingly durable, lightweight, and easy to refill.

them, you can also put in greater distances each day. They are, however, much less durable than hiking boots and usually don't have ankle support.

Socks are a big part of the comfort picture. As with clothing, certain natural and synthetic fibers are moisture-wicking, but cotton is a no-no. Gone, too, are the days when wool felt like it was giving you a rash—contemporary blends keep your feet comfortable in a wide range of temperatures.

Trekking Poles: Your Metal Arm Extensions

Trekking poles can give you more stability—a bonus in these times of lightweight boots and trail-running shoes, which give you less. With trekking poles, you can reach the ground and secure your balance. And they make great splints or tarp supports too.

High-Tech Gadgets

High-tech gadgets aren't so high-tech anymore. Many people hike with smartphones and still others with GPS units and altimeters (or all in one!). Outdoor GPS devices are designed to help you find your way out of a paper bag, should you get lost in the creases, but don't neglect your other navigation skills.

If you do choose to bring the toys, remember that they're only as good as their batteries. You can mail extras ahead in your resupply caches, or you can plan to recharge at populated trailheads and then mail your charger ahead when you're done. Putting your smartphone in airplane mode when you're not using it to receive data can often buy you four or five days of battery power. Portable chargers add weight to your pack and can be fickle, so weigh your options carefully and read reviews before you invest in one.

ON THE TRAIL

You're almost there! You've done all your packing, you know where you're going, and you're headed for rejuvenation. Even so, you still have some things to think about.

Wilderness Ethics and Multiuse Trails

The PCT passes through different federal lands used by many people. Being aware of a few simple principles can ensure a good experience for everyone.

Plan ahead and be prepared. Bring what you need and double-check your lists. Leaving something as simple as fire starter behind can lead to dire consequences in an emergency.

Camping on durable surfaces and using established sites help you adhere to outdoor ethics.

Travel and camp on durable surfaces. Avoid camping on vegetation or in meadows or fragile alpine areas. When you stop for a break, set yourself and your pack on logs, rocks, or other durable surfaces.

Dispose of waste properly. Dig catholes 6–8 inches deep, at least 200 feet away from water sources, to bury human waste. Pack out all toilet paper. Do not use rocks or downed wood to hide waste piles. Pack out everything you brought along, including uneaten food, wrappers, and trash.

Leave what you find. Your pack will be heavy enough, trust me!

Minimize fire hazards. Only use fire pits in areas where fires are permitted. Keep fires small and use only downed, dead sticks and wood. Don't leave any trash in fire pits, and make sure your fire is completely extinguished before you go to bed or leave camp.

Respect wildlife. Don't share your gorp with sweet-faced begging birds or bruins.

Be considerate of other visitors. Keep your voice to a dull roar so that others can enjoy the quiet. If you're hiking in a group, go single file when passing others. Grant uphill hikers the right-of-way.

Horses are permitted on the entire length of the PCT, although particularly steep hillsides, precarious terrain, or washouts may be challenging or inadvisable for them. In places where equestrians are almost as common as hikers, sharing the trail by stepping aside becomes second nature. Sure, horse droppings can be irritating, but volunteer equestrian groups support trail maintenance—they pack in tools, food, and gear to remote backcountry trail crews and are sometimes involved in search-and-rescue efforts.

THE MOUNTAINEERS' TEN ESSENTIALS

If you've done your planning right, odds are that you'll have the Ten Essentials even if you don't know what they are. They can save your bacon should something unforeseen happen.

1. Navigation (map and compass)
2. Sun protection (sunglasses and sunscreen)
3. Insulation (extra clothing)
4. Illumination (headlamp or flashlight)
5. First-aid supplies
6. Fire materials (fire starter and matches/lighter)
7. Repair kit and tools including a knife or multitool
8. Nutrition (extra food)
9. Hydration (extra water)
10. Emergency shelter

Mountain bikes and motorized vehicles are prohibited on the PCT. Ongoing pressure from the mountain-biking community in recent years has sparked debate about allowing bikes on the trail. The Forest Service, however, continues to uphold its 1988 order closing the PCT to mountain bikes in order to protect the recreation experience of the trail's primary users, hikers and equestrians.

Fishing can be a fun diversion on the PCT, and some lakes, creeks, and rivers along the route are popular with anglers. If you choose to try your hand at catching a rainbow or brook trout, follow the Washington Department of Fish and Wildlife regulations (see "Passes, Permits, Regulations" in appendix 1). If you do get lucky and catch dinner, avoid attracting furry, four-legged critters by cleaning and cooking your fish away from where people camp.

Staying Found

In places, the PCT can be challenging to follow, despite the familiar PCT blazes that often mark the route. Some signs are missing or misleading, some trail turns are not second nature, some stretches follow reroutes or rock cairns. Fog and inclement weather can also throw you off, so if it feels wrong, it most likely is! Stop and reassess your surroundings and direction. If for some reason you get lost or find yourself in an uncomfortable situation, here are a few tips that may help.

Always let someone know where you're going and when you plan to return home. Leave your itinerary with a friend, maybe even a map with your route marked. Leave a list of the land-management agencies and contact numbers for the areas you'll be passing through. And specify a date and time to contact rangers should you not return. Be sure to give yourself a buffer for weather or unforeseen circumstances.

Stay put if you're lost or injured! It's easier to locate a fixed target than a moving one. Use your waiting time to gather firewood, filter water, and examine your food situation.

Don't panic. Try to relax your mind with positive, constructive thoughts, and settle into a daily routine that will help ease the situation.

Use your cell phone, satellite phone, or personal locator beacon for help. Almost everyone takes a cell phone into the backcountry these days, but reception can be very spotty. Satellite phones have become cheaper and smaller, making them a better option if you travel frequently in remote areas. Additionally, personal locator beacons such as SPOT messenger devices connect to private satellite networks and alert emergency personnel if you trigger an SOS. They are less expensive to use than satellite phones.

Staying Safe and Crime-Free

Thankfully, most criminals are lazy and committing crimes on trails is usually too much effort. That said, staying vigilant and keeping a healthy level of awareness is always a good idea.

Never leave valuables in your vehicle. Take anything and everything that might look interesting. Even if it's empty, a closed sunglasses case might look like it contains an expensive pair of Maui Jims; a smartphone charger might make a prowler think the phone is still in the car.

Case the place. When you arrive at a trailhead, look for anything or anyone that seems out

BLAZES OF GLORY

Navigating along the PCT is fairly straightforward thanks to trail blazes and signs on trees and signposts, all the way from Mexico to Canada. Blazes come in all shapes, depending on their age. Some very old ones are white and diamond-shaped, with green lettering that says "Pacific Crest Trail System" and an image of a tree. These are my personal favorites because they're so historic—often the trees have grown around or over them and they look like they're getting sucked into the bark. Newer blazes feature the PCT emblem with black, white, and teal coloring, with the wording "Pacific Crest Trail, National Scenic Trail" and an image of a mountain and a tree. In other places, wooden signs say "Pacific Crest Trail" with an arrow. Thanks to those who have traveled this path before us, we can rest assured that, in a roundabout way, we will be right behind them.

PCT blazes come in a variety of shapes and colors, but all point the way.

of place—for example, people sitting in cars as if they're waiting. Criminals rely on stealth and may spook and leave if they see you watching them. If you smell a rat, write down the license plate number, vehicle make and model, and a description of the person in question. A moment of diligence may make the world of difference should something happen later on.

Trust your instincts. If you sense that someone you meet has bad intentions, allow yourself to be guarded and rude if necessary.

Never tell anyone you meet where you're planning to spend the night, especially if you're alone. Be vague—"I'm just hiking until I get tired."

Never mention your party size. If you're hiking alone, using "we" statements might confuse a criminal. Shouting "Hurry up, Mike" or "Let's get going, Chris" into the bushes may deter someone who thinks you're an easy solo target.

Avoid hiking with headphones. Listen to the sweet birdsong, squeaking pikas, and whistling marmots instead. Paying attention to your surroundings will help you hear someone or something coming.

Treating Water

To filter or not to filter, why is that even a question? It only takes one bad swig to ruin your entire trip. Even if water looks clear and clean, it may contain tasteless protozoa such as *Cryptosporidium* and *Giardia*. These waterborne pathogens cause flulike symptoms, including vomiting and diarrhea, lasting one to six weeks or in some cases, up to a year.

With all the fancy-shmancy lightweight options for treating and/or filtering water, why risk it? **Water-treatment devices** range from UV-light pens that kill bacteria and viruses to carbon or ceramic filters that eliminate bacteria and unpleasant tastes. Almost all are lightweight, portable, and extremely effective. Or, opt to use **water-treatment tablets**, usually made with iodine or chlorine. And you could always **boil water**—that's the only 100 percent effective way to kill waterborne pathogens, but it consumes fuel and eats up your trail time if you wait for the water to cool.

If you do use a filter, avoid silted and murky water if possible. Washington's glacier-fed rivers of milky-colored water contain silt, fine sand, and pulverized stone that can clog a filter, fast! So can murky pond water.

Primitive privies, like this one at Mig Lake (section 5), are better than nothing when you've gotta go!

Potty Talk

There are a few backcountry privies along the PCT, especially in the more popular and visited areas, but in general, civilized folks must engage in the backcountry squat.

Find a spot that's at least **100 feet from camps or the trail** and at least **200 feet from water**.

Dig a hole no more than 6 inches deep. If you dig too deep, the bacteria won't be able to properly break down the waste.

Dispose of toilet paper in a small baggie and take it with you.

Cover up the waste completely and stir some dirt in the dung to ensure that it will decompose efficiently.

Apply a squirt of hand sanitizer to your palms and fingers, and you're good to go.

Hazards

Along with the enjoyable adventure you'll be having along the trail, you'll want to keep your wits about you as you encounter the more hazardous challenges.

No Bridge over Troubled Water

Arriving at a healthy, robust bridge is always a comfort and relief. Unfortunately, some bridges on the PCT are crooked, failing, or missing altogether. When you're crossing rivers, a little know-how goes a long way.

Cross early. Cross creeks in the morning, when water levels are at their lowest.

Cross with friends. If you're hiking solo, make some trail friends and cross together. If the river is high, you may want to link arms and choreograph your movements. You could always offer them something delicious from your food bag in exchange for the helping hand.

Look for straight, shallow, wide, and gentle water. Throw a stick into questionable sections to determine the speed and direction of the current.

Watch for hidden debris. Keep a close eye out for small logs or downed trees that might be hidden.

Don't cross if it's above your knees. Any higher than your knees, and the current can suck you downstream. If the water is flat, however, you could probably bend this rule of thumb.

Unbuckle your pack's waist belt. Your pack might shift slightly as you walk, but having an easy exit strategy could save your life if you go for an unexpected swim.

Maintain at least two points of contact. Use trekking poles or find a big stick to help you balance.

Log crossings can be hazardous. Crossing on a downed log might seem like the best bet for keeping your shoes dry, but inspect the log closely. Is the bark completely intact? If not, it could peel off when you step onto it. If you fell off that log, would you be sent sailing toward a waterfall or sustain serious injuries? If yes, find a different option. Make sure you have traction; wet logs without bark are often slipperier than ice. As you cross, focus your gaze on the log or opposite riverbank.

Wear your camp shoes to aid your footing. Once you're across, dry your feet completely before you put your hiking shoes back on, or you may end up cursing blisters.

Landslides Might Bring It Down

In the wet summer of 2013, landslides washed out the PCT between Rocky and Woody passes in Washington. That summer and the following one, hikers were forced to gingerly cross the loose, unstable soil and stone gorges left behind. This was not the first time the PCT washed out in that area, nor the only place where landslides like this have happened.

Should you encounter a landslide, only attempt to cross if you think the ground is stable enough. Slides can be a result of years of soil erosion, water runoff, or seismic activity, and the soil and debris often shifts when you step on it. Probe the debris with your trekking poles or a long stick to ensure that it's stable. Carefully kick in steps and keep your weight centered above your feet as you move. Move as quickly as you can to clear the area.

Wildfires

With warm, dry weather comes the threat of summer wildfires. At least once a season, it seems, fires close part of the PCT. While Southern California is generally the hardest hit, fires can pop up just about anywhere, including in the usually damp Pacific Northwest. In 2012, the third-worst wildfire season in Washington's history, the Cascade Creek Fire closed a long stretch of the PCT near Mount Adams, and the fire charred more than 20,000 acres.

Then, in 2015, the state experienced its worst wildfire season on record. The unprecedented dry weather and record-breaking heat exacerbated fire conditions and led to more than 900,000 acres burned. Three firefighters lost their lives. President Barack Obama declared a federal emergency and additional firefighters arrived to help tackle the blazes. Nearly 265 structures, including primary residences, cabins, and outbuildings, burned to the ground. Air quality reached unhealthy levels in and around Chelan, and entire communities were forced to evacuate as the fires grew larger and larger with no weather break in sight. The PCT was closed in various places in the Central and North Cascades throughout the summer, for fear the fires would overtake the trail. Thankfully, the fires never reached the PCT itself, but hikers who traveled it just ahead of the closures spoke of burning eyes and ash falling like snow.

Dangers remain in past burns. Use extra caution when hiking in areas with blackened, dead, standing trees and loamy, loose soil, as trees may become unstable, especially in high winds. Don't camp in areas with charred trees, even if they look sturdy.

If you encounter or hear about a wildfire anywhere in your vicinity while you're on the trail, head out to a road via the nearest safe route. Wildfires spread incredibly fast, so don't assume that because a fire's in the distance, you're safe. Wildfire updates are posted on the land-management agency and PCTA websites to help you stay on top of new developments and trail closures.

Forest Service Roads

Even for short expeditions, you may find yourself beginning on, ending on, or simply using usually unpaved Forest Service roads as part of your plan. Erosion from small creeks, bad weather, and poor maintenance can break down the road grade or even wash it out completely.

Always call ahead to check on current road conditions. If possible, **take a high-clearance vehicle** to the trailhead, to make the bumps and divots less noticeable. Drive slowly. Gravel and dirt roads, especially in wet weather, can become very slick. Use extreme caution in passing, especially where roadways are narrow. Expect to see others. After driving a half hour on a forest road without another vehicle in sight, you might speed up and drift into the center, using the whole road. Right about then, you'll encounter the only other car for miles, and one of you will end up in the roadside bushes.

Hunting Season

Washington's hunting seasons vary from year to year depending on the health of the population being hunted and other factors, but it's a good idea to wear bright orange in the backcountry in late summer through early fall. I wear a huge, mesh, orange vest over my torso or pack in remote areas that hunters frequent.

Within Washington, black bears are most common near Stehekin (section 6), although they can be found anywhere along the PCT.

For complete hunting regulations and seasonal openings, visit the Washington Department of Fish and Wildlife online (see "Passes, Permits, Regulations" in appendix 1).

Facing the Beasts

On your PCT journey, you'll undoubtedly see wild animals other than humans. Most pose little threat, but always practice good etiquette when you encounter larger beasts.

Bear Know-How

Some folks hike all the way from Mexico to Canada and miss seeing bears, while others section hike and see several; your bear-viewing karma is up to fate and luck. From late spring through midsummer, bear sightings are more common in the morning or early evening hours. In fall, bears work very hard to fatten themselves up on seasonal berries and juicy grubs, as they prepare for the long winter. In Washington, bear-hunting season in most areas starts August 1, just before the berries ripen. Somehow, the bears seem to make themselves extremely scarce during the daylight hours when hunters are in the hills.

Black bears are the most common bears in Washington, with numbers estimated at twenty thousand to thirty thousand. A handful of grizzly bears are said to still roam the North Cascades, although biologists estimate there may be fewer than ten. Be sure to report all grizzly bear sightings to wildlife officials.

Bears prefer to be left alone to forage, feed, and raise their young. In many places along the PCT, except in national parks, they are hunted and are therefore extremely wary of people. Hikers will be lucky to snap a shot of their hind ends as they bound off into the forest. Nonetheless, it pays to play it safe when traveling in bear country.

Make noise, especially where the trail is overgrown or you're hiking around blind corners. Clap, sing, and talk loudly.

Cook meals at least 100 yards from your sleeping area, and don't sleep in the same clothes you cooked in. Never eat dinner inside your tent.

Hang all food and any scented toiletries (toothpaste, lip balm, sunscreen), or use a bear canister. Do not sleep with food in your tent.

In fact, **avoid using scented sunscreen**, perfume, lotion, or lip balm.

Empty your pack's pockets each night to ensure that no leftover food, wrappers, or crumbs are in them. Move your pack away from your tent, in case the former smells of food or garbage.

Clean up with alcohol. If something with a fragrance, such as sunscreen or food, spills in your tent, clean it up with hand sanitizer, which has alcohol in it that can mask smells.

Watch for bear signs. Prints in the mud and scat piles are good indications, but also watch for smaller, easier-to-miss signals such as scratched trees. Bears looking for grubs will overturn and occasionally shred logs. In berry patches, bears will pull bushes downward, sending bits of berry, brush, and leaves to the ground and breaking branches.

Animal carcasses of any kind are bad news, as they attract predators. If you find one, leave the area immediately.

If a bear is aggressive, it's likely feeling threatened and defending its cubs or food source. Startled bears will also act out in agitation. If a bear is jaw popping, huffing, vocalizing, or aggressively slamming its paws to the ground, it's trying to tell you that you've crossed the line. **Avoid eye contact**, which bears perceive as a challenge. **Never turn your back on the bear**, but if it's safe to do so, slowly back up. **Talk calmly and quietly** so the bear can identify you as a human. Occasionally, a bear will bluff charge (charge, stop short, and run away) to try to scare the devil out of you. Stand your ground and avoid eye contact. Don't take even a half step backward. If a black bear does attack, fight back with all you've got.

If hiking in bear country spooks you, you might bring along a can of bear spray. Bear spray comes in large, heavy canisters designed so the spray can reach up to 32 feet. Of course, the wind direction must be perfect or the red, burning pepper spray can leave you, *instead of the bear,* temporarily disabled. The spray won't help unless a bear is close and acting aggressively. In fact, if pepper spray is improperly used as repellent, researchers have shown that it can actually attract bears.

Wildcat Country

While the odds of seeing a cougar (a.k.a. mountain lion) are higher in California than in Oregon or Washington, your overall chance of seeing these solitary, shy creatures anywhere along the mostly hiker-infested PCT are quite slim.

Look for prints in loose soil or mud. The sheer size of an adult cougar print, roughly the width of an adult hand, makes it easy to identify. The cats' recessed toenails cause a lack of nail marks. And the paw pad, beneath the "toes," has two distinctive lobes at the top and three at the base.

If a cougar does get curious about you, there are a few things you can do.

Maintain eye contact. In fact, give the cat the stink eye if you want. Cougars rely on being stealthy and hidden. Staring a cat down tells it you're aware of its presence.

Never run! Running may trigger a cougar's instinctive urge to chase.

Get big and go crazy. Wave your trekking poles or pull your jacket up over your head to make yourself look larger. Shout, bark, scream, do whatever it takes to make yourself a formidable enemy.

Keep children close. Don't let the wee ones, or trail dogs, run ahead on the trail. If you do see a cougar, pick up small children and keep them high by holding them or placing them on a stump to make them appear larger. Cougars usually target the easiest prey.

Back away slowly if it's safe to do so, using care not to trip. Don't turn your back on the animal.

If a cougar does attack, fight back and fight dirty. Those who have survived cougar attacks have duked it out. Throw rocks and punches. Right hooks, haymakers, fingers in eyeballs—it's all fair game.

Far less unnerving to hikers, bobcats are medium-sized cats who make their home along the entire stretch of Washington's PCT. While these wildcats are usually solitary and rarely seen, quiet hikers may occasionally catch a glimpse of one on forest edges or in meadows where rabbits and rodents are often found. Attacks on humans are extremely rare, but if you do encounter an aggressive bobcat, take the same actions as you would for a curious cougar.

Bobcats are generally stealthy, but every once in a while a lucky hiker gets a glimpse of one.

Mountain Goats

Mountain goats are very common in Washington's alpine environments, especially those with snowfields or glaciers. To find goats, stop, look, and listen. Often, the sounds of their clicking hooves will help you spot their bright white coats against gray rocks. Both male and female goats have horns, but the males are larger. Weighing an average of 100–300 pounds, they—like deer and elk—are most active in the early morning and early evening. While seemingly docile, they may behave aggressively, especially if they have young or feel threatened. Always give them plenty of space and never try to shoo one off the trail. In high-alpine environments, goats are suckers for salt. Since human urine contains salt, they will paw at soiled vegetation, tearing up fragile plants. When traveling in goat country, piddle or puddle on the rocks!

Snakes

The PCT runs through landscapes that are home to several varieties of snakes; in Washington watch for them primarily in the southern part of the state, from the Columbia River to Indian Heaven Wilderness, and again around Stehekin north to Rainy Pass. It's possible to encounter gopher snakes, rubber boas, garter snakes, racer snakes, and the most feared, rattlesnakes.

Thankfully, **rattlesnakes** give you a warning tail shake to let you know they're nearby. They usually try to hide or blend into the rocks and warm soil, since rattlesnakes are food for many birds of prey. Like most creatures, they're rarely aggressive unless they feel threatened. Take these precautions to minimize your chances of an encounter.

Watch your footing, especially when in camp and when stopping for potty breaks.

Use extra caution when crossing downed wood, scree fields, and rocky outcroppings.

Keep your pup on a short leash in snake country, and avoid letting him sniff and explore under bushes and rocks.

Use trekking poles. Snakes are sensitive to vibration and might feel you before they hear you.

Learn what a mad rattlesnake sounds like! YouTube is full of examples of rattling rattlers, usually being antagonized by someone. Their rattle sounds a lot like dried grass.

Back away slowly if you get schooled by a rattle, and don't make any sudden movements. Keep your distance!

Snake bites are rare, but if someone gets bit, contact emergency personnel immediately. Keep the patient calm and remove any restrictive clothing such as jewelry, watches, socks, and the like. Immobilize the bitten limb, keeping it below the heart. Cleanse the wound but don't flush it with water. Cover the affected area with a dry dressing and avoid ice. If possible, place a lightly constricting band, with a finger's worth of wiggle room for blood flow, above the bite to help prevent the spread of venom.

Insects

Mosquitos, gnats, black flies, ticks, and horseflies are some of the annoying biting, burrowing, buzzing bugs you may have to battle on the PCT. Thankfully, walking at a good clip tends to discourage most of them from landing or attaching. A little know-how in the biting battalion department is often key to avoiding looking like you have the mumps.

Invest in a **good insect repellent** or **wear a loose-fitting long-sleeved shirt and pants**. The most common and effective repellents contain DEET. This pesticide makes some folks nervous, but the US Environmental Protection Agency has given it a thumbs up and human-health complications are rare. Unless you plan on bathing in it or have extreme sensitivities, you should be dandy. Some products are almost 100 percent DEET, but I prefer a repellent in the 30 percent range—enough to prevent most bites while not burning holes in my shoes.

Another relatively new bug repellent, picaridin, has an almost undetectable odor and is less greasy and sticky than DEET. Manufacturers claim that it works as well, but I'm a bit of a skeptic, since bugs stand in line for a bite of me. More gentle but somewhat less effective mosquito repellents include a wide variety of herbal products, often with ingredients such as essential oils.

Thankfully, Washington's PCT is not heavily populated with **ticks**. While they can technically be found almost anywhere, you're more likely to pick one up on the stretch from the Columbia River to Indian Heaven Wilderness or from Stehekin north to Rainy Pass. There are fewer than twenty cases of Lyme disease reported in Washington per year, so your odds of a journey-ending tick bite are reasonably low. Using insect repellent, wearing long, light-colored pants and a long-sleeved shirt, and frequently checking clothing and skin are the best ways to prevent a tick from latching on.

To combat ticks and mosquitos, you might consider treating your clothing and gear with a chemical called permethrin. One application is usually effective for up to six weeks and through six washings. This insecticide is so effective that several outdoor clothing lines bake it right in.

Bee stings and horsefly bites can cause severe allergic reactions. If you get stung or bitten and develop hives, wheezing, or swelling of the lips, throat, or tongue, seek help immediately. Also, keep a close eye out for infections at the bite site, such as weeping or discoloration, which might require a doctor's care.

Off You Go

Since every single ounce counts on the trail, you likely won't be carrying this guide with you. Then again, you might just photocopy the pages you need and tuck them in with your maps to read each evening. Or perhaps, invest in a lightweight e-reader and download the book along with other reading material to keep you entertained. Some of today's e-readers have battery lives of up to eight weeks and weigh less than 7.5 ounces. Your hiking companions may swoon at the nightly story-time ritual.

With a little planning, a little know-how, and a little get-up-and-go, you'll soon be on your way to enjoying the spectacular Pacific Crest Trail and its grand landscapes. As you wander amid fragrant wildflowered hillsides and take in misty-eyed views of river valleys, you'll be making memories for years to come. Your journey awaits!

SECTION 1

COLUMBIA RIVER TO FOREST ROAD 23

THIS WASHINGTON PCT SECTION does not have stunning alpine views or scenery that will make you misty-eyed. In fact, it has its share of clear-cuts and forest roads. But skipping it does it and you a disservice. From the state's PCT start on the north bank of the Columbia River, Bonneville Dam hovers in the distance as you wander deeper into the woods. Near Gillette Lake, deciduous trees lend an East Coast feel to the usual Pacific Northwest evergreen canopy. Big Huckleberry Mountain and Panther Creek Experimental Forest are lush with quiet woods intent on renewing your soul. The lively voices of gentle streams and peaceful rivers overtop the whispering forest. Indian Heaven Wilderness abounds with lakes and meadows—a fantastic treat for the eyes. The final stretch places your feet at the base of Mount Adams, off of Forest Road 23, in the shadow of the towering volcano. This section of the PCT has much to offer, so take the time to enjoy it!

ACCESS

North Bank of Columbia River

From the north end of the Bridge of the Gods over the Columbia River, on the Oregon-Washington border, turn west on State Route 14 (Evergreen Highway) and locate the PCT Trailhead in 0.1 mile on the north side of the highway. Parking is limited to a couple of cars, on the side of the road.

PCT Trailhead off Forest Road 23

From the town of Trout Lake, head north at the Y near the only gas station onto Mount Adams Recreation Highway. At 1.2 miles, bear left on Forest Road 23. Proceed 12.6 miles to FR 521, signed "PCT North Trailhead." Turn right (east) and follow this unpaved but well-maintained spur road 0.3 mile to the trailhead on the north side of the road. Parking is plentiful.

DISTANCE 81.8 miles

STATE DISTANCE 0–81.8 miles

ELEVATION GAIN/LOSS +17,230/–13,370 feet

HIGH POINT 5150 feet

BEST TIME OF YEAR July–Oct

PCTA SECTION LETTER H

LAND MANAGERS Columbia River Gorge National Scenic Area, Gifford Pinchot National Forest (Mount Adams Ranger District, Indian Heaven Wilderness)

PASSES AND PERMITS NW Forest Pass to park at PCT Trailhead off FR 23. Free self-issue wilderness permits at wilderness area trailheads.

MAPS AND APPS

- Halfmile's WA Section H
- USFS PCT Map #9 Southern Washington
- Green Trails Bonneville Dam #429, Bridal Veil #428, Lookout Mountain #396, Wind River #397, Indian Heaven #365S, Mt Adams West #366
- Halfmile's PCT app, Guthook's overall PCT app and PCT WA app

LEGS

1. Columbia River to Rock Creek
2. Rock Creek to Panther Creek Road
3. Panther Creek Road to Forest Road 60 at Crest Campground
4. Forest Road 60 at Crest Campground to Forest Road 24
5. Forest Road 24 to Forest Road 23

Opposite: *During peak season, hikers could eat their weight in berries all the way along the PCT between the Oregon and Canada borders.*

SECTION 1
COLUMBIA RIVER
TO FOREST ROAD 23
SECTION 2
Mount Adams
Forest Road 23
Mount Adams Wilderness
LEG 5
Forest Road 24
Swift Reservoir
To Yale
Twin Buttes Rd
LEG 4
Indian Heaven Wilderness
Gifford Pinchot National Forest
Trout Lake
Wind River Rd
Wind River
Carson - Guler Rd
Forest Road 60 at Crest Campground
Little Soda Springs Rd (Szydlo Rd)
Panther Creek Rd
LEG 3
Big Huckleberry Mtn
Panther Creek Road (Panther Creek Campground)
LEG 2
Rock Creek
LEG 1
Yacolt Burn State Forest
Salmon River
White Salmon River
Carson
White Salmon
Columbia River
Stevenson
Hood River
Columbia River Gorge National Scenic Area
Cascade Locks
Bridge of the Gods
To Camas
Columbia River
0 2 4 MILES
0 2 4 KILOMETERS

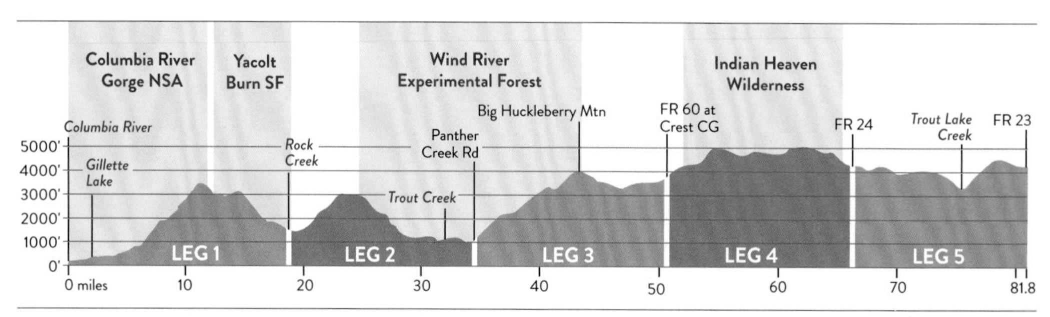
Columbia River Gorge NSA
Yacolt Burn SF
Wind River Experimental Forest
Indian Heaven Wilderness
Columbia River
Gillette Lake
Rock Creek
Trout Creek
Panther Creek Rd
Big Huckleberry Mtn
FR 60 at Crest CG
FR 24
Trout Lake Creek
FR 23
5000'
4000'
3000'
2000'
1000'
0'
LEG 1
LEG 2
LEG 3
LEG 4
LEG 5
0 miles
10
20
30
40
50
60
70
81.8

SUGGESTED ITINERARIES

Where noted, distances are to camp trail spurs; camp may be up to 0.1 mile from junction.

8 DAYS

		Miles
Day 1	Columbia River to Camp 4	9.3
Day 2	Camp 4 to Rock Creek Camp	9.2
Day 3	Rock Creek Camp to Trout Creek Camp	10.4
Day 4	Trout Creek Camp to Panther Creek Campground spur	5.4
Day 5	Panther Creek Campground spur to Big Huckleberry Camp	11.0
Day 6	Big Huckleberry Camp to Blue Lake	12.2
Day 7	Blue Lake to Mosquito Creek Camp	13.5
Day 8	Mosquito Creek Camp to FR 23	10.8

7 DAYS

		Miles
Day 1	Columbia River to Camp 4	9.3
Day 2	Camp 4 to Rock Creek Camp	9.2
Day 3	Rock Creek Camp to Trout Creek Camp	10.4
Day 4	Trout Creek Camp to Camp 14	13.8
Day 5	Camp 14 to Blue Lake	14.8
Day 6	Blue Lake to Mosquito Creek Camp	13.5
Day 7	Mosquito Creek Camp to FR 23	10.8

6 DAYS

		Miles
Day 1	Columbia River to Camp 7	14.3
Day 2	Camp 7 to Trout Creek Camp	14.6
Day 3	Trout Creek Camp to Big Huckleberry Camp	16.4
Day 4	Big Huckleberry Camp to Blue Lake	12.2
Day 5	Blue Lake to Mosquito Creek Camp	13.5
Day 6	Mosquito Creek Camp to FR 23	10.8

From Randle, turn south onto State Route 131. After 0.9 mile, bear left at a junction onto Forest Road 23. Stay on FR 23 for roughly 33 miles, passing onto a long gravel stretch of road and then regaining pavement. Turn left (east) onto FR 521, signed "PCT North Trailhead." Turn right (east) and follow this unpaved but well-maintained spur road 0.3 mile to the trailhead on the north side of the road.

NOTES

Cities and Services

Near the southern trailhead, find gas, groceries, dining, and lodging in Cascade Locks (Oregon) and Stevenson (Washington). Near the northern trailhead, find gas, a convenience store, dining, and lodging in Trout Lake. Other cities near the southern trailhead are Hood River (Oregon) and Carson and White Salmon (both in Washington).

Camping Restrictions

Near Blue Lake in Indian Heaven Wilderness, camping is limited to designated sites only. No permits required.

Water

At 7.4 miles from the trailhead, 0.7 mile north of Camp 3, you'll encounter the last water source for the next 11.3 miles. Water may also be scarce 2.6 miles north of Rock Creek for a 6.7-mile stretch. In some years, there's another waterless stretch for 11 miles north of reliable Panther Creek.

1 COLUMBIA RIVER TO ROCK CREEK

DISTANCE 18.6 miles

ELEVATION GAIN/LOSS
+4900/–3560 feet

HIGH POINT 3475 feet

CONNECTING TRAILS AND ROADS
Tamanous Trail #27, Three Corner Rock Trail (Stebbins Creek Trail), CG 2090 (unpaved)

ON THE TRAIL

A big, beautiful PCT sign starts you off! Be sure to stop and pose for the quintessential picture before you begin your adventure. Because you're starting at nearly sea level, you'll soon be climbing, but for now, the trail is mostly level as it cruises through brushy landscape in the Columbia River Gorge National Scenic Area. Watch for stinging nettles as you make your way—if you brush up against their leaves, they'll leave you with burning, small welts that are a real buzzkill (usually not a serious health

A trail close to Rock Creek is beautifully landscaped in lush vanilla leaf.

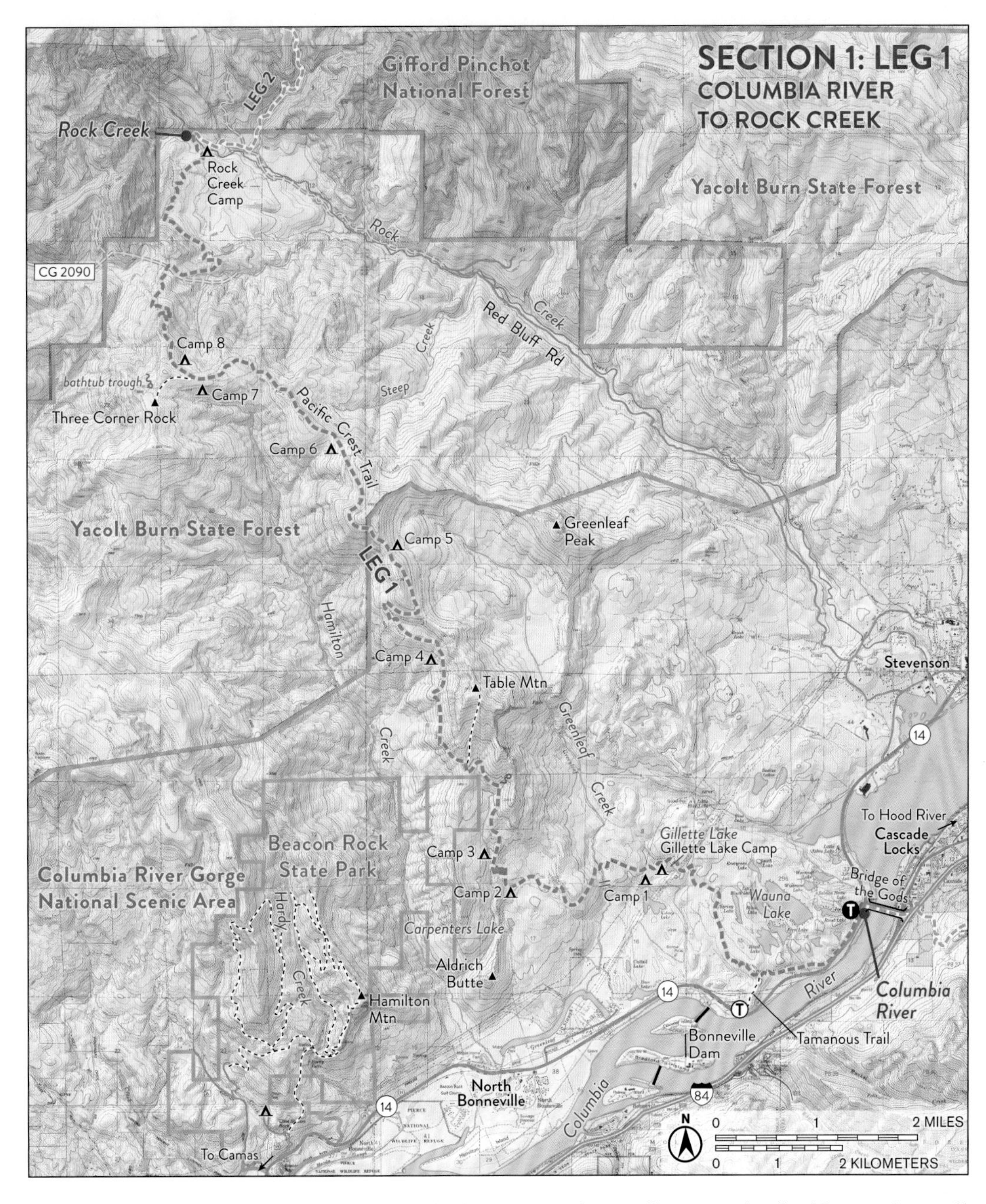

issue). A couple of creeklets dribble through the brush, useful water sources if you're desperate.

The humming of cars on the highway just out of sight and the telephone poles along the trail remind you that civilization is not far off. In 0.9 mile, you'll see a utility building and a small house through the trees on the left (south) side of the trail. Just beyond, cross a paved driveway and continue on the other side. Just when you start to wonder if you'll ever get away from it all, you arrive at a junction with **Tamanous Trail #27**, 1.3 miles from the trailhead. (The Tamanous Trail leads to the Bonneville Butte Trailhead.)

The PCT heads northwest now. In 0.6 mile from the Tamanous junction, cross a dirt road, the first of many in this section. The landscape alternates between clear-cut meadows, powerlines, riparian brush, and mixed deciduous-evergreen forests, with views beyond of the mountains you're heading for. Trust me, the scenery gets better up ahead.

In 1.8 miles beyond the Tamanous junction, the trail crosses a dirt road under humming powerlines. Below you is decent-sized Gillette Lake, sitting at the base of clear-cut hillsides. Thankfully, there are enough trees on its shores to make it seem worthy of a look, a break, or a restful night. In 0.2 mile from the dirt road, reach the lake's western side and find two well-used trailside campsites beneath big-leaf maples (**Gillette Lake Camp**). A spur trail to the south of the camp leads to a small creek, a plentiful water source 💧. The PCT turns a rather sharp right here and isn't signed. If you go the wrong way, you'll end up either on the spur for the creek or at the lake, and you'll quickly figure it out. A couple more campsites are scattered around the lakeshore if the trailside spots are taken.

The bountiful but unnamed creek bounces along the trail's south side and in 0.1 mile from Gillette Lake Camp, a log bridge guides hikers over the flowing water. Just after the bridge, a short spur trail heads left (south) to **Camp 1**, a very spacious camp with a robust fire pit. The PCT then gently climbs, leading to more clear-cuts and powerlines, and 0.1 mile past Camp 1 the trail crosses a defunct dirt road. Come to another one 0.1 mile farther. At most of the dirt-road crossings, the PCT is very obvious on the other side, but this one might throw you for a loop. To find the PCT, head left (southwest) and follow the dirt road approximately 50 feet, looking for the trail on the road's right (west) side. Views of the Columbia River and Bonneville Dam are now visible in the distance, to the south.

Cross another old dirt road 0.5 mile from the last one. Go left a few steps on the road to pick up the trail and continue on the other side. There are so many old roads in this section that you might think I'm stuttering when I repeat myself again and again. Trust me, it's yet another scrappy old road!

In 4.2 miles from the Columbia River Trailhead, and 0.1 mile from the last road crossing, arrive at a sturdy bridge across Greenleaf Creek 💧. This creek flows year-round and is surrounded by trees producing (wait for it . . .) green leaves! Ferns, moss, and Oregon grape make this area a spectacular emerald-lime color, very Northwest rainforest-esque.

More views of Bonneville Dam show up to the trail's south as you make your way through the varied forest understory. In 1.2 miles from Greenleaf Creek (5.4 miles from the trailhead), arrive at an unsigned junction with a trail heading left (southwest). This trail once connected with the Dick Thomas Trail, but is now off-limits to hikers due to private land ownership. In another 0.2 mile, reach a small bridge, a dribbling seasonal creek, and a trailside camp (**Camp 2**). The camp is big enough for at least two tents and the creek usually trickles enough to filter what you need. In 0.3 mile beyond Camp 2, reach a small boardwalk, followed by a little bridge over another seasonal creek. The landscape still has that riparian and deciduous feeling as you cruise through the emerald tunnel.

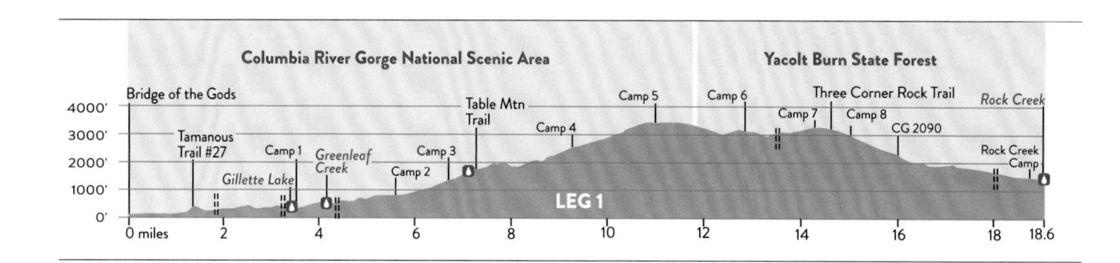

Scree fields pop up here and there along the PCT near Table Mountain.

A huff-and-puff begins up a ridgeline toward Table Mountain. In 1.1 miles from Camp 2 (6.7 miles from the trailhead), find another camp (**Camp 3**), this one only big enough for one tent and very close to the trail. Beyond the camp, the trail crosses an old jeep road and then meets up with it, using a small portion as the PCT. The trail quickly turns back to its skinny, single-track self.

In 0.7 mile from Camp 3 (7.4 miles from the trailhead), stop and get water 💧. **The next water is in 11.3 miles**, so fill 'er up and don't wither away on the coming climbs—there's much more to see! The watering hole is a great place to meet people, since almost everyone stops for a top-off and a chat with like-minded, trail-obsessed fellow travelers. The creek, a tributary of Cedar Creek, dribbles across the trail from the hill to the right (northeast). Some wonderful person with time on her hands created a small catch basin with a rock border, creating a sink of sorts, useful for dipping bottles if the flow isn't pumping.

In roughly 300 feet from your water rendezvous is the announcement that you are entering the **Table Mountain Natural Resources Conservation Area**. A large, well-constructed log sign to the trail's right (northeast) tells about the land, explaining that it protects animal habitat, sensitive foliage, and geological and scenic features. The PCT blazes right on past the sign through the forestland and meets up with another Table

Mountain sign in 0.5 mile. A labyrinth of confusing trails to the right (north) from this sign lead to the top of Table Mountain, a flat summit with views of the neighboring peaks and the Columbia Gorge. The PCT continues northwest of the sign and ambles into the forest. The route is fairly straightforward, but if you get discombobulated, look for the familiar PCT blaze nailed to a trailside evergreen.

The next mile traverses the southwestern edges of Table Mountain, passing several talus fields and rocky cliff bands, all amid lowland forest. After that, the true climbing and sweating begins, making you grateful you filled up back at the watering hole. In roughly 1.9 miles from that water stop, just as you really start to climb, a well-used campsite shows up to the trail's left (west). **Camp 4** is suitable for two small tents and has a fire pit and log benches for sitting. Even if you're not stopping for the day, this camp makes a fine place for a sip of water and a Scooby snack.

Next, the trail continues its climb, crossing under powerlines, past a jeep road, and through old clear-cuts before things get interesting. Views start to open up to the Columbia Gorge and Table Mountain. Mount Hood's snowy slopes to the southwest, with barren cliff bands in the foreground, make for a fine snapshot.

In 1.7 miles beyond Camp 4, arrive at the saddle of an open-feeling, unnamed peak. A small one-tent campsite (**Camp 5**) is to the trail's right (northeast). While no signs or landmarks announce its arrival, shortly after Camp 5 enter Yacolt Burn State Forest. Rich history in this area dates back to September 1902, when dozens of wildfires ravaged nearly 240,000 acres, causing thirty-eight deaths and destroying structures, homesteads, and livestock. Shortly after that, in 1908, a group of landowners founded the Washington Fire Protection Association, which helped establish a system of fire prevention and management.

From here, the trail opens up to a great view of Mount Hood before ducking back into the forest, where it continues and then crosses two defunct forest roads. The first is an old road swallowed by plants, at 1.2 miles beyond Camp 5; the second is an ample dirt road, 0.3 mile beyond that. Just prior to crossing the second forest road is **Camp 6**, with room for at least three tents, but no fire pit or, of course, water. That last watering hole is now some 5.1 miles back.

In 0.9 mile from Camp 6 and the last road crossing, the trail spits you out at a gravel road with several large excavated rock piles. Look for the rock cairns leading to the continuation of the often overgrown PCT on the north side of the road. Back into the forest you go, crossing another defunct forest road and then walking through a clear-cut area where tiny trees are making a resurgence. Within this clear-cut, 0.9 mile from the rock-pile road crossing, is **Camp 7** to the trail's left (south), with room for just one tent. It could be, and has been, used in a pinch by those who don't have the gumption to go any farther, but it's nothing to write home about. The tight space and slightly sloping ground are less than ideal, but it's worthy of mention in case you're beat. When the body says it's done, it's done.

In 0.3 mile past Camp 7, reach a junction with the **Three Corner Rock Trail**, which eventually links with the lightly used **Stebbins Creek**

THREE CORNER ROCK

If time is on your side, you may want to scoot up to Three Corner Rock, an interesting jumble of stone atop a peak that previously housed a fire lookout. The tower is long gone, but the concrete steps to the summit are still firmly in place. To check it out, take the Three Corner Rock Trail left and follow it past the water trough spur to its dead-end, a jeep road, 0.4 mile from the PCT. Turn right (west) at the road and walk a short 0.3 mile to a four-way junction. To the right (north) is Three Corner Rock, complete with grand views of Mount St. Helens and neighboring peaks.

Opposite: *Gillette Lake is a peaceful oasis set in the midst of decommissioned dirt roads.*

The old water trough near Three Corner Rock is no longer a good source of water; the sign for it hidden in the trees may give you some false hope.

Trail as it leads southwest to the **Washougal River** area. For years, PCT hikers took this trail 0.3 mile to get piped water from a bathtub-style trough. It's still there, but much deteriorated. The bathtub is completely rusted out with no bottom, and the water coming from the pipe is a cruddy brown color. Don't waste your time unless you are in dire need and have a good way to purify the sediment.

From the Three Corner Rock junction, the PCT begins a gradual if long descent to Rock Creek. Little light makes it through the canopy of dense conifers, making for an understory of woody duff. To the right, 0.2 mile from the Three Corner Rock junction, someone took the time to clear some fallen sticks and make a spot flat and wide enough for one tent (**Camp 8**). There's nothing aesthetically pleasing about this spot at all; to be blunt, it's downright ugly and dark, but if your knees are crying, you might be thrilled to see it.

The PCT continues its descent through deep forest and, 1.4 miles from the Three Corner Rock junction, crosses the road **CG 2090**. In roughly 0.4 mile beyond the road, a sign, the first of several, shows up trailside noting the date of logging, burning, and planting, courtesy of the Washington Department of Natural Resources (DNR). The old signs call attention to how long it takes a renewable resource to, well, renew, and they give you something to look at besides the evergreens.

Down, down, down you go through the mossy forest of mature hemlocks, ferns, and Oregon grape, crossing the occasional scree field and passing the random large boulder until you reach another forest road 1.9 miles beyond the last one (3.3 miles past Three Corner Rock junction). You're now very close to Rock Creek, but it keeps you guessing, since its sound doesn't carry very far. Another DNR sign shows up trailside as evergreens and emerald foliage guide you along the PCT.

In 0.6 mile from the last road crossing (3.9 miles from Three Corner Rock junction), arrive at **Rock Creek Camp**. Three lovely campsites sit along the shores of purring **Rock Creek**. Spectacular natural pools near the water's edge make ideal bathtubs, provided the flow isn't too high and there aren't too many looky-loos ogling your grubby nakedness. If this isn't home for the night, a sturdy, well-crafted bridge, located 0.1 mile beyond the camp, leads you over the playful water as you continue on your merry way.

CAMP-TO-CAMP MILEAGE

Columbia River to Gillette Lake Camp	3.3
Gillette Lake Camp to Camp 1	0.1
Camp 1 to Camp 2	2.2
Camp 2 to Camp 3	1.1
Camp 3 to Camp 4	2.6
Camp 5 to Camp 6	1.5
Camp 6 to Camp 7	1.8
Camp 7 to Camp 8	0.5
Camp 8 to Rock Creek Camp	3.7
Rock Creek Camp to Rock Creek	0.1

2 ROCK CREEK TO PANTHER CREEK ROAD

DISTANCE 15.7 miles

ELEVATION GAIN/LOSS
+3190/–3740 feet

HIGH POINT 3120 feet

CONNECTING ROADS
Red Bluff Road (FR 2070, unpaved), FR 417 (unpaved), Old Bunker Hill Road (unpaved), Little Soda Springs Road (Szydlo Road), Wind River Road, Warren Gap Road (unpaved), Panther Creek Road (FR 65)

ON THE TRAIL

Cross **Rock Creek** and in 0.4 mile you'll see a trailside state Department of Natural Resources (DNR) sign about the regenerating forest. Afterward, rock hop across **Snag Creek** and reach another sign as you mosey along. Apparently, the DNR is proud of its efforts and wants to be sure you know it! In 0.7 mile past Rock Creek, reach the lightly traveled, dirt Red Bluff Road (FR 2070). Déjà vu! It looks just like all the others that you have and will cross in this section. Some of these roads are active, while others are private logging roads.

There's a campsite just a short distance northwest of Red Bluff Road, to the left (northwest) of the PCT. It's not highlighted in this guide because its convenience is deceptive. The site is small, with a tree root smack dab in the middle of it. A tiny tent will balance precariously on the shelf created by the root, but if the occupant moves, the whole enchilada will likely tumble toward the trail. Unless you fancy discombobulating shenanigans when you're exhausted, it's best to walk right past it.

In 1.1 miles beyond Rock Creek, pass a creeklet and reach a short spur leading right (southeast) to a gorgeous little one-tent camp in the trees (**Camp 9**). Water is plentiful here most years. Trickling water drips off neighboring hillsides and you reach an even larger creek 0.4 mile beyond Camp 9.

The PCT gently twists and turns and crosses a couple more creeks, the last at 2.6 miles from Rock Creek (1.5 miles from Camp 9). **Be sure to fill up here**, or at one of the creeks before this, as the next 6.7 miles are waterless most seasons.

March onward past a couple of interesting moss-laden lava fields before the trail starts its ascent toward a high, unnamed ridge. Above, a lava cliff with jagged rocks provides interest for your eyes as your legs do the hard work. Head north through dry gullies dotted with ferns and vine maples and reach a flat spot among the bear grass 3.6 miles from Rock Creek. To call this a camp is ridiculous, and this guide doesn't, although

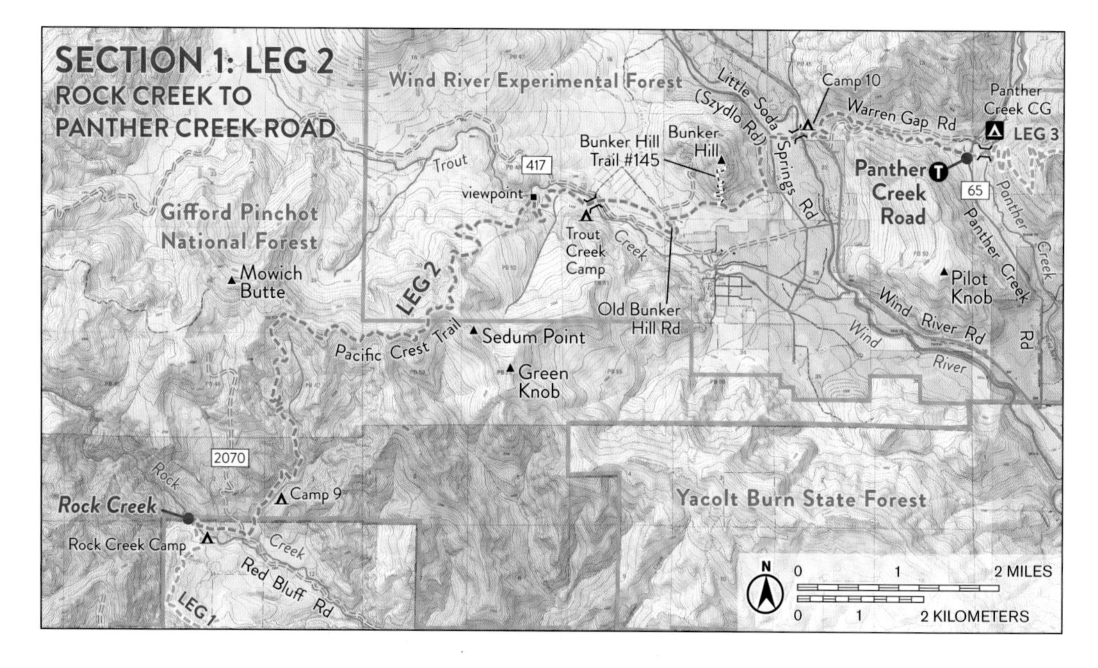

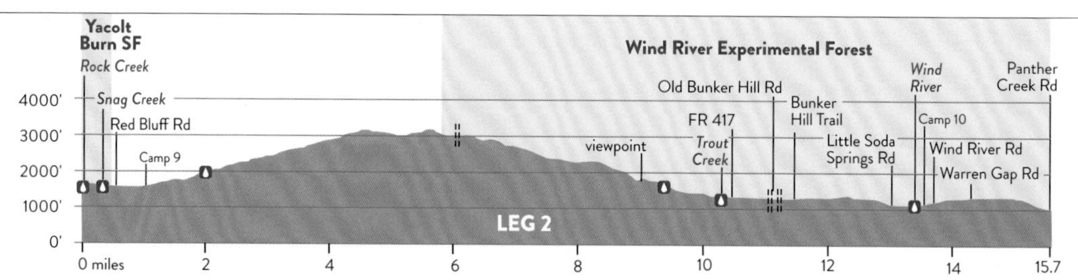

any place could technically be called a camp if it's flat. Very few camps exist in this area, so it's likely that at some point a discouraged hiker pitched a tiny tent in this spot and the trend caught on. The site is almost on the trail; in fact, it's so close that it looks like the trail has been slightly altered to go around it.

Just beyond the flat spot in the bear grass, the trail heads east, levels out, and traverses the shoulders of the ridge just above. Your quads will be grateful for the reprieve as you wander through kinnikinnick, mossy boulders, and evergreens, reaching an abandoned dirt road at 6.1 miles from Rock Creek (5 miles from Camp 9). Anything relatively flat along the PCT constitutes a camp, and the road has been used for one many times. You certainly could throw your tent down here, but though the road is rustic, someone may use it at some point. Since tire tracks across your forehead would mess up your selfies, this guide skips calling this an official camp. There are beautiful camps and water at Trout Creek, just 4.2 miles downhill.

The PCT crosses the road and cruises back into the hemlocks and Douglas-firs, beginning to gently head downhill. The gentle grade makes this 4-plus miles feel longer, as the trail takes its time delivering you to Trout Creek. One foot in front of the other works like a charm.

In 2.8 miles from the road crossing, arrive at a rocky **viewpoint**, just off a well-worn spur that goes straight (northeast). The PCT deceivingly turns right (south), causing trail-brained hikers to visit the viewpoint straight ahead whether they want to or not. But it's a good stop anyway. The viewpoint boasts sights down onto Trout Creek and homesteaded, pastoral lands. Evergreen-rich high peaks protect wide-open fields dotted with ranches and horse barns. This brush with civilization seems completely out of place. Thankfully, when you get to the valley, the PCT does a decent job of hiding the creature comforts and keeping you, for the most part, sheltered from manufactured creations.

After the viewpoint, continue your PCT evergreen party and find the first of several seasonal creeks in just 0.4 mile. Several of these creeks are large enough to grab a drink if you can't wait for Trout Creek, roughly 1 mile ahead. When you get there, you'll find two spectacular campsites (**Trout Creek Camp**), both big enough for two tents each and close to the cold, purring water. If you aren't calling this home for the night, you may want to stop here anyway—grab a bite, filter some water, or splash around. When you're ready to move on, cross the sturdy concrete footbridge that delivers you to a parking lot and well-traveled, unpaved **FR 417**.

The area you're walking through is part of the **Wind River Experimental Forest**, a significant epicenter of forest research in the Pacific Northwest. Scientific field studies of old-growth forest,

A large concrete bridge over Trout Creek escorts hikers across the often swift water.

plant and animal habitat, and water health are conducted here to aid forest management. North of here, you'll walk through another of these important areas, the Panther Creek Experimental Forest.

For now, cross FR 417 and note a sign pointing the way to the continuation of the PCT. An arrow also points right (southeast), toward the Wind River Work Center, a Forest Service training facility. The PCT makes its way north through hemlocks with vanilla leaf and ferns near their roots. Shortly after the road crossing, a fence shows up trailside, on the left, making a very clear distinction between the PCT and private property and giving you peeks into the fields beyond.

The next few turns are a bit confusing as you work your way through the woods, dodging property boundaries and forest roads. In 0.8 mile after crossing FR 417, arrive at the dirt **Old Bunker Hill Road**, and go left along the road (southeast). Follow it 50 feet or so and locate the PCT in overgrown brush to the road's left (southeast) again. These minor twists and turns can throw off your mental compass a bit, but you really are continuing in a southeasterly direction. Cruise through the tall bracken fern and maples until you arrive at Old Bunker Hill Road again, just 0.1 mile beyond where you previously met it.

A sign says "**Whistle Punk Trail No. 59**," with an arrow and a tiny PCT emblem that are easy to miss. Help other hikers scratching their heads in bewilderment by telling them to follow the road to the left (north) and then walk about 100 feet to locate the PCT on the road's right (northeast) as it ambles through a tall, grassy meadow. A small birdhouse-shaped sign with a stick figure of a hiker simply says "Hiking Trail." A closer look reveals the PCT emblem nailed to the signpost. Jackpot, you've found it! With most of the confusion behind you, enjoy the meadow walk that soon cuts back into the forest. In 0.5 mile from Old Bunker Hill Road, arrive at **Bunker Hill Trail #145**, which heads steeply to the top of Bunker Hill to the north.

From the junction with the Bunker Hill Trail, follow the PCT to the right (east) and continue traversing through the towering conifers. Pastures and rooftops are visible through branches and leaves here and there. At 1.3 miles from the Bunker Hill Trail junction (1.8 miles from Old Bunker Hill Road), pop out onto the paved **Little Soda Springs Road (Szydlo Road)**. No Trespassing signs are hung in almost every direction around this confluence of the trail and road. The PCT in this area is adjacent to private property and the owners make sure you know it! After you cross the road, the No Trespassing signs make more sense. You are very close to people's driveways, outbuildings, and private gates. The trail is nearly level here and you'll make good time with each step.

BUNKER HILL

The views from near the top of Bunker Hill are similar to what you've just seen coming down into Trout Creek, but beautiful all the same. Not only is the viewpoint a worthy distraction for the eyes, but the old-growth forest you'll climb through is impressive. The roundtrip is 3.4 miles with 1200 feet of elevation gain.

In 0.3 mile from Little Soda Springs Road, arrive at a sturdy, well-constructed footbridge over Wind River. Whoever built this beauty did so with Northwest weather in mind: horizontal wood slots placed perpendicular to the bridge deck help you avoid doing a triple toe loop in wet weather. In prime hiking season, **Wind River** is an idyllic place to grab a drink, splash, and cool off. The shallow, wadable water and beckoning gravel banks are good places to take a load off. Unfortunately, the shorelines are brushy, and following the spur trails to the water requires some trekking pole whacks and some bobbin' and weavin' to avoid stinging nettles. A couple of campsites (**Camp 10**) are just beyond the bridge, off spur trails. The PCT continues straight ahead and spits you out at the paved **Wind River Road** in 0.3 mile from the bridge (0.6 mile from Little Soda Springs Road).

Relatively flat terrain and a soft, narrow trail guide you through typical Northwest foliage in the midst of mixed deciduous-conifer forest. At

0.8 mile from Wind River Road, cross the unpaved **Warren Gap Road** and continue in similar terrain for the next 1.3 miles until you reach the paved **Panther Creek Road (FR 65)**.

If you're looking for a place to camp, you're in luck! The Forest Service **Panther Creek Campground** is just a hop, skip, and a jump away. You can either go left (north) on FR 65 for 0.1 mile, or cross the road and continue on the PCT, taking one of the spur trails to the car campground. There are thirty-three campsites here, as well as potable water, picnic tables, vault toilets, fire pits, and a campground host who usually sells firewood. Ahhhh, the luxuries of home! It'll cost you to camp here, though. Those wanting to camp for free will be happy to find a tent site along the PCT just past the road crossing, with room for two small tents.

This campground makes a fantastic starting or ending point for those wanting to hike the PCT legs to the south and north. It's also a perfect place to talk a friend into meeting you with a carload of drool-worthy dining options.

CAMP-TO-CAMP MILEAGE

Rock Creek to Camp 9	1.1
Camp 9 to Trout Creek Camp	9.2
Trout Creek Camp to Camp 10	3.0
Camp 10 to Panther Creek Road	2.4

3 PANTHER CREEK ROAD TO FOREST ROAD 60 AT CREST CAMPGROUND

DISTANCE 15.9 miles

ELEVATION GAIN/LOSS
+4320/–1760 feet

HIGH POINT 3995 feet

CONNECTING TRAILS AND ROADS
Panther Creek Road (FR 65), FR 68 (unpaved), Cedar Creek Trail #149A, Grassy Knoll Trail #146, FR 6801 (unpaved), FR 60 (Carson–Guler Road, unpaved)

ON THE TRAIL

From Panther Creek Road (FR 65), head east along the PCT and immediately notice a very lightly used, unsigned trail coming in from the left (north), a backdoor trail to **Panther Creek Campground**. A small two-tent campsite is also located here and is your free option (**Camp 11**).

In 0.2 mile from Panther Creek Road, arrive at **Panther Creek**. To the left is an unsigned but very well-defined trail that heads north along the river, ducking into the Panther Creek Campground. Straight ahead the PCT continues by crossing a wide wooden bridge with metal side rails. Before heading across, **fill up on water**, as the next reliable water is in roughly 11 miles. You have a long huff-and-puff before that, making your way toward Big Huckleberry Mountain.

Once beyond the bridge, the climbing starts on the trail's eight varying-length switchbacks to a ridgeline high above. Removing some clothing layers now will make you much more comfortable as you climb—the hill is a doozy in places and you'll be sweating rivers. Tip your hat to the large old-growth trees providing you shade as you grunt up the slope.

In roughly 3.4 miles from the Panther Creek Bridge (3.6 miles from Panther Creek Road), reach the ridgeline and reap your reward—less intense climbing and views of surrounding evergreen peaks and the very ice-cream-cone tip of Mount Hood. The PCT traverses the ridgeline, sometimes atop the ridge proper, sometimes just below it, until it reaches **Camp 12**, with its fire pit and room for two small tents. Just beyond, cross a lightly traveled dirt spur road off FR 68, 3.7 miles from Panther Creek Bridge. Trail Angels occasionally have water service here, but don't count on it. In busy

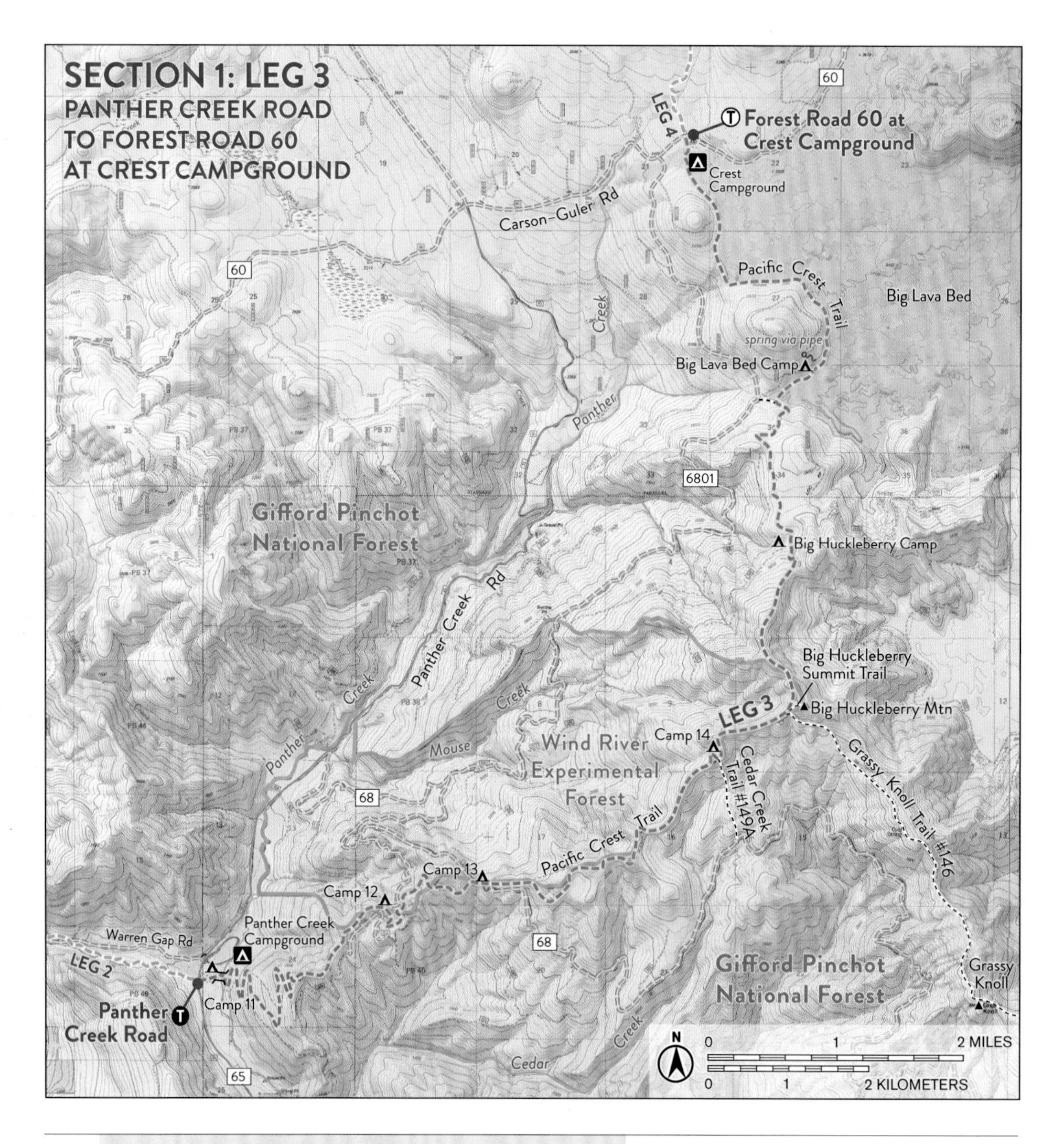
SECTION 1: LEG 3
PANTHER CREEK ROAD
TO FOREST ROAD 60
AT CREST CAMPGROUND
Forest Road 60 at
Crest Campground
Crest
Campground
LEG 4
60
Carson–Guler Rd
Pacific Crest Trail
Big Lava Bed
spring via pipe
Big Lava Bed Camp
Panther Creek
6801
Gifford Pinchot
National Forest
Big Huckleberry Camp
Panther Creek Rd
Big Huckleberry
Summit Trail
Big Huckleberry Mtn
LEG 3
Mouse Creek
Camp 14
Wind River
Experimental
Forest
Cedar Creek
Trail #149A
Grassy Knoll Trail #146
68
Camp 13
Camp 12
Panther Creek
Campground
Warren Gap Rd
LEG 2
Camp 11
Panther
Creek Road
Grassy
Knoll
Cedar Creek
65
0 1 2 MILES
0 1 2 KILOMETERS

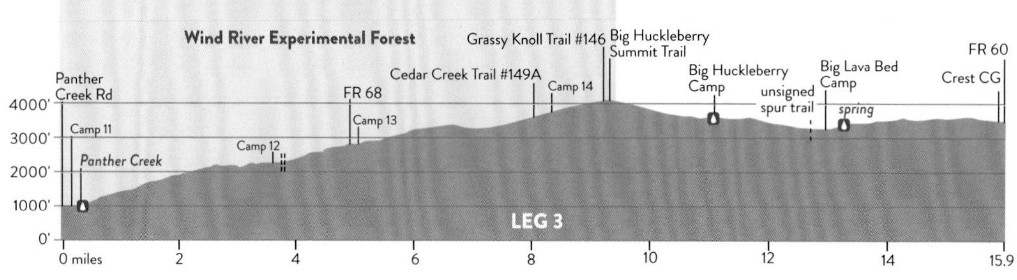
Wind River Experimental Forest
Panther
Creek Rd
Camp 11
Panther Creek
Camp 12
FR 68
Camp 13
Cedar Creek Trail #149A
Camp 14
Grassy Knoll Trail #146
Big Huckleberry
Summit Trail
Big Huckleberry
Camp
unsigned
spur trail
Big Lava Bed
Camp
spring
FR 60
Crest CG
4000'
3000'
2000'
1000'
0'
LEG 3
0 miles
2
4
6
8
10
12
14
15.9

Glimpses of Mount Adams entice you to follow the trail toward its base.

summers, the water will be long gone before you arrive, unless you have a lucky trail feather tucked into your pack.

The next 1.4 miles gently gain elevation until you cross the fairly well-traveled gravel **FR 68**. A large sign announces that you are in the Wind River Experimental Forest, Panther Creek Division, and the PCT continues on the other side of the road. Many have used the road shoulders to camp, but the best camp is just beyond the sign to the trail's left (north). A fire pit and room for two small tents make this primarily level **Camp 13** a great destination for a sleepy hiker. Panther Creek Road is now 5.1 miles behind.

After Camp 13, views of Mount Hood continue to pop through the evergreen forest as you work your way to a grassy saddle at 1.8 miles from FR 68. At 3 miles from FR 68, arrive at a trail junction with **Cedar Creek Trail #149A**, leading to the right (south).

CEDAR CREEK

If you're eager for water, you could head down this trail approximately 0.3 mile, losing 300 feet of elevation, to find the seasonally flowing Cedar Creek. Near the creek crossing is a small one-tent camp where you could easily find the Sandman.

At 0.3 mile past the Cedar Creek Trail junction, a couple of spur trails head left (west) up a small rocky knoll and arrive at a wonderful old lava shelf. The shelf is a good place for lunch, a break, or a snapshot of Mount Hood, provided it's not too hot or windy. A small camp (**Camp 14**) with room for a couple of tents is to the shelf's right (north) near tree line. If you stay here and the weather is clear, you'll have a front-row seat for grandeur: Mount Hood and the surrounding skyline, glowing at sunrise and sunset. Of course, there's no water near this camp, save for the trek down to Cedar Creek (see "Cedar Creek" sidebar).

Back on the PCT, nibble your way through huckleberries in late summer, passing a couple of spots where folks have created makeshift camps by moving sticks, crushing bear grass, and settling for less than desirable sleeping situations. Nothing says backache like the screaming of thoracolumbar fascia crushed by a bear-grass root ball. Much better camping options are up ahead, so give the footsies a rubbin' and keep 'er rollin'.

A moderate climb traverses southeast under a dense evergreen canopy until you arrive at **Grassy Knoll Trail #146**, 1 mile beyond the Cedar Creek Trail junction (4 miles from FR 68). The Grassy Knoll Trail, the route of the former Cascade Crest Trail, heads right (east). Almost immediately beyond the junction, a sign on a tree notes the northeast direction of the **Big Huckleberry Mountain** summit, as well as the PCT's continuation.

BIG HUCKLEBERRY MOUNTAIN SUMMIT

If time permits, a side trip to the top of Big Huckleberry Mountain, the site of a former L4-style fire lookout, offers decent vistas of the South Cascades. To obtain the grassy summit, take the Big Huckleberry Summit Trail for roughly 0.2 mile, gaining 200 steep feet as you go. Once on top, enjoy your quiet perch.

The PCT continues northeast, traversing the shoulders of Big Huckleberry Mountain, easing up on the grade and alternating between thick forest, grassy saddles, and sweeping views of Mount Adams, which now seems just a couple of ridges away.

In 1.9 miles from the Grassy Knoll/Big Huckleberry junction (5.9 miles from FR 68), descend to a deeply forested plateau, boasting multiple campsites (**Big Huckleberry Camp**),

Weary hikers will be thrilled to have the picturesque Big Lava Bed Camp all to themselves.

some with metal fire rings. To the trail's left (west), someone has carved the word "water" into a flat piece of wood and tied it to an old tree with parachute cord. If the homemade sign isn't there, wander around following game trails until you find the reliable little spring to the west. The plateau makes a fine destination for a break and fill-up of the belly and bottle.

In 0.2 mile past Big Huckleberry Camp, cross a former road that nature has taken back, making it almost unidentifiable. Descend in forest cover of Douglas-firs and hemlocks, and in roughly 1.5 miles beyond the camp, pass a delightful patch of trailside Pacific rhododendrons. Rhodies are relatively unusual in this part of the Cascades, so they're worth a look. In a few spots, it almost looks like someone has landscaped the trail edges.

Shortly after the rhododendron patch, 1.7 miles beyond Big Huckleberry Camp, an unsigned, unmaintained spur trail branches off left (west). This is a shortcut to FR 6801, which if taken northbound, leads to FR 60 (Carson–Guler Road), a main road that the PCT crosses near Crest Campground. As a side note, FR 6801 is washed out for passenger cars south of where the spur trail meets up with it.

In 2.1 miles beyond Big Huckleberry Camp, the large, well-developed **Big Lava Bed Camp** shows up to the left (west) of the trail. This camp could easily hold at least three tents, but its log-bordered tent pad is intended for a medium-sized one. This spacious forested camp also has a metal fire ring as well as benches for sitting and resting your exhausted carcass. As luck would have it, you are only 0.2 mile south of a water source!

Open pockets of sunlight give your eyes a change of pace as you break from the evergreen tunnel of trees. Maple, alder, and mountain ash reacquaint you with lime-green shades. In 0.2 mile from Big Lava Bed Camp, arrive at a trailside water source to the left (west). Thankfully, someone has tapped a spring and brought the water to the trail via a PVC pipe. Water playfully drips and dribbles enough to fill bottles and reservoirs. If it's prime thru-hiker season, you might meet a few new friends as you wait your turn.

Beyond the PVC watering hole, the PCT skirts the edges of the **Big Lava Bed**, formed when a cinder cone erupted some eighty-two hundred years back. The massive jumble of rocks contains hidden caves, odd stacked lava formations, and drought-tolerant plants trying their hand at growing among the stone gardens. For roughly 2 miles, the PCT walks adjacent to this rocky wonder, which looks more like a familiar talus field than a massive volcanic deposit.

TRAIL ANGELS ARE HEAVEN-SENT

Any PCT thru-hiker will express overwhelming gratitude for people called Trail Angels. Occasionally, you'll follow your nose to a trailhead and find that some decent person has set up a barbeque in a parking lot and is flipping burgers and serving cookies to hungry trail traipsers. Other times you might come across lonely totes full of snacks or gallon water jugs along the trail, offered up to passing hikers. One time I was offered a soda and an orange from some horsemen who were helping with trail maintenance and bestowing delicious snacks upon weary hikers who passed their camp.

This joy that pops up along the PCT is called "trail magic," and over the years I've wondered if it was for me too, as a section hiker. Should I skip partaking of the bounty because I'm not hiking the full trail? I've talked to several Trail Angels whose message shares a theme: they find happiness in helping hikers, period. Their charity is open to anyone who delights in their services and whose mouth waters at the thought of a burger instead of a steaming bag of hiker goo. Trail Angels understand that your challenges are personal and that by being outdoors and putting in miles, you're a backpacker and deserve to be treated as such. That said, if you encounter trail magic in person, you may want to ask if the offerer minds if you partake, but I bet I already know the answer.

A hiker enjoys a colorful sunset with views of Mount Hood near Camp 14.

In 2.5 miles beyond the PVC watering hole (10.7 miles beyond FR 68), arrive at **Crest Campground** and the well-traveled gravel **FR 60** (Carson–Guler Road). Crest Campground is a car-camping area consisting of four campsites fitted with picnic tables and fire rings. And there's a vault toilet—a welcome break from taking care of duty rustic-style. Years ago this used to be a horse camp, and some maps call it "Crest Horse Camp," but now it's just for people. There's no fee for camping here, so treat the area well and thank the Forest Service for real tables and a real potty. There's also no trash service, so please pack it out.

Crest Campground is a great spot for starting or ending a PCT journey, or a good place for syncing up with friends. FR 60 gets a fair share of traffic. Both the towns of Trout Lake (to the northeast roughly 18 miles) and Carson (the same distance to the south) make good jumping-off points for someone meeting you here. Both towns have gas stations and food, as well as lodging options for hikers who want solid walls and running water.

CAMP-TO-CAMP MILEAGE

Panther Creek Road to Camp 11	0.1
Camp 11 to Camp 12	3.6
Camp 12 to Camp 13	1.4
Camp 13 to Camp 14	3.3
Camp 14 to Big Huckleberry Camp	2.6
Big Huckleberry Camp to Big Lava Bed Camp	2.1
Big Lava Bed Camp to Crest Campground	2.7
Crest Campground to FR 60	0.1

4 FOREST ROAD 60 AT CREST CAMPGROUND TO FOREST ROAD 24

DISTANCE 16.8 miles

ELEVATION GAIN/LOSS
+2580/–1810 feet

HIGH POINT 5140 feet

CONNECTING TRAILS AND ROADS
FR 60 (Carson–Guler Road, unpaved), Shortcut Trail #171A, Thomas Lake Trail #111, East Crater Trail #48, Indian Heaven Trail #33, Cultus Creek Trail #108, FR 24 (Twin Buttes Road, unpaved)

ON THE TRAIL

From **Crest Campground**, cross Forest Road 60 (Carson–Guler Road) and be sure to pick up your free self-issue wilderness permit at the kiosk. You'll be in the Indian Heaven Wilderness in no time, but for now, head into the forest and climb at a gentle grade. Pacific silver, subalpine, and Douglas-firs are the primary conifers, with a twist here and there of white pine. The landscape at your feet alternates between patches of oval huckleberry, vanilla leaf, and bear grass. The forest feels light and open, and as you head north you'll high-step a few times on the narrow trail's erosion-resistant log steps.

At 1.7 miles, the trail meets up with **Sheep Lake** 🅞 to the left (west). Like most lakes you'll find in Indian Heaven, Sheep Lake is more of a shallow pond than deep lake and sports grassy vegetation around its edges and peninsulas. The mucky water might look less than appetizing, but once it's treated, it goes down the hatch without creating a gut ball. Green Lake up ahead is even grassier and smaller, so Sheep Lake is the best water option before your climb up Berry Mountain.

Sheep Lake is also a good place for a snack, and there's a bench in **Camp 15** to the trail's right (east). This small camp is not very desirable, as it's very close to the trail, with little privacy. It is, however, suitable for one or two small tents and has a rock fire pit as well as the nearby lake for water.

In 0.2 mile beyond Sheep Lake (1.9 miles from FR 60), enter the **Indian Heaven Wilderness**, announced by a sign mounted to a tree. You are now in a storied land with great history! For more than nine thousand years, Native American tribes—including the Yakama, Klickitat, Cascades, Wasco, Wishram, and Umatilla—came together here to fish, hunt, pick berries, and commune with one another. The Native people originally called this area Sahalee Tyee, which loosely translates to "the Chief's high, heavenly ground." Designated a wilderness in 1984, today Indian Heaven is 20,960 acres of wilderness land boasting more than 175 lakes, ponds, and tarns and countless meadows and marshes. Thankfully, the PCT runs right through the middle of it all. If you happen to be passing through at the end of July or beginning of August, be forewarned that this is a premier mosquito nursery. Waltzing with bug goo or long sleeves and long pants should keep your cursing to a minimum.

At 0.7 mile from the wilderness boundary (2.6 miles from FR 60), find a one-tent, no-frills camp (**Camp 16**) in the trees. Sure, it's a tiny flat spot, but it's moderately private. A small grassy pond known as **Green Lake** is to the right (east), just 0.1 flat mile farther along the trail. In very dry summers, this pond becomes a mud puddle—all the more reason to fill up back at Sheep Lake.

In 0.1 mile past Green Lake (2.8 miles from FR 60), arrive at a large meadow and stop for a minute and take a look around. **Red Mountain** towers to the west. This extinct shield volcano has a rocky, red top and sports a fire lookout. The lookout was Washington's very first one, built in the early 1900s by hauling split cedar siding and roofing more than 20 miles of rugged terrain with horse and wagon. During World War II, it served as a post in the US Army's Aircraft Warning Service, part of the

Indian Heaven Wilderness touts copious shallow lakes and meadows for hikers to enjoy along the PCT.

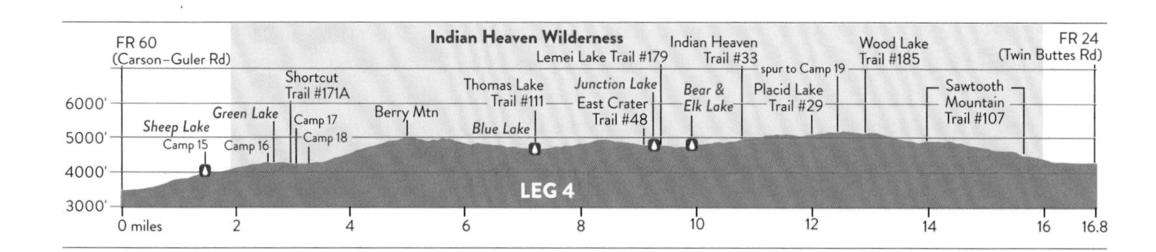

mainland defense system. The original tower was replaced in 1959 to accommodate wear and tear. Then, in December 2006, a fierce windstorm nearly shook the lookout off the map. For the next two summers, volunteers donated labor and expertise to reconstruct the structure using salvaged authentic materials. Today, the Red Mountain Lookout lives on and is visible from many vistas along the PCT. This is the first glimpse of it as you head north.

In 3.2 miles from FR 60, arrive at a junction with **Shortcut Trail #171A**, leading to Indian Race Track. If time permits, take the 0.5-mile one-way trip out to the Race Track, a large meadow where Native Americans held competitions for horsemanship. While Mother Nature has primarily reclaimed the deep ruts cut into the meadow by fast hooves, it's fun to let your imagination run wild. A side trip up to Red Mountain is also

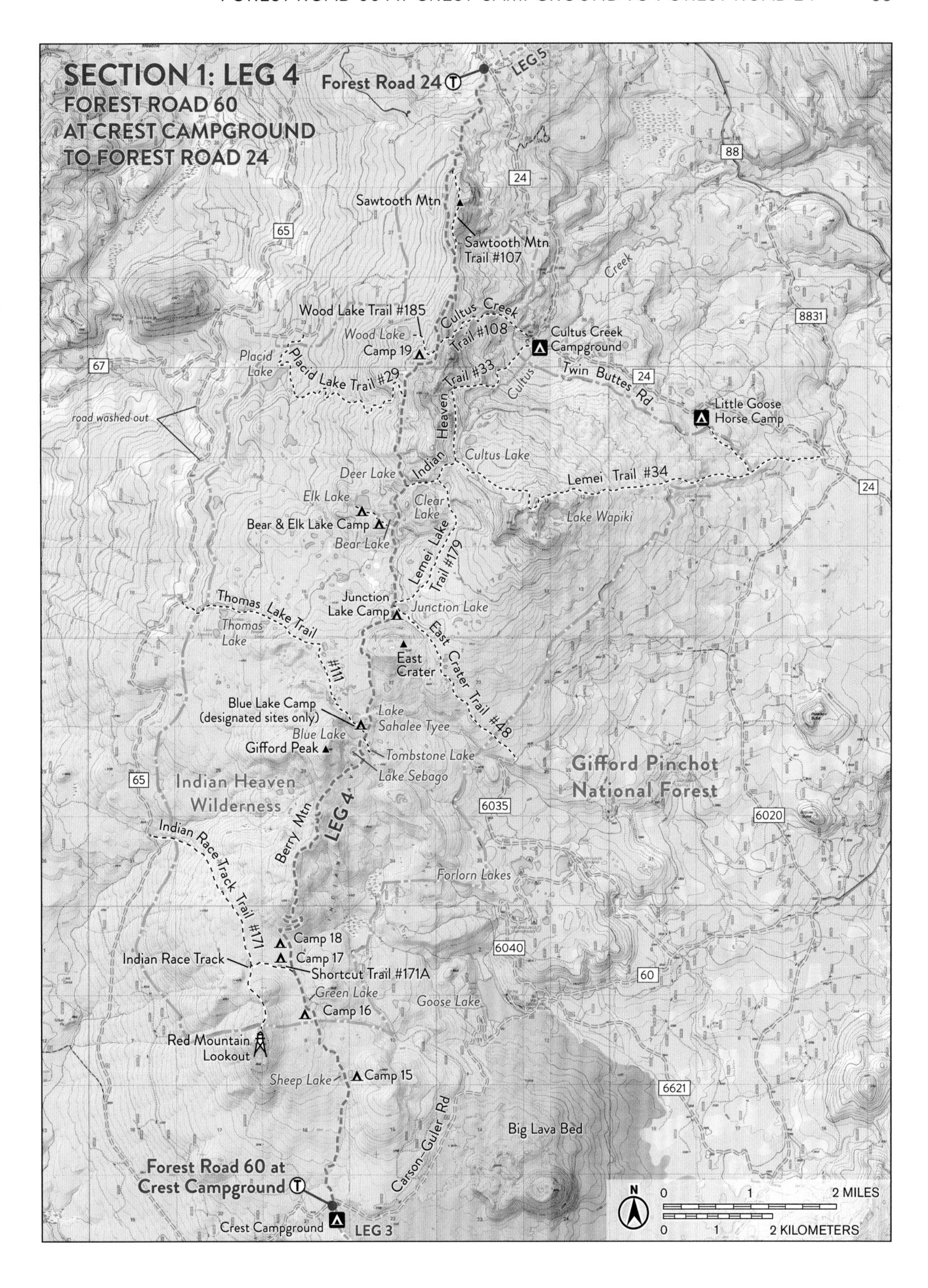
SECTION 1: LEG 4
FOREST ROAD 60
AT CREST CAMPGROUND
TO FOREST ROAD 24
Forest Road 24
LEG 5
88
24
Sawtooth Mtn
65
Sawtooth Mtn
Trail #107
Creek
Wood Lake Trail #185
Cultus Creek
8831
Wood Lake
Camp 19
Trail #108
Cultus Creek
Campground
Placid
Lake
Placid Lake Trail #29
67
Trail #33
Twin Buttes Rd
24
Cultus
Heaven
Little Goose
Horse Camp
road washed out
Indian
Cultus Lake
Deer Lake
Lemei Trail #34
24
Elk Lake
Clear
Lake
Lake Wapiki
Bear & Elk Lake Camp
Bear Lake
Lemei Lake
Trail #179
Junction
Lake Camp
Junction Lake
Thomas Lake Trail
Thomas
Lake
East
East
Crater
Crater Trail #48
#111
Blue Lake Camp
(designated sites only)
Lake
Sahalee Tyee
Blue Lake
Gifford Peak
Tombstone Lake
Gifford Pinchot
National Forest
Lake Sebago
65
Indian Heaven
Wilderness
LEG 4
6035
6020
Indian Race Track Trail #171
Berry Mtn
Forlorn Lakes
Camp 18
6040
Indian Race Track
Camp 17
Shortcut Trail #171A
60
Green Lake
Goose Lake
Camp 16
Red Mountain
Lookout
Sheep Lake
Camp 15
6621
Carson-Guler Rd
Big Lava Bed
Forest Road 60 at
Crest Campground
Crest Campground
LEG 3
N
0 1 2 MILES
0 1 2 KILOMETERS

INDIAN RACE TRACK AND RED MOUNTAIN

If you want to check out the Race Track and Red Mountain, the total roundtrip adventure will be 3.8 miles from the PCT intersection. Take Shortcut Trail #171A east for 0.5 mile until you arrive at a large meadow. This meadow was chosen out of so many in the area because of its level softness—the perfect place for horses to avoid injury while powerfully sprinting to the finish line. Not long ago, the Race Track ruts were clear and visible, but today, thanks to Mother Nature's takeover, it takes a keen eye to find them. Since you're here, you may as well head up and check out the Red Mountain Lookout. Continue for 0.1 mile on the Shortcut Trail, just beyond the meadow, and look to the left (south) for a lightly traveled trail heading into the forest. Head south here, and in 1 mile arrive at a gravel road. Unfortunately, the Red Mountain Lookout didn't make the cut to stay inside the Wilderness Boundary, but thankfully the road access is gated and only accessible by service vehicles. Follow the road uphill until you reach the tower located just 0.3 mile ahead.

possible by following the Shortcut Trail to Indian Race Track Trail #171.

In just 0.1 mile beyond the Race Track junction, arrive at a one-tent campsite to the trail's left (**Camp 17**). It's extremely close to the trail, with no privacy, but it's under trees for shade and has cushioned tree needles for bedding. **Camp 18**, a twin to Camp 17, also on the left, is just 0.2 mile beyond. Neither camp is optimal, and they were most likely made by thru-hikers, but they're flat, open spots where you could flop down with the setting sun.

From here, the trail begins a series of three long switchbacks leading you up to the top of Berry Mountain. On your climb, be sure to stop and note the various Cascade peaks, including Mount St. Helens, Mount Adams, and Mount Hood. Red Mountain and its lookout are clearly visible, even more so the higher you go. The trail guides you through swales of terra-cotta-colored mineral deposits on open hillsides, dusty pebbles underfoot, and landscaping of bear grass, huckleberry, pine, and fir. Rocky cliffs along the shoulders of Berry Mountain are more signs of past volcanic activity and give your eyes something to focus on as you try to ignore your heavy breathing.

The trail grade eases as you crest the forested ridge of **Berry Mountain**. The ridge has at least two spots where you could put a tent if you were creative and moved a few sticks. It seems like folks have used them before, but not often, and since these sites aren't presently established, we won't call them camps. Along the ridge, peekaboo views of Mount St. Helens to the northwest and Mount Adams to the northeast are pleasant attention grabbers. A few gentle ups and downs battle it out across the ridge until the downhill wins and you find yourself descending five short switchbacks toward popular Blue Lake.

In 4 miles from the Race Track junction, a tree sign announces that overnight camping is permitted only at designated sites. In Indian Heaven, there are two areas near the PCT where **camping is restricted to designated sites**—Blue Lake, Thomas Lake, and their environs. This sign marks the southern boundary of the designated area near Blue Lake. In this area, camps are signed with a symbol of a tent.

Immediately beyond the overnight camping sign, an unnamed outlet lake-swamp-pond can be seen through the trees to the right (east). Beyond that a signed tree points the way to a designated camping area in between Lake Sebago and Blue Lake, followed by the lapping sapphire-colored shores of **Blue Lake** itself to the trail's left (west), 4.1 miles from the Race Track Junction (7.3 miles from FR 60). More campsites are to the south, east, and north of the lake (**Blue Lake Camp**) **O**. A day-use picnic area along the eastern shore makes a pleasant place to grab a snack and take a break if this isn't home for the night. If it is and you want more options, there are two more campsites at Tombstone Lake, 0.2 mile away via a trail to the southeast. And more sites are to the west along

A ribbon of trail runs through one of the many meadows in Indian Heaven Wilderness.

Thomas Lake Trail #111. One is at the very western tip of Blue Lake and another is just beyond at Lake Sahalee Tyee. The Thomas Lake Trail is just north of the Blue Lake day-use area.

Blue Lake is very popular with the day-hiking and weekend-warrior crowd, since it's an enjoyable hike from the Thomas Lake Trailhead to the northwest. North of the picnic area are three signs. One tree sign notes the PCT with arrows, one free-standing sign points toward distant trails to the north (Trail #48) and south (Trail #171A), and lastly another tree sign indicates Thomas Lake Trail #111, which wraps around Blue Lake's northern shore and heads west. Continue north along the PCT once you've enjoyed Blue Lake and are ready to venture onward.

Birds are all around you—dark-eyed juncos, winter wrens, hairy woodpeckers, and Steller's jays carry on their mission of finding food throughout the forest nursery. In 0.3 mile, an unsigned anglers' trail shows up to the PCT's right (east), leading east to an unnamed lake.

Gentle elevation gain and loss rolls you along through the huckleberries, heather, and hemlocks until you arrive at a junction, 1.8 miles from Blue Lake, with **East Crater Trail #48** to the right (east). Immediately past the junction is **Junction Lake** and **Junction Lake Camp** , complete with two campsites 80 yards toward the water along a spur trail to the right (east). At 0.1 mile north of the East Crater Trail junction, the PCT crosses a small wooden bridge over Rush Creek, a small, slow-moving outlet stream, and wraps around the western tip of Junction Lake for another 0.1 mile to a junction with **Lemei Lake Trail #179**.

Blue Lake in Indian Heaven Wilderness is one of the most popular in the area.

The Junction Lake area has a wide-open feeling because vegetation on the lake's western shores is limited to grasses and huckleberries, thanks to boggy marshes. After hard rains, the trail can be a muddy hot mess here and you might have to hopscotch to avoid sinking in past your ankles. Then again, people fork over big bucks to get mud baths, so count yourself lucky. Junction Lake is very typical of Indian Heaven—shallow in depth, buggy during summer, and swampy around the edges. It is, however, a beautiful lake, which photographs well due to its sky-blue reflections and the lime-green shoreline.

In 0.9 mile beyond the East Crater Trail junction, pass a seasonal creek on a bend and stop for water if you need it and if the creek is flowing.

CULTUS CREEK CAMPGROUND

Located roughly 3.5 miles northeast on Indian Heaven Trail #33, Cultus Creek Campground is a popular car-camping spot for summertime recreationists. Should you want to meet up with someone or hop off the trail, you could deviate from the PCT at this junction. You can also reach the campground by heading north along the PCT for 2 miles and then following Cultus Creek Trail #108 for 1.5 miles. This latter option has more elevation gain and loss than the first, if you fancy more of a challenge.

HUCKLEBERRY HARVEST OFF FOREST ROAD 24

If you happen to be cruising through this area during huckleberry harvest (mid-August to mid-September), you'll definitely see people with buckets, as this is some of the best wild-berry picking in the country. The most desired berry of them all, out of the twelve species that grow in Washington, is the thin-leaved huckleberry, which is found in this spot. The berry's perfect purple coloration, sweet flavor, and large size make it coveted by both recreational and commercial harvesters.

Huckleberries started with fire. Thousands of years ago, uncontrolled fires burned through this area, charring trees and opening up the barren, acidic soil to sunlight, and up popped the huckleberries. As the berries flourished, people and wildlife became dependent on them for survival.

In subsequent years repeated fires, either set off naturally by lightning or intentionally by tribal members, kept the area open to sunlight and led to healthy crops. Today, researchers are working to determine the best way to keep huckleberries a viable and renewable resource.

North of FR 24, a **Handshake Agreement** with Native tribes is in place. For thousands of years, Native Americans spent summers and falls harvesting berries in this region. Harvesting berries not only provided sustenance but also became a ritual, cultural, and spiritual practice. The Sawtooth Berry Fields east of FR 24, as well as anywhere you see Handshake Agreement signs, are part of a historical understanding between the Forest Service and the tribes. These lands are protected and reserved for tribal harvesters to respect their long-standing culture and traditions.

A few rules apply if you want to take some berries home:

- You may not harvest berries in wilderness areas, including Indian Heaven. That said, a few here and there as a snack is not considered a harvest. Berries can't be removed from the area, however.
- In areas where harvesting is permitted, each person is allowed 3 gallons of huckleberries free of charge per year. That's way more than any gluttonous PCT hiker could possibly eat, assuming you're popping handfuls as well as putting them in your oatmeal at breakfast. And if you eat more than that, you'll want to have your trowel handy.
- If you want to sell berries or products containing berries, such as jams or fruit leather, you must secure a Special Forest Products Permit, available at the Mount Adams Ranger District in Trout Lake.
- The Gifford Pinchot National Forest doesn't issue commercial permits until mid-August.
- Respect the Handshake Agreement signs. Reserve those berries for Native American harvesters.

If not, you'll have to continue drawing from the sketchy lakes.

On the left (west), Elk Lake Trail #176 drops 50 feet from the PCT to the large and lovely Bear Lake, located 1.2 miles beyond the East Crater Trail junction. A couple of large woodsy campsites are located here (**Bear and Elk Lake Camp**) ⓿ and make fine choices for enjoying the ambiance of Indian Heaven. Another campsite is at Elk Lake, to the east roughly 0.5 mile farther along the Elk Lake Trail. While that particular campsite isn't as grand as those at Bear Lake, Elk Lake is a spectacular lake–deeper, clearer, and more private than most in the area—and may be well worth a visit.

On the PCT, continue through a sea of hemlocks and huckleberries until **Indian Heaven Trail #33** takes off on the right (east), 0.6 mile beyond the Elk Lake Trail junction. A couple of camps are at Clear Lake, 0.3 mile east along the Indian Heaven Trail.

Conifers, meadows, talus fields, and wetlands pepper the landscape, giving you the essence of the Indian Heaven ecosystem. As you gently climb around the shoulder of **Bird Mountain**, you'll reach **Placid Lake Trail #29** on the left (west), 1.7 miles beyond the Elk Lake Trail junction. Placid Lake is 2.6 miles to the west and there are no established camps or water before the lake itself, so if you are northward bound, then onward along the PCT you go!

Next up, the trail traverses the slopes of Bird Mountain and then begins a moderate descent. Look for an unsigned spur trail on the left (northwest), 0.5 mile from the Placid Lake Trail junction. This narrow spur leads downhill roughly 0.1 mile to a well-established campsite (**Camp 19**) with room for at least two tents near an unnamed pond. A small rock fire pit, the privacy in the trees, and the water source make this a good place to lay your head.

The mixture of hemlock and fir are thick as hairs on a Sasquatch's back as you head north, passing through boulder fields and the occasional patch of fragrant seasonal bear grass blooming trailside. At 0.9 mile from the Placid Lake Trail junction, reach **Wood Lake Trail #185** and **Cultus Creek Trail #108**. If you seek privacy in camping, Wood Lake has a woody one-tent campsite along its shoreline, 0.5 mile left (west) of this intersection. The lake itself might not knock your socks off, but it's restful and quiet at the edge of the conifers. Cultus Creek Campground is to the right (east) at this junction, 1.5 miles along the Cultus Creek Trail.

A similar landscape continues as you head north on a forgiving grade, allowing you to make good time and distance. In 1.3 miles from the Wood Lake/Cultus Creek junction, **Sawtooth Mountain Trail #107** joins the PCT to the right (northeast). This trail is an alternative to the PCT, since its purpose is purely scenic. It's longer by 0.3 mile and steeper by 325 feet than sticking to the PCT, but it may be worth checking out if time and gumption are on your side.

Along the PCT, spindly trees line the way as you descend toward FR 24. In 1.4 miles, meet up with the northern end of the Sawtooth Mountain Trail and then cruise through huckleberry thickets. Keep your eyes open for deer, elk, and bear in this dense, berry-laden forest, especially during harvest season—they like them as much as you do! Eye-popping views of Mount Adams show up to the trail's right (northeast), so close it looks like a hologram and takes your mind off the trek for a few minutes.

In 1.2 miles from the northern end of the Sawtooth Mountain Trail (2.6 miles from its southern end), arrive at **FR 24 (Twin Buttes Road)**. This gravel road is one of the area's main thoroughfares. Don't linger too long near its edges, or you'll be covered in dust as the trucks go zipping by. If need be, you could use this road as a meeting place or a pickup destination, because getting here by car from the nearby town of Trout Lake is pretty straightforward.

SAWTOOTH MOUNTAIN

Folks looking for lofty views of Indian Heaven Wilderness, Mount Adams, Mount St. Helens, and Mount Rainier might relish the trek to the crest of Sawtooth Mountain, where numerous viewpoints along the way allow your eyes a feast. The trail climbs approximately 380 feet to the forested summit of Sawtooth Mountain before rejoining the PCT 1.6 miles from where it started. Due to light usage, this trail has become slightly overgrown over the years—wear your shins' blue huckleberry tattoos with honor.

CAMP-TO-CAMP MILEAGE

Segment	Miles
FR 60 to Camp 15	1.7
Camp 15 to Camp 16	0.9
Camp 16 to Camp 17	0.7
Camp 17 to Camp 18	0.2
Camp 18 to Blue Lake Camp	3.8
Blue Lake Camp to Junction Lake Camp	1.8
Junction Lake Camp to Bear and Elk Lake Camp	1.2
Bear and Elk Lake Camp to Camp 19 spur	2.2
Camp 19 spur to FR 24	4.3

Opposite: *Huckleberry bushes add pops of burgundy to the trail's edges.*

5 FOREST ROAD 24 TO FOREST ROAD 23

DISTANCE 14.8 miles

ELEVATION GAIN/LOSS
+2240/–2500 feet

HIGH POINT 4540 feet

CONNECTING TRAILS AND ROADS
FR 24 (Twin Buttes Road), FR 8851, Steamboat Lake Trail #70, FR 88, FR 8810, FR 23

ON THE TRAIL

From **Forest Road 24 (Twin Buttes Road)**, the PCT immediately crosses near a small dirt parking lot and then guides hikers through relatively flat, Handshake Agreement huckleberry fields. During summer months, Native American berry pickers are often here bringing in the bounty of the bushes. The trail crosses three access roads in 0.3 mile before ducking back into spindly second-growth forest.

SURPRISE LAKE

Surprise Lake and Surprise Lake Campground are located off a dirt access road east of the PCT and are respectfully reserved for Native Americans during the summer months, especially during the berry harvest. Vehicle access is limited to high-clearance, four-wheel-drive vehicles only.

Those looking to camp will find a few cleared-out small tent sites tucked in along both sides of the trail (**Camp 20**). The 3.8 miles from FR 24 to the crossing of FR 8851 are somewhat forgettable, especially if you're deep in thought. Shaggy tree branches cling to the lower trunks of tall firs, while bear grass, lupine, and huckleberries dot the pathway. The ups and downs are gradual and gentle, allowing your mind to roam apace with your breathing, a metronome-like cadence. A seasonal creeklet, often stagnant and horsey, is just before paved FR 8851. If you can wait just another 0.2 mile, you'll find better water.

In 0.1 mile after crossing FR 8851, pass through a meadow and then arrive at a small bridge over the slow-moving, seasonal Mosquito Creek. The access can be a little muddy and the creek quite shallow, but it's not the worst place to draw a drink. Plenty of seasonal water is available for the next several miles, so if you aren't dry, there are more options. In 0.2 mile beyond FR 8851 (4 miles from FR 24), a beautiful, large three-tent campsite (**Mosquito Creek Camp**) shows up to the trail's right (south). This camp, surrounded by large conifers, comes complete with logs for sitting and a primitive rock fire pit.

Moving onward, the PCT's grade is mellow as it passes through evergreens, riparian brush, grassy meadows, and pockets of slide alder. Seasonal water trickles under brushy stream banks in at least five different locations along the trail before you pass another single-tent site (**Camp 21**) to the trail's right (south), 0.9 mile from Mosquito Creek Camp (4.9 miles from FR 24). This campsite isn't worth crowing about, since it's fairly close to the trail, but water is nearby and it's a fine enough place to crash if you aren't picky.

The landscape continues to be very similar as you wind your way east, crossing a defunct old road at 6.1 miles from FR 24 (2.3 miles from FR 8851). In 0.4 mile beyond the defunct road, cross a hardy seasonal outlet creek flowing from Steamboat Lake above. This is a great place for water provided the season isn't too dry.

Immediately after the creek, reach a junction with **Steamboat Lake Trail #70**, a feeder trail leading to **Steamboat Lake**. The midsized lake, complete with a primitive campground, is popular with the angling and 4x4 crowd. It's roughly 0.3 mile north of the PCT via this access trail.

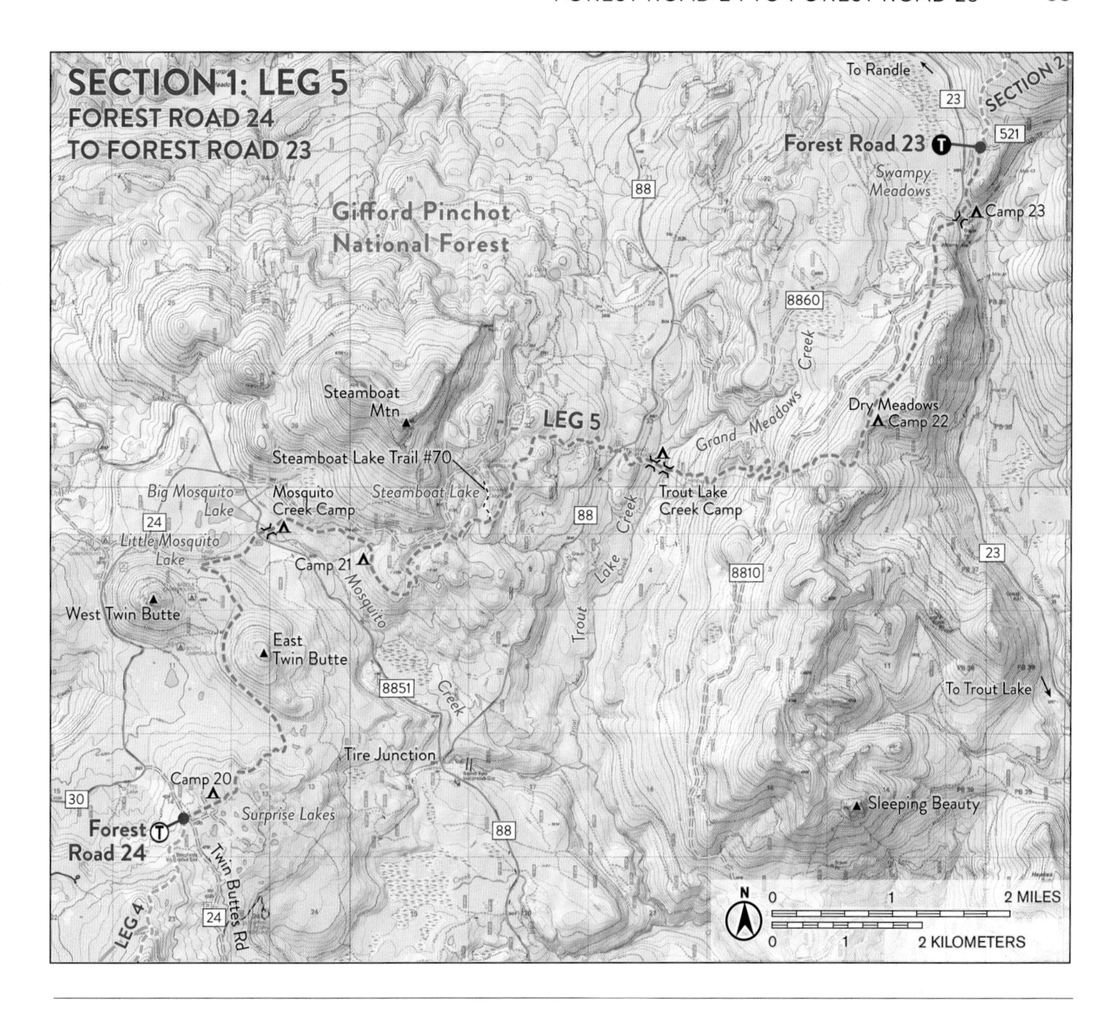

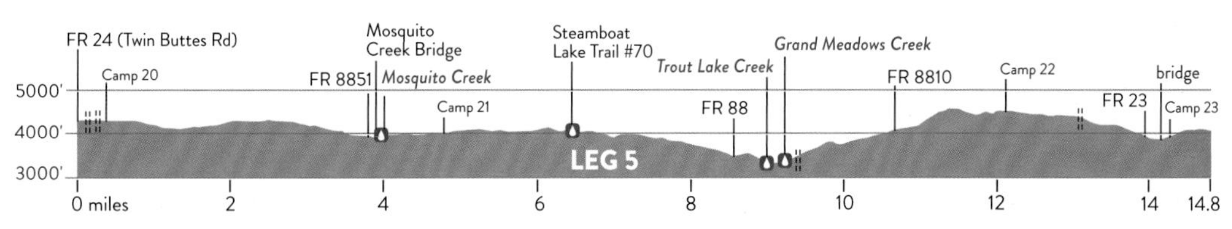

Over the next 2 miles, the trail gradually descends through the shade of tall timbers until it reaches the paved **FR 88**. From here, head left (north) for roughly 50 yards to find the PCT recommencing on the east side of the road. Back into the filtered sunlit forest you go, descending roughly 200 feet to reach the reliable **Trout Lake Creek**, 0.5 mile from FR 88. A small wooden bridge guides you across the creek to a spacious camp (**Trout Lake Creek Camp**) on the trail's left (north). This large camp, tucked into the trees, is big enough for four tents and has logs for sitting and a primitive rock fire pit. As far as PCT camps go, this one has all the comforts of home.

Immediately after passing the camp, cross another small wooden bridge over the small **Grand**

Meadows Creek and begin climbing up, up, up. Because you've been cruising on such a forgiving grade, this huff-and-puff feels worse than it really is. In 0.3 mile from Trout Lake Creek Camp, cross the no-longer-used FR 071 and continue your uphill grunt.

At 1.8 miles beyond Trout Lake Creek Camp, cross the gravel **FR 8810** and enjoy the flat surface for a minute or two before continuing the uphill jaunt along the PCT, positioned directly across the road. A sign on a tree notes the distances from road to road, but it's hard to read because of sap and tree growth. The tree is trying to eat this sign!

In roughly 0.5 mile from FR 8810, the trail finally gives you a reprieve from climbing and allows your calves and quads to relax. The trail takes a turn to the north and cruises through mossy, light-filled forest sprinkled with thickets of bear grass and huckleberries. In 1.2 miles from FR 8810, pass a small campsite (**Camp 22**) to the trail's right (east), just before the expanse of **Dry Meadows**. The camp is close to the trail and has space for two small tents. There's no water, so carry some if you plan to shoot for this destination. The meadow just beyond is a good place to check out starry skies at night.

Dry Meadows is teeming with wild strawberries, tempting all who walk by to sample. If you haven't experienced them before and they are ripe, do your taste buds a favor and eat a few! They are tiny but oh so sweet, and they make a great snack for hungry, produce-starved hikers. As always, be sure you make a positive ID before throwing berries down the hatch.

Looking at old maps, you can see how many logging and Forest Service roads once crisscrossed this area. Mother Nature has reclaimed many timeworn roads, including one you cross at 2.4 miles beyond FR 8810 (1.2 miles from Dry Meadows). Some of the defunct roads are so disguised with downed logs, brush, and debris, you might not even know you're crossing one. The conifer cruise continues along a lenient grade, spitting you out at gravel

Brush tries to overtake the trail near Mosquito Creek.

SYNCING UP AT FOREST ROAD 23

If folks are meeting you at FR 23, or you're leaving a car for a shuttle, you'll want to continue to the PCT parking area located farther north along the trail. Car access is via the short FR 521, which branches off FR 23 just north of where the PCT crosses the road. Occasionally, Trail Angels station themselves along FR 23, offering rides to PCT hikers into the town of Trout Lake, roughly 14 miles to the southeast.

FR 8810, 3 miles farther along than where you last crossed it (1.8 miles beyond Dry Meadows). Follow the gravel road to the right (east) and arrive at paved FR 23.

FR 23 gets a fair amount of traffic, so if hiker brain has set in be sure to stop, look, and listen to avoid becoming a hood ornament as you cross. Locate the PCT on the other side of the road and almost immediately cross a sturdy wooden bridge over a reliable water source. Just after the bridge, the PCT connects with an old roadway where camping (**Camp 23**) options are plentiful. This spacious area could easily accommodate four or five tents, but privacy is limited because of proximity to the trail. FR 23 is just a grove of trees away and you can hear the cars as they scoot by, an unfamiliar noise until now. Thankfully, the creek, especially after a rain, does its best to muffle engine noises and you fall asleep to white noise as you hit your pillow. If for some reason you want to get back out to FR 23 at this point, the old roadway still connects a couple of hundred feet to the west.

After the camp, the PCT climbs, gaining roughly 240 feet in the quiet forest before descending 50 feet and delivering you to the PCT parking lot, 0.8 mile beyond FR 23. There are no facilities at this trailhead, but parking is plentiful. Car access is via the short FR 521, which branches off FR 23. Dance a jig with those sore hiker feet if this is your destination. A smoothie in Trout Lake awaits!

CAMP-TO-CAMP MILEAGE

FR 24 to Camp 20 .... 0.3
Camp 20 to Mosquito Creek Camp 3.7
Mosquito Creek Camp to Camp 21 .... 0.9
Camp 21 to Trout Lake Creek Camp 4.2
Trout Lake Creek Camp to Camp 22 .... 3.0
Camp 22 to Camp 23 .... 2.0
Camp 23 to FR 23 .... 0.7

SECTION 2

FOREST ROAD 23 TO WHITE PASS

THIS WASHINGTON STATE PCT SECTION is unquestionably one of the most picturesque and memorable of the entire Mexico–Canada route. Ask thru-hikers which sections of the PCT are the most scenic, and you're sure to hear them say "Goat Rocks." Goat Rocks itself, in the wilderness area of the same name, is an extinct stratovolcano, with a rainbow of seasonal wildflower meadows framed by jagged peaks and sweeping views of rugged, distant mountains.

Before you get to the Goat Rocks Wilderness, you'll traipse through the Mount Adams Wilderness, complete with in-season fields of lupine and aster, giving you a window on renewal as the area bounces back from recent fires. Mount Adams, the state's second-highest volcano, will mesmerize you with its asymmetrical broad shoulders and ancient cascading glaciers.

Near the Coleman Weedpatch, your mind marinates in quietness save for a peck or two from a northern flicker as the views give way to tranquil tarns and small ponds. Your hand, rather than your pocket, will be your camera's new home as you enjoy all that this section has to offer.

ACCESS

PCT Trailhead off Forest Road 23

From the town of Trout Lake, head north at the Y near the area's only gas station onto Mount Adams Recreation Highway. At 1.2 miles, bear left on Forest Road 23. Proceed 12.6 miles to FR 521, signed "PCT North Trailhead." Turn right (east) and follow this unpaved but well-maintained spur road 0.3 mile to the trailhead on the north side of the road. Parking is plentiful.

From Randle, turn south onto State Route 131. After 0.9 mile, bear left at a junction onto FR 23. Stay on FR 23 for roughly 33 miles, passing onto

Opposite: *Lush foliage and tall conifers landscape the trail's edge near Forest Road 23.*

DISTANCE 65 miles

STATE DISTANCE 81.8–146.8 miles

ELEVATION GAIN/LOSS +11,100/–10,730 feet

HIGH POINT 7230 feet

BEST TIME OF YEAR July–Oct

PCTA SECTION LETTER H

LAND MANAGERS Gifford Pinchot National Forest (Mount Adams Ranger District, Cowlitz Valley Ranger District, Goat Rocks Wilderness, Mount Adams Wilderness)

PASSES AND PERMITS NW Forest Pass to park at White Pass Trailhead. Free self-issue wilderness permits at wilderness area trailheads.

MAPS AND APPS

- Halfmile's WA Section H
- USFS PCT Map #9 Southern Washington
- Green Trails Mt Adams West #366, Mt Adams #367S, Walupt Lake #335, White Pass #303, Goat Rocks/William O. Douglas Wilderness #303S
- Halfmile's PCT app, Guthook's overall PCT app and PCT WA app

LEGS

1. Forest Road 23 to Killen Creek
2. Killen Creek to Walupt Lake Trail
3. Walupt Lake Trail to Snowgrass Flat Trail
4. Snowgrass Flat Trail to White Pass

a long gravel stretch of road and then regaining pavement. Turn left (east) onto FR 521, signed "PCT North Trailhead." Turn right (east) and follow this unpaved but well-maintained spur road 0.3 mile to the trailhead on the north side of the road. Parking is plentiful.

White Pass

From Packwood, drive northeast on US Highway 12 for 20.4 miles to just past the summit of White Pass. Look for a small dirt parking area to the south signed "Pacific Crest Trail South" and "Cascade Crest Trail."

From Interstate 82 in Yakima, take exit 31A and follow the signs for "US 12 West/Naches." Drive approximately 17 miles, through the town of Naches, to a junction with State Route 410. Turn left (south) and continue on US 12 for 34 miles to a small dirt road to the north signed "Pacific Crest Trail North." Follow the narrow dirt road for 0.2 mile, passing Leech Lake, and locate the PCT parking area to the right (northeast).

NOTES

Cities and Services

Near the southern trailhead, find gas, a convenience store, dining, and lodging in Trout Lake. Near the northern trailhead, find gas, a convenience store, and lodging at the White Pass summit and ski area. Other cities near the northern trailhead are Randle, Packwood, and Yakima.

Camping and Other Restrictions

Camping is restricted in Snowgrass Flat and at Shoe Lake and Shoe Lake basin. **Campfires** are prohibited in Shoe Lake basin and within 0.25 mile of Goat Lake. Camping is prohibited within 100 feet of the PCT and within 100 feet of lakes. **Grazing, hitching, or tethering of stock** within 200 feet of all lakes in the Gifford Pinchot National Forest is prohibited. Please respect the no camping areas near Snowgrass Flat, marked on this guide's maps. Funding has dwindled and backcountry camping enforcement has been cut. It's up to us to keep our meadows and backcountry pristine. If you're interested in becoming a volunteer ranger in this area, contact the Cowlitz Valley Ranger District.

Water

At 2.7 miles from the trailhead, there's a spring, after which the trail is waterless for 6.4 miles north until Sheep Lake. North of Midway Creek, water is limited to murky ponds for roughly 7 miles or, in very dry summers, for up to 11 or more miles. And north of Snowgrass Flat Trail, water is scarce for 4.5 miles until north of the Goat Rocks Spine.

Hazards

This section's alpine terrain delivers permanent snowfields; narrow, rocky trail tread; and early- and late-season snow crossings. Trail washouts are common. Be prepared for any weather, check mountain forecasts, and check with land managers for possible trail issues before heading out. Additionally, at 12.4 miles north of the PCT Trailhead off FR 23, you'll have to cross Adams Creek, a silty, glacier-melt waterway that can be hazardous, especially after heavy rains or in early-season snowmelt. Rock or log hopping is very challenging and can be dangerous; most folks wade. See this guide's introduction for tips on water crossings.

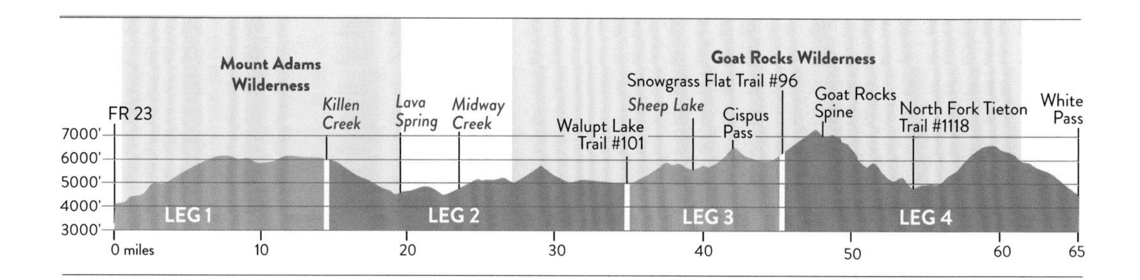

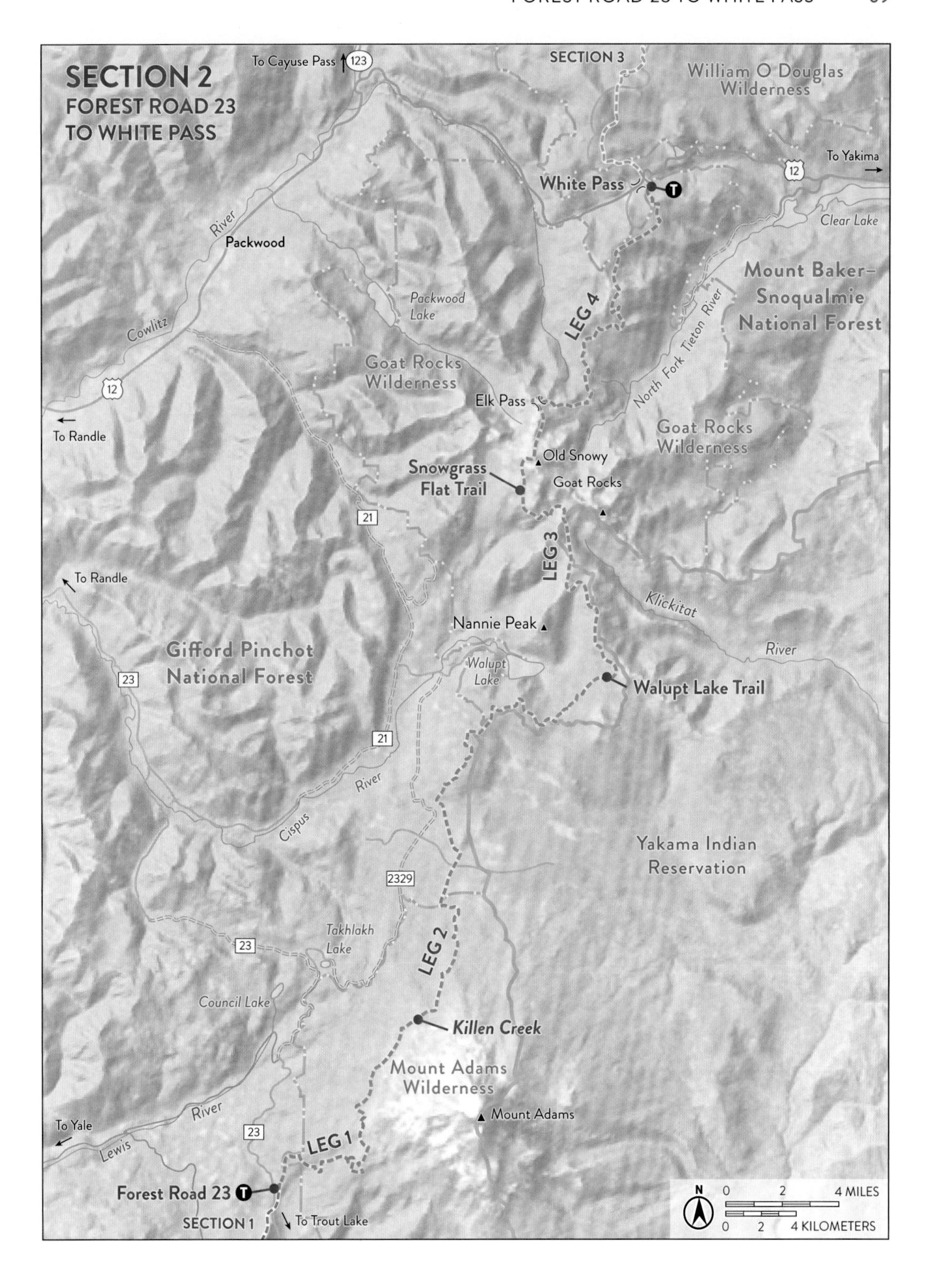
SECTION 2
FOREST ROAD 23
TO WHITE PASS
To Cayuse Pass 123
SECTION 3
William O Douglas Wilderness
To Yakima
12
White Pass
Clear Lake
River
Packwood
Mount Baker–Snoqualmie National Forest
Packwood Lake
LEG 4
Cowlitz
North Fork Tieton River
Goat Rocks Wilderness
12
Elk Pass
To Randle
Goat Rocks Wilderness
Old Snowy
Snowgrass Flat Trail
Goat Rocks
21
LEG 3
To Randle
Klickitat
Nannie Peak
River
Gifford Pinchot National Forest
Walupt Lake
Walupt Lake Trail
23
21
River
Cispus
Yakama Indian Reservation
2329
Takhlakh Lake
LEG 2
23
Council Lake
Killen Creek
Mount Adams Wilderness
Mount Adams
River
To Yale
23
Lewis
LEG 1
Forest Road 23
SECTION 1
To Trout Lake
N
0 2 4 MILES
0 2 4 KILOMETERS

Killen Creek Trail is just one of many connecting trails in Mount Adams Wilderness.

SUGGESTED ITINERARIES

Where noted, distances are to camp trail spurs; camp may be up to 0.3 mile from junction.

7 DAYS

		Miles
Day 1	FR 23 to Sheep Lake Camp (Mount Adams)	9.1
Day 2	Sheep Lake Camp to Lava Camp	10.5
Day 3	Lava Camp to Camp 7	9.9
Day 4	Camp 7 to Sheep Lake Camp (Goat Rocks) spur	10.0
Day 5	Sheep Lake Camp spur to High Country Camp	6.2
Day 6	High Country Camp to Hidden Springs Camp spur	11.3
Day 7	Hidden Springs Camp spur to White Pass	8.0

6 DAYS

Day 1	FR 23 to Sheep Lake Camp (Mount Adams)	9.1
Day 2	Sheep Lake Camp to Lava Camp	10.5
Day 3	Lava Camp to Camp 7	9.9
Day 4	Camp 7 to Sheep Lake Camp (Goat Rocks) spur	10.0
Day 5	Sheep Lake Camp spur to Lutz Lake Camp	13.2
Day 6	Lutz Lake Camp to White Pass	12.3

5 DAYS

Day 1	FR 23 to Sheep Lake Camp (Mount Adams)	9.1
Day 2	Sheep Lake Camp to Midway Creek Camp	14.8
Day 3	Midway Creek Camp to Sheep Lake Camp (Goat Rocks) spur	15.6
Day 4	Sheep Lake Camp spur to Lutz Lake Camp	13.2
Day 5	Lutz Lake Camp to White Pass	12.3

1 FOREST ROAD 23 TO KILLEN CREEK

DISTANCE 14.6 miles

ELEVATION GAIN/LOSS
+2890/–990 feet

HIGH POINT 6150 feet

CONNECTING TRAILS
Riley Shortcut Trail #64A, Stagman Ridge Trail #12, Riley Trail #64, Divide Camp Trail #112, Killen Creek Trail #113

ON THE TRAIL

Locate the large PCT trailhead sign and fill out your free self-issue wilderness permit before heading into the hinterlands. Another sign reminds you that the trail is open to hikers and horsemen and that the terrain is considered "more difficult." New hikers might find the grade a bit challenging, but one foot in front of the other gets you where you need to go, no worries, no hurries!

Enter the fir and hemlock forest and in 0.2 mile reach a large camp (**Large Forest Camp**) to the left (west), suitable for at least four tents and set beneath the tall conifers. The camp boasts log benches and ample room for larger groups. Just beyond is a sturdy wooden bridge over a seasonal tributary, which can be an unreliable water source in dry summers. If water is flowing, you may want to grab some, because the next dependable water is 2.5 miles beyond.

In 0.5 mile from the trailhead, the **Mount Adams Wilderness** welcomes you via a tree sign. Technically, you're still roughly 0.5 mile from the actual boundary, but it's fun to play along. Note the beautiful contrast between the rusty coloration of decaying soil sprinkled with conifer needles and the bright-green foliage of trailside perennials as you gradually gain elevation. In 1.2 miles from the trailhead, a flat spot cleared of debris to the trail's left (west) could be used for one tent in a pinch. The site is very small, lacks privacy, and is close to the trail, so it's not an official camp in this guide.

The conifer ramble continues and in 1.4 miles from the trailhead, a shallow, unreliable seasonal creek dribbles near the trail. Just beyond it, to the trail's left (west), is a one-tent campsite (**Camp 1**). It's nothing to write home about, since it's close to the trail and lacks privacy, but it is relatively flat, is free of debris, and gets regular use by thru-hikers. It's a good place to saw some logs (figuratively, of course; actually sawing logs in a wilderness area is frowned upon).

A short 0.1 mile beyond Camp 1 (1.5 miles from the trailhead), arrive at a junction with **Riley Shortcut Trail #64A**, a connector to the Riley Trail. The official PCT heads right, while the shortcut to the left shaves 2.4 miles.

RILEY SHORTCUT TRAIL #64A

To detour off the PCT, follow the Riley Shortcut Trail north for roughly 2 miles to intersect Riley Trail #64 (also called the Riley Camp or Riley Creek Trail). Once there, go right (east) and reenter the wilderness area via gently graded switchbacks. In 1.8 miles from the Riley Trail intersection, arrive at the first of several unnamed small lakes and ponds. From there, gentle ups and downs guide you to Riley Creek Meadows, offering Mount Adams views and several pleasant, although sometimes buggy, camps near the silted Riley Creek. The Riley Trail meets up with the PCT 3.5 miles from its junction with the Riley Shortcut Trail, making this detour about 5.5 miles, which is 2.4 miles shorter than the official PCT route.

Shortly after passing the Riley Shortcut Trail, the PCT turns southeast and climbs high, somewhat steeply at times, into a burn zone. The landscape is rebounding from the hot fires of 2012, and small plants and saplings are thriving in the sooty, acidic soil. Around you, songbirds trill, woodpeckers peck, and butterflies flutter.

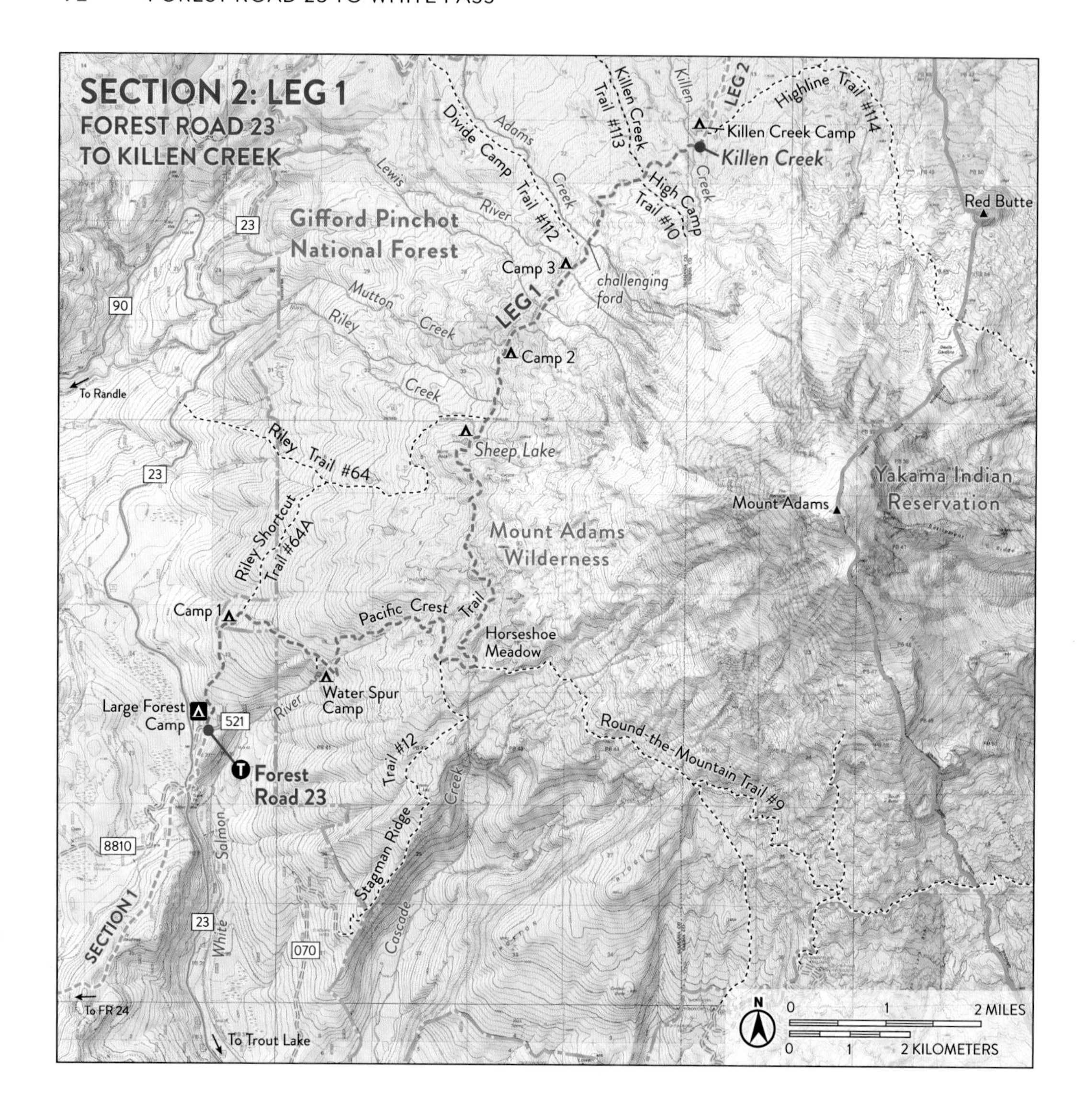
SECTION 2: LEG 1
FOREST ROAD 23
TO KILLEN CREEK
Gifford Pinchot
National Forest
Mount Adams
Wilderness
Yakama Indian
Reservation
Killen Creek Camp
Killen Creek
Highline Trail #114
Killen Creek Trail #113
High Camp Trail #10
Divide Camp Trail #112
Adams Creek
Lewis River
Camp 3
challenging ford
LEG 1
LEG 2
Mutton Creek
Riley Creek
Camp 2
Sheep Lake
Riley Trail #64
Riley Shortcut Trail #64A
Camp 1
Pacific Crest Trail
Horseshoe Meadow
Water Spur Camp
Large Forest Camp
Forest Road 23
Round-the-Mountain Trail #9
Trail #12
Stagman Ridge
Cascade Creek
White Salmon River
Mount Adams
Red Butte
To Randle
To FR 24
To Trout Lake
SECTION 1
23
90
521
8810
070
0 1 2 MILES
0 1 2 KILOMETERS

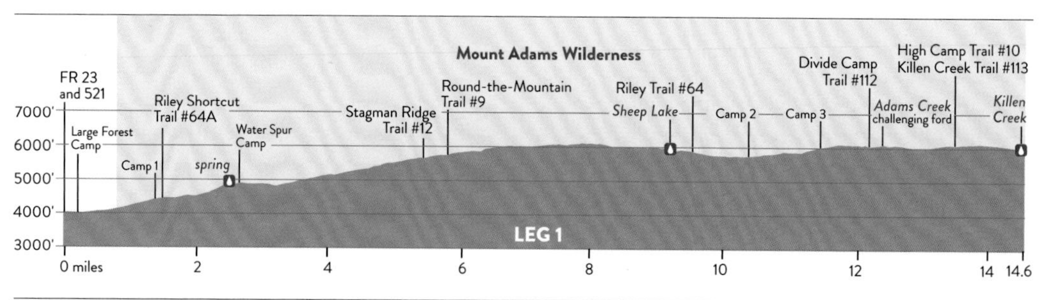
Mount Adams Wilderness
FR 23 and 521
Large Forest Camp
Camp 1
Riley Shortcut Trail #64A
spring
Water Spur Camp
Stagman Ridge Trail #12
Round-the-Mountain Trail #9
Sheep Lake
Riley Trail #64
Camp 2
Camp 3
Divide Camp Trail #112
Adams Creek challenging ford
High Camp Trail #10
Killen Creek Trail #113
Killen Creek
LEG 1
7000'
6000'
5000'
4000'
3000'
0 miles
2
4
6
8
10
12
14
14.6

Reach an easy-to-miss water source 🅞 2.7 miles from the trailhead. A small, makeshift sign that simply says "Water" is attached to a tree and points the way via a spur trail to the right (south). Access this reliable spring by leaving the main trail and dropping 50 yards through brushy vegetation. This is the last water until Sheep Lake, 6.4 miles beyond this point. So top off!

Back on the PCT, a well-used one-tent camp (**Water Spur Camp**) is 0.1 mile beyond the water spur, to the PCT's right (south). The camp is relatively flat and was spared from the hot fire.

For the next several miles, you'll pass through scorched trees, some without bark, some standing erect as if frozen in time, and some crisscrossing the fire-scarred ground. As in all fire zones, proceed with caution. The dead standing timbers are unstable and may topple over in an ample wind.

The PCT climbs north for a bit and then turns east again and wanders through large boulders spread about randomly, providing visual interest among the charred trees. Keep your eyes open for elk and deer that come here to feast on the tender new shoots of the rebounding plants. Enjoy the reprieve of a lush green meadow, spared from fire, before the charcoaled trees again guide you along.

At 5.4 miles from the trailhead, arrive at a junction with **Stagman Ridge Trail #12**, to the right (south). This trail, like so many in Mount Adams Wilderness, is popular with the horsemen, so don't be surprised if you meet some clippity-clopping hooves and riders. The next 0.4 mile climbs through fields of aster, Solomon's seal, and dwarf huckleberries before arriving at a junction with **Round-the-Mountain Trail #9**. This intersection is marked only with PCT signs, so it's easy to miss it and just continue on. The PCT makes a hard left (north) here and offers a gentle grade.

To the right (east) is the lovely **Horseshoe Meadow**, a favorite of photographers and wildflower enthusiasts. In season, the large meadow is teeming with aster and lupine, creating a blanket of purple in the foreground of Mount Adams. A sprinkle of burned trees adds to the visual spectacle.

Heading north, the PCT flirts with the western shoulders of Mount Adams and graciously guides hikers through open forest and wonderful pockets of seasonal wildflowers. Lupine, aster, paintbrush, bistort, valerian, and many more varieties provide a showy, fragrant trailside rainbow as you meander up and down the forgiving grade. Occasional views of Mount Adams to the east and Mount Hood to the south are trail treats. Rock gardens left years ago by receding glaciers look as if, in places, landscape architects have been strategically at work among the wildflowers. Along the way, viewpoints with stones for sitting make good snack or pack-off breaks, while gray jays call hollowly from barren

Brilliant wildflower gardens are common in Mount Adams Wilderness.

limbs above. The Mount Adams high country rewards your climb with an enveloping tranquility.

In 3.3 miles from the Trail #9 junction (9.1 miles from the trailhead), Sheep Lake ◘ shows up to the left (west), along with the large and well-used **Sheep Lake Camp** (there's another Sheep Lake Camp later on, in the Goat Rocks Wilderness). The camp fits roughly three small tents and provides access to the calm shoreline. Other water seekers may wander through your site in their efforts, so be prepared to make some happy hiker friends. Sheep Lake is fairly small, stagnant, and buggy, especially during the early season. At least two other campsites are located around Sheep Lake, so wander until you find one to call home.

From Sheep Lake, the PCT continues north and rock hops its way across the silted Riley Creek in 0.2 mile. Like many volcanoes, Mount Adams sheds silty water thanks to fine sediment deposited in the creeks by melting glaciers high on the mountain's flanks. Water color ranges from completely opaque to slightly dingy and can clog a water filter lickety-split. Filter water from lakes and clear streams, or use iodine tablets or UV-purification devices and expect a little crunch in your tetrazzini.

In 0.3 mile beyond Sheep Lake, arrive at a junction with **Riley Trail #64** to the left (west) (this is the end of the shortcut route you passed some 8 miles back). Roughly 0.4 mile along this trail are a couple of pleasant camps near Riley Creek Meadows. The camps have room for several tents and would be a good destination for a larger group. Back on the PCT, you'll encounter three small seasonal creeks over the next 0.2 mile, which, if flowing, are clear enough to filter. Hooray for hydration!

The trail winds through grassy meadows dotted with fir trees and boulders until it arrives at a jumble of volcanic lava left by mudflows up to thirty-five hundred years ago. The soft sandy soils between the rocks provide several places where you could squirrel away your tent for the night, with one of the largest (**Camp 2**) located 1.1 miles from the Riley Trail junction (10.5 miles from the trailhead). The flat campsites, to the left and right of the trail, can support two small tents each. Because the sites are visible from the trail, they aren't optimal for privacy, but hey, this is the PCT, so we take what we can find when we're sleepy. The ambiance isn't too bad, and the thickets of trees provide a little shelter from wind and a place to hang your hat.

The lava promenade continues, reminding you of how close you are to a potentially active stratovolcano. **Mount Adams** is the second-highest peak in Washington, only about 2130 feet shorter than Mount Rainier. While Adams hasn't erupted in fourteen hundred years, scientists don't consider it to be extinct. They monitor occasional thermal anomalies and gas emissions to predict any signs of instability. The odds of Adams erupting while you're on your mountain rendezvous are very slim, so enjoy the tranquility and don't worry your sweet head.

Over the 1.4 miles beyond Camp 2, you'll rock hop across six milky-colored, glacier-melt creeks and rivers, the largest being Lewis River, before arriving at another camp (**Camp 3**). The Mount Adams–style sandy, flat spot is immediately left (northwest) of the trail and easily accommodates five or six small tents. Like most camps in this area, this one isn't going to knock your socks off in terms of views or location. It's near the trail, so neither secluded nor private, but the camp's ability to accommodate a larger group is tempting if you have worn-out Boy Scouts in tow.

Continue your gentle mountain ramble, reaching **Divide Camp Trail #112**, 0.3 mile from Camp 3 (2.8 miles from the Riley Trail junction). With a name like "Divide Camp," you might think that majestic camp awaits! Not so. The camp—0.7 mile to the left (northwest) along the Divide Camp Trail and then another 0.3 mile left (south) at a signed spur—is a typical set of campsites in the trees, complete with a small seasonal dribble nearby. Scenic meadows near the camp trail spur make for great photo souvenirs if the wildflowers are blooming and Mount Adams is not hiding its rugged face.

Opposite: *The sunset adds scintillating spectrums of color to the wildflower fields and rugged summit of Mount Adams.*

THE 2012 FIRES IN MOUNT ADAMS WILDERNESS

I was sound asleep in my tent on the night of September 8, 2012. After an exhausting day of hiking nearly 16 miles on various trails, I'd fallen asleep almost as soon as my head hit the pillow.

I became aware of a crow cawing overhead as if in distress, and I woke up to massive thunderclaps and strikes of lightning across the sky. "This is going to be ugly," I remember thinking. Since I was in no danger, I put my pillow over my head and tried to go back to sleep amid the crashes and flashes. The next morning at my camp near Randle, I woke to the news I'd feared: several pocket fires were quickly merging and spreading on Mount Adams's high slopes. Days went by and smoke filled the air. Hazy skies showed the peril by day, while flames illuminated the slopes by night. The PCT and several connecting trails were closed to all foot traffic, save for those brave men and women trying to dig fire lines. By the time the rains and first snow finally fizzled the smoldering mess, 20,038 acres, almost half of the Mount Adams Wilderness, had burned.

Charcoaled trees and loamy, acidic soils in burn zones invite an abundance of new life.

The next summer, I drove back to the area with a heavy heart to see the damage in the fire zone. To my surprise, my spirits were lifted. Just a few months later, new life was springing up. It was fascinating to walk through the charred remains and loamy soils, as the creaking trees seemed to relate their mesmerizing stories. Amid the destruction, bees and hummingbirds buzzed around the new plant shoots. Beetles and ants raced around charred logs, and above me I heard the insistent drumming of the black-backed woodpecker. The nutrient-rich soils brought strength and fervor to foliage roots as new light hit the forest floor. Many of the trees in this area were dead on their feet before the fire, so Mother Nature had done some necessary housekeeping.

In subsequent years, the Mount Adams area has suffered even more fire damage. In the dry, hot summer of 2015, in early July, the west side of the mountain, near the Riley Trail, burst into several small spot fires that quickly merged, charring 340 acres. And on August 10 that same year, lightning aimed its fiery strength at Adams's southeast side, severely burning more than 53,500 acres.

As you hike and camp in fire zones, be sure to use caution as trees may become unstable, especially in high wind. Check with an area's land managers before setting out to learn the latest trail conditions or closures. And, whatever you do, stop to listen. The new life that springs back after tragedy is a wonderful lesson. The fire zone might just be nature's finest teacher.

Open meadows along the PCT offer views of the mighty glaciers of Mount Adams.

Along the PCT, subalpine firs intermittently dot the rocky landscape as you head into a large swath of boulders and glacial deposits. Give a mental high five to the folks who help hikers navigate this stretch by outlining the gravel trail with boulders. Follow the stone cairns, otherwise known as purposefully placed rock piles, if you happen to lose the route. Note the brilliantly colored stones—burgundy, rust, tan, and pink. Beauty is found in this lifeless, desolate setting!

In 0.2 mile from the Divide Camp Trail junction (12.4 miles from the trailhead), arrive at the big kahuna of water crossings in this area, **Adams Creek**. This silted creek is the largest around and has **no bridge**, challenging hikers to pick their way across in the fashion that best suits them. Some years, skinny logs wash downstream, helping those with good balance cross on slippery beams. Other years, rocks can be used as stepping-stones for those with long legs and extensive jumping abilities. Many, though, prefer to play it safe and wade across, avoiding an unexpected tumble into the drink. Water levels fluctuate seasonally, sometimes gushing forcefully and obligating hikers to cross several branches of swift water before declaring victory on the opposing bank. For the best crossing opportunities, don't follow the crowd. My experience with this creek has been to walk up and down the bank until I find a crossing that looks manageable for my personal abilities. Sometimes, that's much farther up or down than you'd think. PCT hikers tend to want to cross right where the trail spits them out, but that's not always the best option. See this guide's introduction for tips on water crossings, and manage your risk by knowing your abilities and following your gut instinct about what's best for you personally. Your hiking partner might have the grace of an elegant swan, while

Early morning rays light up the horizon near Killen Creek.

you might take after a water buffalo. Embrace that wonderful you and entertain your companions.

Once you're safely across Adams Creek, the PCT pops in and out of grassy wildflower meadows and thickets of conifers. In 0.8 mile beyond the creek, a seasonal tarn is to the trail's left (northeast). If you need water, you could filter here, but it's best to wait for flowing water if possible, since this tarn is stagnant. The trail rambles on and in 0.3 mile from the tarn arrives at a junction with **High Camp Trail #10** to the right (southeast), which leads 1.1 miles to some spectacularly scenic camping high on the shoulders of Mount Adams. **Killen Creek Trail #113** arrives on the left (northwest), roughly 100 feet beyond the High Camp Trail junction.

From here the trail descends through meadows speckled with dwarf evergreens until passing a couple of tarns to the trail's right (southeast), 1 mile from the Killen Creek Trail junction. **Killen Creek** itself is immediately past the tarns, spanned by a wooden bridge. The creek lightheartedly bounces down rocks just below the trail, forming a small waterfall bordered by wildflowers. At 0.1 mile beyond Killen Creek, a spur trail leads to plentiful campsites (**Killen Creek Camp**) in a meadow to the trail's left (northwest). This is an ideal camping area, complete with several private tent sites tucked into tree thickets and bountiful clear water from the nearby creek.

CAMP-TO-CAMP MILEAGE

FR 23 to Large Forest Camp	0.2
Large Forest Camp to Camp 1	1.2
Camp 1 to Water Spur Camp	1.4
Water Spur Camp to Sheep Lake Camp (Mount Adams)	6.3
Sheep Lake Camp to Camp 2	1.4
Camp 2 to Camp 3	1.4
Camp 3 to Killen Creek Camp	2.7

2 KILLEN CREEK TO WALUPT LAKE TRAIL

DISTANCE 20.2 miles

ELEVATION GAIN/LOSS
+1880/–2850 feet

HIGH POINT 5950 feet

CONNECTING TRAILS AND ROADS
Muddy Meadows Trail #13, FR 5603, FR 115, Coleman Weedpatch Trail #121, Walupt Lake Trail #101

ON THE TRAIL

From **Killen Creek Camp**, the PCT meanders through spindly firs before arriving at a junction with **Highline Trail #114** in 0.2 mile. From here, a mild descent takes you past a shallow, unnamed lake that's set about 80 feet down a slope to the left (west), with no obvious spur trail. Another lake just after the first, 0.3 mile from the Highline Trail junction, is much closer to the trail and has a spur trail leading to a small one-tent lakeside camp (**Camp 4**).

Hairy firs with moss on their lower limbs dot the trail's edges, and bear grass and huckleberries grow at their feet. In 2.4 miles from the Highline Trail junction, reach another junction, this one with **Muddy Meadows Trail #13**. In 0.8 mile beyond this junction, the PCT continues descending and crosses through a silver forest—the white ghost trees frozen in time from long ago.

At 1.5 miles from the Muddy Meadows Trail junction, cross a small, shallow, seasonal creeklet, which could serve as a watering hole if you're low; but it's unreliable, so don't count on it. In another 0.1 mile (1.6 miles beyond Muddy Meadows Trail junction), a sturdy wooden bridge crosses the **South Fork Muddy Creek**. Muddy is right! This dog looks like churning chocolate milk and should not be considered a water source . . . even though chocolate milk does sound delicious.

Caught in a rocky basin, the spring near Lava Camp is some of the clearest water on the entire PCT.

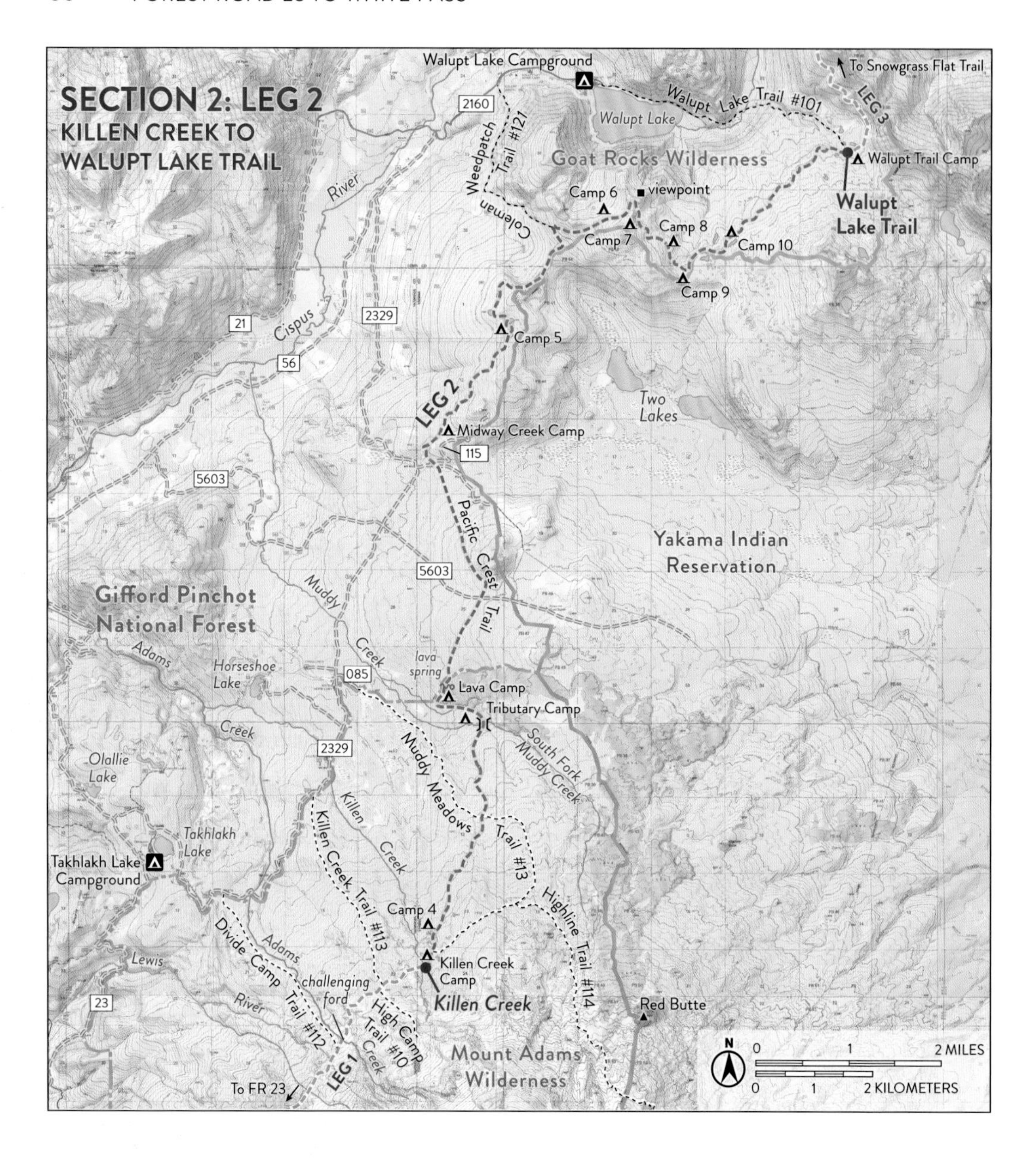
SECTION 2: LEG 2
KILLEN CREEK TO
WALUPT LAKE TRAIL
Walupt Lake Campground
To Snowgrass Flat Trail
Walupt Lake Trail #101
LEG 3
Walupt Lake
Goat Rocks Wilderness
Walupt Trail Camp
Walupt
Lake Trail
Camp 6
viewpoint
Camp 7
Camp 8
Camp 10
Camp 9
Coleman
Weedpatch
Trail #121
2160
River
Cispus
21
56
2329
Camp 5
LEG 2
Two
Lakes
Midway Creek Camp
115
5603
Pacific Crest Trail
Yakama Indian
Reservation
Gifford Pinchot
National Forest
Muddy
Creek
lava
spring
Lava Camp
Tributary Camp
085
Adams
Horseshoe
Lake
Creek
2329
South Fork
Muddy Creek
Olallie
Lake
Muddy Meadows
Trail #13
Killen
Creek
Killen Creek Trail #113
Takhlakh
Lake
Takhlakh Lake
Campground
Camp 4
Highline Trail #114
Killen Creek
Camp
Killen Creek
Adams
Lewis
River
Divide Camp
Trail #112
challenging
ford
High Camp
Trail #10
Creek
23
Red Butte
Mount Adams
Wilderness
LEG 1
To FR 23
0 1 2 MILES
0 1 2 KILOMETERS

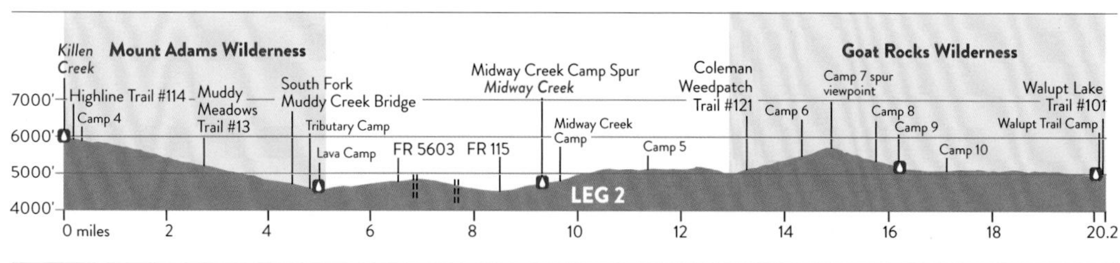
Killen
Creek
Mount Adams Wilderness
Goat Rocks Wilderness
Highline Trail #114
Camp 4
Muddy
Meadows
Trail #13
South Fork
Muddy Creek Bridge
Tributary Camp
Lava Camp
FR 5603
FR 115
Midway Creek Camp Spur
Midway Creek
Midway Creek
Camp
Camp 5
Coleman
Weedpatch
Trail #121
Camp 6
Camp 7 spur
viewpoint
Camp 8
Camp 9
Camp 10
Walupt Lake
Trail #101
Walupt Trail Camp
LEG 2
7000'
6000'
5000'
4000'
0 miles
2
4
6
8
10
12
14
16
18
20.2

After the forested areas of the Coleman Weedpatch, the PCT wanders up along a ridgeline to give hikers a sneak preview of the coming attractions of Goat Rocks Wilderness.

The trail reaches another wooden bridge over a silted tributary in 0.5 mile from Muddy Creek, followed by a large, well-used camp (**Tributary Camp**) to the trail's left. This camp, visible from the trail but off the beaten path via a short spur, has room for three or four small tents, trees for privacy, and purring white noise from the creek to put you to sleep. Unfortunately, this tributary is slightly silted and isn't great for filters. You could boil water from it, or treat it with iodine tablets or UV light, if you don't mind a little grit. Some of the best water along the entire PCT is 0.3 mile north at a lava spring. You could always play rock, paper, scissors with your hiking partner—rules say that two out of three wins a rest while the other person fetches the drink!

In 0.3 mile from Tributary Camp, the trail twists and turns through huckleberries and spotty evergreens until it reaches a spur on the right (north), diving into the trees. This spur goes to a large, very well-used camp (**Lava Camp**) set amid a jumble of lava stones, with room for approximately five small tents. A lovely crystal-clear spring is along the PCT roughly 100 feet beyond the camp spur. Applaud the trail crews who built a rocky retaining wall to create a small pond, making it easier to fill bottles. The natural filtration from deep in the earth makes this water especially pure and tasty, although filtering/treating for surface contaminants is always recommended. On the edge of the lava field is a tree sign noting the Mount Adams Wilderness boundary—say goodbye and look forward to Goat Rocks, coming soon!

The next 1.6 miles takes you past the lava field and then onward through sparse subalpine fir and lodgepole pine. Elevation gain and loss are hardly worth a mention as you wander through intermittent bear grass, huckleberry shrubs, and lupine blossoms, soon reaching a memorial placard, a trailhead sign, and FR 5603. The placard is dedicated to Matt Delson and the Delson Family for their efforts in trail maintenance along the PCT. The neatly stacked lava rocks and placard in concrete are reminders that volunteering a little extra love can make history. The trailhead sign is your typical wooden-style billboard, with a box of wilderness permits and information for those headed south.

FR 5603 is a well-maintained but lightly used gravel road taking eastbound car travelers 0.8 mile to the guard station of the Yakama Indian Reservation and westbound travelers to various other forest roads and, eventually, the towns of Randle and Packwood. Cross the road and find the continuation of the PCT on the north side, along with a small gravel parking lot and another trailhead sign.

You are very close to the **Yakama Indian Reservation** on this next stretch, and small metal signs are there to remind you. In 1972, under the direction of President Richard Nixon, the reservation boundary was relocated based on the Indian Claims Commission's account of its being incorrectly placed during the Treaty of 1855. As you travel through this area, please be respectful of the boundaries and travel and camp on Forest Service land only.

For the next 6 miles or so, until you reach the Goat Rocks Wilderness boundary, this stretch of the PCT is not very aesthetically pleasing. In fact, the trail seems in the midst of a desperate identity crisis, going from defunct old road to trail and back, crossing a couple of abandoned spur roads on its way. Thankfully, the grade is a piece of cake, with minimal elevation gains and losses that quickly move you along.

After the trailhead north of FR 5603, begin your ramble through meager lodgepole pines and Douglas-firs around the base of the uninspiring Potato Hill. Shortly after, the trail magically turns into a double-track old jeep road, heading northeast before turning back into a single-track trail. If you're desperate to camp, a couple of lackluster one-tent spots of flattened bear grass can be found along this stretch, but they aren't optimal or recommended.

In 1.9 miles from FR 5603, cross the scarcely used dirt **FR 115** and continue on the PCT. Immediately after the road junction, traverse a small, sloping grassy meadow and reenter the forest landscape, now looking familiar for this stretch. At 0.3 mile from FR 115, arrive at a **trailside sign** containing free self-issue wilderness permits. The Goat Rocks Wilderness is up ahead, so fill yours out. The Forest Service uses the information collected for educational purposes and to apply for additional trail-maintenance funding. Past the sign is a shallow, trickling seasonal creek. A much better option is Midway Creek, 0.4 mile ahead.

In 0.3 mile from the trailside permit station (0.6 mile from FR 115), arrive at a short spur to the right (east), which leads to a meadow with camping aplenty (**Midway Creek Camp**). This open meadow, not visible from the trail, can easily accommodate five or six tents and is near Midway Creek. Because the camp is so large, you may end up sharing it with other hikers looking for a place to crash. Employ the Golden Rule, make some friends, and get to know your fellow travelers. Their DNA is likely quite similar to your own!

Just past the camp spur is another seasonal creeklet. This isn't Midway Creek, although in wet seasons it may have enough flow to supply water if you're too tired to take your poor aching feet another 0.1 mile (now *that's* tired). In that 0.1 mile, you'll reach the second part of Midway Creek Camp (to the trail's left, several flat sites in a meadow), which is just before **Midway Creek** ◘. This creek is beyond the camp, through the trees, and most years is about 3 feet wide, the widest creek along this trail stretch. **Stopping to fill up is recommended**, as the next water you'll pass, except for seasonal trickles, is in stagnant ponds—ick!

Immediately beyond Midway Creek is yet another meadow with campsites, still what I'm calling Midway Creek Camp, as well as a couple of abandoned, unmaintained connecting trails. Make sure you're a wiz with a compass if you intend to explore the hinterlands beyond your camp, or you'll find yourself between a creek and a hard place.

From here the PCT passes a couple of grassy meadows before diving deeply into a second-growth forest. In 0.8 mile from Midway Creek, cross a small seasonal trickle, unreliable in warm seasons. The trail rolls up and down now, alternating between deep forest and huckleberry-laden meadows on the evergreen edges. In places, tall firs swallow the daylight, darkening the trail, while in other stretches they graciously let in the sun.

Starting at 1.9 miles beyond Midway Creek, pass a series of stagnant ponds that range in size and color. Insects love this perfect nursery, so most hikers hoof it past as fast as possible, trying to avoid pesky biters. In 2.3 miles beyond Midway Creek, a two-tent campsite shows up to the trail's left

Fragrant meadows and large rocky buttresses help make the Goat Rocks Wilderness so memorable.

Many shallow lakes greet northbound hikers just after they enter the Goat Rocks Wilderness.

(**Camp 5**). The site is surrounded by evergreens and the vibe is decent, except for the lack of privacy owing to its being next to the trail.

Beyond Camp 5, more tarns sit quietly undisturbed, some light brown, some a dark rust color. Don't consider them for water unless you're in dire straits. Where there are bodies of water, there are usually camps. In this case, most of the flat spots around are very lightly used because of the abundant bitty biters and the lack of clean water.

At 3.7 miles past Midway Creek, enter the Goat Rocks Wilderness, announced by a tree sign to the trail's right (east). Immediately, the conifers seem larger and the ecosystem healthier as the trail guides you through huckleberries and bear grass beneath the forest canopy. The PCT traverses the west side of a forested hill before climbing a moderate switchback to reach a junction with **Coleman Weedpatch Trail #121**, 0.6 mile beyond the wilderness boundary (4.3 miles past Midway Creek).

The trail ascends gradually beyond the Coleman Weedpatch Trail junction and passes two more murky ponds in roughly 0.8 mile. A lightly used two-tent camp (**Camp 6**) is along a spur trail, through the trees toward the pond on the left. It's nothing to crow about, but it will work if you're hard pressed to find a spot to snooze.

From here, the PCT heads east and crests a conspicuous ridgeline, 1.3 miles from the Coleman Weedpatch Trail junction. To the right (south) via a spur trail is a lightly used one-tent camp (**Camp 7**) near a meadow. The camp is not well defined and has no water, but you would have a quiet evening, since the spot is private and not visible from the trail.

Directly across the PCT from this camp spur, to the left (north), is a short trail to a **viewpoint**, where you can catch your first real glimpse of the spectacle of Goat Rocks. Old Snowy and the jagged remnants of the ancient stratovolcano are on the horizon, and Walupt Lake is visible in the valley below. It all seems so far away, but you'll be there in a hop, skip, and a jump!

The PCT turns southeast after the viewpoint and ambles just below the ridge crest in the heart of subalpine country. Mount Adams shows off her flat summit in the distance as wildflowers give a pop of color to the foreground. Just when you thought there would be more time in the subalpine country, the trail drops you back down into the forest. Thankfully, a few meadows show up here and there to break the monotony.

In roughly 1 mile from the viewpoint, a three-tent camp (**Camp 8**) is visible to the trail's left in the middle of a patch of tall trees. Since the camp is lightly used and is more of a cleared-out flat spot than a well-constructed campsite, you'll want to look closely to find it. Just beyond Camp 8 is another flat spot, this one immediately to the trail's left (northwest). Based on the cleared debris, it's been used for camping several times, but it's close to the trail and so not optimal. Several flat spots around here could be used for campsites if the Sandman is closing in on your evening.

In 1.4 miles from the viewpoint (0.4 mile from Camp 8), a stream trickle often dribbles enough to fill a water bottle or two. It's the only flowing water anywhere around, so I'm listing it as a water source and crossing my fingers for you. Let's put it this way: I've never seen it dry in the several times I've passed by here, but I've heard rumors that it dries up in unusually hot, drought-stricken summers. Immediately beyond the creek to the trail's right (southeast) is a well-used camp (**Camp 9**) complete with a fire pit and room for two tents.

The trail levels off some and passes a pond, arriving at **Camp 10** in 0.4 mile from the water trickle. Two campsites are on either side of the trail, very close to it. They're not often used but they're obvious enough to a hiker scanning for a place to rest weary bones. The pond is like so many in the area—stagnant and murky.

From here, pass several grassy meadows and arrive at a somewhat confusing intersection where an adjacent trail, blocked by sticks as a warning, tries to lure you. This trail, 0.4 mile from the Camp 10 pond, heads off to a shallow lake within the Yakama Indian Reservation. Stay left at the intersection and pay close attention so you don't take a wrong turn and head into the grassy yonder.

Gentle ups and downs through cedar and fir are followed by patches of overgrown huckleberry as you make your way to the junction with **Walupt Lake Trail #101**, 3.3 miles from the Camp 10 pond. A large clearing with trail signs makes a good place to stop and take a break, provided you aren't getting nailed by bloodsucking pests. A couple of spur trails to the right (south and southeast) lead to different objectives. The one to the south arrives at the one-tent **Walupt Trail Camp**, complete with a fire pit. The other, to the southeast, is unmaintained and heads toward the large Howard Lake, well within the Yakama Indian Reservation. If you're looking for the camp and choose the wrong trail, you'll know very soon: the camp spur is only about 20 yards long, while the other trail is seemingly never ending. Water is north on the PCT another 0.1 mile. If the Walupt Trail Camp is occupied, another small campsite is near a pond 0.4 mile west along the Walupt Lake Trail, off a short spur to the right (north).

WALUPT LAKE TRAIL

Walupt Lake Trail #101 heads west, arriving in 4.4 miles at Walupt Lake Campground and a busy parking area for hikers and horsemen heading into the Goat Rocks Wilderness. This trail makes a good PCT entrance or exit. You'll have a fairly decent chance of bumming a ride to town from the busy trailhead, if you need one. The closest town is Packwood, about 23.5 miles on forest roads from the parking area.

CAMP-TO-CAMP MILEAGE

Killen Creek Camp to Camp 4	0.5
Camp 4 to Tributary Camp	4.2
Tributary Camp to Lava Camp	0.3
Lava Camp to Midway Creek Camp	4.1
Midway Creek Camp to Camp 5	2.2
Camp 5 to Camp 6	3.0
Camp 6 to Camp 7	0.5
Camp 7 to Camp 8	1.0
Camp 8 to Camp 9	0.4
Camp 9 to Camp 10	0.5
Camp 10 to Walupt Trail Camp	3.5

3 WALUPT LAKE TRAIL TO SNOWGRASS FLAT TRAIL

DISTANCE 10.4 miles

ELEVATION GAIN/LOSS
+2550/–1110 feet

HIGH POINT 6470 feet

CONNECTING TRAILS
Walupt Lake Trail #101, Nannie Ridge Trail #98, Bypass Trail #97, Snowgrass Flat Trail #96

ON THE TRAIL

Roughly 240 feet past the junction with **Walupt Lake Trail #101**, an unsigned spur darts off the PCT toward a small pond to the west. Just beyond that, 0.1 mile from the Walupt Lake Trail junction, a seasonal creek with decent water is usually flowing. While it's not completely reliable, in normal seasons it flows enough to draw water. If it's dry, and you're desperate for a sip, a spur to the left (west) is just ahead, 0.2 mile from the Walupt Lake Trail junction; it leads to a small stagnant pond with a one-tent camp (**Camp 11**). This camp is not very aesthetically pleasing and can be muddy. It's best to keep moving or head back to Walupt Trail Camp.

The landscape opens up as you wind your way northbound on the west side of a high ridge with a rocky cliff face. Bear grass and huckleberries guide you as you huff and puff between clumps of evergreens. In the valley to the southwest below, a

The PCT curves like a winding ribbon along the subalpine terrain near Snowgrass Flat, while Mount Adams looks on.

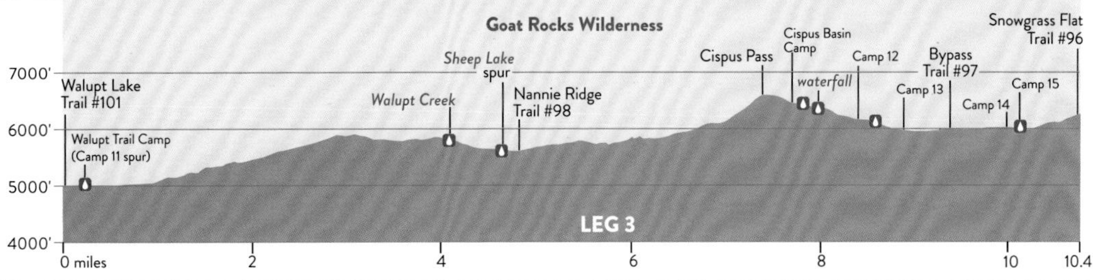

large blue pond twinkles and glistens, surrounded by a marshy meadow. As you climb higher, rocky open hillsides give way to views of Walupt Lake to the southwest and Nannie Ridge to the west. To the south, Mount Adams shows her flat summit as she peeks over an unnamed ridgeline. These views only get better as Goat Rocks Wilderness weaves its way into your soul.

The trail plays hopscotch between forest and open hillsides as it continues climbing, sometimes

GOAT ROCKS BLISS

The Goat Rocks ridgeline is reflected in a small, quiet tarn at sunset.

From here on out, you're in the beating heart of Goat Rocks country. This part of Washington has a deserved reputation for grandeur, its jagged ridges and subalpine hillsides teeming with dancing creeks and fragrant wildflower meadows. Because this landscape is a soul salve for so many, it's very popular and can be downright crowded during the summer. Day hikers flock to this area via easy access from trailheads near Walupt Lake. Weekend warriors and backpackers set up base camps along the PCT and spend their days marinating in backcountry bliss.

As a result, PCT hikers may have a tough time finding a camp, especially on a weekend. Get creative with your camps and look very hard—some of the best places to park your tent are away from the obvious locations. Whatever you do, take your time as you travel through here. This is the PCT stretch you'll be talking about for years to come and one that you'll never forget.

gently, sometimes moderately, passing at least three tiny dripping seasonal creeklets not worthy of a stop. Eventually, meadows take over and the trail delivers you to seasonal **Walupt Creek** 💧, 4.1 miles beyond the Walupt Lake Trail junction. In hot summers, this creek can be dry as a bone, but most years it has at least a trickle. Rock hop your way across to find a one-tent campsite to the left and another one-tent campsite off a trail spur to the right (**Walupt Creek Camp**). If the sites are full or the creeks are dry, you may want to keep going to Sheep Lake, 0.7 mile to the north.

From Walupt Creek, the PCT traverses several wildflower meadows, complete with the familiar favorites—paintbrush, aster, Sitka valerian, and mountain bistort. Mount Adams, fully visible now, makes a delightful backdrop as the trail takes a turn to the west and arrives at an unsigned spur to the left (west), 0.6 mile past Walupt Creek. If you intend to camp at Sheep Lake, this is a well-used and well-defined shortcut leading you to the lake 0.1 mile beyond.

Sheep Lake is a gorgeous little lake in a subalpine wildflower meadow—a fairy-tale setting. Because it's so grand, it's very popular with day hikers and backpackers, who mostly approach via Nannie Ridge Trail #98. Campsites (**Sheep Lake Camp**) around the lake are plentiful but might be full, especially on a weekend. Be diligent in your search—some sites are tucked well away from the lake in clumps of trees. The lake is also home to northwestern salamanders, who struggle to live in this picturesque but populated setting. They count on responsible hikers to keep bug spray, sunscreen, and body scum out of their home—and I can't tell you the number of times I've seen grubby hikers doing the backstroke in the soup. Doing your part to bathe elsewhere will help the salamanders continue to be part of this delicate ecosystem.

NANNIE RIDGE TRAIL

Nannie Ridge Trail #98 heads southwest and in 4.6 miles leads to Walupt Lake, Walupt Lake Campground, and a bustling parking area for hikers heading into the Goat Rocks. This is an excellent trail to use for starting or ending your PCT trek or for syncing up with friends. Additionally, if you needed help for some reason, you'd likely be able to find a Good Samaritan near busy Walupt Lake.

In 0.1 mile from the unsigned shortcut trail to Sheep Lake, the PCT arrives at **Nannie Ridge Trail #98**, coming in from the south. This junction is a little confusing because it seems like a T or a dead-end. PCT hikers will want to take a sharp right at this point and head north.

From the Nannie Ridge Trail junction, the PCT begins a gentle ascent through grassy wildflower meadow toward a high, jagged unnamed ridge above. The path cuts into the hillside and

A hiker climbs the last stretch of trail northbound before Cispus Pass.

Cispus Basin is perhaps one of the most beautiful places in Washington State, if not along the entire PCT.

traverses Walupt Creek Canyon, which has several small coulees, at least two of which contain seasonal dripping creeks. Wildflowers such as Lewis's monkeyflower, larkspur, scarlet gilia, and lupine grow like weeds as you climb higher and higher into a landscape so perfectly picturesque that you might want to stay a few days.

Ahead, a prominent unnamed peak beckons you forward through grassy meadows dotted with trees, until you crest a saddle with spectacular open views to the north and east of green hillside meadows, stony and rugged peaks, dancing distant waterfalls, and pockets of evergreen thickets. Andesite columns from long-ago lava flows are visible to the trail's left (west). This kind of awesome beauty is one of the reasons we hike. It's so spectacular it almost doesn't feel real—a movie soundtrack could start playing any minute. Stop and enjoy every second, using all of your senses.

The PCT crosses into the Yakama Indian Reservation at this point, exiting in 0.9 mile at Cispus Pass on the north side of the cirque. Trail signs remind you that hunting and trespassing beyond the PCT are prohibited. A couple of signs also remind you to stay on the trail. Because this area is high-elevation, it receives a lot of snow, some of which usually sticks around throughout the whole hiking season.

Watch where you're walking—it's easy to get so caught up in views that you forget to watch your feet. Pockets of talus and scree mixed with sandy soils make up the tread, while white and red heather dot the trail edges. Deep in the canyon to the east are the headwaters of the Klickitat River, while ahead of you to the north is the craggy profile of Gilbert Peak. In the meadows below the trail, lupine and aster fields make patchy throw rugs of purple amid the apple-green grasses.

A bare hillside deteriorating from erosion challenges you to take your eyes off the grandeur and focus on your feet. Be aware of the instability of the hillside you're crossing and move through the area swiftly.

LANDSLIDES AND EROSION

Over the years, a few stretches of the PCT in Washington have suffered from landslides and erosion. From just south of Cispus Pass through the Goat Rocks Spine, or Knife Edge, you'll find places where water and snow have tried to wipe the PCT off the map. Use extra caution with your foot placement and ensure the hillside is stable by probing with your trekking poles before crossing suspect areas. If all else fails, find another way around and don't put yourself at risk. Equestrians should contact the Forest Service to find out the trail status before attempting to ride through washed-out sections.

Reach the summit of **Cispus Pass** in 2.3 miles from the Nannie Ridge Trail junction. A weathered sign on the highest tree around announces the pass along with the elevation, 6473 feet. From here, the trail begins a gradual descent into a giant subalpine cirque known as Cispus Basin. Grassy wildflower meadows adorn every hillside, while primeval peaks make up the high horizon. This spectacular place is filled with majestic sweeping views everywhere you look! What's the rush? Stop, take off your pack, grab some photos, and soak it in.

Midway around the cirque, 0.6 mile from Cispus Pass, the trail descends slightly and arrives at an open, unsigned, but very popular camping area (**Cispus Basin Camp**), with room for many tents. Nearby, two tributaries of the Cispus River cross the PCT, providing water for thirsty hikers.

The trail takes a westward turn and continues traversing the cirque, which feels smaller now that you're deep inside it. Use care on several short sections of washed-out trail as you move along. Seasonal creeks playfully dribble in normal years. In 1.1 miles from Cispus Pass, rock hop your way across the base of a 20-foot-high waterfall, tumbling with purpose from the slopes above. There's almost always water here, so if the season is especially dry, this is a good place to fill up.

Traverse a scree slope and, at 1.3 miles from Cispus Pass, find a one-tent camp (**Camp 12**) to the trail's left. This camp is visible from the trail but aesthetically pleasing, with a flat tent site, a view into Cispus Basin, and evergreens for protection. In 0.1 mile beyond Camp 12, a trail leads to a lovely lunch spot. Some may have tried to camp here, but the lack of a flat sleeping spot makes it a less than desirable place to call home for the night.

Continue rambling westward through increasing hemlocks and subalpine firs, passing at least five more seasonal creeks before arriving at another camp (**Camp 13**), to the trail's left (south), 0.5 mile from Camp 12 (1.8 miles beyond Cispus Pass). The camp, also a rocky viewpoint into the Cispus River drainage, can fit two small tents and boasts a wind block in the form of neighboring conifers.

At 0.2 mile past Camp 13, pass a seasonal creek just before a well-constructed shale wall arrives on the trail's right (northeast). Stop to admire this trail-building marvel—well done, trail crews, well done! In another 0.3 mile, reach a junction with **Bypass Trail #97**, which heads left (west) and connects to Snowgrass Flat Trail #96 in 1 mile.

The Bypass Trail junction can be a little confusing—the Bypass Trail is straight ahead and the PCT is to the right, continuing its northbound trek. If you're deep in thought, you might accidentally end up on the Bypass Trail, so pause "trail brain" for a moment when you arrive at this intersection. If you're looking for a camp, there

BYPASS TRAIL TO SNOWGRASS FLAT TRAILHEAD

If you need to hop off the trail or connect with friends, follow Bypass Trail #97 until it reaches Snowgrass Flat Trail #96 in 1 mile. From there, turn left (south) and head down 3.8 miles to a parking area and trailhead. The Snowgrass Flat Trail intersects the PCT 1 mile north of the Bypass Trail, but as its name implies, the latter is the shortest route to the Snowgrass Flat Trailhead.

Talus fields are common in the high subalpine terrain just north of Cispus Basin.

are a couple of decent tent sites near a seasonal creek 0.5 mile west on the Bypass Trail. There are also more ahead along the PCT, so you have options.

The PCT climbs now, somewhat steeply at times, and passes a couple more seasonal creeks.

WHAT THE HECK IS SNOWGRASS?

Snowgrass Flat was named for a plant that was popular with stockmen of yesteryear. It's unknown, however, exactly what plant they called "snowgrass." Technically, snowgrass is a nickname for tussock, which is native to New Zealand and not found in cold Northwest climates. Bear grass is the closest thing around that resembles tussock, and it's snowy white in color. Perhaps we can thank a mistaken plant ID for naming these striking meadows.

The landscape alternates between wildflower meadows and dwarf evergreens that struggle to grow tall in the short growing season. Beautiful shale cairns serve as fine art, trail sculptures that guide you toward the Snowgrass Flat area.

In 0.5 mile beyond the Bypass Trail junction, a spur heads left (west) into a grove of trees to a secluded two-tent camp (**Camp 14**). In 0.2 mile beyond that (0.7 mile from the Bypass Trail junction), another spur, this time to the right (east), climbs a steep slope and arrives at two more secluded single-tent campsites (**Camp 15**). Water crosses the PCT immediately north of the Camp 15 spur and is a reliable source for both camps. **Load up on water here, as it's scarce for roughly the next 4.5 miles**.

From here the trail ascends to a junction with **Snowgrass Flat Trail #96**, 1 mile from the Bypass Trail junction. Stop and swoon. Seasonal wildflower meadows lightly perfume the air and offer a spectacular rainbow in all directions. Behind you to the south, Mount Adams shines like a hologram; to the northeast, Old Snowy and his band of pointed brothers rise up from the meadows; and to the west, Mount St. Helens shows off her missing top. Sights in all directions blow you away and make you grateful you're healthy enough to stand in this wild place. No wonder it's so popular!

The Snowgrass Flat Trail, and Lily Basin Trail #86 just beyond it, are popular with day hikers, so you're likely to see wildlife of the human variety perched on rocks nearby, nibbling on snacks. Give 'em a wave and keep 'er rolling! One of the best features of Goat Rocks—the Knife Edge, a.k.a. the Spine—is ahead and begs for your footprints.

CAMP-TO-CAMP MILEAGE

Walupt Trail Camp to Camp 11 spur 0.2
Camp 11 spur to Walupt Creek Camp........ 3.9
Walupt Creek Camp to Sheep Lake Camp spur 0.6
Sheep Lake Camp spur to Cispus Basin Camp 3.0
Cispus Basin Camp to Camp 12............. 0.7
Camp 12 to Camp 13...................... 0.5
Camp 13 to Camp 14...................... 1.1
Camp 14 to Camp 15...................... 0.1
Camp 15 to Snowgrass Flat Trail 0.3

4 SNOWGRASS FLAT TRAIL TO WHITE PASS

DISTANCE 19.8 miles

ELEVATION GAIN/LOSS
+3780/–5780 feet

HIGH POINT 7230 feet

CONNECTING TRAILS AND ROADS
Snowgrass Flat Trail #96, Coyote Trail #79, North Fork Tieton Trail #1118 (access road is washed out), Hidden Springs Trail #1117 (access road is washed out), Round Mountain Trail #1144, US 12

ON THE TRAIL

Get ready for the crowning jewels of the Goat Rocks Wilderness on this leg of the PCT! After the junction with Snowgrass Flat Trail #96, the trail climbs, moderately at times, through subalpine country sprinkled with firs and scattered boulders. Moving quickly through this stretch is difficult because that camera keeps magically coming out of your pocket. Higher and higher you go, moving from grassy patches to glacier-polished boulders. Permanent snowfields, even well into a hot summer, are part of this trail leg, so proceed across them with caution and look for cairns to help you navigate.

The 1.5 miles after the Snowgrass Flat Trail junction are sprinkled with campsites where you can take in the wonder (**High Country Camp**). The sites are often near boulders, behind tree patches, or in wide-open spaces where privacy is limited but views are worthy. Many are hidden off-trail 100 feet or so, while some are visible from the PCT. These campsites are primarily dry, although water is available along the trail just south of the Snowgrass Flat Trail junction. Sadly, this area is suffering from overuse, and Forest Service funding to patrol prohibited camps is extremely limited. Please practice meticulous Leave No Trace ethics: camp only on durable surfaces and use existing camps.

Subalpine scenery eventually hands the torch to an alpine landscape and you find yourself walking through an expansive rock garden on the broad shoulders of the spikey Old Snowy. In 1.4 miles from the Snowgrass Flat Trail junction, stop to catch a view out to the northwest of the often snowy Goat Lake basin, with emerald-green cirques, dancing waterfalls, and the profile of a peak named Hawkeye Point, a former fire lookout site. Just when you think your eyes might melt and your heart might pop out, Mount Rainier appears like a vision on the horizon behind it all, and a patch

This view just south of the Goat Rocks Spine could be described as "nature's masterpiece."

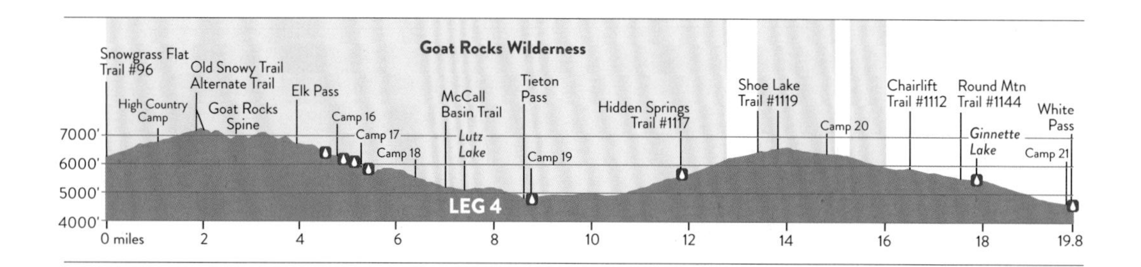

of lupine jumps in with a pop of majestic purple! Those who have not stood here can't begin to imagine such wild exquisiteness and peaceful isolation.

You'll encounter permanent snowfields here and there as you pick your way through the rocks and arrive at a junction with the **Old Snowy Trail** and **PCT Alternate Trail**, marked by a sign, 1.8 miles from the Snowgrass Flat Trail junction. This is the official start of the Goat Rocks Spine (a.k.a. Knife Edge) and you have two choices. The first is the PCT Alternate Trail, and the second is the official PCT route, which climbs over the Packwood Glacier. The Alternate Trail is much more popular because it avoids the challenges and hazards of the changing glacier. The Alternate Trail climbs to the right (southeast), 550 feet up Old Snowy, before dropping back to the left (north) to reconnect with the Spine 0.8 mile beyond this point. The panoramic views from the top are swoon-worthy and well worth the burn.

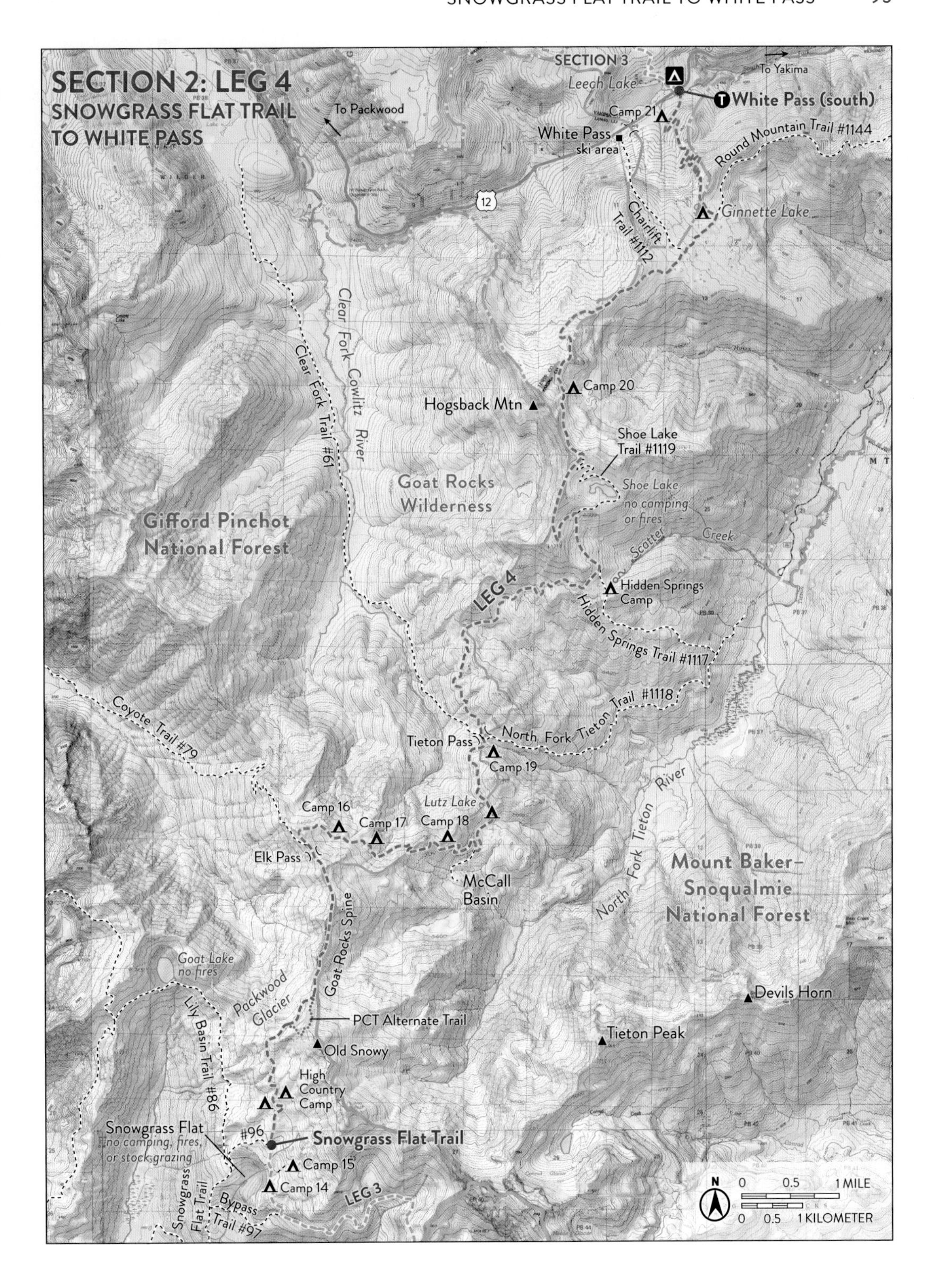
SECTION 2: LEG 4
SNOWGRASS FLAT TRAIL TO WHITE PASS
SECTION 3
Leech Lake
To Yakima
White Pass (south)
To Packwood
Camp 21
White Pass ski area
Round Mountain Trail #1144
12
Ginnette Lake
Chairlift Trail #1112
Clear Fork Cowlitz River
Clear Fork Trail #61
Camp 20
Hogsback Mtn
Shoe Lake Trail #1119
Shoe Lake no camping or fires
Goat Rocks Wilderness
Gifford Pinchot National Forest
Scatter Creek
LEG 4
Hidden Springs Camp
Hidden Springs Trail #1117
North Fork Tieton Trail #1118
Coyote Trail #79
Tieton Pass
Camp 19
River
Camp 16
Camp 17
Lutz Lake
Camp 18
Elk Pass
McCall Basin
North Fork Tieton
Mount Baker–Snoqualmie National Forest
Goat Rocks Spine
Goat Lake no fires
Packwood Glacier
Lily Basin Trail #86
PCT Alternate Trail
Devils Horn
Tieton Peak
Old Snowy
High Country Camp
Snowgrass Flat no camping, fires, or stock grazing
#96
Snowgrass Flat Trail
Camp 15
Camp 14
LEG 3
Snowgrass Flat Trail
Bypass Trail #97
N
0 0.5 1 MILE
0 0.5 1 KILOMETER

WHAT'S THE GOAT ROCKS SPINE ALL ABOUT?

Grit your teeth and lace up your boots for the most harrowing, yet exhilarating, stretch of trail along the PCT in Washington.

If you've chosen to do this section of the PCT, odds are you've heard folks talking about the Goat Rocks Spine, or the Knife Edge, which guides PCT hikers for 2.4 miles across a harrowing traverse of barren mountain peaks and cliff bands. The trail across the Spine has little margin for error in places, often crossing above sheer drops on either side of narrow, crumbling ridges. Add to that the washouts and erosion issues on this high-country trail, and you might be stopping to gnaw on your fingernails. That said, thousands of people cross this desolate tightrope every year and live to tell about it. In fact, they even get splendid pictures and fodder for blogs, since the route is such an adventure and takes hikers high into alpine terrain with sweeping views. Seriously, the panoramas, the ambiance, and the magnificence are ta-die-fer.

The eroded rocky peaks the PCT crosses are the undigested leftovers of a spitting two-million-year-old stratovolcano, nicknamed the Goat Rocks Volcano. Back in the day, Goat Rocks Volcano may have looked similar to its cousins, Mount Rainier and Mount Adams, but then it started erupting. Once the eruptions stopped, glacial erosion knocked away the outer layers of ash and lava, leaving behind the rocky lava spine on which we now travel.

In the not too distant past, equestrians also traveled across this stretch of trail. When you get here, you'll be shaking your head at the thought of horses attempting to cross this precarious section—wings would be nice. Sadly, over the years several horses succumbed to the treacherous edges. In fact, a few years ago, a horse skeleton at the bottom of the Coyote Trail junction signpost served up a morbid reminder that crossing with a horse can be a deadly proposition.

While I wish every man, woman, child, and guinea pig had a chance to see the Spine in their lifetime, avoid it like the plague if abundant snow is present, the area is shrouded in dense fog, you suffer from equilibrium issues, or your friends agree you have the coordination of a walrus on ice skates. One slip could really be a buzzkill.

After the Forest Service blasted the new trail through the Packwood Glacier and just beyond, the PCT avoided the steep climb up Old Snowy and took a more direct line. The Packwood Glacier crossing, which comes almost immediately after the junction with the Alternate Trail, can be icy, dicey, and frightening, especially early in the season. Other times, the snow can be soft, forgiving, and easy-peasy to walk across. Whichever route you take, be sure to take your time, watch your footing, and don't necessarily follow the footprints of others.

Once across the snowy glacier, continue hiking on the steep, narrow stretch of trail, clanking and clambering over the talus—it sounds like you're walking on broken dinner plates. Mount Rainier, floating off in the distance, pulls your eyes away from the trail on many occasions, but focusing on your feet is a good idea amid any loose rock and crumbling trail. Stop ogling unless you stop walking, or you might start teetering. Several wide stretches here and there will calm your nerves and allow you to take a rest with little risk. Below you to the west, several glaciers light up the barren mountain shoulders, while adjacent meadows benefit from melting runoff. Keep an eye out for herds of elk that graze on the green hillsides below and for surefooted mountain goats that frolic around these crumbling peaks.

Up, down, and around you go, across narrow, washed-out, steep, crumbling trail, all with grand views. At 1.3 miles, a weathered and nearly illegible Cascade Crest sign shows up atop a pile of rocks. Beyond that, in 0.8 mile (2.1 miles from the Alternate Trail junction), reach **Elk Pass** and a junction with **Coyote Trail #79**, which descends toward Packwood Lake in the valley to the northwest. The PCT continues along the Spine, until it finally takes a sharp turn to the right (west), 2.4 miles from the Alternate Trail junction, and begins to descend, putting an end

Snowfields linger well into late summer near the appropriately named Old Snowy.

You may have to use your imagination to see the shoe shape of Shoe Lake, especially from this vista, just north of the lake basin.

to your heart palpitations. Congratulations! You made it across one of the most epic stretches along the entire PCT!

The trail leaves the ridge and descends in the open meadowy country, passing a cool, clear stream to the trail's right, 0.6 mile beyond the Coyote Trail junction. Stop to fill up here, or keep rolling—more stream crossings are ahead. At 0.8 mile past the Coyote Trail junction, come to a small one-tent camp (**Camp 16**) on the left, followed by two more creek crossings and a two-tent camp (**Camp 17**), located 0.4 mile beyond Camp 16. Both camps are visible from the trail, near patches of trees, and private enough that they make fine choices for bedding down.

Cross two more streams just beyond Camp 17, the first one viable for water, the second one slightly silted. The trail then ascends a small hill, reaches a saddle, and drops over the other side. The meadowy subalpine scenery begins to concede to the forest and a camp arrives to the trail's left (north), 1.2 miles from Camp 17. This three-tent camp (**Camp 18**) is ideal, tucked quaintly under large evergreens on the edge of a grassy meadow. However, for a couple of years now, it has had a dirty little problem. A large quantity of decaying, flattened camping gear has been left here and has yet to be removed. Rumor has it the gear was left behind during an emergency rescue and that the Forest Service is aware of the trash. By the time you get here, let's hope it's gone so you can enjoy this spot if you need a place to crash.

In 0.6 mile from Camp 18, arrive at an unsigned, well-used trail coming from the right (south). This is the unofficial 0.4-mile trail to **McCall Basin**, a vision of colorful wildflowers, tree thickets, dripping creeks, and cranking waterfalls. Tieton Peak stands guard to the southeast, while the ridges south of the basin make up the skyline toward Old Snowy. Mountain goats, herds of elk, and even black bears are common in this remote, peaceful meadow. If time permits and the mosquitos aren't too vicious, it's worth the side trip to throw down camp in this majestic landscape.

Just after the trail to McCall Basin, the PCT turns northward and dives deeper into forest until it arrives at the swampy Lutz Lake to the trail's left (west) in 0.5 mile. The lake, which dries up to almost nothing in hot summer months, is stagnant and not optimal for drawing water unless you have a great filter. It does, however, have several ideal campsites (**Lutz Lake Camp**) nearby. The first three-tent camp is located off a spur just to the PCT's left (west), within view of Lutz Lake. Two more two-tent camps are 0.1 mile north along the PCT, on both sides of the trail.

From Lutz Lake, the trail ducks into hemlocks and cedars and meanders up and down through treetop shadows, until it descends to **Tieton Pass** and a junction with **North Fork Tieton Trail #1118** coming in from the right (east) and **Clear Fork Trail #61** arriving from the left (west). Spur trails to the right, near the junction, lead to two well-used one-tent camps (**Camp 19**), 1 mile past Lutz Lake Camp.

If you need water, two dribbling seasonal creeks are nearby. The best one is roughly 120 yards to the right (east) on the North Fork Tieton Trail. The second is approximately 200 yards to the west on the Clear Fork Trail. As with all seasonal creeks, they may run dry in hot summers.

Leave Tieton Pass, with the scenery now a familiar blend of conifers, bear grass, and huckleberries. Pass two seasonal dribbling creeklets: the first in 0.2 mile from Tieton Pass, the other in 0.9 mile. The second is the bigger and better of the two, if it's flowing. Neither is optimal due to low flow volumes, but they'd work in a pinch.

Pass two unnamed brown ponds to the trail's left (west) as you gently roller-coaster up and down through the hemlocks, firs, and cedars. A rocky buttress visible to the trail's left (west) through the trees breaks the oh-so-green monotony and gives your eyes a treat.

In 3.3 woodsy miles beyond Tieton Pass, arrive at a junction with **Hidden Springs Trail #1117**, heading to the right (east). Because Shoe Lake and Shoe Lake basin up ahead are off-limits to camping, the camping opportunities in this area are limited to **Hidden Springs Camp**, found by descending roughly 110 feet in 0.2 mile east along Hidden Springs Trail. Thankfully, there's a true spring here, along with approximately three to four well-used tent sites.

From the Hidden Springs Trail junction, the PCT moderately ascends slopes of mixed conifer and grassy meadows until it arrives at **Shoe Lake Trail #1119** in 0.8 mile. If you need water, you could take a side trip to the serene shores of Shoe Lake by following this trail northeast for 0.5 mile and either making a loop (see sidebar) or hiking back out to the PCT. Shoe Lake truly does look like a thick high-heeled shoe, if you use your imagination. If you skip it, you'll still get to see it and its subalpine basin as you climb higher northward along the PCT.

After the Shoe Lake Trail junction, the PCT takes a westward turn through grassy lupine-filled slopes before turning steeply north again. The open slopes give you a reprieve from the forest trek and begin to offer up views as you climb high into subalpine country. Thank the trail crews and volunteers who have constructed sturdy walkways over wet areas—turnpikes to elevate and stabilize the moisture-rich soil on the sloping hillsides. Lush

SHOE LAKE TRAIL

Shoe Lake Trail and Shoe Lake basin offer subalpine beauty extraordinaire! If you have time and gumption for a detour, this is a fantastic side trip to see some varied scenery. Follow Shoe Lake Trail #1119 as it wraps itself around the lapping shores of Shoe Lake for 0.5 mile. After reaching the toe of the shoe, the trail makes a hairpin turn and heads northwest, zigzagging up an open grassy slope high above the lake, rejoining the PCT again in 1.3 miles. The total detour is 1.8 miles, whereas staying on the PCT gets you to the northern tip of the Shoe Lake Trail in 1.2 miles.

Magnificent scenery, such as what hikers will see on this traverse on the shoulder of Hogsback Mountain, provide a treat for the eyes as you head toward White Pass.

green meadows draw you farther north, as views give way to the distant, rugged slopes of the Goat Rocks to the south. Crest an open ridgeline just west of an unnamed peak and descend the other side. Traverse north along the slope's talus-filled western flanks, huffing and puffing as you click and clack through the stones until you reach the ridgeline again. This time, the ridgeline offers views into the Shoe Lake basin and makes you want to stop and take in every inch of rugged beauty. Reach the northern end of **Shoe Lake Trail #1119**, 1.2 miles from its southern end.

The PCT now wanders through lavish vegetated meadows complete with arnica and lupine, with peeks into Shoe Lake basin, until it reaches a saddle and begins traversing north on the shoulders of blush-colored **Hogsback Mountain**. Scree slopes and wildflower meadows alternate along the open slopes, while the verdant grassy valley below begs you to stop and take a look. Mountain goats frequent this area; so keep your eyes open.

In 0.9 mile from Shoe Lake Trail's northern end, reach a one-tent camp (**Camp 20**) to the PCT's right (east).The trail then crosses a few more grassy meadows before it bobs back into hemlocks and subalpine firs and rides the outskirts of the Goat Rocks Wilderness boundary, noted by aging signs. A poorly defined saddle officially ends the subalpine romp, and **Chairlift Trail #1112** arrives from the left (north), 2.7 miles past the

CROSS-COUNTRY TO WHITE PASS

Some folks hike to the beat of a different drummer and choose a cross-country route to White Pass. If your toes are tapping out of rhythm, follow the Chairlift Trail to its end and then hike cross-country along the base of the Great White Express Chairlift to White Pass. This alternative route delivers you to food, lodging, and civilization faster but comes at the price of periodically steep and unkempt brushy slopes. That said, routefinding is fairly straightforward, since you'll have a visual on the pass and you'll be following chairlifts. It's sure to make for adventurous exploration.

north end of Shoe Lake Trail. You're getting closer to US 12—the ski lifts are the first signs of civilization in a while, so bust out a jig in anticipation. The Chairlift Trail takes off northward and arrives at the Great White Express Chairlift in roughly 0.5 mile from the PCT.

Almost immediately after the Chairlift Trail junction, a stagnant puddle appears through the trees to the PCT's left (north). It's the first of several mosquito-laden dabbles in this area, which help to break up the forest's green tunnel. **Round Mountain Trail #1144**, which travels east toward Clear Lake, arrives on the PCT's right (east) at 1.1 miles after the Chairlift Trail junction.

In a short, forested 0.2 mile beyond Round Mountain Trail, arrive at the shores of **Ginnette Lake**, and **Ginnette Lake Camp**, to the left (west). Ginnette Lake—a shallow, 100-yard-long lake with downed logs and grassy banks—provides the first true on-trail water source since the dribbles near Tieton Pass. If you're running low, decide if you want to stop and filter the stagnant water here or keep rolling toward US 12. Two more creeks, one seasonal, are better options up ahead, not to mention the plethora of mouth-watering beverages at the White Pass convenience store. If you choose to camp, a pleasant three-tent campsite, tucked just into the trees along the lakeshore, awaits your somnolent snores.

Back on the PCT, wander through thick mossy hemlocks before a series of switchbacks delivers you to a clear seasonal stream, left (southwest) of the trail, 0.9 mile from Ginnette Lake. In hot summers, it may be dry, so don't put all your eggs in this basket.

The final stretch of conifer-lined trail descends to a one-tent camp (**Camp 21**) and a bridge over the rushing South Fork Clear Creek, immediately before the PCT parking area off US 12, 2 miles beyond Ginnette Lake. If you need food or lodging, **White Pass** is 0.5 mile along the highway to the left (southwest). A well-stocked convenience store and a mediocre hotel are on the north side of the highway.

CAMP-TO-CAMP MILEAGE

Snowgrass Flat Trail to High Country Camp	0.5
High Country Camp to Camp 16	4.2
Camp 16 to Camp 17	0.4
Camp 17 to Camp 18	1.2
Camp 18 to Lutz Lake Camp	1.2
Lutz Lake Camp to Camp 19	1.0
Camp 19 to Hidden Springs Camp spur	3.3
Hidden Springs Camp to Camp 20	2.9
Camp 20 to Ginnette Lake Camp	3.1
Ginnette Lake Camp to Camp 21	2.0
Camp 21 to White Pass	0.05

SECTION 3

WHITE PASS TO CHINOOK PASS

DISTANCE 28.8 miles

STATE DISTANCE 146.8–175.6 miles

ELEVATION GAIN/LOSS +5060/–4080 feet

HIGH POINT 5880 feet

BEST TIME OF YEAR July–Oct

PCTA SECTION LETTER I

LAND MANAGERS Okanogan-Wenatchee National Forest (Naches Ranger District, William O. Douglas Wilderness), Mount Rainier National Park

PASSES AND PERMITS NW Forest Pass to park at White Pass and Chinook Pass. Free self-issue wilderness permits at wilderness area trailheads.

MAPS AND APPS

- Halfmile's WA Section I
- USFS PCT Map #9 Southern Washington
- Green Trails White Pass #303, Mt Rainier East #270, Bumping Lake #271
- Halfmile's PCT app, Guthook's overall PCT app and PCT WA app

LEGS

1. White Pass to Bumping River
2. Bumping River to Chinook Pass

THE SECTION OF THE PCT between White Pass and Chinook Pass is the land of quiet shallow lakes and depthless ponds, with a relatively easy trail grade that makes for leisurely traveling. For many folks, this section is a favorite for introspection, due to the inviting, reflective lakeshores and the quietness of the landscape. Some excitement comes with crossing the Bumping River near Fish Lake, a cold, manageable wade in midsummer, or a rock/log-hopping, balance-y adventure to those gifted with grace. As you amble north, the trail brushes the border of Mount Rainier National Park and then crosses sweeping subalpine terrain that gives the eyes a feast and the camera a snap-happy experience. Hikers with kids, folks with physical challenges, and backpacking newbies will appreciate the merciful trail slope and laid-back vibe as each turn leads to a new water discovery and opportunity for exploration. Because of the pockets of puddles (a.k.a. lakes and ponds), this section can be extremely buggy in late July and early August. If you can, save your trip here for late August or September, when the hemoglobin hunters are on their way out. Otherwise, fox-trot with your bug-be-gone, eat plenty of garlic, and sweat like you're eating five-star Thai food. That way, the bugs will drown a salty death before they can chaw on your colorful cheeks.

ACCESS

White Pass

From Packwood, drive northeast on US Highway 12 for 20.3 miles to just past the summit of White Pass. Look for a small dirt road to the north signed "Pacific Crest Trail North." Follow the narrow dirt road for 0.2 mile, passing Leech Lake, and locate the small PCT parking area to the right (northeast). Parking is limited. If the lot is full, continue 0.1 mile on US 12 to the southern PCT parking area, where space is more plentiful, signed "Pacific Crest Trail South" and "Cascade Crest Trail."

From Interstate 82 in Yakima, take exit 31A and follow the signs for "US 12 West/Naches." Drive

Opposite: *With Mount Adams behind you, Mount Rainier takes center stage as you continue your northbound journey.*

A wooden boardwalk guides hikers across marshy terrain near Bumping River.

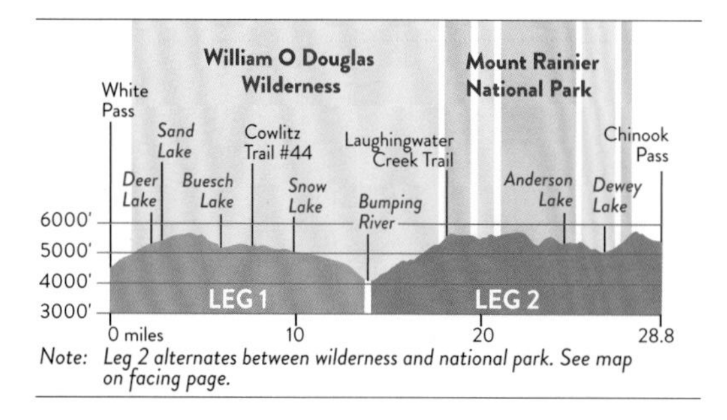

approximately 17 miles, through the town of Naches, to a junction with State Route 410. Turn left (south) and continue on US 12 for 34 miles to a small dirt road to the north signed "Pacific Crest Trail North." Follow the narrow dirt road for 0.2 mile, passing Leech Lake, and locate the PCT parking area to the right (northeast).

Chinook Pass

From Enumclaw, follow State Route 410 east toward Chinook Pass for roughly 45 miles, passing Tipsoo Lake. Just beyond Tipsoo Lake, begin descending and look to the left (north) for a large PCT parking area.

From Interstate 82 in Yakima, take exit 31A and follow the signs for "US 12 West/Naches." Drive approximately 17 miles, through the town of Naches, to a junction with State Route 410. Bear right and stay on SR 410 for roughly 45 miles to the large PCT parking area to the right (north).

Note that SR 410 to Chinook Pass closes during winter and may be slow to open after a heavy snow year.

NOTES

Cities and Services

Near the southern trailhead, find gas, a convenience store, and lodging at the White Pass summit and ski area. There are no services at the northern trailhead, Chinook Pass. Other cities near the southern trailhead are Randle, Packwood, and Yakima; near the northern trailhead, Enumclaw.

Camping Restrictions

No permits are needed for travel or camping in Mount Rainier National Park, but camping is prohibited within 0.25 mile of any designated trail within the park.

Hazards and Inconveniences

A wade across the Bumping River headwaters is required, generally only calf- to knee-high during summer. Check with the land manager before heading out, especially in heavy snowpack years. This White Pass to Chinook Pass section can also be very muddy in places, due to horse traffic.

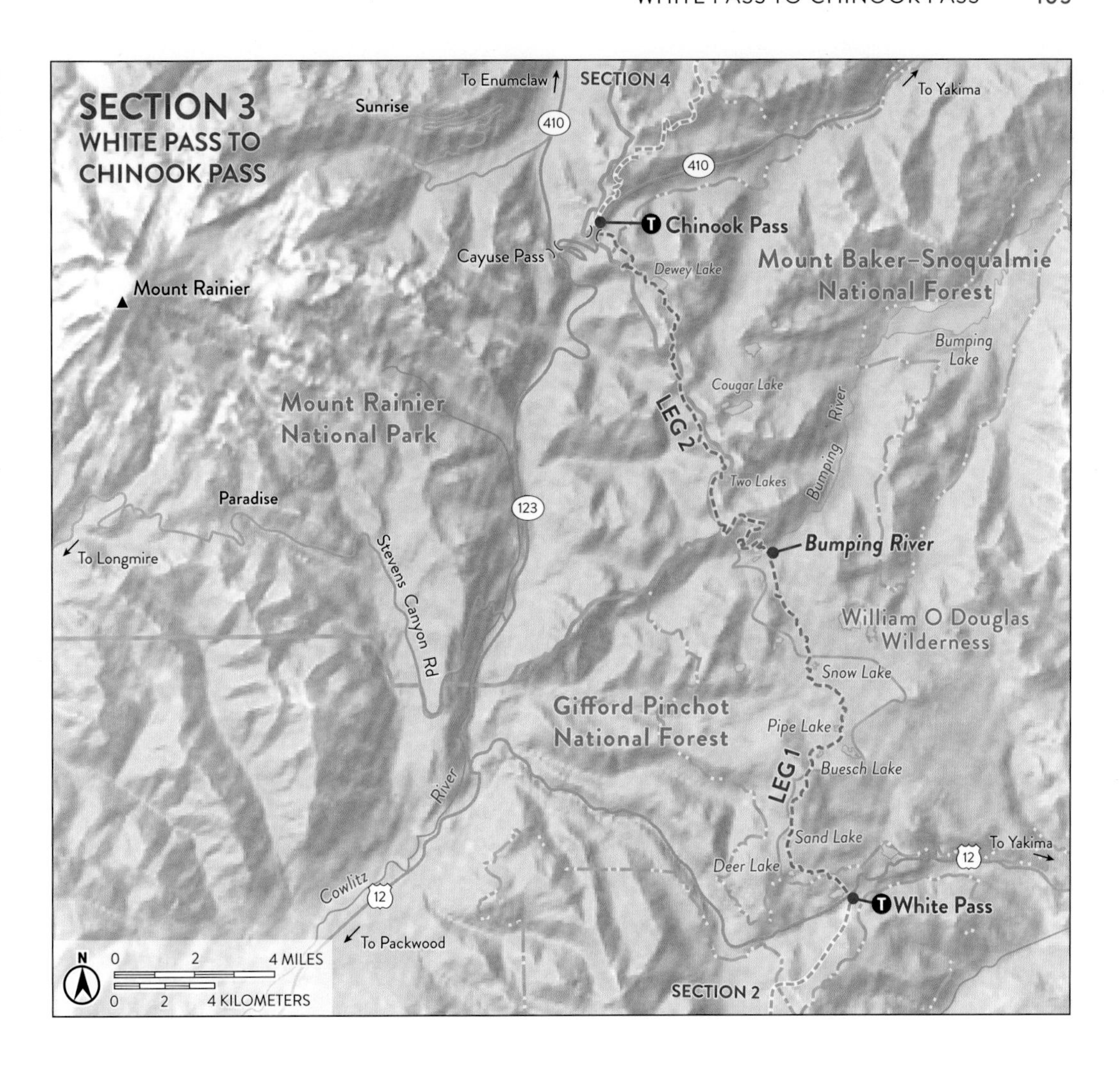

SUGGESTED ITINERARIES

Where noted, distances are to camp trail spurs; camp may be up to 0.2 mile from junction.

3 DAYS

		Miles
Day 1	White Pass to Snow Lake Camp	9.6
Day 2	Snow Lake Camp to Anderson Lake Camp	14.0
Day 3	Anderson Lake Camp to Chinook Pass	5.2

2 DAYS

Day 1	White Pass to Bumping River Camp	13.5
Day 2	Bumping River Camp to Chinook Pass	15.3

1 WHITE PASS TO BUMPING RIVER

DISTANCE 13.5 miles

ELEVATION GAIN/LOSS
+1330/–1640 feet

HIGH POINT 5500 feet

CONNECTING TRAILS
Sand Lake Trail #60, Cortright Creek Trail #57, Dumbbell Lake Trail #1156, Cowlitz Trail #44, Twin Sisters Trail #980, Pot Hole Trail #45, Jug Lake Trail #43, Bumping River Trail #971

ON THE TRAIL

After grabbing your free self-issue wilderness permit at the trailhead, duck into the graceful hemlocks and swaying Douglas-firs to begin a gentle, shaded ascent. In 0.4 mile, cross a dirt road, which in winter serves as a busy thoroughfare for Nordic skiers, who swish their way along a vast system of cross-country ski trails. A few switchbacks continue pulling you northbound until you arrive at the William O. Douglas Wilderness boundary, marked by a tree sign, followed by a junction with Dark Meadows Trail #1107, 1.1 miles from the trailhead. Unless you're hiking at night, dark it is not! Bear left at the junction, continuing on the PCT.

In 0.6 mile from the Dark Meadows Trail junction (1.7 miles from the trailhead), an unnamed creek arrives to the trail's right (north). There are a couple of spots here where you could throw down a tent; however, it's not very private, and muddy soils during the rainy season may have you sleeping in a swamp. Rolling onward is a much better idea.

Pass a couple of grassy meadows, visible through the trees to the trail's right (north), and watch your step if you're gawking—the tread is uneven when dry and slippery with mud when wet, struggling to recover from muddy stock prints. In 0.9 mile from the Dark Meadows Trail junction (2 miles from the trailhead), Deer Lake greets you on the left (south). **Deer Lake** is shallow and muddy bottomed, good for dipping your toes, with a treed shoreline sporting several decent one- to two-tent campsites (**Deer Lake Camp**).

From Deer Lake, the PCT is mostly level for the next 0.5 mile as it wanders through pockets of grassy meadows and evergreen glades before it pops out at the open, lupine-filled shoreline of **Sand Lake**. This shallow lake is fed only by snowmelt and rainwater, so it can be completely bipolar in appearance. On one visit, the water can be almost all the way across the trail, swampy and flooded, while on the next, the lake might be a mere shallow puddle bulging with grasses. Love it for what it is.

In 0.1 mile beyond entering Sand Lake's basin, arrive at a trail junction with **Sand Lake Trail #60** to the PCT's left (west). If you follow this little ditty west for roughly 250 feet, you'll arrive at an old shelter on its last legs, built by the Civilian Conservation Corps back in the 1930s. It's a fun novelty to find such a structure way out here in the boonies, although camping in the shelter is not

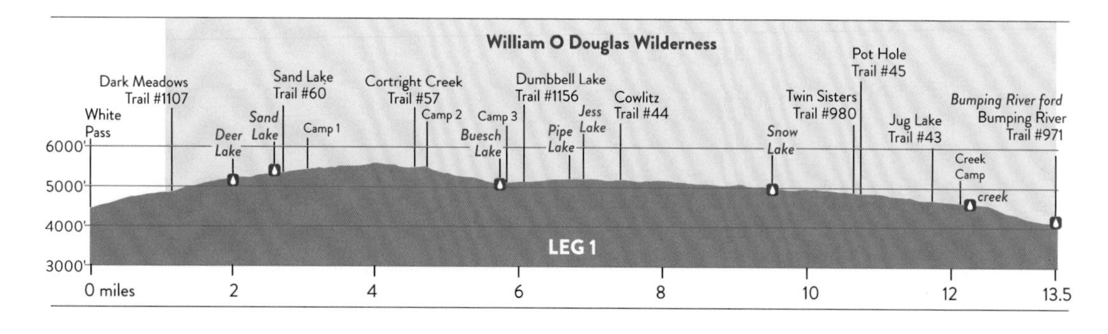

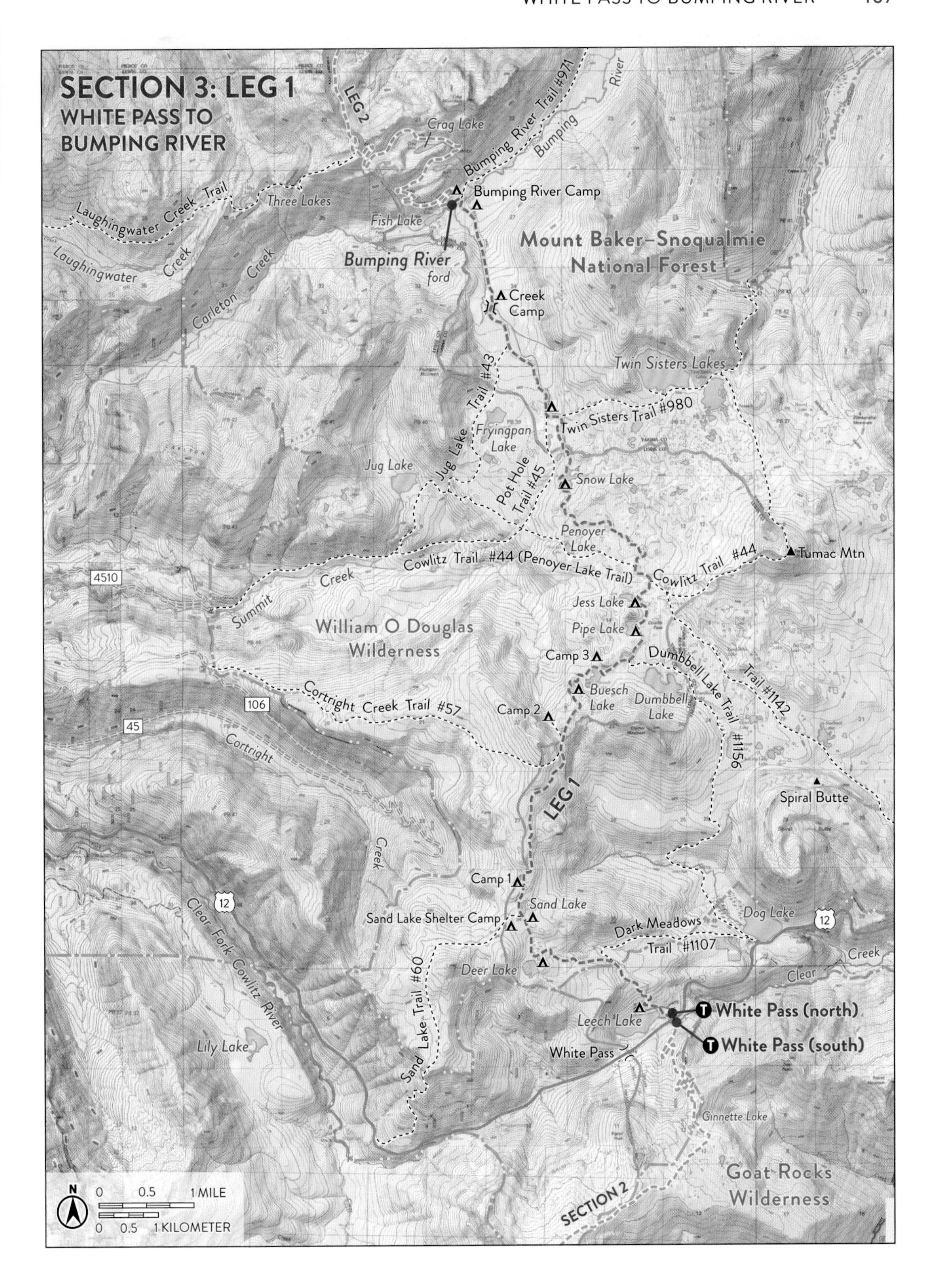
SECTION 3: LEG 1
WHITE PASS TO BUMPING RIVER
LEG 2
Crag Lake
Bumping River Trail #971
Bumping River
Laughingwater Creek Trail
Three Lakes
Bumping River Camp
Fish Lake
Laughingwater Creek
Carleton Creek
Bumping River ford
Mount Baker–Snoqualmie National Forest
Creek Camp
Twin Sisters Lakes
Jug Lake Trail #43
Twin Sisters Trail #980
Fryingpan Lake
Jug Lake
Pot Hole Trail #45
Snow Lake
Penoyer Lake
Cowlitz Trail #44 (Penoyer Lake Trail)
Cowlitz Trail #44
Tumac Mtn
4510
Summit Creek
William O Douglas Wilderness
Jess Lake
Pipe Lake
Camp 3
Dumbbell Lake Trail #1156
Trail #1142
Buesch Lake
Dumbbell Lake
Camp 2
Cortright Creek Trail #57
106
45
Cortright Creek
LEG 1
Spiral Butte
Camp 1
Sand Lake
Sand Lake Shelter Camp
12
Dog Lake
Dark Meadows Trail #1107
Clear Creek
Clear Fork Cowlitz River
Deer Lake
Sand Lake Trail #60
Leech Lake
White Pass (north)
White Pass (south)
Lily Lake
White Pass
Ginnette Lake
Goat Rocks Wilderness
SECTION 2
0 0.5 1 MILE
0 0.5 1 KILOMETER

WILLIAM O. DOUGLAS WILDERNESS

For more than thirty-five years, US Supreme Court Justice William O. Douglas ruled on cases involving everything from civil rights to environmental protections. He was known for his energy, intellect, and dominance in the courtroom, but his fervor, knowledge of law, and sense of justice for citizens are not the only reason he is remembered. Mr. Douglas made his home in Goose Prairie, a tiny don't-blink-you'll-miss-it community on the outskirts of the Bumping River area, not far from the PCT. As a child, he nearly perished when he suffered a paralysis that caused him to lose leg strength. Through hiking, he regained muscle power and built back his ailing body, which in turn helped renew his spirit. As a true nature lover and explorer, he knew every hilltop and valley in this area by heart and penned the now famous book *Of Men and Mountains*. In 1984, just four years after his passing, at eighty-one years old, Washington State designated nearly 170,000 acres as the William O. Douglas Wilderness, a fitting tribute to a man who considered every inch of this area his backyard.

recommended. The mice might want to spoon in your cozy sleeping bag, and one strong wind gust could blow the whole place down. Nearby, there are plenty of spots to set up your tent, and there's even a fire pit for ambiance (**Sand Lake Shelter Camp**). This area could easily support four or more tents, so if your Boy Scout troop is hoping to tell ghost stories, there might be no better place.

To the right on the PCT, across from Sand Lake Trail, a peninsula with a small one-tent campsite juts out into the lake. Another well-established two-tent site is in the trees to the trail's right via a short, well-defined spur (**Sand Lake Camp**). The water here, of course, is Sand Lake, which isn't great, but a little filtering takes away a lot of the nasty.

From Sand Lake, ramble north on a kind trail grade that rolls up and down so mildly you might not even notice. A one-tent camp (**Camp 1**) is to the trail's left 0.4 mile from the Sand Lake Trail junction, near a swampy pond. The water is disgusting here, so cart some from elsewhere if you intend to call this home.

The PCT guides you north through a variety of towering conifers, while bear grass and huckleberries landscape the trail edges. Rocky cliff walls above you here and there contribute to the ambiance and provide a welcome break from the oh-so-green forest. At 1.9 miles from the Sand Lake Trail junction, arrive at a chunky wooden post to the left (west), missing a trail sign for the lightly used **Cortright Creek Trail #57**.

Immediately afterward, a swampy pond shows up to the left (west), a mosquito nursery extraordinaire! In 0.2 mile from the Cortright Creek Trail junction, the PCT curves around a stone buttress to a small pass. A spur trail heads up the hill 50 feet to the left (west) and arrives at a small, dry but private one-tent campsite (**Camp 2**).

Northward you go, descending a few switchbacks until the trail finds its familiar, rather level, easygoing grade. The landscape alternates between evergreen thickets, grassy meadows, and brown ponds until Buesch Lake, one of the largest lakes in this stretch, is visible through the trees to the right (southeast), 1.1 miles from the Cortright Creek Trail junction. Even though it's large, you'll likely scratch your head and wonder if this really is Buesch Lake, because you've seen so many pockets of water. The shoreline's wavy configuration adds to the confusion. Campsites (**Buesch Lake Camp**) via spur trails abound, so if you're ready to call it a night, follow their lead. The lake is your water source, even though, like so many in this area, it has a muddy, brown, silted bottom and grassy edges. It's not great, but it's the largest and best we've got, so filter away, friends!

Opposite: *Tranquil lake shorelines, like this one at Snow Lake, are abundant north of White Pass.*

Late in the season when the weather is hot, wading across the Bumping River will refresh you.

In 1.3 miles beyond the Cortright Creek Trail junction (5.8 miles from the trailhead), rock hop your way across a slow-moving outlet of Buesch Lake, and find a one-tent campsite (**Camp 3**) to the left (north).

From here, the PCT contours around the northern tip of Buesch Lake and gently climbs past more meadows, ponds, and swamps until it meets up with **Dumbbell Lake Trail #1156**, arriving on the right (southeast), 0.5 mile beyond Buesch Lake's outlet. Bear left to keep your wandering feet firmly on the PCT.

The next big lake, **Pipe Lake**, is 0.6 mile farther, to the PCT's left (east). It has several campsites (**Pipe Lake Camp**) around its edges via spur trails, and a couple more sites are visible along the PCT. There is no holy grail of perfect lake camp in this stretch, because the lakes are all shallow and very similar—déjà vu, each camp looks like the next! Pipe Lake is shallow but more emerald in color than Buesch Lake.

The PCT runs along the east shoreline of Pipe Lake before brushing the east edge of **Jess Lake** in 0.3 mile. Spur trails lead to tucked-away campsites at both Jess and some reflective unnamed ponds nearby (**Jess Lake Camp**). By now, you're probably struggling to keep track of which lake/pond/puddle/swamp is named what! There are so many small bodies of water in this giant parcel of land that if you walked cross-country in any direction, you'd find more. You aren't the first to be confused, so don't sweat the befuddlement and just enjoy the landscape.

At 1.1 miles from the Dumbbell Lake Trail junction, arrive at **Cowlitz Trail #44** coming in from the right (southwest). The PCT turns northwest for 0.2 mile and then arrives at a junction with the continuation of **Cowlitz Trail #44 (a.k.a. Penoyer Lake Trail)**, which appears straight ahead and almost tricks you into following it. Instead, bear right and continue on the

PCT along a twisty swath of trail that heads north for a spell and then makes a northwesterly turn. The landscape is familiar, sporting the same bear grass, huckleberry, and heather that you've been enjoying for miles.

In 0.4 mile from the Penoyer Lake Trail junction, rock hop across a trickling seasonal creek. Some years, this little rascal flows heartily, while other years it's just a dribble. Three more itty-bitty seasonal creeklets, all smaller than the first, cross the trail before you start noticing large **Snow Lake** to your right and some conspicuous spur trails leading to camps (**Snow Lake Camp**), 2 miles beyond the Penoyer Lake Trail junction. Snow Lake has a lot of arms for camping and is slightly deeper than most lakes in the area. The PCT flirts with an outlet on Snow Lake's westernmost arm, where rock hopping keeps your shoes dry. Immediately across, more spur trails darting into the brush provide additional water and camp access.

The PCT next gracefully offers a relatively flat path until you reach a trail junction with **Twin Sisters Trail #980** to the right (east), 0.8 mile beyond Snow Lake's outlet. A seasonal creek is just to the right (east), immediately north of the junction. The PCT then jogs to the west very briefly, reaching a junction with **Pot Hole Trail #45** to the left (southwest), 0.1 mile beyond the Twin Sisters Trail junction. The signpost for Pot Hole Trail is a mass of weathered wood and has fallen down over the years, so watch for it on the down low.

Huckleberry, heather, and lupine meadows alternate between conifer groves and at least three seasonal creeks before you reach **Jug Lake Trail #43**, to the left (southwest). The traveling is still easygoing, ultimately losing more elevation than climbing in this stretch.

In 0.5 mile from the Jug Lake Trail junction, a large five-tent campsite (**Creek Camp**) is to the trail's right, in the midst of several large conifers that border a grassy, wet meadow. Immediately beyond the large camp, the trail crosses a sturdy wooden bridge with a hardy, flowing unnamed creek, reaching another five-tent campsite (also Creek Camp). Both of these campsites could be divided into several autonomous tent sites, so if you have a small party, Creek Camp is a fine goal for day's end. Both campsites have a pleasant ambiance, water, and large trees for a bit of privacy.

After passing Creek Camp, the trail meanders through evergreens before reaching a wooden boardwalk that takes you across swampy meadows. Your poles click-clack across the planks and in the distance you'll catch occasional mountain views. You're getting somewhere, hooray! Beyond the boardwalk, the PCT begins a steep descent and passes a two-tent campsite (**Bumping River Camp**) to the right (east), just before the Bumping River, 1.2 miles from Creek Camp (1.7 miles beyond the Jug Lake Trail junction).

Fiddlesticks! The **Bumping River** is missing its bridge, so hikers must figure out their way across. During most summers, the water is no deeper than midcalf or knee-high and flows quietly in places, so a **wade** across can actually be enjoyable for hot feet. Do your best river dance and embrace the adventure! Those with more coordination than a drunk rhino might be able to use a combination of river rocks and fallen logs to teeter their way across with dry shoes.

Once across, find a small one-tent campsite (also Bumping River Camp) to the right, along with a junction for **Bumping River Trail #971** and two more campsites (also Bumping River Camp) to the left.

CAMP-TO-CAMP MILEAGE

White Pass to Deer Lake Camp 2.0
Deer Lake Camp to
Sand Lake Shelter Camp 0.6
Sand Lake Shelter Camp to
Sand Lake Camp 0.0
Sand Lake Camp to Camp 1 .... 0.4
Camp 1 to Camp 2 .... 1.7
Camp 2 to Buesch Lake Camp 0.9
Buesch Lake Camp to Camp 3 .... 0.2
Camp 3 to Pipe Lake Camp................ 0.8
Pipe Lake Camp to Jess Lake Camp......... 0.2
Jess Lake Camp to Snow Lake Camp........ 2.8
Snow Lake Camp to Creek Camp 2.6
Creek Camp to Bumping River Camp 1.3

2 BUMPING RIVER TO CHINOOK PASS

DISTANCE 15.3 miles

ELEVATION GAIN/LOSS
+3730/–2440 feet

HIGH POINT 5880 feet

CONNECTING TRAILS
Bumping River Trail #971, Laughingwater Creek Trail, American Ridge Trail #958, Tipsoo Lake Trail

ON THE TRAIL

From **Bumping River Camp**, the PCT steepens and ascends six long switchbacks before it takes a northeastern turn toward Buck Lake, which lies to the trail's right (south). The large **Buck Lake Camp** is reached via a small spur trail to the right, 1.8 miles from the Bumping River.

Just 0.3 mile farther north, a one-tent campsite (**Camp 4**) is immediately to the trail's right. A small fire pit and the level ground make it inviting, but privacy is limited due to its proximity to the PCT. Immediately beyond, a seasonal creek dances over stones, usually providing enough of a dribble to serve as this camp's water source.

Three more seasonal creeks trickle across the trail before you reach **Crag Lake** and its outlet creek, both to the PCT's left (southwest), 2.6 miles from Bumping River. Several pleasing campsites are here (**Crag Lake Camp**), including a large one suitable for groups just before the lake comes into view. A couple of lightly used spur trails drop 20 feet to the lake, where water is usually reliable.

From Crag Lake, the PCT ascends into rocky, subalpine country, dappled with huckleberries, Solomon's seal, corn lily, aster, lupine, bear grass, heather, and paintbrush. A seasonal tarn is in the valley to the trail's left, visible through the trees, while the rocky hillsides continue to draw your gaze. Look closely, as resident mountain goats often dot the cliffs. The stony trail can be rough on your ankles, so while you're gawking, watch your step.

What a paradise! The green hills continue to reward your huff-and-puff as you climb higher and higher, reaching several viewpoints that show off peaks near Bumping River, such as the jagged Mount Aix. Golden-mantled ground squirrels scamper around the rocks, waiting for you to set down your bag of gorp when you stop for a break.

In 4.2 miles from Bumping River, the trail zigzags up a few switchbacks with grand views before it ducks into **Mount Rainier National Park**, noted by a "US Boundary NPS" sign. In 0.1 mile past the boundary, reach a junction with **Laughingwater Creek Trail**. The sign proudly notes the direction of White Pass and Chinook Pass and begs for a picture! Mount Rainier is clearly visible and will tempt your eyes as you move northbound. What a vision!

MOUNT RAINIER NATIONAL PARK

You might be excited to know that your feet are treading within the borders of one of the most magnificent national parks in the United States. Established in 1899, the park boasts more than 236,000 acres of magnificent wild backcountry, centered around the highest and one of the most active stratovolcanoes in the Pacific Northwest. Because Mount Rainier is an active volcano and is so close to a large metropolis, geologists carefully monitor all signs of increased activity. Presently, there's no evidence that an eruption is imminent, so you can enjoy the spectacular panoramas the park provides without biting your nails. Dogs are not permitted on park trails, but are allowed along the PCT in this stretch.

From the Laughingwater Creek Trail junction, the PCT crosses a wooden boardwalk and then traipses through high subalpine terrain, wandering through apple-green meadows. Barren, rocky, unnamed peaks pull your attention from the trail and make you want to stop for photos. One Lake,

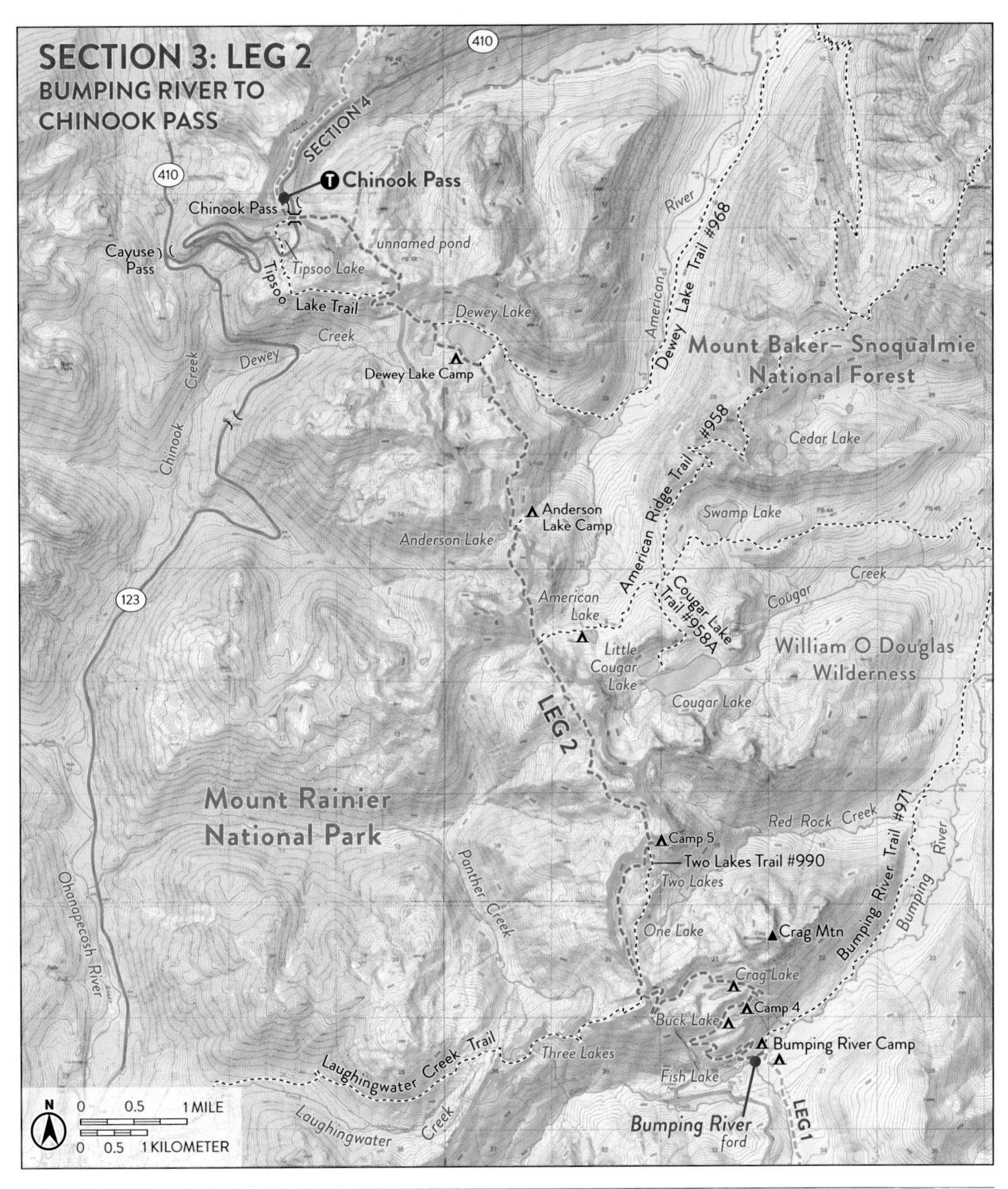
SECTION 3: LEG 2
BUMPING RIVER TO CHINOOK PASS
SECTION 4
410
Chinook Pass
Chinook Pass
Cayuse Pass
unnamed pond
Tipsoo Lake
Tipsoo Lake Trail
Dewey Lake
Dewey Lake Camp
Dewey Creek
Chinook Creek
American River
Dewey Lake Trail #968
Mount Baker– Snoqualmie National Forest
American Ridge Trail #958
Cedar Lake
Swamp Lake
Anderson Lake Camp
Anderson Lake
123
American Lake
Cougar Lake Trail #958A
Cougar Creek
Little Cougar Lake
Cougar Lake
William O Douglas Wilderness
LEG 2
Mount Rainier National Park
Red Rock Creek
Camp 5
Two Lakes Trail #990
Two Lakes
Panther Creek
Bumping River Trail #971
Bumping River
Ohanapecosh River
One Lake
Crag Mtn
Crag Lake
Camp 4
Buck Lake
Bumping River Camp
Three Lakes
Laughingwater Creek Trail
Fish Lake
Bumping River ford
LEG 1
Laughingwater Creek
0 0.5 1 MILE
0 0.5 1 KILOMETER

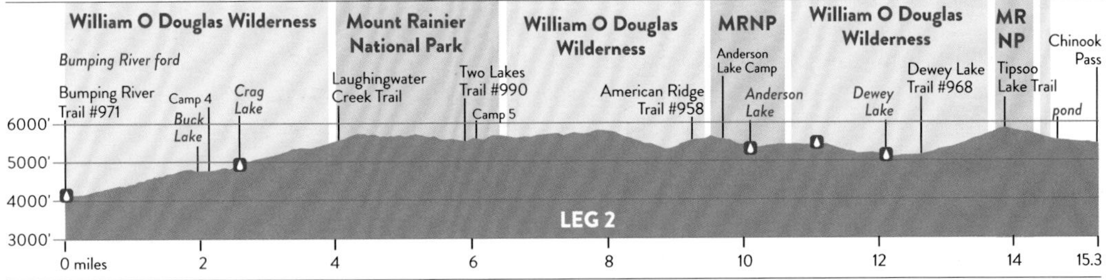
William O Douglas Wilderness
Mount Rainier National Park
William O Douglas Wilderness
MRNP
William O Douglas Wilderness
MR NP
Bumping River ford
Bumping River Trail #971
Camp 4
Buck Lake
Crag Lake
Laughingwater Creek Trail
Two Lakes Trail #990
Camp 5
American Ridge Trail #958
Anderson Lake Camp
Anderson Lake
Dewey Lake
Dewey Lake Trail #968
Tipsoo Lake Trail
pond
Chinook Pass
6000'
5000'
4000'
3000'
LEG 2
0 miles
2
4
6
8
10
12
14
15.3

American Lake is a quiet vision during summer.

actually the name, not just the number, in the valley to the east tempts you to walk cross-country for a visit. The PCT only flirts with Mount Rainier National Park along this stretch, bouncing to and fro across the park's perimeter. Just before the next trail junction, you step out of the park, but you'll soon be back inside. Back and forth you go, with a toe in and a toe out.

In 1.6 miles from the Laughingwater Creek Trail junction, arrive at a junction with **Two Lakes Trail #990**. This trail heads south, while the PCT heads slightly northwest. A well used, one-tent campsite (**Camp 5**) is along a spur to the right (east), just beyond the signed junction. In 0.2 mile from the Two Lakes Trail junction, reenter the park and arrive at more great views of Mount Rainier to the northwest. Resident hoary marmots, popping up from their lunch of lupine, sound their high-pitched alarms and then waddle to the safety of their burrows. Some are conditioned to passing hikers, sunning themselves on rocks lackadaisically, permitting a few camera snaps.

The PCT enters the park again, although you likely didn't know you ever left, because signs only announce when you enter. Intermittently, the trail cruises between grassy meadows and subalpine firs, twisting and turning north with occasional views.

AMERICAN LAKE

Make it your mission to visit **American Lake** and, if possible, **Little Cougar and Cougar lakes.** American Lake, 0.5 mile (+40/–145 feet) east from the PCT, is a vision to behold! Surrounded by unnamed peaks, this little subalpine lake has a handful of campsites tucked in the trees near the shoreline. An outlet creek provides dribbling water for filtering, and a sky full of stars begs you to figure out the slow shutter setting on your camera. Little Cougar and Cougar lakes are also glorious, but finding them can be tricky unless you're good with a map and compass or use a GPS unit to help guide you. There is a trail, but it's not marked and isn't well used, which can cause confusion. Follow American Ridge Trail 0.9 mile beyond American Lake and arrive at an unsigned four-way intersection. The right-hand trail is Cougar Lake Trail #958A. Follow it south for 1 mile and arrive at the gorgeous pair of sapphire lakes, backed by large, stony peaks. Many of the campsites in this area are closed for restoration, so please obey the signs and camp only on durable surfaces.

In 1.1 miles from the Two Lakes Trail junction, arrive at a lunch spot (or emergency campsite) immediately to the trail's right (west), with logs for sitting. Take a gander out to the north for your first views of Chinook Pass! Pat yourself on your sweaty back if that's your goal. You've left the national park again, but hold tight—you'll be back in it soon enough.

At 2.8 miles from Two Lakes Trail's south end, arrive at a junction with **American Ridge Trail #958** to the right (east). A signpost points toward American Lake and Cougar Lake Trail #958A, roughly 1.5 miles along the American Ridge Trail.

Technically, you could pitch a small tent at a barren spot near the PCT's intersection with the American Ridge Trail, to the left (west). It's good to know this spot is here, in an emergency, but it's not an optimal place to camp.

The PCT next gradually descends through grassy meadows, subalpine firs, and huckleberry thickets until it flirts with the national park boundary again and arrives at a sign for camping to the right (east), 1.3 miles from the American Ridge Trail junction. A short spur heads east to well-established sites at **Anderson Lake Camp**. The sites are relatively flat and spaced apart, and even though this is an established camp on the outskirts of the park, it doesn't require a permit. **Anderson Lake** itself is 0.1 mile farther along the PCT, within the park. Camping at the lake itself is not permitted.

After Anderson Lake, the PCT leaves the park and wanders back into the William O. Douglas Wilderness. Without warning it seems, you find yourself huffing and puffing up a couple of hills, traversing meadowed wetlands, and crossing three seasonal creeks before descending to **Dewey Lake** and its basin in 2 miles.

Curious hoary marmots pop up from their burrow to check out nearby hikers.

The lake offers an abundance of camping along almost its entire perimeter (**Dewey Lake Camp**). The PCT traces the lake's southwestern shoreline, where at least ten camps are waiting for you; some are tucked into evergreen thickets, offering a good deal of privacy. A trail at the lake's southeastern shore leads east, around the lake to other campsites, also linking up with Dewey Lake Trail. Or, follow **Dewey Lake Trail #968** itself, which intersects with the PCT at the north end of the lake, just after a small wooden bridge over a calm creek. It's not obvious or well marked, so if the trail you're following isn't a spur leading to a campsite, it's likely the Dewey Lake Trail. Wilderness area regulations apply: no camping within 100 feet of the lake and no fires within 0.25 mile. Due to overuse, the Forest Service has worked hard at restoration in this area. Please respect the signs; camp and walk elsewhere.

As you hike along Dewey Lake, it's almost impossible not to stop and snap a photo or pause for a quiet rest. Despite its being very popular with day hikers and weekend warriors, the lake still offers a good deal of serenity; it's a place where you can breathe deeply and relax the soul.

The PCT climbs rather abruptly out of the Dewey Lake basin into dark conifers before popping out into subalpine terrain. To the south, behind you now, is Dewey Lake and the prominent peaks near Bumping River, such as the mighty Mount Aix. In 1.6 miles from the southern end of Dewey Lake, a wilderness permit sign and box show up nailed to a tree to the trail's right (south), for those heading southbound.

In 0.1 mile beyond the wilderness permit sign, the PCT comes to a junction with **Tipsoo Lake (Naches Loop) Trail**, heading off to the left (west). The junction is well marked with a sturdy metal sign. Stay on the PCT and immediately after the junction, arrive at a sweeping viewpoint of the Dewey Lake basin and surrounding peaks. You may want to sit here all afternoon. But the PCT calls, so onward you go.

From this point to Chinook Pass, the grassy wildflower meadows tucked between rock gardens and subalpine firs take your breath away. As you pass through, marmots carry on with their primitive mission of finding food before winter hibernation, while deer graze on trailside greens.

Keep your eyes out for herds of mountain goats in rocky terrain like this talus-covered slope as you head north toward Chinook Pass.

The gently lapping shores of Dewey Lake provide a soundtrack as you walk its southwestern edge.

In 0.6 mile from the Tipsoo Lake (Naches Loop) Trail junction, an unnamed pond is visible to the right. This small body of water is surrounded by open meadows, shiny boulders, and small evergreens, creating an oasis of visual bliss. Due to the fragile nature of this ecosystem, and the constant day-hiking pressure it receives, camping here is discouraged.

Chinook Pass is getting ever closer. You'll soon see the roadcut in the hillside and hear the cars whipping along the highway. Yet the trail continues to proudly guide you through high-country meadows, reaching a wilderness regulation sign 0.7 mile from the pond. In 0.2 mile, carefully cross the busy, buzzing SR 410 and arrive at a very large paved parking area on the northwest side. There are garbage cans and clean pit toilets here for your convenience.

TIPSOO LAKE

If time permits, or if you end up having to wait for a ride, you might want to check out Tipsoo Lake, located just southwest of Chinook Pass. Find the PCT on the north side of the Chinook Pass parking area, or simply follow one of the many small trails leading up the mounded dirt bank. Follow an unsigned trail left (southwest) for 0.3 mile until you arrive at Tipsoo Lake, set amid abundant seasonal wildflowers. Because the lake is in view of Chinook Pass and the highway, day hikers pop up like daisies. They, too, come for this soul-food buffet. Enjoy every bite!

CAMP-TO-CAMP MILEAGE

Segment	Miles
Bumping River Camp to Buck Lake Camp	1.9
Buck Lake Camp to Camp 4	0.3
Camp 4 to Crag Lake Camp	0.4
Crag Lake Camp to Camp 5	3.3
Camp 5 to Anderson Lake Camp	4.2
Anderson Lake Camp to Dewey Lake Camp	2.0
Dewey Lake Camp to Chinook Pass	3.2

SECTION 4

CHINOOK PASS TO SNOQUALMIE PASS

THIS SECTION OF THE PCT has a reputation that might make you want to skip it. You've probably heard the 40 miles of clear-cuts and uninspiring terrain south of Snoqualmie Pass described as the worst of Washington's PCT. But I'll let you in on a little secret: Chinook Pass to Snoqualmie Pass is actually a fun place to explore, a surprisingly enriching stretch of trail. For the first 30 miles, the PCT travels through meadowlands with vast views, lakes, whistling hoary marmots, herds of mountain goats, and gorgeous countryside. Sure, there are clear-cuts after that, but they open up views and they're busy regenerating—elk seem to love the small saplings. Camps in this section aren't always pristine, but knowing that prepares you for the requisite night or two of camping near logging areas. There is plenty of wonder to be found here, and fewer people means more solitude. Your efforts will be worth your while!

ACCESS

Chinook Pass

From Enumclaw, follow State Route 410 east toward Chinook Pass for roughly 45 miles, passing Tipsoo Lake. Just beyond Tipsoo Lake, begin descending and look to the left (north) for a large PCT parking area.

From Interstate 82 in Yakima, take exit 31A and follow the signs for "US 12 West/Naches." Drive approximately 17 miles, through the town of Naches, to a junction with SR 410. Bear right and stay on SR 410 for roughly 45 miles to the large PCT parking area to the right (north), complete with vault toilets.

Note that SR 410 to Chinook Pass closes during winter and may be slow to open after a heavy snow year.

Opposite: *Silver forests from wildfires of years past provide rich soils where berry bushes thrive and saplings work to renew the hillsides.*

DISTANCE 68.9 miles

STATE DISTANCE 175.6–244.5 miles

ELEVATION GAIN/LOSS +12,870/–15,280 feet

HIGH POINT 6415 feet

BEST TIME OF YEAR July–Oct

PCTA SECTION LETTER I

LAND MANAGERS Okanogan-Wenatchee National Forest (Naches Ranger District, Norse Peak Wilderness), Mount Baker–Snoqualmie National Forest (Snoqualmie Ranger District), Tacoma Public Utilities (Green River Watershed), Seattle Public Utilities (Cedar River Watershed)

PASSES AND PERMITS NW Forest Pass to park at Chinook Pass and Snoqualmie Pass. Free self-issue wilderness permits at wilderness area trailheads.

MAPS AND APPS

- Halfmile's WA Section I
- USFS PCT Map #9 Southern Washington
- Green Trails Bumping Lake #271, Mount Rainier East #270, Lester #239, Snoqualmie #207
- Halfmile's PCT app, Guthook's overall PCT app and PCT WA app

LEGS

1. Chinook Pass to Arch Rock Trail
2. Arch Rock Trail to Bear Creek Trail
3. Bear Creek Trail to Spongy Water Spring
4. Spongy Water Spring to Mirror Lake
5. Mirror Lake to Snoqualmie Pass

Basin Lake shines like topaz nestled in evergreen-dotted hillsides.

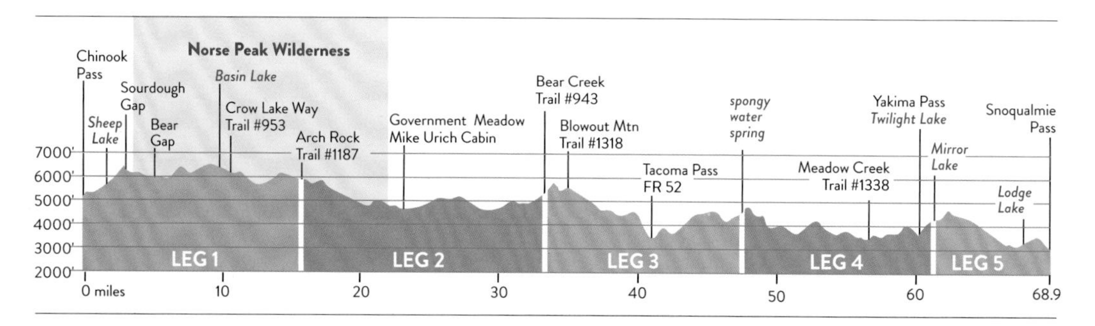

Snoqualmie Pass

From Seattle, drive east on Interstate 90 toward Snoqualmie Pass. Take exit 52 (Snoqualmie Pass West) and turn right at the end of the exit ramp. Head south and turn right again in roughly 100 yards onto a dirt road leading to the ski area's westernmost parking area. The trailhead and large log PCT sign are on the west side of the parking area.

NOTES

In summer 2017, lightning caused more than 55,000 acres of timber and understory to burn near Norse Peak Wilderness. The PCT was affected but has since reopened. Proceed with caution through weakened and dead standing trees.

Cities and Services

There are no services at the southern trailhead, Chinook Pass. The closest cities are Enumclaw and Yakima. At the northern trailhead, Snoqualmie Pass has gas, convenience stores, dining, and lodging. The closest town is North Bend.

Camping Inconveniences

Campsites in the middle of this section are not always pristine or aesthetically pleasing due to nearby forest roads and clear-cuts.

Water

North of Sheep Lake, 1.8 miles from the trailhead, on-trail water is scarce for 8.5 miles. And north of Government Meadow the spring 3.1 miles past FR 7080 is the last water for 11.8 miles.

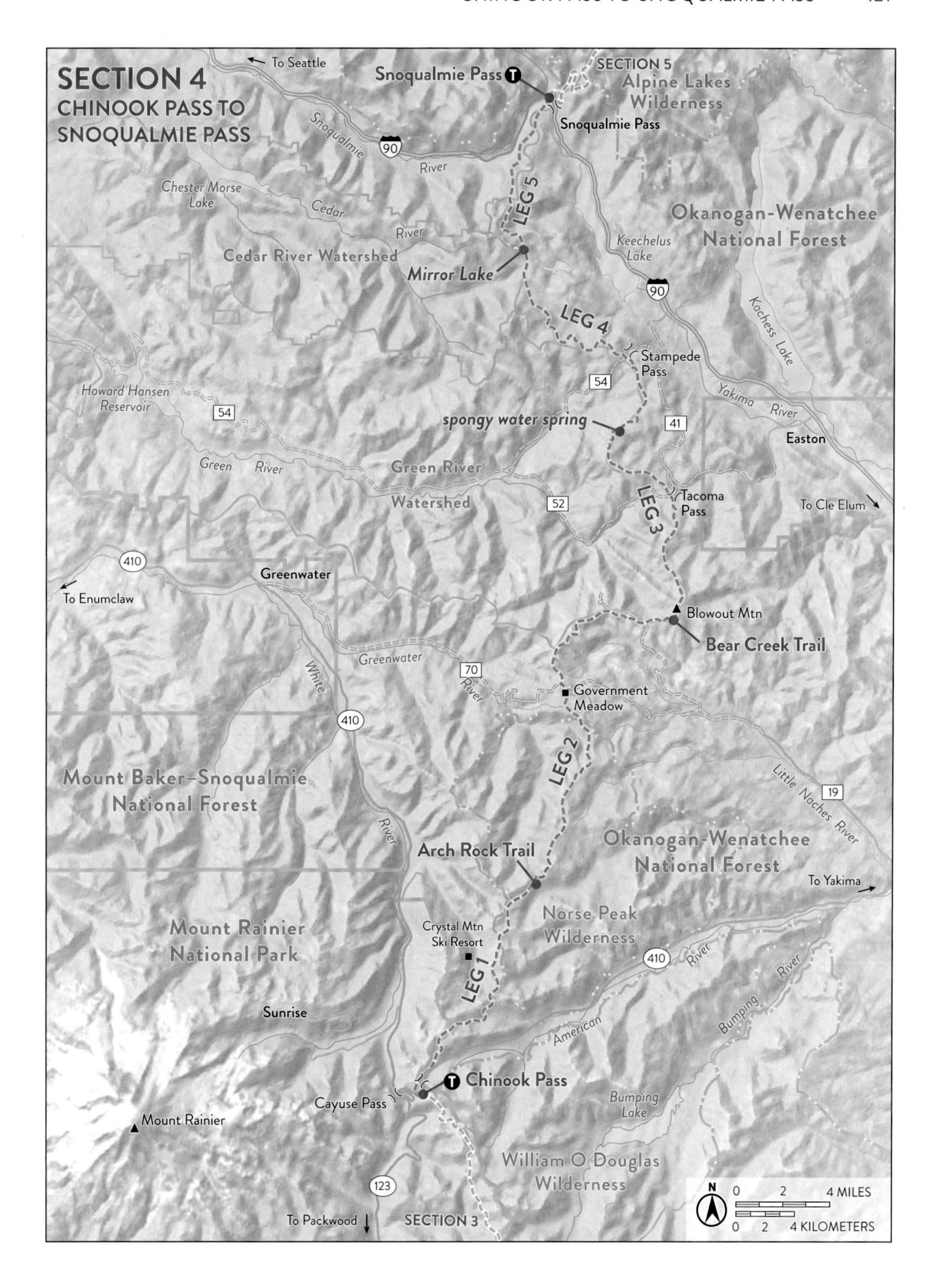
SECTION 4
CHINOOK PASS TO SNOQUALMIE PASS
To Seattle
Snoqualmie Pass
SECTION 5
Alpine Lakes Wilderness
Snoqualmie Pass
Snoqualmie River
90
Chester Morse Lake
Cedar River
LEG 5
Okanogan-Wenatchee National Forest
Keechelus Lake
Cedar River Watershed
Mirror Lake
90
Kachess Lake
LEG 4
Stampede Pass
54
Howard Hansen Reservoir
54
Yakima River
spongy water spring
41
Easton
Green River
Green River Watershed
52
LEG 3
Tacoma Pass
To Cle Elum
410
Greenwater
To Enumclaw
Blowout Mtn
Bear Creek Trail
Greenwater River
70
White River
Government Meadow
410
LEG 2
Little Naches River
19
Mount Baker–Snoqualmie National Forest
Okanogan-Wenatchee National Forest
Arch Rock Trail
To Yakima
Norse Peak Wilderness
Mount Rainier National Park
Crystal Mtn Ski Resort
410
LEG 1
American River
Bumping River
Sunrise
Chinook Pass
Cayuse Pass
Bumping Lake
Mount Rainier
William O Douglas Wilderness
123
To Packwood
SECTION 3
N
0 2 4 MILES
0 2 4 KILOMETERS

A pika carries a leafy treasure as he scoots across talus to his burrow.

SUGGESTED ITINERARIES

Where noted, distances are to camp trail spurs; camp may be up to 0.2 mile from junction.

7 DAYS

		Miles
Day 1	Chinook Pass to Basin Lake Camp spur	9.6
Day 2	Basin Lake Camp spur to Arch Rock Spring Camp	8.4
Day 3	Arch Rock Spring Camp to Spring Camp	9.9
Day 4	Spring Camp to Tacoma Pass Camp	12.6
Day 5	Tacoma Pass Camp to Camp 12	12.7
Day 6	Camp 12 to Mirror Lake Camp	7.4
Day 7	Mirror Lake Camp to Snoqualmie Pass	8.3

6 DAYS

Day 1	Chinook Pass to Basin Lake Camp spur	9.6
Day 2	Basin Lake Camp spur to Camp Mike Urich	13.6
Day 3	Camp Mike Urich to Camp 6	13.9
Day 4	Camp 6 to Camp 11	10.2
Day 5	Camp 11 to Mirror Lake Camp	13.3
Day 6	Mirror Lake Camp to Snoqualmie Pass	8.3

5 DAYS

Day 1	Chinook Pass to Basin Lake Camp spur	9.6
Day 2	Basin Lake Camp spur to Camp Mike Urich	13.6
Day 3	Camp Mike Urich to Tacoma Pass Camp	17.3
Day 4	Tacoma Pass Camp to Camp 13	15.7
Day 5	Camp 13 to Snoqualmie Pass	12.7

1 CHINOOK PASS TO ARCH ROCK TRAIL

DISTANCE 15.8 miles

ELEVATION GAIN/LOSS
+2600/–2190 feet

HIGH POINT 6420 feet

CONNECTING TRAILS
Unsigned pass trail, Silver Creek Trail #1192, Union Creek Trail #956, Bullion Basin Trail #1156, Basin Trail #987, Crow Lake Way Trail #953, Goat Lake Trail #1161

ON THE TRAIL

Fill out your free self-issue wilderness permit at the trailhead, and hop on the PCT to begin your gradual ascent, traversing northward across a shrubby hillside of aster, elderberry, and pearly everlasting. A couple of switchbacks steepen the grade and wind you in and out of fir and cedar before a sign on a tree reminds you that camping is prohibited within 100 feet of Sheep Lake.

In 1.8 miles from the trailhead, arrive at the stunning subalpine **Sheep Lake** **O**, where campsites are plentiful (**Sheep Lake Camp**). **Fill up on water here, as the next on-trail water is in 8.5 miles.** The meadowy lakeshore, dotted with evergreens and sporting a backdrop of rocky unnamed peaks, is a vision worthy of more than just a snap or two. Stop for a pace and take it in. Day hikers frequent this area, and for good reason!

The PCT caresses the lake's southeastern edge and then climbs out of the lake basin on switchbacks, taking you higher and higher, where views abound. Behind you now to the southwest is the tiny dot of the trailhead parking area and the ribbonlike highway at Chinook Pass. Farther south are the flat summit of Mount Adams and the rugged peaks of the Goat Rocks Wilderness, lending definition to the horizon. Wildflower fields abound near your feet as you climb high into the hinterlands. Suddenly, to the southwest, Mount Rainier's dome appears over foreground peaks, reminding you how close you are to the national park.

At 1.2 miles beyond Sheep Lake, arrive at the craggy **Sourdough Gap** and pop over to the north side. Interestingly, Sourdough Gap was named after gold prospectors who often carried a small amount of sourdough bread starter with them as they traveled from place to place. Several mining claims were staked near here by the "sourdoughs."

Relief for your hard-working calves comes as the trail levels out and the grade becomes much easier. New views, now into **Placer Lake** basin to the east, and more open cirques bring a change of scenery. In just 0.1 mile beyond Sourdough Gap, an unsigned trail heads north toward another pass. If time permits, you may want to follow this trail toward the unnamed pass, which offers views of Mount Rainier National Park's Crystal Lakes and Crystal Peak, a vision worthy of a few more steps.

CRYSTAL LAKES AND CRYSTAL PEAK

If you have time and stamina, follow the unsigned pass trail as it crosses over the ridge and drops into Mount Rainier National Park, offering up wide-open views of Crystal Lakes and Crystal Peak. In 1 mile, after losing roughly 600 feet of elevation, the trail arrives at the larger and more scenic of the two Crystal Lakes, where you'll find a wilderness camp and backcountry toilet. Camping here requires a permit and must be prearranged with the Park Service. The smaller Crystal Lake, and another wilderness camp with a toilet, lies 0.7 mile farther into the basin, a descent of another 400 feet. Ultimately, you could end or begin hiking the PCT via this route, as SR 410 is roughly 4 miles from the PCT junction with the unsigned pass trail.

After the unsigned pass trail, the PCT descends through sweeping views and whistling hoary marmots who stand at attention near their dirt

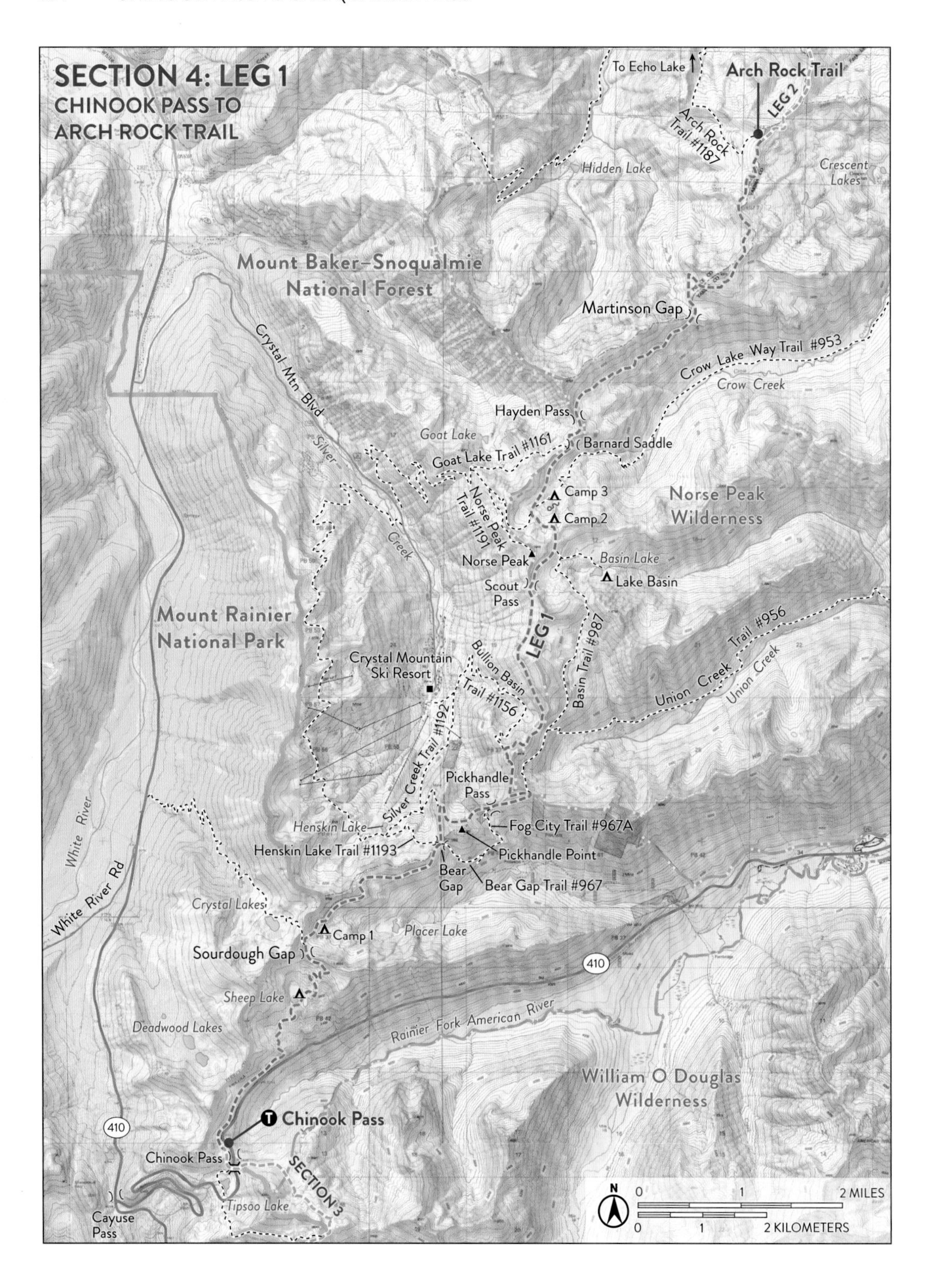
SECTION 4: LEG 1
CHINOOK PASS TO ARCH ROCK TRAIL
To Echo Lake
Arch Rock Trail
LEG 2
Arch Rock Trail #1187
Hidden Lake
Crescent Lakes
Mount Baker–Snoqualmie National Forest
Martinson Gap
Crow Lake Way Trail #953
Crow Creek
Crystal Mtn Blvd
Hayden Pass
Goat Lake
Goat Lake Trail #1161
Barnard Saddle
Silver
Camp 3
Camp 2
Norse Peak Wilderness
Norse Peak Trail #1191
Norse Peak
Basin Lake
Lake Basin
Scout Pass
Creek
Mount Rainier National Park
LEG 1
Basin Trail #987
Union Creek Trail #956
Union Creek
Crystal Mountain Ski Resort
Bullion Basin Trail #1156
Silver Creek Trail #1192
Pickhandle Pass
Fog City Trail #967A
Henskin Lake
Pickhandle Point
Henskin Lake Trail #1193
Bear Gap
Bear Gap Trail #967
White River
White River Rd
Crystal Lakes
Camp 1
Placer Lake
Sourdough Gap
410
Sheep Lake
Deadwood Lakes
Rainier Fork American River
William O Douglas Wilderness
410
Chinook Pass
Chinook Pass
SECTION 3
Tipsoo Lake
Cayuse Pass
N
0 1 2 MILES
0 1 2 KILOMETERS

burrows. Placer Lake twinkles in the distance as you continue walking through high subalpine terrain, traversing grassy hillsides and winding your way northeast. In 2.2 miles beyond Sheep Lake, find a trailside one-tent campsite (**Camp 1**)—with no privacy, but a lovely viewpoint to the trail's right (east).

In 3.3 miles beyond Sheep Lake, reach a confusing junction where several paths intersect. **Bear Gap Trail #967** leads southeast; **Henskin Lake Trail #1193** drops northwest toward, you guessed it, Henskin Lake; and **Silver Creek Trail #1192** heads north and switchbacks toward the **Crystal Mountain Ski Resort**, now very visible on the opposite hillside. If a friend wanted to hike in and meet you, say, with a juicy pear, a fresh cinnamon roll, or a piping-hot pizza, this is a very obtainable meeting spot, relatively close to the ski area and to paved roads and civilization.

To the west, beyond Crystal Mountain's ski runs, Mount Rainier shows off her many glaciers and turbulent river valleys. Onward you go, traversing green, open slopes, rolling along gently, until the PCT dives southeast through the steep hillsides of **Pickhandle Point**, yet another name attributed to the mining claims in this area. The trail then gently turns northeast and continues through open terrain near **Pickhandle Pass**, where it meets up with **Fog City Trail #967A**, 1.1 miles beyond the confusing junction at Bear Gap Trail. Fog City was a miners' tent camp not far below Pickhandle Pass, so named because of the constant socked-in weather here. Today, the Fog City Trail is rarely used.

Next, traverse an open, meadowed slope before reaching a hairpin turn to the west on the shoulders of Crown Point. Here, 0.4 mile from the Fog City Trail junction, the PCT meets up with **Union Creek Trail #956** to the right (north), which heads northeast into distant lake basins and eventually circles back to SR 410 east of Chinook Pass. Views of the grand, snowcapped Mount Rainier get better with each turn, keeping things interesting.

Crystal Mountain Ski Resort is still visible across the valley, with its ski lifts and access roads. The PCT stays high and passes three unsigned trails on the left (west), which arrive from the ski area far below. The first, at 0.6 mile beyond Union Creek, is **Bullion Basin Trail #1156**, followed by two more unsigned turnoffs, which do not appear on most maps. In 2.6 miles from the Fog City Trail junction,

CRYSTAL MOUNTAIN SKI RESORT

The Crystal Mountain Ski Resort first opened in 1962 and provides Seattle and surrounding metro areas with 2600 acres of slippery winter terrain that gets an annual snowfall of 486 inches. During the summer, the resort offers gondola rides to a stunning Mount Rainier vista, mountain biking, and horseback riding. Lodging and dining are open in summer months, if you want to detour off the PCT for a real meal or a comfy bed. Simply hike roughly 2 miles on Silver Creek Trail #1192 into the basin located 1500 feet below the PCT.

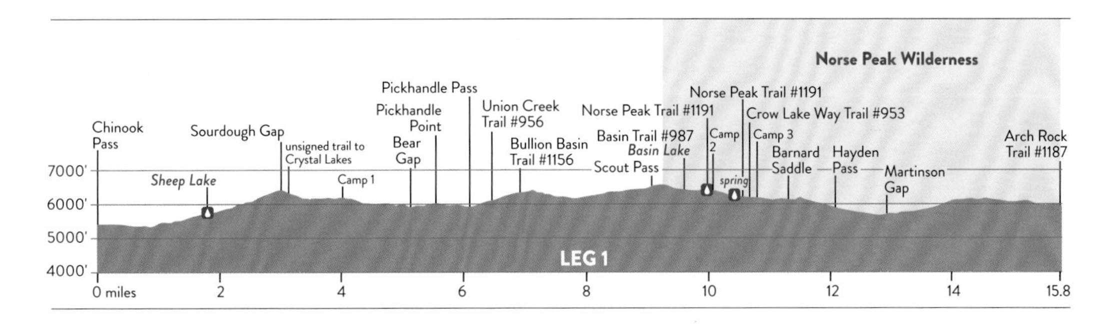

Caption

arrive at the unsigned **Scout Pass**, a lovely, open mixed grass and conifer area that drops you over to the eastern side of Norse Peak. A decrepit stock hitching post has seen better days but reminds you that everyone needs a break from time to time . . . including you! Suck in those Rainier views and fish out a snack from your pack as you gawk.

On the east side of the pass, more sprawling subalpine slopes allow views of the surrounding hills and distant peaks to the east. Keep an eye out for mountain goats, which often visit this area in large herds. Before long, your hillside traverse leads to views of **Basin Lake** and the appropriately named **Lake Basin**. The twinkling aqua lake set amid grassland and conifers is a vision and begs you to visit. In 0.4 mile, you'll get your chance when a signed spur for **Basin Trail #987** shows up to the PCT's right (east). If you're looking to throw down your tent, there are lovely **campsites at Basin Lake**, located 0.4 mile east of the PCT. You'll lose roughly 600 feet of elevation but find a tranquil place to drift off and count sheep, or perhaps mountain goats.

The wonderful meadow rambles continue as you wander in and out of lupine, arnica, aster, and subalpine fir, gently descending into Big Crow Basin. In 0.4 mile from the Basin Trail junction, a sloping one-tent campsite (**Camp 2**) is on the trail's right. It doesn't offer much privacy, but it could work for a snooze if you're losing daylight.

In 0.7 mile beyond the Basin Trail junction (0.3 mile past Camp 2), keep your eyes peeled for a small spur trail leading to the right (east) on a hillside traverse. You'll walk right by it if you aren't looking or if someone else isn't stopped there already. A small **spring** gurgles with reliable, delicious water. Trail crews have installed a metal pipe near the spring's headwaters, allowing for a constant fountain. Drink up, fill up, and then giddyup for more trail adventures ahead.

Immediately beyond the spring, **Crow Lake Way Trail #953** connects to the PCT on the right (east). In 0.1 mile beyond the junction, a spectacular camp (**Camp 3**) in the evergreens awaits your tent. A cozy campsite has space for two small tents, logs for sitting, some privacy, and plenty of shade. Claim it, stake it, and call it home . . . or JKW (just keep walking).

Grasslands continue as you climb out of Big Crow Basin across occasional scree fields and rocky terrain before the trail drops into mossy conifers. From here, the PCT rolls gradually up and down, obtaining the forested, unsigned **Barnard Saddle** as well as the unsigned **Goat Lake Trail #1161** in 0.9 mile beyond the Crow Lake Way Trail junction.

The PCT now traverses a couple of large, rock-strewn ravines and darts in and out of evergreen pockets before it arrives at the unsigned **Hayden Pass**, where it offers previews of the coming attraction: Little Crow Basin. You'll cross open, rocky hillsides with brushy avalanche slopes and pockets of conifers. In season, scarlet gilia and pearly everlasting splash the nearby hillsides a patriotic red and white against the blue sky.

In 2.9 miles beyond the Crow Lake Way Trail junction, arrive at the forested **Martinson Gap**, complete with a new sign announcing its presence and elevation of 5720 feet. The quiet isolation and lack of traffic in this area are a cleansing soul shampoo.

NORSE PEAK TRAIL

Two unsigned, lightly used spur trails arrive from the PCT's left (west) and connect to **Norse Peak Trail #1191**. One is 0.5 mile before the spring (0.2 mile past the Basin Lake Trail junction), and one is immediately after the spring. They look like camping spur trails but will lead you and your heavy pack on a wild goose chase if you're looking for a spot to snooze. Since they aren't used often, it's easy to get lost trying to make a side trip out of them. Stick to the PCT unless you're a wiz with a map and compass or have fairly extensive knowledge of the backcountry near here.

Opposite: *The PCT overlooks bustling Crystal Mountain Ski Resort, as Mount Rainier looms in the background.*

Brilliant high-country meadows welcome hikers just north of Basin Lake.

From Martinson Gap the PCT traipses under rocky cliffs and begins slowly climbing tan, barren-soil slopes sprinkled with subalpine firs. In places, expansive views give you a reason to stop and gawk. Eventually, the trail returns to dense evergreen forest and arrives at **Arch Rock Trail #1187**, which heads off toward Echo Lake, 3 miles northwest of the PCT.

CAMP-TO-CAMP MILEAGE

Chinook Pass to Sheep Lake Camp	1.8
Sheep Lake Camp to Camp 1	2.2
Camp 1 to Camp 2	6.0
Camp 2 to Camp 3	0.4
Camp 3 to Arch Rock Trail	5.4

2 ARCH ROCK TRAIL TO BEAR CREEK TRAIL

DISTANCE 17.4 miles

ELEVATION GAIN/LOSS
+2840/–3430 feet

HIGH POINT 5940 feet

CONNECTING TRAILS AND ROADS
Raven Roost Trail #951, Louisiana Saddle Trail #945A, Maggie Creek Trail #1186, FR 70 (unpaved, near Government Meadow), FR 7080 (unpaved), FR 7038 (FR 784, unpaved), Bear Creek Trail #943

ON THE TRAIL

The PCT leaves the **Arch Rock Trail #1187** junction and in short order arrives at a sign for Airplane Meadows. The meadows aren't expansive, but the elk like to frolic in them, so keep your senses honed for their ruckus. The trail gradually descends, alternating between thickets of firs and sloping grassy hillsides, until it reaches **Raven Roost Trail #951**, coming in from the right (east) in 0.7 mile.

The forest offers up a couple of peekaboo views to the northeast, where countless distant peaks invite you to pause and enjoy the scenery. In 1.3 miles beyond the Raven Roost Trail junction, arrive at **Arch Rock Spring**, noted by a couple of tree signs. Here, a spur trail leads left (west) and in a handful of feet arrives at a reliable, dribbling spring. At least two campsites (**Arch Rock Spring Camp**) are along the PCT north of the spring spur trail. The campsites are well used and suitable for a couple of tents each.

In 0.9 mile from Arch Rock Spring, the PCT passes over a wonderfully odd series of mud and sand hills. It feels like you're walking on a hard-packed sandy beach. These tan mounds are geological formations left behind by melting glaciers many moons ago and are a treat to see. On windy days, when the sand has swirled over the trail, yours might be the only footprints, as if you were the first person to ever walk this path.

Onward through firs and hemlocks you go, gently rolling up and down until you reach a thick, forested pass known as **Louisiana Saddle**. Here, **Louisiana Saddle Trail #945A** heads to the right (east), traversing forested hillsides on a relatively easy grade until reaching Rods Gap, an uneventful, equally forested notch, where someone has squirreled away sticks to make space for one small tent. There's no water, and it's not an optimal place to camp, but it's good to know that a flat spot exists in this area if you find yourself elbow deep in darkness.

Next up, the PCT strolls through more mixed conifers and over a recently built turnpike before arriving at **Maggie Creek Trail #1186**, to the left (southwest), 3 miles from the Louisiana Saddle Trail junction. Almost immediately after, bid adieu to the Norse Peak Wilderness and continue your romp through the Mount Baker–Snoqualmie National Forest.

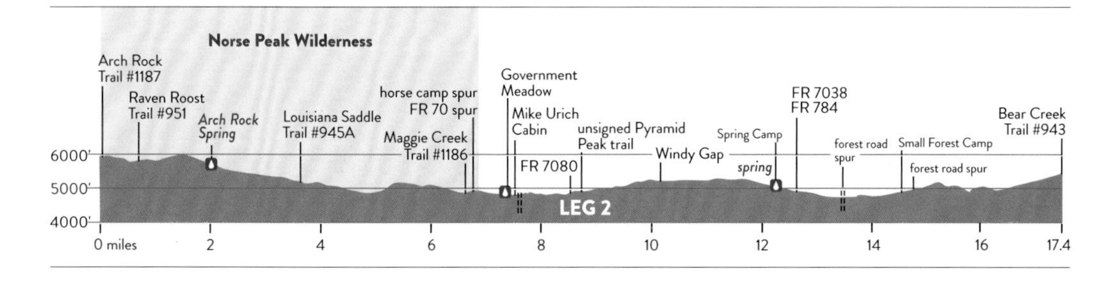

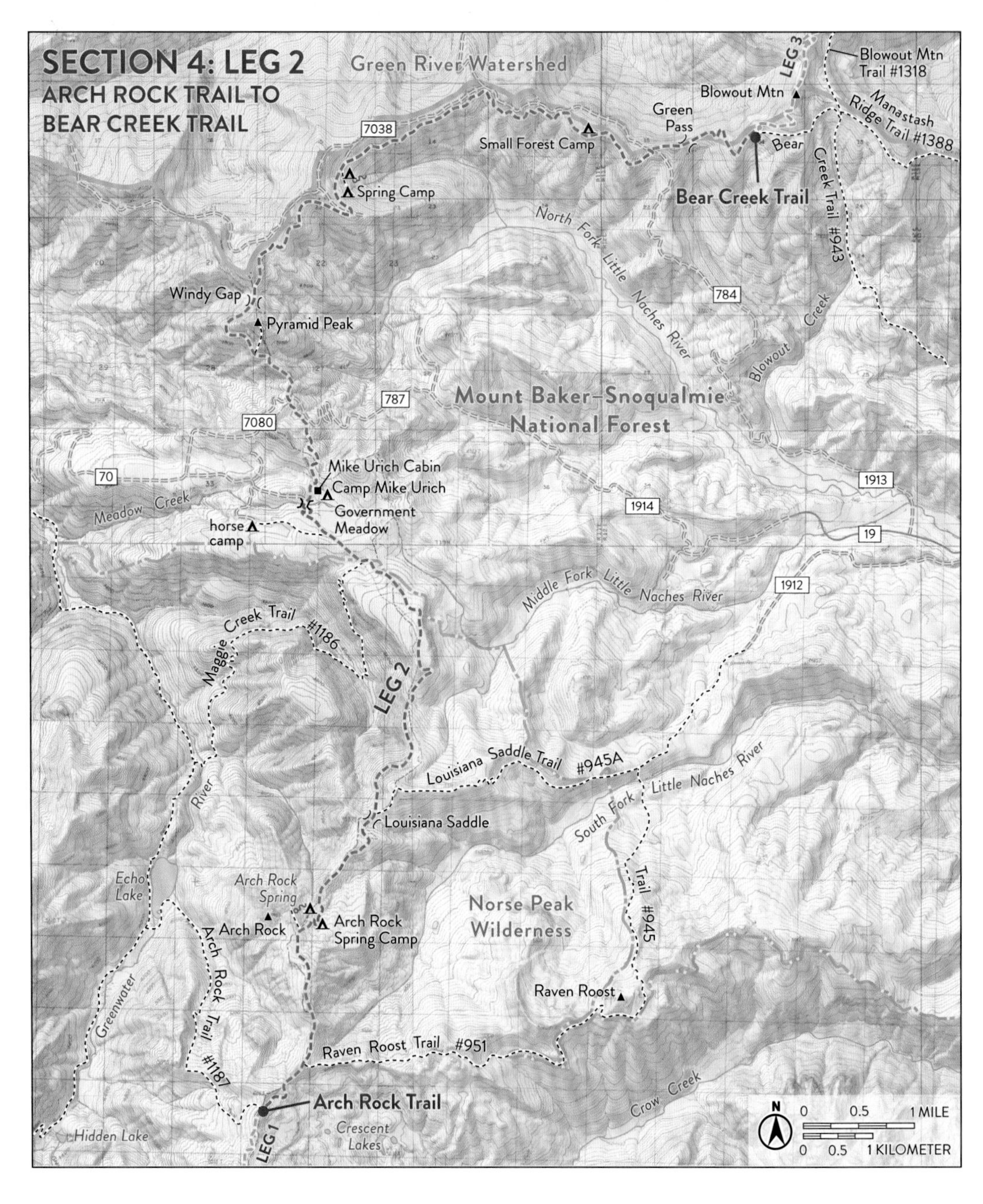

From here all the way to Snoqualmie Pass, you'll cross so many forest and logging roads that your head will spin. A few clear-cuts join the party as the PCT leads through public and private lands used for a plethora of purposes, including hunting, target shooting, and harvesting trees. You may also encounter a handful of dirt bike and ATV riders having fun on backcountry forest roads. But don't fret or turn back. I saw two herds of elk on this stretch of trail and met a

A fritillary butterfly dines on a sweet treat of wildflower nectar.

hunter who offered me a big juicy pear. There's always something interesting to be discovered, or perhaps even eaten. Your adventure is all about what you make it.

In 0.2 mile from the Maggie Creek Trail junction, a **spur trail** noted by a tree sign branches left (west) to a horse camp located 0.35 mile beyond the junction. If you're looking to start or end your trip on the well-traveled but unpaved **FR 70** out of the town of Greenwater, follow this unnamed trail toward the horse camp for less than a mile to its junction with FR 70 at a parking area. A sign here notes the road with an arrow, so you'll be sure to find it.

At roughly 0.5 mile beyond the horse camp spur trail, the PCT descends to a wooden bridge over a creek at the edge of **Government Meadow**. **Stop for water**, as this is the best place to fill 'er up for a while. Immediately beyond the bridge, a spur trail leads to the **Mike Urich Cabin**, which is often home to horsemen or trail workers. If no one has claimed the casa, you're in luck! The cabin is available on a first-come, first-served basis, so make yourself at home. Share if you wish, especially if the weather is not cooperating. The little log cabin—complete with a wood stove, outhouse, and surrounding flat ground for tent sites—makes a fine place to camp (**Camp Mike Urich**), with plenty of space for all who want to stay. You may find the area a little "horsey," so watch where you put your tent. Oh yes, and a word to the wise . . . keep your tent zipped up as much as possible to avoid the snuggly mice that seek out your warm toes in your sleeping bag.

The PCT winds its way around the back of the cabin and continues on an old roadbed past a couple of signs noting the history of the area. In 0.1 mile, the trail arrives at a rough-and-tumble parking area for off-road vehicles and then passes a trail sign for the PCT. In another 0.1 mile (0.2 mile beyond the cabin), the trail crosses a rutted dirt road and continues on the other side. Signs for the PCT point you in the right direction if you get confused. Don't hesitate to call on the spirit of Mike Urich too—I hear he's great with invisibly steering you in the right direction.

Dip back into the forest filled with subalpine and silver fir and pass a couple of open meadows before finding yourself at gravel **FR 7080**, 1.2 miles north of the Mike Urich Cabin. Unlike many roads along this stretch, this one actually gets used, albeit lightly. Logging trucks, motorcycles, pickup trucks, and ATVs zip by about once an hour. Use caution when you cross and avoid camping on the road edges.

This may also be a good time to mention that while most folks mean you no harm, there can be bad grapes in every healthy bunch. This area is well known for rustic target-practice sites, and mischievous local yokels occasionally come up here to camp and party. Stick to the trail and pay attention to your raised hackles if something doesn't feel right.

After FR 7080, continue through clear-cuts on the other side. The evergreens here have started

THE MIKE URICH CABIN AND GOVERNMENT MEADOW

Mike Urich was a forest worker in the 1940s and 1950s who made great contributions to the land and trails in these parts, and the cabin is a memorial of his legacy. In partnership with the Forest Service, the current cabin was built by volunteers from the Sno-Jammers Snowmobile Club in 1992. A fabulous poem near the entrance warns those who pass not to rouse the ire of Mike's spirit by mistreating the land or leaving a fire unattended. Folks who use the cabin are protective of it, keeping a close eye out for potential vandals or those who otherwise misuse it. Thanks to the care and contributions of so many, the structure has not been trashed.

Government Meadow is one of the most popular snowmobiling areas in the state come winter. The sledders flock to the wide-open meadows to tear up fresh powder and hang out in the cabin, warming their digits. In the summer, 4x4s and ATVs take to the forest roads leading to the cabin and sometimes bring morsels of goodness, which sometimes get shared with PCT hikers. Visitors to Government Meadow also include the elk herds, which graze at dawn and dusk. This, of course, brings hunters, who frequent the cabin in the fall.

Government Meadow is a significant part of Washington's history. This area was part of a Native American cross-country and trade route known as the Naches Pass Trail. In 1853, the Longmire party of pioneers, with their train of nearly thirty wagons, spent a couple of days resting at Government Meadow, then known as Summit Prairie. This was the first successful wagon-train crossing through the rugged Naches Pass area of the Cascade Mountains. Three weeks later, a second wagon train followed, and a rustic wagon road was soon created. The Longmires eventually settled in the Yelm Prairie area and went on to become instrumental in developing parts of today's Mount Rainier National Park.

Opposite: *The Mike Urich Cabin, as seen here in use by horsemen, is available on a first-come, first-served basis.*

You are at
GOVERNMENT
MEADOWS
CABIN.
18 Inches Of Snow
Required To Ride
In Meadows
CAMP
MIKE URICH
DEDICATED TO THE
MEMORY OF
MIKE URICH

Mount Rainier pops up against a pink morning sky near Pyramid Peak.

to regenerate but aren't tall enough to block views of Mount Rainier to the southwest. Fireweed and pearly everlasting bring pink and white color pops to the trail and try to distract you from the logged landscape. In 0.4 mile from FR 7080, arrive at a defunct gravel spur road, which dead-ends at an old parking area. Turn left and walk the road roughly 25 feet north-northeast, and then continue on the well-marked PCT as it darts back into the forest.

Keep an eye out to the right (east) in 0.4 mile for the narrow and infrequently used unsigned trail that scoots to the top of **Pyramid Peak**. This primitive trail climbs steeply to the site of a former L4-style forest lookout that was torn down in 1968. The Mount Rainier views from the top are decent, but the clear-cuts in every direction are an eyesore. Skip the side trip.

Instead, continue your traverse around the broad base of Pyramid Peak and keep a sharp eye out for herds of elk, which graze among the regenerating trees in the nearby valleys. Trailside elderberries, with their brilliant red clusters, pull your focus from the hillsides here and there. Reach **Windy Gap** a short distance later, where you'll cross over to the northeast side of the ridge.

In roughly 2.3 miles from FR 7080, the PCT enters a spectacular silver forest **burn zone**. During the summer of 1988, while Yellowstone National Park was suffering from the largest wildfire in recorded park history, a smaller but just as heated fire raced through this landscape, destroying every tree in its path. This fire, accidentally started by loggers near Windy Gap, managed to burn 3000 acres. Like the Yellowstone fire zones, this forest is rebounding beautifully. Saplings thrive in the acidic soils, huckleberries are sweet as cotton candy, and bear grass shows off its slender stalks as you walk among the ghost trees.

On the ridge above the burn zone, **FR 7038** hugs the PCT. Occasional cars and trucks rumble along the dirt road as they make their way to hunting, camping, or berry-picking grounds. After a hairpin turn, walk through more clear-cuts as the trail trends northeasterly and arrives at two lovely one- and two-tent campsites (**Spring Camp**) to the right (southeast), 3.1 miles past FR 7080. There's a spring nearby, which you can easily zip by if you're not paying attention. You definitely want to **stop here and get water, because the next source is more than 11.8 miles** away. Bottoms up!

From here, the PCT descends to FR 7038, which has a split personality and on some maps is also named FR 784. Walk left (north) along the road for roughly 30 feet to find the PCT again on the opposite side. Back into a recently logged forest you go, walking through fireweed and small sapling-filled, clear-cut hillsides. Through the stumps, distant views open up, including of Mount Rainier to the southwest. In 1.1 miles after crossing FR 7038 (FR 784), cross another forest road, a spur off FR 7038.

In 2.2 miles beyond FR 7038, the trail passes a pleasant, forested one-tent campsite (**Small Forest Camp**) located up a small spur to the left (north) but visible from the main trail. The camp is dry, but if you filled up back at the spring, you're all set. In 0.3 mile beyond the camp, reach another gravel forest road spur. There are so many forest roads in this area that five different topo maps, one state gazetteer, and Forest Service personnel can't keep them all straight by number. Some disagree that a couple even exist, but I've seen them with my own two eyes, mates!

Now you're in for a climb, a descent, and another climb as you crest the broad western shoulders near Blowout Mountain. Up, up, up you go through the evergreens before arriving at yet another gravel forest road located 1.1 miles beyond the last one. More climbing ensues as you move through bountiful huckleberries that attempt to take over the trail. In 5.1 miles past FR 7038, arrive at signed **Bear Creek Trail #943**.

CAMP-TO-CAMP MILEAGE

Arch Rock Trail to Arch Rock Spring Camp 2.2
Arch Rock Spring Camp to Camp Mike Urich 5.2
Camp Mike Urich to Spring Camp 4.7
Spring Camp to Small Forest Camp 2.4
Small Forest Camp to Bear Creek Trail 2.9

3 BEAR CREEK TRAIL TO SPONGY WATER SPRING

DISTANCE 14.1 miles

ELEVATION GAIN/LOSS
+2950/–3650 feet

HIGH POINT 5660 feet

CONNECTING TRAILS AND ROADS
Blowout Mountain Trail #1318, FR 52 (at Tacoma Pass)

ON THE TRAIL

From the **Bear Creek Trail #943** junction, continue ascending through conifers and huckleberries until you reach a saddle near the top of Blowout Mountain. Finally, you're rewarded for your huff-and-puff with views of rocky neighboring peaks, through trees kind enough to part for a vista.

A small, waterless one-tent campsite (**Camp 4**) lies to the trail's left, 0.9 mile from the Bear

Sometimes the little things—like this showcase of recently bloomed beargrass—are what hiking is all about.

Creek Trail junction. The camp sports views from the ridge but is rather wide open and visible from the trail. Another campsite (**Camp 5**) is 0.2 mile farther, to the right. It's tucked into a grove of trees and is a bit more out of the way. In fact, if you plan to stay there, keep a close lookout or you might walk right by it. More great views pop up as you travel along the ridge.

In 1.5 miles from the Bear Creek Trail junction, arrive at **Blowout Mountain Trail #1318**, heading off to the right (east). The forest thickens as you begin a descent through conifers, fireweed, and typical Northwest ground cover, until a camp (**Camp 6**) comes into view on an incline, to the trail's right (east). The large, open six- or seven-tent camp is technically a parking or turnaround area for a defunct forest road that you'll cross in a few more steps. The turnaround area has regrown itself into a sparse, grassy open space, so if you use your imagination, you could call it a meadow. I've included it as a camping option, because camps for large groups are hard to find in these parts.

SECTION 4: LEG 3
BEAR CREEK TRAIL TO SPONGY WATER SPRING
LEG 4
spongy water spring
Camp 11
Snowshoe Butte
Camp 10
Bearpaw Butte
Camp 9
Camp 8
Camp 7
41
Cabin Creek
52
Tacoma Pass
Tacoma Creek
Green River
5220
Okanogan-Wenatchee National Forest
5230
Camp 6
Mount Baker–Snoqualmie National Forest
Green River Watershed
Pioneer Creek
LEG 3
Camp Creek
Blowout Mtn Trail #1318
Camp 4
Camp 5
Blowout Mtn
Bear Creek Trail
Manastash Ridge Trail #1388
LEG 2
Green Pass
784
Bear Creek Trail #943
0 0.5 1 MILE
0 0.5 1 KILOMETER

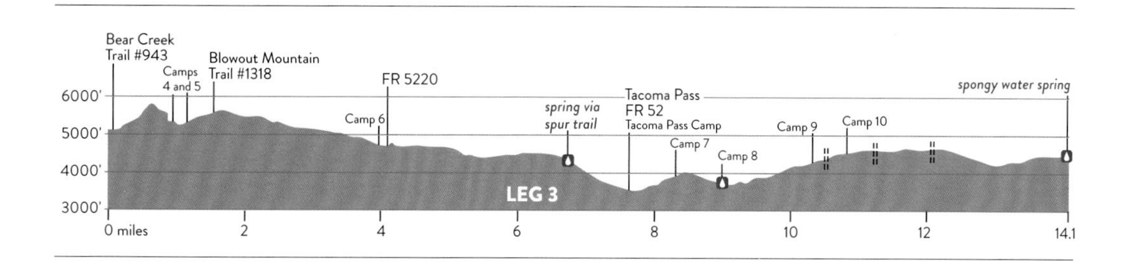
Bear Creek Trail #943
Camps 4 and 5
Blowout Mountain Trail #1318
FR 5220
Camp 6
spring via spur trail
Tacoma Pass FR 52 Tacoma Pass Camp
Camp 7
Camp 8
Camp 9
Camp 10
spongy water spring
6000'
5000'
4000'
3000'
LEG 3
0 miles
2
4
6
8
10
12
14.1

Cross the little-used dirt forest road, 2.5 miles beyond the Blowout Mountain Trail junction, and continue for another 0.4 mile to cross yet another forest road, this one with a large, used, but unsigned parking area for the PCT off FR 5220. You could, and some have, camped near the turnaround spot, but this road clearly gets some use, so be careful you don't end up with tire tracks across your forehead.

From the parking area, the PCT climbs into a logged tract, which offers meager views through the trees northeast of the second-highest nonvolcanic peak in Washington, Mount Stuart. Bear-grass stalks and huckleberries decorate the trail edges where sunlight breaks through, while conifers reach high into the blue sky.

The PCT plateaus and then begins a gentle descent through thick evergreens until reaching a very **important water spur trail** on a switchback to the PCT's left (west), 5 miles past the Blowout Mountain Trail junction and roughly six switchbacks into the descent. This is the first water that's reasonably close to the trail since you left the small spring nearly 11.8 miles south. By now, your mouth probably feels like you've been sucking on soda crackers! Some years, the water spur is unmarked, with no indication of nearby relief except for the obvious spur and an audible trickle of running water. Other years, hikers leave notes that point the way. Whatever the case, keep a close lookout for the spur so you don't miss it! The trail leads approximately 400 feet to a clear, cold, reliable creek fed by a spring.

In 0.8 mile past the spring, reach two small one-tent campsites (**Tacoma Pass Camp**), one to the left and one to the right, just before you cross the largest and most maintained gravel forest road in these parts, FR 52, at Tacoma Pass. But although the road is well maintained, it's very lightly traveled—if you needed help for some reason, your odds of someone driving by are very slim.

After crossing FR 52, the PCT begins climbing through sparse evergreens and brushy open slopes, evidence of yesteryear's clear-cuts, as you make your way to the ridgetop. Up you go, huffing and puffing through the waterless terrain, fighting mosquitos and black flies and hoping for views to take your mind off the drudgery. They'll come, eventually, so hang in there.

In 0.9 mile from FR 52, the trail drops to a decommissioned logging road, which becomes the trail for a bit before single-track takes over and the climbing starts up again. Pearly everlasting, saplings, wild strawberries, and lupine dot the trail edges where sunlight penetrates. In due course, the PCT pops back into thick evergreens with bear grass for ground cover. A one-tent primitive camp (**Camp 7**) is 1.2 miles beyond FR 52, to the right, offering a shady, quiet trailside spot. A bigger camp ahead is used more frequently, but if the trail seems busy it may already be claimed.

Pleasant forest walking continues through an area known as Sheets Pass and in 0.5 mile from Camp 7 (1.6 miles from FR 52), a well-used one-tent camp (**Camp 8**) shows up to the right, complete with a stump for sitting and a fire pit. This forested camp is a fine place to call home for the night and features a small seasonal creek nearby, just north along the PCT. Don't count on the creek in a unusually dry, hot summer. The dribble of water makes it hard to scoop with a water bottle, but you can usually shimmy the bottle around to get enough. Water pickins are slim in these parts, so we take what we can get!

The trail ascends past the thicket of evergreens onto open slopes filled with weeds, wildflowers, and bracken ferns trying to take over the narrow dirt path. Don't stop for pictures—you'll get no Facebook likes for snaps from here. Keep rolling. There *is* beauty up ahead, once you get to Mirror Lake! Bear-grass stalks cover hillsides as the trail opens up to views of forested hills, clear-cuts, and logging roads. The open slopes fill with ripening huckleberries in late summer, introducing your mouth to nature's sweetest candy.

In 3 miles from FR 52, the PCT climbs to a high point near the shoulders of Bearpaw Butte and finds itself next to a tent site on the trail's right, in a wide, weedy dirt patch that long ago was part of a forest road parking lot. This spot could host four or five

Opposite: *South of Snoqualmie Pass, old clear-cuts open up light, allowing conifers to regrow and shrubs and wildflowers to flourish.*

tents (**Camp 9**), useful for a large group. Privacy and shelter are limited, but the area is in high country, which gives it at least one redeeming quality.

From Camp 9, the trail drops to touch an old logging road twice before regaining single-track once more. PCT markers are on posts around here, but they have been damaged by snow and storms over the years. Look on the ground for them if you get discombobulated. The trail then follows a narrow ridge as it climbs northwest and passes a barren one-tent spot (**Camp 10**) to the trail's right, 3.5 miles beyond FR 52. This is where the PCT challenges a guidebook author. Is this a camp or just a dirt patch? You decide and call it what you want. Since others have used it, I'll call it a camp.

Don't be fooled by the plateau—your climb is not done until the fat birdy sings. Keep rolling along through clear-cuts and saplings until you finally, yes, finally begin a gentle descent through evergreens and open slopes, crossing two decommissioned logging roads and through dense huckleberry shrubs to arrive at your next water source.

Thankfully, the earth has given us water in the form of a spring amid a small, mossy, spongy, grassy slope to the right (south) of the trail, just after the PCT makes a sweeping turn to the northeast. You'll walk right by it if you aren't paying attention, so watch really closely. The spongy spring is just below the trail in a swampy meadow, with a beaten-down grassy path leading to the trickles, 6.5 miles from FR 52. If you want to camp, walk approximately 0.3 mile farther along the PCT to a short spur trail on an abandoned road, which leads to a fairly private one-tent camp (**Camp 11**).

CAMP-TO-CAMP MILEAGE

Bear Creek Trail to Camp 4	0.9
Camp 4 to Camp 5	0.2
Camp 5 to Camp 6	2.8
Camp 6 to Tacoma Pass Camp	3.4
Tacoma Pass Camp to Camp 7	1.2
Camp 7 to Camp 8	0.5
Camp 8 to Camp 9	1.3
Camp 9 to Camp 10	0.5
Camp 10 to Camp 11	3.3

4 SPONGY WATER SPRING TO MIRROR LAKE

DISTANCE 13.3 miles

ELEVATION GAIN/LOSS +2900/−3250 feet

HIGH POINT 4710 feet

CONNECTING TRAILS AND ROADS FR 54 (unpaved), Meadow Creek Trail #1338

ON THE TRAIL

Leave the spongy spring feeling well hydrated and with a renewed pep in your step. This leg is about to cross so many logging and forest roads that you might try to stick your spork in your eye, but don't bust a cornea yet. Nearer Snoqualmie Pass the scenery redeems itself and you might once again be tempted to pull out the camera.

Pass the right-hand trail spur to one-tent **Camp 11**, and then alternate between meadows dotted with huckleberries and thickets of conifers. In 1.2 miles from the spongy spring, cross a dirt forest road and find the PCT on the other side. Onward you go, through more bear grass and evergreens. For the first time since the start of this section, you'll see the trimmed areas of powerlines near I-90 and Stampede Pass, a popular snowmobiling mecca.

In 0.5 mile from the last dirt forest road, cross another. The trail descends steeply at times,

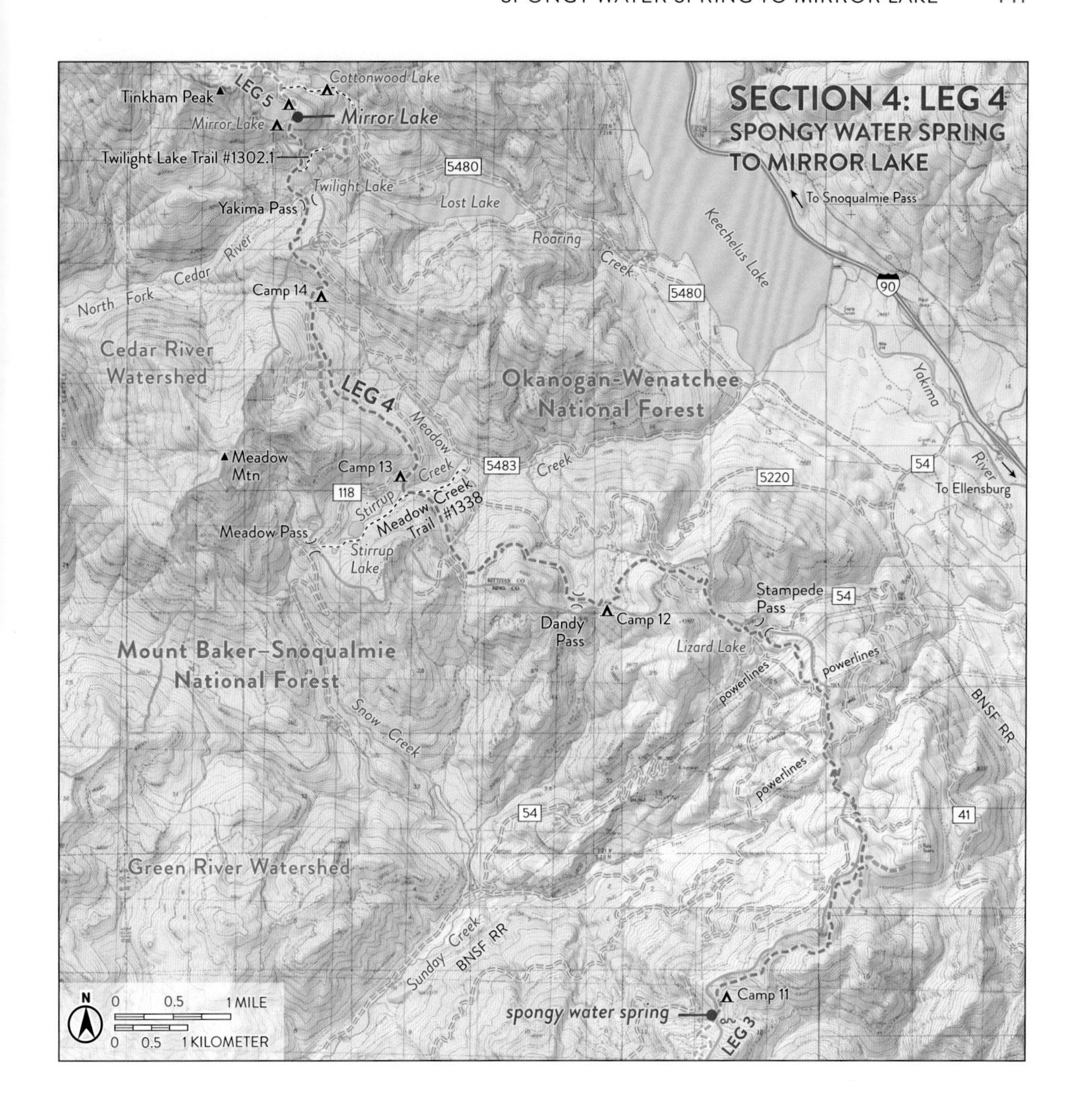
SECTION 4: LEG 4
SPONGY WATER SPRING TO MIRROR LAKE
Tinkham Peak
LEG 5
Cottonwood Lake
Mirror Lake
Mirror Lake
Twilight Lake Trail #1302.1
5480
Twilight Lake
Lost Lake
Yakima Pass
To Snoqualmie Pass
Keechelus Lake
Roaring Creek
North Fork Cedar River
Camp 14
5480
90
Cedar River Watershed
LEG 4
Okanogan-Wenatchee National Forest
Yakima River
Meadow Creek
Meadow Mtn
Camp 13
5483
Creek
54
To Ellensburg
118
Stirrup Creek
Meadow Creek Trail #1338
5220
Meadow Pass
Stirrup Lake
Stampede Pass
54
Dandy Pass
Camp 12
Lizard Lake
Mount Baker–Snoqualmie National Forest
powerlines
powerlines
BNSF RR
Snow Creek
powerlines
54
41
Green River Watershed
Sunday Creek
BNSF RR
0 0.5 1 MILE
0 0.5 1 KILOMETER
Camp 11
spongy water spring
LEG 3

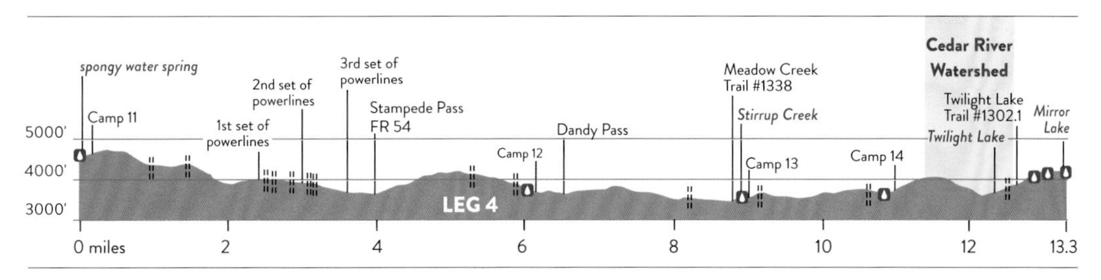
spongy water spring
Camp 11
1st set of powerlines
2nd set of powerlines
3rd set of powerlines
Stampede Pass FR 54
Camp 12
Dandy Pass
Meadow Creek Trail #1338
Stirrup Creek
Camp 13
Camp 14
Cedar River Watershed
Twilight Lake Trail #1302.1
Twilight Lake
Mirror Lake
5000'
4000'
3000'
LEG 4
0 miles
2
4
6
8
10
12
13.3

Morning sunshine crests the eastward peaks giving life to a new day.

weaving through a thick grove of spindly conifers, until you break out onto a hillside under buzzing powerlines. Thankfully, the PCT is very evident as it guides you through the slope's foliage.

This is where I start sounding like a broken record. Over the next 0.6 mile, you'll cross four more dirt roads, with groves of Douglas-firs breaking the monotony before you reach a second set of powerlines. Same drill, different buzzing wires. More of the same follows, this time with two road crossings before you reach the third and final set of powerlines, 0.4 mile beyond the prior set.

In 0.6 mile from the third powerline crossing, arrive at the unsigned, dirt **FR 54**, the most traveled road in this area, which isn't really saying much. You'd likely spend all day watching grass grow if you were waiting for someone to pass by. You've seen so many forest roads that you may not recognize this one as the main thoroughfare, but it is.

After crossing FR 54, the trail climbs moderately through bear grass and spindly trees. Huff and puff your way through the second-growth forest, reaching a notch near the ridgetop, and then work your way through an old clear-cut. After crossing two more logging roads, one of them very old, descend to a small seasonal creek, 1.9 miles beyond FR 54 (2.5 miles after the third set of powerlines). Stop for a fill-up if this cold, relatively clear creek is flowing. In 0.1 mile beyond the creek, the PCT continues descending and passes a grassy meadow camp (**Camp 12**) to the left (south), with space for two tents. Camping in a meadow is a big no-no for leaving no trace, but this particular meadow has seen so many overnighters that its tent spots are barren, and another low-impact principle is to use existing sites instead of creating new ones.

The PCT winds its way west past the forested, uneventful, and unsigned **Dandy Pass** before crossing a logging road, 2 miles from Camp 12. Immediately after the road, a lovely creek flows over mossy rocks into a stony catch basin, waiting for your water bottle. From here, the trail turns north through a more mature forest and arrives at a sign for **Meadow Creek Trail #1338**, 0.9 mile from the last logging road. Also noted on the sign is Stirrup Lake, found by cruising through clear-cuts for 0.5 mile southwest of the PCT. The lake, more like a puddle in dry summers, sits amid chainsawed terrain, and the berry bushes have taken over. Save your energy and instead grind your carcass to the camp at Mirror Lake.

In 0.1 mile from the Meadow Creek Trail junction, rock hop across **Stirrup Creek** and find a small but pleasant one-tent camp (**Camp 13**) to the left. It's small and near the PCT, but the forest is mature, the camp is well used, and the ambiance gives off a good vibe.

Ascend to pass another gravel forest road, 0.2 mile past Stirrup Creek, and duck back into conifers. Huff and puff your way through aging second-growth forest and newer timbers regenerating in logging zones as you make your way north. Various peekaboos along the route show the rocky summits of Tinkham and Silver peaks, an exciting glimpse of the wonders ahead.

In 2 miles beyond Stirrup Creek, the trail crosses, you guessed it, another dirt logging road and then drops to a small stream in another 0.1 mile. Rock hop across and enter the forest on a gentle ascent. Immediately to the right is a small one-tent, slightly sloping camp (**Camp 14**), complete with a fire ring. The forest is pleasantly shady and water is nearby, but the Mirror Lake campsites offer more for scenery—so if you can muscle up the vigor, keep on rolling.

Up, up, up you go in the sunlight filtering through the trees. Clumps of bear grass and patches of moss give the understory plenty of green. In 0.8 mile from the last logging road, the PCT leaves national forest land for a bit and teeters along the border of the **Cedar River Watershed**. The meticulously managed 90,638-acre watershed supplies water to 1.4 million people in Greater Seattle and is home to a rich diversity of plants and animals. Keep your eyes open for critters, great and small.

Pass a sign noting your exit from national forest land, and descend steeply at times to the marshy western shores of **Twilight Lake** and its shallow basin, known as **Yakima Pass**

Dawn breaks brilliantly across the summer sky in early morning near Dandy Pass.

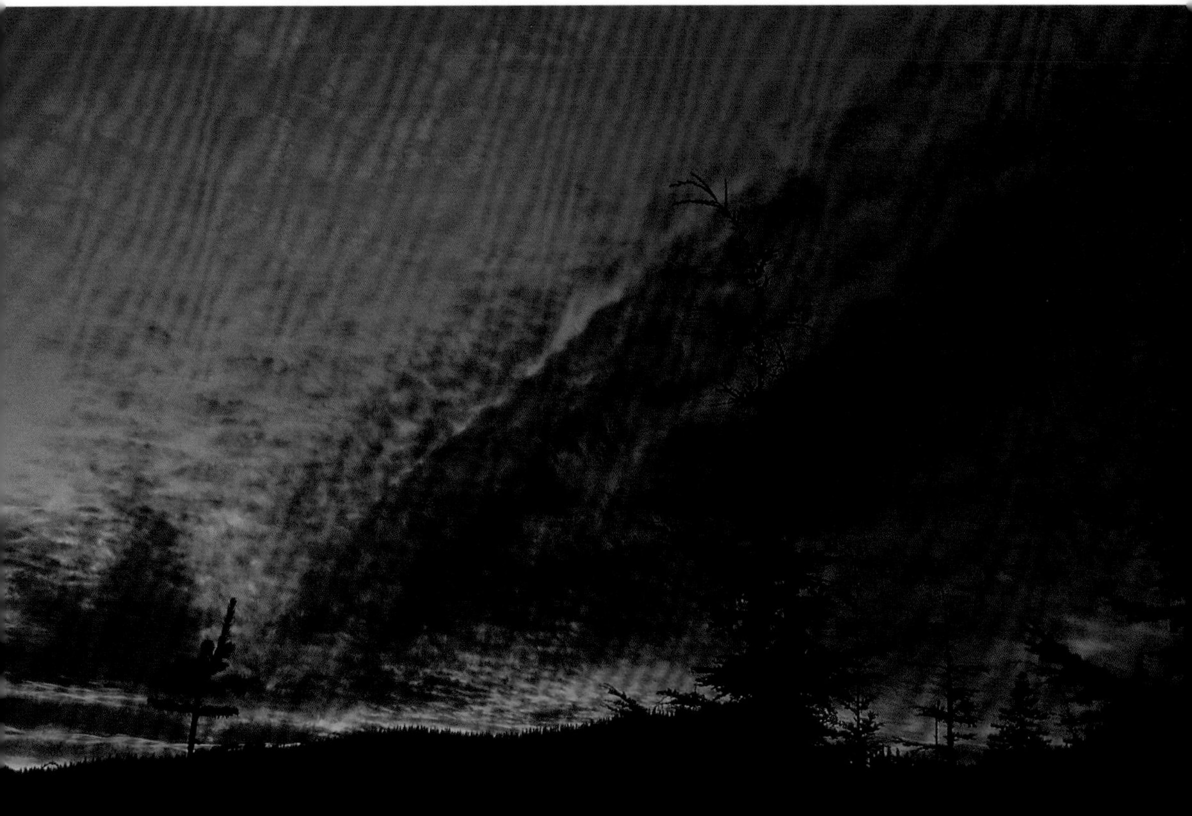

New growth springs to life in a formerly logged landscape south of Snoqualmie Pass.

and noted by a sign. From here to Mirror Lake, water is plentiful, so fill up wherever you find the best flow.

At Twilight Lake there's a nearly extinct path out to what looks like an island, where a large camp still exists. If you can get to it with dry feet, it's your lucky day, since this area is overgrown with reeds in swamp water. You could wade out to it if you're exhausted, but easily accessible and more appealing campsites await at Mirror Lake. On the northwest shore of Twilight Lake, cross a wooden footbridge over a dribbling outlet creek and begin climbing out of the basin.

Cruise across an old logging road, now returning to its natural roots, 0.3 mile beyond Twilight Lake and Yakima Pass, and climb more steeply now, arriving at a seasonal creek. Another old roadbed follows, and then the PCT arrives at signed **Twilight Lake Trail #1302.1**, looking sadly like it hasn't seen a pair of hiking boots in years.

Next, the PCT traverses open hillsides brimming with fireweed, thimbleberry, and boulders. You'll cross a Mirror Lake outlet creek twice before arriving at several well-used campsites (**Mirror Lake Camp**) and the tranquil, treed shoreline of **Mirror Lake**, 0.9 mile from

Twilight Lake and Yakima Pass. If these first campsites are full, follow a boot-beaten path around the lake's southern shore, past the logjam to a couple more sites, or stay north along the PCT and find a few more shoreline sites to the trail's left (west).

Dust off the camera! Welcome back to large, mature conifers and a worthy backdrop, a far cry from the clear-cut scars you've been traveling through. Mirror Lake itself is a vision and on clear days does its name justice by reflecting the rugged slopes of Tinkham Peak to its west. Day hikers access this area easily via Mirror Lake Trail #1302 or from FR 9070, both north of here. You'll know them by their crisp linen and treats like cut-up watermelon; unlike us, they don't look and smell like they badly need a bar of soap.

Sleep well if this is home for the night. Otherwise, carry on to Snoqualmie Pass.

CAMP-TO-CAMP MILEAGE

Camp 11 to Camp 12	5.9
Camp 12 to Camp 13	3.0
Camp 13 to Camp 14	2.1
Camp 14 to Mirror Lake Camp	2.3

HEAD ON UP TO TINKHAM PEAK!

If "adventure" is your middle name and you like a navigational challenge, try the primitive hands-and-feet scramble to Tinkham Peak. Seen from Mirror Lake, the treeless, rocky summit is a real tease, practically daring you to find it. A couple of routes to the top leave from the PCT, but the easiest approach is from Mirror Lake. Follow the PCT to the lake's outlet and walk the southern shore on a narrow trail past the logjam. Marked most years by surveyors' tape, the trail then heads south, away from the lake, and begins climbing steeply on vague tread. Up, up, up you go until you reach the ridgeline and an open, meadowy slope leading to the summit, with views in all directions. You're very close to the Cedar River Watershed on this route, and No Trespassing signs abound. Respect the boundaries and stay on the faint pathways.

5 MIRROR LAKE TO SNOQUALMIE PASS

DISTANCE 8.3 miles

ELEVATION GAIN/LOSS
+1580/–2760 feet

HIGH POINT 4580 feet

CONNECTING TRAILS AND ROADS
Mirror Lake Trail #1302, Cold Creek Trail #1303, FR 9070 (unpaved), I-90

ON THE TRAIL

The PCT leaves Mirror Lake's southern shore and wanders through mature forest, arriving at **Camp 15** in 0.3 mile, a site where folks have previously pitched tents. There's room for roughly two small tents, but the sites are near the trail and not private. Mirror Lake Camp, in your rearview, is a much better option.

Immediately after the tent sites, **Mirror Lake Trail #1302** arrives from the right (east), noted by a tree sign. This is a popular day-hiking route for folks who want to eat lunch at Mirror Lake or huff and puff up the rocky shoulders of Tinkham and Silver peaks. If a busy weekend has all the campsites at Mirror Lake occupied, you could follow Mirror Lake Trail east approximately 0.4 mile to a couple of pleasant sites near the shallow, treed shores of Cottonwood Lake, but you'll lose roughly 300 feet of elevation doing so.

A rock-lined pathway beckons you to follow near Twilight Lake.

HEAD ON UP TO SILVER PEAK!

Silver Peak sure makes you work for it, but boy oh boy, does it reward too! Follow the faint unsigned trail west from the PCT (marked by a cairn 1.7 miles south of FR 9070 and 0.9 mile north of the Cold Creek Trail junction). You'll break out onto a saddle roughly 0.7 mile beyond the PCT. From this saddle, you can climb other peaks, such as Tinkham, but since our goal is Silver Peak, turn right (northwest) and follow the steep, rocky trail to the summit, roughly 0.7 mile beyond and up.

Important: The final 0.3 mile is a class 2 or 3 scramble, requiring use of hands to make your way. If you're not comfortable with such hazards, you can stick to the lower slopes and still reap your view reward. To the east is Mount Stuart, the second-highest nonvolcanic peak in the state. To the south are Mount Rainier and Mount Adams. Visible to the north on a clear day are Mount Shuksan, Glacier Peak, and Mount Baker. To the southwest, below you, is the sapphire sparkling water of Annette Lake. Head back the way you came when you've sucked in enough of that fresh alpine air.

The PCT climbs gently past large Douglas-firs and hemlocks and then turns west and reaches a junction 0.8 mile from Mirror Lake. The signed **Cold Creek Trail #1303** comes in from the right (north), another day-hiking approach to favorite PCT haunts. Cold Creek Trail drops north roughly 1400 feet in 1.5 miles to the Cold Creek Basin, home to the small Twin Lakes.

Traverse a large cirque and make your way north, click-clacking through scree fields under the shoulders of Tinkham Peak. Ahead, the pointy stone top of Silver Peak is visible and tempts you to find its summit. Next, 0.4 mile from the Cold Creek Trail junction, cross the headwaters of Cold Creek, usually dry or just a tiny dribble most summers.

Immediately beyond, the PCT achieves an easier grade and passes several tarns, ponds, and puddles. During early summer, this area can be a buggy mess, and you'll want to put your feet in overdrive through this often muddy stretch. The stagnant puddles provide an interesting visual break, and faint paths head into the brush to more bitty-biter breeding grounds.

Climbing commences and up you go, hitting a few switchbacks before continuing your northbound hillside traverse. In 0.9 mile from the Cold Creek Trail junction, notice a peculiar cairn and a faint trail to the left (west). If you aren't looking, you'll likely walk right by it. This is an unmaintained yet frequently used path that

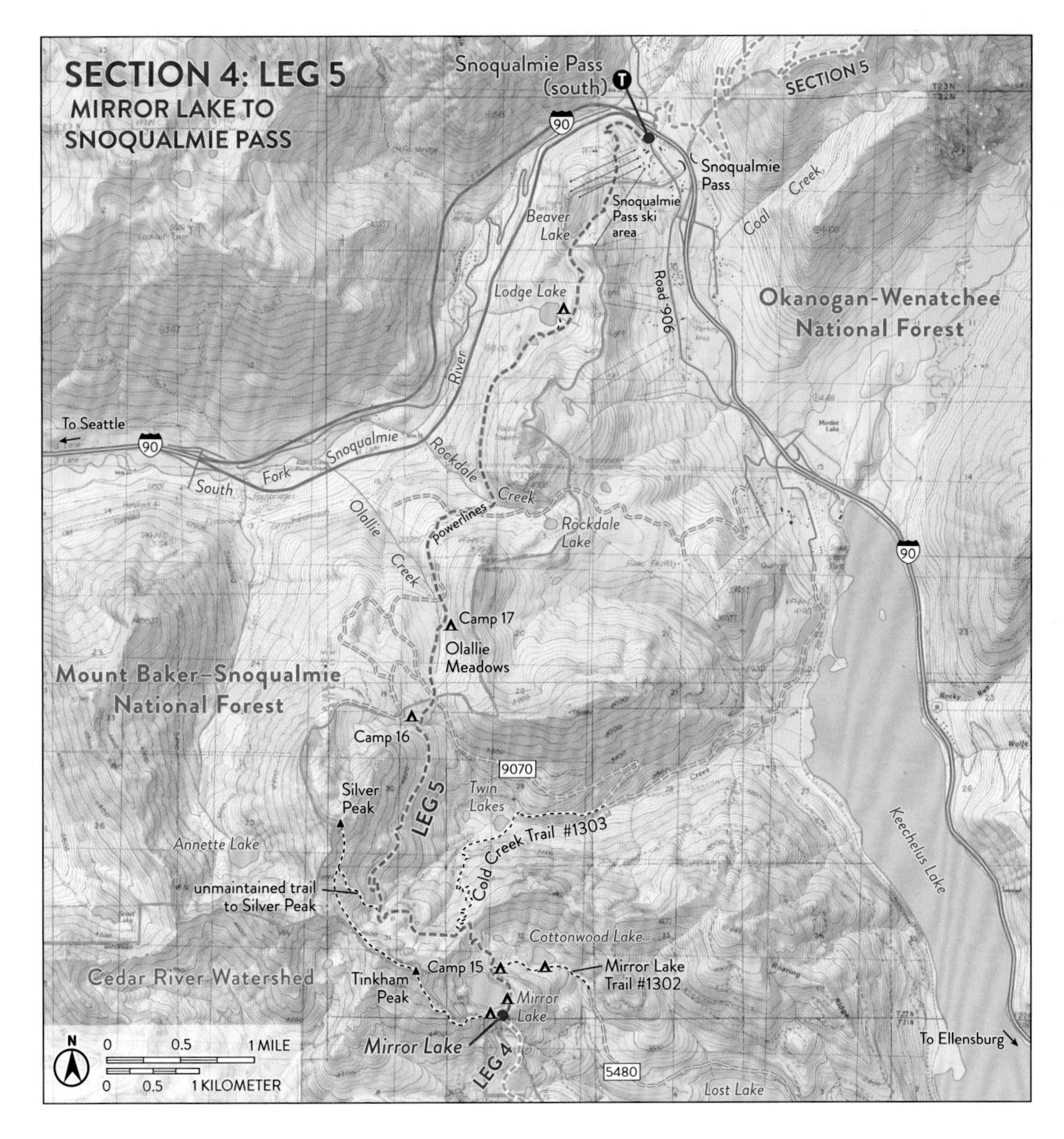

accesses the trail to Silver Peak. If time and gumption allow, you might want to haul yourself up the broad, open shoulders of Silver Peak and enjoy the vista.

Continue roaming northbound along the PCT, cutting across several rock-strewn talus slopes with seasonal dribbles before arriving at a one-tent camp (**Camp 16**) to the left, 2.5 miles past the Cold Creek Trail junction (1.6 miles past the Silver Peak spur trail). Immediately

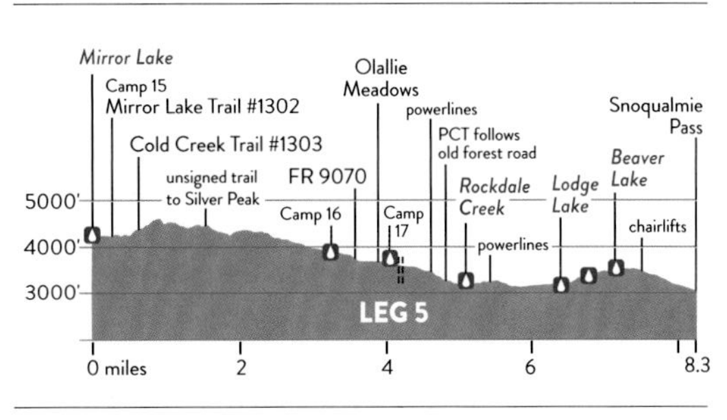

The PCT passes under the chairlifts of the Summit at Snoqualmie ski area.

before the camp, a seasonal creek flows with relatively reliable water, except in extremely warm summers. You're very close to FR 9070 here, popular access for the summer day-hiking crowd. Privacy and quiet might be limited should you choose to camp here.

In 0.1 mile from Camp 16, cross the dirt **FR 9070** and find the PCT on the other side. Wander through brushy huckleberry, spirea, and bear-grass shrubbery, which at times can be slightly overgrown, and cross a creek, on a small wooden bridge located 0.2 mile from FR 9070. The path opens up now, and a shallow, grassy bog to the right (east) comes into view, as well as Olallie Meadows just ahead. In the distance to the north, a clear day brings views of Chair Peak and the Tooth, both popular destinations for rock climbers and adventure seekers.

Pass Olallie Meadows, noted by a sign 0.5 mile from FR 9070, and cross lazy Olallie Creek immediately beyond. The word *olallie* means "huckleberry" in Chinook Jargon, a Native American trading language. These meadows are more like thick huckleberry bogs, and they support at least three different species of *Vaccinium* that feed birds, bears, and hikers alike. Feel free to graze until your lips are blue.

Just beyond Olallie Creek, a spur trail leads through brushy shrubs to a primitive one-tent camp (**Camp 17**), to the trail's right (east). The site is quite private save for the occasional hiker checking to see if it's taken or exploring where the spur leads.

Beyond Camp 17, duck back into the evergreen forest before traversing the base of a sloping talus field. Next up, cross yet another old forest road, this one looking like it hasn't seen a vehicle in years. The stony, old road is 0.3 mile beyond Olallie Meadows (0.8 mile beyond FR 9070). The next stretch of trail is bedecked with brushy foliage and adolescent regenerating evergreens which is soon interrupted by the buzz of unsightly powerlines. Bear with the PCT as things turn ugly for a span before they get scenic again.

In 1.3 miles past FR 9070 (0.8 mile from Olallie Meadows), the PCT hits an old forest road and follows it, confusingly, to the right (northeast) for 0.2 mile. Classic PCT trail markers are found along the road, but they aren't in-your-face visible. So unless you know where to go, you might stand here with your maps and scratch your head for a minute. The road walk isn't all that bad, and it allows you to catch your first clear glimpse of I-90 near Snoqualmie Pass. In late summer, goldenrod and fireweed bring some brilliant color and cheer into this man-made landscape. People have camped along the road, evidenced by the barren dirt spots; but with Lodge Lake just ahead, save these for emergencies.

From the road, the continuation of the PCT is clearly visible as it runs across a large talus field on a slope ahead. In 0.2 mile after starting its road walk, the trail darts back into the brushy swale to the left (north). Look for a brown post near the ground, proudly bearing the PCT emblem, to confirm that your tootsies are headed in the right direction.

From here, the PCT drops to cross **Rockdale Creek** 🄾, almost always a sure bet for water. Rock hop across and then traverse the talus field you saw from the road. Give a look left and see if you can spot the classic L4-style forest lookout rising tall on the tippy-top of Granite Mountain, to the northwest. The challenging climb to the lookout

In late or early season snow can linger in places along the trail, like this icy scene at Lodge Lake.

Patches of early season snow dot the hillsides in late fall near Snoqualmie Pass.

doesn't stop the herds of hardy hikers who trundle to the top nearly every day of the year, come sun, snow, sleet, hail, or sadly, dangerous avalanche conditions. The fall colors visible from the PCT signal some of the sweetest huckleberry bushes on the planet.

Wave hello to the lookout hikers and goodbye to the distant berries as you mosey upward through the talus field, past another set of powerlines, and finally into the cool shade of the forest. You're now back into scenery that triggers a sigh of relief, underneath your uphill grunting. You'll be in thick forest until you reach the Snoqualmie Pass ski area; for now it's pleasant hiking and little evidence of anything man-made.

In 1.4 miles beyond Rockdale Creek, the trail levels out, crosses a puncheon bridge over a wet area, and passes a small pond to the right through the trees. Immediately beyond, arrive at a left-hand (northwest) spur trail to **Lodge Lake**, noted by a tree sign. Several shady campsites (**Lodge Lake Camp**) are down this spur, which heads roughly 500 feet to the tranquil lake.

After the Lodge Lake spur trail, climbing commences as you cruise through cool shade thanks to mature forest. In 0.3 mile from the spur trail, cross a hardy creek that often provides clear, cold water throughout the summer. Onward you go, up a moderate slope, until reaching a saddle 0.9 mile north of Lodge Lake, where the PCT levels out, pops out of the forest, and passes **Beaver Lake** to the left (west). The small Beaver Lake is more like a pond, but it's a pretty little body of water, with birds flitting around its shrubby banks.

From Beaver Lake and the saddle, the PCT begins its descent toward the **Snoqualmie Pass ski area**, technically called Summit West. In

LODGE LAKE LODGE

In 1914, the Mountaineers Club volunteers constructed a gorgeous log lodge almost entirely out of trees found on the site. It sat on a knoll about 0.3 mile southwest of Lodge Lake and featured a kitchen as well as separate dorms for men and women. There was no plumbing or electricity, but that wasn't considered a challenge back then. For years, the lodge housed organized outings of climbers, hikers, skiers, and snowshoers. During Presidents Week in February, the club held an annual snowshoeing carnival that included races across the frozen lake, followed by dancing to the music of a wind-up Victrola and storytelling by the huge stone fireplace. In those days, Snoqualmie Pass was quite remote and the lodge was a wilderness retreat accessible by a lengthy train ride or by driving unpaved, rutted roads.

On a very warm September day in 1944, as a caretaker was burning trash in the large fireplace, a spark cruised through the chimney, hitting the roof and burning the lodge to smithereens. No structure, nor any lingering evidence of one, is found at the lake today. Instead, the picturesque sapphire waters beg you to stop for a photo.

summertime, the ski area turns to meadows, with flowers such as pearly everlasting, goldenrod, mountain ash, rosy spirea, and fireweed spreading a carpet of brilliant color. The mountains in front of you include the crimson-colored Red Mountain and the bold stone face of Guye Peak, both grand and swoon-worthy sights. You'll almost forget that you're crossing two ski area access roads and beneath three chairlifts. The small residential and commercial area of Snoqualmie Pass is in view now, directly below you to the north. Folks jonesin' for real food may be tempted to cut downslope and find the nearest deep fryer. If that's not you, stay on the PCT as it slices across the slopes, leads into forest again, and finally pops out at the official trailhead, 0.9 mile past Beaver Lake. If this is the end of your journey, congratulations on a job well done! If you're headed for more, well, then let the good times roll!

CAMP-TO-CAMP MILEAGE

Mirror Lake Camp to Camp 15 .... 0.3
Camp 15 to Camp 16 .... 3.0
Camp 16 to Camp 17 .... 0.7
Camp 17 to Lodge Lake Camp.............. 2.5
Lodge Lake Camp to Snoqualmie Pass 1.8

SECTION 5

SNOQUALMIE PASS TO STEVENS PASS

IF YOUR WANDERLUST has you dreaming of hiking 70-plus miles of roadless backcountry, past high mountain lakes, through deep river valleys, and with spectacular alpine views, look no further than the Snoqualmie Pass to Stevens Pass section of the PCT. This section is the state's most popular, primarily because of its proximity to the Seattle metro area, its reputation for unfathomable beauty, and the distance (which most folks can hike in less than a week). Lakes abound, with Spectacle Lake the unquestioned loveliest of them all: framed by the rugged snowcapped shoulders of Lemah Mountain and Three Queens, it boasts bold granite slabs for sunning and tucked-away quiet nooks for rest. Other rugged peaks in this section are alpine visions: Chikamin, Bears Breast, Mount Daniel, and Cathedral Rock. And water sources include two major waterways you'll cross: Lemah Creek and Waptus River.

The trail-building marvel that is Kendall Katwalk starts you off, its sheer rock-face-turned-hiker-friendly-shelf blasted out of the granite with dynamite. Later, near Pieper Pass, as you click-clack across a mountainside of scree, you'll again appreciate the trail builders responsible for the switchbacks, built in the 1970s. In July, waterfalls and creeks are at their peak runoff; while in late August or early September, huckleberry feasts near Deception Pass will turn your lips and fingers blue. Avoiding mosquito swarms near Hope and Mig lakes is a challenge any month. But whatever the season, you can count on meeting fellow hikers: this section is one of the most traveled in the state. So have a plan B for camping: you may have to hike farther than you intended if your preferred campsite is already taken.

DISTANCE 71.3 miles

STATE DISTANCE 244.5–315.8 miles

ELEVATION GAIN/LOSS
+19,130/–18,100 feet

HIGH POINT 5930 feet

BEST TIME OF YEAR Aug–Sept

PCTA SECTION LETTER J

LAND MANAGERS
Mount Baker–Snoqualmie National Forest (Snoqualmie Ranger District, Skykomish Ranger District, Alpine Lakes Wilderness)

PASSES AND PERMITS NW Forest Pass to park at Snoqualmie Pass and Stevens Pass. Free self-issue wilderness permits at wilderness area trailheads.

MAPS AND APPS
- Halfmile's WA Section J
- USFS PCT Map #10 Northern Washington
- Green Trails Snoqualmie Pass #207, Kachess Lake #208, Stevens Pass #176
- Halfmile's PCT app, Guthook's overall PCT app and PCT WA app

LEGS
1. Snoqualmie Pass to Spectacle Lake
2. Spectacle Lake to Waptus River
3. Waptus River to Deception Pass
4. Deception Pass to Hope Lake
5. Hope Lake to Stevens Pass

Opposite: *Sitting in a picturesque basin, Spectacle Lake lives up to its name.*

SECTION 5
SNOQUALMIE PASS
TO STEVENS PASS
To Everett
Henry M Jackson Wilderness
SECTION 6
Wild Sky Wilderness
Stevens Pass
Stevens Pass
To Leavenworth
Skykomish
Skykomish River
Foss River
LEG 5
Lake Susan Jane
Mig Lake
Hope Lake
Trap Lake
Surprise Lake
Glacier Lake
LEG 4
Deception Lakes
Mount Baker–Snoqualmie National Forest
Deception Pass
challenging ford
Cathedral Rock
Hyas Lake
Alpine Lakes Wilderness
Deep Lake
LEG 3
Cle Elum River
Middle Fork Snoqualmie River
Waptus River
LEG 1
LEG 2
Lemah Creek
Gravel Lake
challenging ford
Ridge Lake
Kendall Katwalk
Spectacle Lake
Okanogan-Wenatchee National Forest
Snoqualmie Pass
To Seattle
Snoqualmie Pass
Copper River
South Fork Snoqualmie River
Snoqualmie River
SECTION 4
To Cle Elum
0 2 4 MILES
0 2 4 KILOMETERS
N

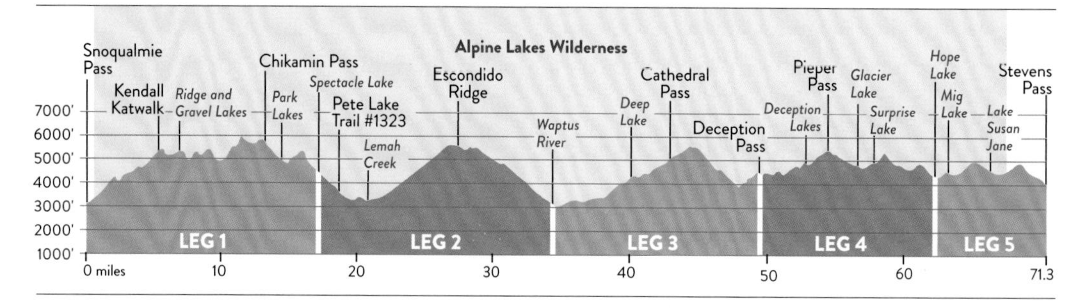
Alpine Lakes Wilderness
Snoqualmie Pass
Kendall Katwalk
Ridge and Gravel Lakes
Chikamin Pass
Park Lakes
Spectacle Lake
Pete Lake Trail #1323
Lemah Creek
Escondido Ridge
Waptus River
Deep Lake
Cathedral Pass
Deception Pass
Deception Lakes
Pieper Pass
Glacier Lake
Surprise Lake
Hope Lake
Mig Lake
Lake Susan Jane
Stevens Pass
7000'
6000'
5000'
4000'
3000'
2000'
1000'
LEG 1
LEG 2
LEG 3
LEG 4
LEG 5
0 miles
10
20
30
40
50
60
71.3

A quaint camp near Gravel Lake offers charming views of surrounding peaks.

ACCESS

Snoqualmie Pass

From Seattle, drive east on Interstate 90 toward Snoqualmie Pass. Take exit 52 (Snoqualmie Pass West) and turn left at the exit ramp's end. Head north, underneath the freeway. Turn right in roughly 100 yards onto a dirt road, signed for the PCT, and drive into the parking area. The trailhead is on the east side of the parking area. Parking is plentiful. Vault toilet available.

Stevens Pass

From Seattle, head east across Lake Washington to Interstate 405 in Bellevue. Drive north on I-405, take exit 23 (for State Route 522 East), and continue to the exit for US Highway 2 (Stevens Pass Highway). Drive east on US 2 for 50 miles to Stevens Pass. Turn right (south) into the ski area and drive to the far left (northeastern) corner of the huge parking area signed for the PCT. Vault toilet available.

NOTES

Cities and Services

Near the southern trailhead, find gas, convenience stores, dining, and lodging at Snoqualmie Pass. There's limited dining at the northern trailhead, Stevens Pass. Other cities near the southern trailhead are North Bend and Cle Elum; near the northern trailhead, Skykomish and Leavenworth.

Camping and Campfire Restrictions

Camping is limited at Ridge and Gravel lakes to designated sites. Camping is restricted for a 2-mile stretch near the Escondido Tarns. And at Surprise Lake, camping is permitted in designated sites only; camping with pack-and-saddle stock is prohibited within 0.5 mile of the lake. **Campfires** are prohibited from the Alpine Lakes Wilderness boundary north to Delate Meadows, roughly 1 mile north of Spectacle Lake. Campfires are also prohibited within 0.5 mile of any lake and above

4000 feet on the west side of the Cascade Crest and 5000 feet on the east side.

Water

North of Ridge and Gravel lakes, water is scarce until Park Lakes 7.6 miles farther. North of Deep Lake's outlet, there's no on-trail water for 6.3 miles.

Hazards

In early season, snow can linger in alpine areas for the first 15 miles north of Snoqualmie Pass, making for potentially dangerous steep and narrow traverses. Check with land managers for trail conditions before heading out. There are also two potentially challenging water fords in this section. The first is north of Spectacle Lake at Lemah Creek, where the bridge bit the dust long ago; hikers must wade or find a downed log and teeter across. The second is an ice-cold unnamed creek that rips down a granite drainage north of Cathedral Pass. This creek has several branches and hikers must choose the best path across—occasionally, there are logs, but they're usually small and very slippery. Wading is often the best way to cross.

SUGGESTED ITINERARIES

Where noted, distances are to camp trail spurs; camp may be up to 0.5 mile from junction.

8 DAYS

		Miles
Day 1	Snoqualmie Pass to Ridge and Gravel Lakes Camp	6.9
Day 2	Ridge and Gravel Lakes Camp to Spectacle Lake Camp spur	10.0
Day 3	Spectacle Lake Camp spur to Escondido Camp	12.4
Day 4	Escondido Camp to Deep Lake Camp	12.3
Day 5	Deep Lake Camp to Deception Pass Camp	8.2
Day 6	Deception Pass Camp to Surprise Lake Camp spur	7.9
Day 7	Surprise Lake Camp spur to Mig Lake Camp	6.2
Day 8	Mig Lake Camp to Stevens Pass	7.4

7 DAYS

Day 1	Snoqualmie Pass to Ridge and Gravel Lakes Camp	6.9
Day 2	Ridge and Gravel Lakes Camp to Camp 7	13.7
Day 3	Camp 7 to Escondido Camp	8.9
Day 4	Escondido Camp to Deep Lake Camp	12.3
Day 5	Deep Lake Camp to Deception Lakes Camp	11.7
Day 6	Deception Lakes Camp to Hope Lake Camp	9.7
Day 7	Hope Lake Camp to Stevens Pass	8.1

6 DAYS

Day 1	Snoqualmie Pass to Small Park Lakes Camp	14.5
Day 2	Small Park Lakes Camp to Escondido Camp	14.8
Day 3	Escondido Camp to Deep Lake Camp	12.3
Day 4	Deep Lake Camp to Deception Lakes Camp	11.7
Day 5	Deception Lakes Camp to Mig Lake Camp	10.6
Day 6	Mig Lake Camp to Stevens Pass	7.4

1 SNOQUALMIE PASS TO SPECTACLE LAKE

DISTANCE 16.9 miles
(17.4 miles with Spectacle Lake Camp)

ELEVATION GAIN/LOSS
+6090/–4670 feet

HIGH POINT 5820 feet

CONNECTING TRAILS
Mineral Creek Trail #1331

ON THE TRAIL

Once you've got your pack ready and you've double-checked your list, give your quads and feet a little pep talk, because you start out with a long, moderate climb containing switchbacks aplenty. Duck into the forest and in no time begin your ascent under the swaying Douglas-firs.

In 1.7 miles, arrive at the Alpine Lakes Wilderness boundary, announced with an official sign. **Campfires are prohibited from this point all the way to Delate Meadows, roughly 1 mile north of Spectacle Lake.** At 2.2 miles, arrive at flowing Silver Creek, a reliable water source crossed by rock hopping. Around the creek, the tall bluebells, slide alder, and salmonberries greet you in early August and beg you to stop and take their picture. Immediately after the creek, arrive at a junction with **Commonwealth Basin Trail #1033**. It might be tempting to wander to the left, since that way goes downhill and would be a nice reprieve. Instead, stay right, climbing on the PCT until Red Mountain to the north reveals its cinnamon color and becomes your focal point, taking your mind off the burn.

Here, the trail opens up to pockets of wildflowers, such as Sitka valerian, enjoying the

It's easy to misstep on shale fields when breathtaking views draw your eyes in every direction but down.

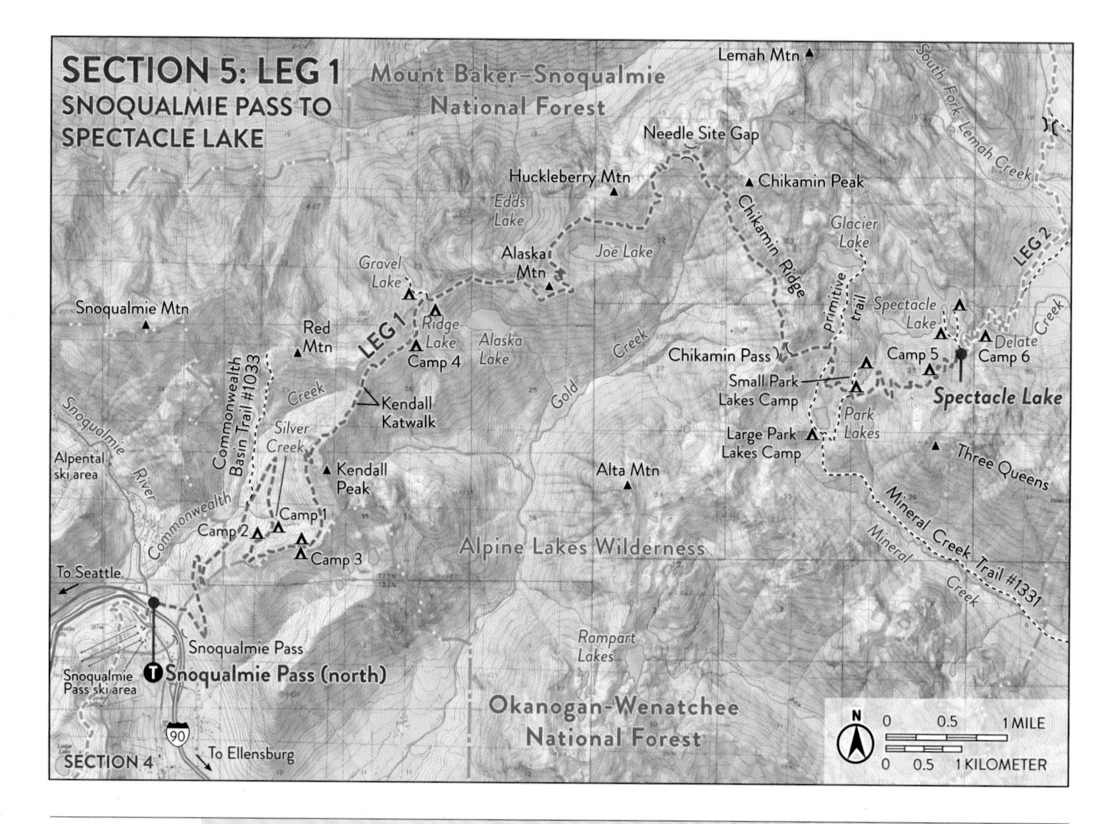

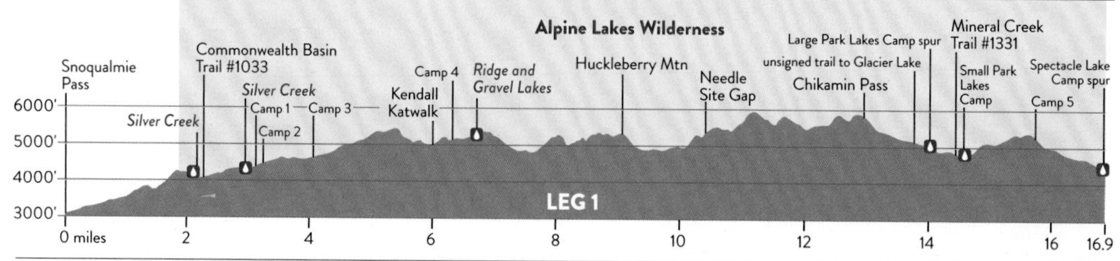

southern exposure and sunlight. Thankfully, when the flowers show up the grade eases slightly, and the views become more vast; you'll see Lundin Peak and Snoqualmie Mountain just west of Red Mountain. In roughly 0.9 mile from the Commonwealth Basin Trail junction, **Silver Creek** again provides reliable water and a rest from the climb, if you need either.

Immediately afterward, cross an avalanche slide area where a tributary of Commonwealth Creek trickles from above. A mediocre campsite (**Camp 1**), with room for one small tent, is just beyond the chute, via a short spur to the left (east). Just past the chute are two more campsites (**Camp 2**), located trailside to the right (west) in the forest. The first of these two sites is obvious, as it sits right next to the trail. But the second camp, which could fit three or four small tents, is not used often; find it by looking southwest when you're standing at the obvious site. The spur trail to it is not well established, so tread carefully. Camps at Gravel and Ridge lakes are better goals, but these initial spots will do in a pinch if you can't make it. This is also a good place to find an old knotty tree stump to perch upon and dig out your gorp.

Continue on through a bit more forest before the PCT angles up to a ridge, where you'll find a couple more small one-tent sites (**Camp 3**), less than a mile from the last camp. Both are directly next to the trail, one to the left (north) and a slightly larger one to the right (south). There's no water on the ridge, so if you intend to camp here, be sure to fill up at the stream just before the avalanche chute. The ridge hands the forested torch to a series of subalpine meadows just under Kendall Peak's ridgeline. In season, spreading phlox, rosy spirea, lupine, and paintbrush splash the foreground of the fantastic views of the peaks.

The rock garden continues as the PCT crests the ridge and drops over the other side, where you get your first good look at the **Kendall Katwalk**, which starts 6 miles from the trailhead. In the late 1970s, a trail crew suspended themselves on ropes and placed dynamite into the sheer granite face to blast this route—an impressive feat and an impressive stretch of trail! The best photos of the exposed crossing are from the Katwalk's northern side, looking back to the south, which shows off the sheer wall and imposing scale.

Past the Katwalk, the trail trends northeast and stays high, keeping you near the ridge amid a mix of conifers, wildflowers, talus fields, and hardy day hikers. At 6.4 miles, there are campsites (**Camp 4**) to the right (east), via a small path, and 0.2 mile farther, on the left (west), just off the trail. These sites are overflow areas if those at Ridge and Gravel lakes are full, but you could also stay here if you want a shorter hiking day. The water for Camp 4 is at the lakes, 0.4 mile farther north along the PCT.

At 6.9 miles from the trailhead, arrive at the first of two lakes, both named by Captain Obvious. **Ridge Lake** sits directly trailside to the right (southeast), on the ridge; and **Gravel Lake** is trailside to the left (northwest), near a gravel slope. Both lakes offer optimal camping, with at least a dozen sites (**Gravel and Ridge Lakes Camp**). The sites at Gravel Lake get less traffic from the day-hiking crowd and may be the quieter option. Both lakes have established sites—which the Forest

The Kendall Katwalk, blasted by dynamite, is just one of the many highlights in this section.

A hiker makes his way across a large cirque while Alaska Lake glistens in a valley below.

Service requires you to use; flip a coin if you're undecided. To find the designated camping areas, follow small "Camp" signs with a hiker symbol at the northern ends of both lakes.

If you're pushing onward to Spectacle Lake, this is a great place to **fill up on water**, as it's one of the last sources until Park Lakes, 7.6 miles farther. There will likely be some snowmelt dribbles and a small pond near the Huckleberry Mountain gap, but those sources aren't reliable; play it safe and don't turn into a prune.

After Ridge and Gravel lakes, things get even more interesting. A giant alpine cirque awaits, where you'll encounter some tricky footing, at least for those hikers not nicknamed "Grace." Scree fields, and plenty of them, draw your eyes down to your feet as you clickity-clack along on the narrow trail, while alpine views in all directions tempt you to look up. Don't give in unless your feet aren't moving. Below you, **Alaska and Joe lakes** twinkle like sapphires as you stay high along the shoulders of Alaska and Huckleberry mountains. You're in the beating heart of the high country. Draw in that fresh air and enjoy every minute of the gorgeous scenery all around you. But ups and downs abound, so don't think you're done climbing yet!

The contour lines tighten on your topo map as the way gets steeper and the vegetation turns to wildflowers, with rocky outcroppings shooting skyward. In 0.8 mile beyond Gravel and Ridge lakes, the PCT crests a ridge, where you'll find a small spur to the left to a viewpoint of **Edds Lake**, tucked into the valley far below and twinkling deep blue in the sunshine. From the ridge, drop into a saddle with views of Joe and Edds lakes, again. There's a small one-tent campsite to the left (northwest)—a tiny site with no water, practically on the trail, only attractive if you're desperate for a snooze.

Next, cross the shoulders of the appropriately named **Huckleberry Mountain**, which teems with delicious berries and even smells like them, a fantastic treat for your senses. Just beyond Huckleberry Mountain, 3 miles past Ridge and Gravel lakes (roughly 9.9 miles from the trailhead), come to a parklike landscape dotted with light gray granite, juniper, heather, and wildflowers. Tarns exist here until late in the hiking season, but water is not optimal or consistently available. Several boot-beaten paths lead to views and lunch spots, but camping here is strongly discouraged because of the area's fragile nature. Remember to camp only on durable surfaces and treat stagnant water.

Just 0.5 mile beyond the tarns, arrive at an awesome view below craggy Chikamin Peak of the Middle Fork Snoqualmie River valley and a plethora of granite spires beyond. Older PCT sources call this **Needle Site Gap**, although it's never been officially named. Call it what you want. I just call it "wow!" Look for hoary marmots munching lupine during their very short season before hibernation. To the south, Mount Rainier is in view, as are the ski slopes at Snoqualmie Pass—how far you've come! From here to Chikamin Pass, the tread is shaley, rough on the bottoms of your feet, and narrow, making it tricky to pass others coming from the opposite direction. A sign warns stock users that there's no turnaround and that pack trains can't pass each other. Thankfully, the dung here is minimal, an indication that few are brave enough to challenge themselves and their "neigh-sayers."

At 6.3 miles from Ridge and Gravel lakes (13.2 miles from the trailhead), crest the saddle of Chikamin Ridge, known as **Chikamin Pass**, and enjoy the view of Park Lakes basin to the southeast before dropping down toward it. In 0.6 mile from the pass, notice a well-used but unsigned trail heading left (north). This unmaintained trail leads to Glacier Lake, Chikamin Lake, and beyond to a climbers' approach to Lemah Mountain. In places, this trail is very primitive and exposed, so only head off here if you have plenty of time to spare, are a good navigator, and your trail name isn't Klutzy McFall.

The high, subalpine Ridge Lake is a popular destination for the first night along the trail.

Just 0.2 mile beyond the unsigned trail, reach a signed junction, with a 0.4-mile spur trail leading to a stock and hiker camping area near the larger of the Park Lakes (**Large Park Lakes Camp**) ◘, with plentiful campsites and water. If the Boy Scouts are in tow, this area can support your group. If you're only on two feet and in a small group, you may want to keep rolling to a smaller version of Park Lakes 0.5 mile farther north, closer to the PCT.

In 0.5 mile from the Large Park Lakes Camp spur trail, arrive at a junction with **Mineral Creek Trail #1331** to the right (south), followed immediately by a sign indicating a hikers' camp to the left (northeast) at one of the small Park Lakes (**Small Park Lakes Camp**) ◘. You can either follow the short spur toward the lake to find two campsites, one on the south side of the lake and one on the north side, or backtrack roughly 350 feet on the PCT to a trailside site in the trees, on the hillside to the southwest.

MINERAL CREEK TRAIL

Mineral Creek Trail #1331 can be used as an access point, allowing for a shorter trip. The trail begins off FR 46 near Kachess Lake and climbs 2685 feet in 5.4 miles to the PCT near Park Lakes. It's often brushy and lightly used, so you may want to contact the Forest Service before you head out.

If the scenery hasn't knocked off your socks yet, climb a scant 300-plus feet out of Park Lakes basin to a subalpine area sporting a couple of seasonal tarns that reflect the granite spires of Lemah Mountain, a worthy photo stop.

In the high country east of Small Park Lakes Camp, a couple of faint trails tempt you to head left (north) to viewpoints, but don't waste the footsteps: the view at the upcoming ridge is almost the same. Roughly 0.8 mile from Park

An inviting parklike setting greets you almost all the way to Spectacle Lake.

DANCING WITH SOOTY GROUSE

Sooty grouse are often seen in subalpine areas along the trail.

The high country above Park Lakes is very popular with the sooty grouse, a chicken-like ground forager that dines on a buffet of leaves, flowers, conifer needles, and invertebrates. This species is the third-largest grouse in North America—some individuals grow to almost 20 inches long. These birds are born with more beauty than brains, and their simplemindedness is always entertaining.

Should you fail to see her camouflaged against the rocks, a female grouse may vocalize with a quiet, sustained whine before eventually winging off in clumsy flight. Usually when this happens, her chicks, which also may have gone unnoticed, get nervous and go running and flapping alongside her in every direction, scaring the liver out of you and anyone else in the vicinity. Once your heart rate returns to normal, you'll notice that despite the commotion, she and her chicks have only flown a few yards away, allowing for a great picture.

Lakes, crest the ridge at 5280 feet. Below you, shining brightly, is Spectacle Lake, along with waterfalls, glaciers, and lingering distant snow patches—all of which should take your mind off your burning quads as you begin a steep, switchbacking descent. In 0.5 mile past the ridgetop, as you make your way downhill, arrive at three waterless trailside campsites (**Camp 5**) tucked between boulders.

Before long, the boulder fields give way to sparse forest, and in 1.1 miles beyond Camp 5, you'll arrive at an easy-to-miss sign to the left (north): it says "Hiker trail, closed to pack and saddle stock" and "Fires prohibited within 1/4 mile of Spectacle Lake." This is the trail to **Spectacle Lake**—keep your eyes open!

The spur trail descends roughly 0.5 mile and then splits near the lake into a gaggle of smaller paths in all directions. Optimal camping (**Spectacle Lake Camp**) is to the lake's east and west, so follow a path and see where it leads. Most of the campsites are perched on outcroppings above the lake; you can see some of the most picturesque sites from the spur trail before you head down to the lake, so stop and scope things out before descending. Since Spectacle Lake is so large and has so much camping, finding a spot to pitch your tent is rarely a challenge, even on busy weekends. The lake itself is simply gorgeous and it would be a real shame to cruise by it, unless you're on a mission involving time or distance. If you choose to stay here, explore Spectacle to your heart's content, or just relax at camp and get your camera ready for alpenglow on the hovering peaks.

CAMP-TO-CAMP MILEAGE

Snoqualmie Pass to Camp 1	3.1
Camp 1 to Camp 2	0.2
Camp 2 to Camp 3	0.8
Camp 3 to Camp 4	2.4
Camp 4 to Ridge and Gravel Lakes Camp	0.4
Ridge and Gravel Lakes Camp to Large Park Lakes Camp spur	7.1
Large Park Lakes Camp spur to Small Park Lakes Camp spur	0.5
Small Park Lakes Camp to Camp 5	1.3
Camp 5 to Spectacle Lake Camp spur	1.1

2 SPECTACLE LAKE TO WAPTUS RIVER

DISTANCE 17.6 miles

ELEVATION GAIN/LOSS
+3590/–4980 feet

HIGH POINT 5600 feet

CONNECTING TRAILS
Pete Lake Trail #1323,
Lemah Meadow Trail #1323.2,
Waptus Burn Trail #1329C (#1329.3 on some maps), Dutch Miller Gap Trail #1362

ON THE TRAIL

In 0.8 mile past the junction with the **Spectacle Lake** spur trail, a trailside camp (**Camp 6**) is to the right, at an elbow bend in the PCT. This is not a pretty camp; in fact, whoever created it is probably still laughing. A large tree came to rest near a flat spot and the branches and duff have been moved aside to create a well-used pad suitable for one tent, with the trail for a view (like having front-row seats for a parade). But you probably won't know the difference if you're dead tired. In 0.1 mile beyond the Camp, **Delate Creek** sports a gorgeous waterfall, flowing from Spectacle Lake high above. A well-built bridge guides you over the rushing water and provides a platform for waterfall photos, with railing posts for a makeshift tripod—what luck! On the north side of the bridge a small path leads down to water, where you can fill your tank if you need to. There's plenty of water all the way to Lemah Creek, so you can lighten up on what you carry and save your feet.

Immediately past Delate Creek, enter the burn zone of the Lemah Creek Fire. On August 28, 2009, lightning and whipping wind sparked a fire so hot and fast that it went from 30 to 600 acres in a couple of days. The PCT was closed for the remainder of that hiking season, for good reason. Today, the black trees contrast starkly with nutrient-loving plants such as purple fireweed and white pearly everlasting, while hummingbirds buzz around sucking nectar from the tall shoots. Small saplings are popping up everywhere as nature tries to heal her scars.

Roughly 300 yards after Delate Creek, rock hop across another small creek and look to the left (northwest) for an old sign that says "Hiker trail, closed to pack & saddle stock," which remarkably survived the blaze. The sign is nearly buried under fireweed and hangs on a tree amid brambles, with no trail in sight. It's a relic from years ago when a path from here led to the outlet of Spectacle Lake. That trail has long been abandoned, but finding the sign is a fun game, since so many miss it.

For the next mile, switchback downhill toward Delate Meadows. At 1.9 miles from the official Spectacle Lake spur trail, you'll pass a sign that says "Campfires are prohibited beyond this point." It's a good reminder, especially since it's in the middle of a fire zone. The way then levels out for a distance and in about 0.6 mile from the campfire sign, another sign announces that the Lemah Creek bridge is out and that stock must use an alternate route. Don't panic. Hikers can still either wade or log-hobble in another mile. For now, continue on gentle grade and at 2.7 miles beyond the spur to Spectacle Lake, arrive at a junction with **Pete Lake Trail #1323**, which goes straight. The PCT, rather confusingly, goes left (north) here and the signage doesn't provide much clarity. Bear left (north) and continue on the PCT through riparian landscape and, at last, healthy conifers.

With that particular fire zone mostly behind you, arrive at **South Fork Lemah Creek**, 0.8 mile past the Pete Lake Trail junction. There are two campsites near the creek (**Camp 7**). The least desirable is to the left (west), just before the creek, with room for only one tent and serving as a junkyard for wooden planks from an old footbridge. This site gets plenty of use, however, and may end up being yours if the other site across the creek is "horsey." In the winter of 2007–2008, Lemah Creek's robust bridge was wiped off the map and has yet to be replaced. For kicks, go stand at the edge of the trail near the remaining bridge supports and imagine the powerful flow that ripped the

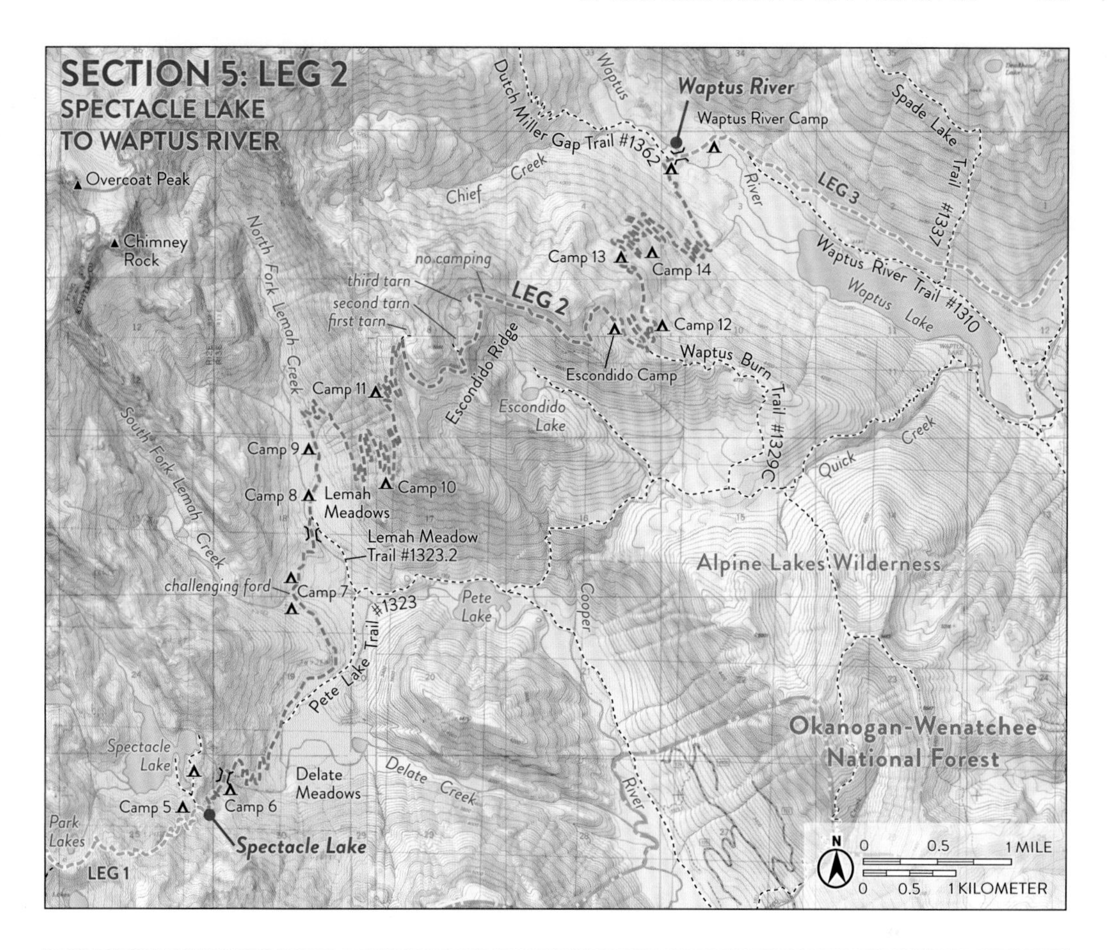

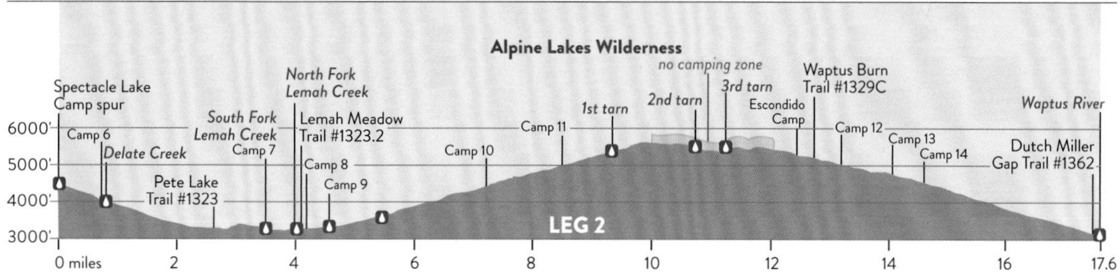

thing off its structure. Shudder at the thought, and then contemplate your crossing.

For years, a large log downstream has been a hiker's savior for crossing with dry feet, but it can be tricky to find and somewhat precarious to cross. Fording is also an option, but use caution, especially after rains or in early season, because this baby pumps fast and cold and can be hazardous. To find the log, just before the creek look to the right (east) very carefully and notice a bush-beaten path through shrubs. Sometimes, a red flag tied to vegetation marks the start of the bushwhack. Push the scratchy bushes back and follow the barely visible trail to the large log, its bark still intact for traction. Cross gingerly, and then slip and slide on the loose dirt of the makeshift trail on the other

side, going straight up the bank, until you're victoriously standing on the PCT again. Woohoo, take that, Lemah Creek!

The second site of Camp 7 is obvious here, as big and well established as any camp on this stretch. With room for three or four tents, a fire pit, and several logs for sitting, it's a PCTer's dream provided that horses haven't left any presents behind. Because of this site's popularity, be prepared to camp elsewhere if you roll in late in the day.

Beyond South Fork Lemah Creek, the grade rolls gently up and down through conifers mixed with low-growing riparian shrubs for 0.5 mile before crossing North Fork Lemah Creek, which thankfully has a bridge. In a short 0.1 mile from the bridge, arrive at a trail junction with Lemah Meadow Trail #1323.2, which heads toward Pete Lake to the southeast. Just beyond it another 0.1 mile (now 4.2 miles past the Spectacle Lake spur trail) are two very desirable campsites (**Camp 8**). The one to the right (east) comes first, via a short, obvious spur trail leading to a forested area large enough for four or five tents and boasting a "backyard" of large, grassy meadow. Because of its size, horse campers often use it, so watch for deposits from the bank of horse hiney. For water, either retrace your steps to North Fork Lemah Creek or crash the next campsite for a visit. That cozy, creekside, one-tent site is approximately 60 feet farther along the PCT, where a spur trail goes left (west) through riparian brush.

If the Camp 8 sites are full, there are more options, so don't sweat it. Ahead just 0.4 mile are two forested sites (**Camp 9**) to the left (west), with room for one tent each and a creek just a few feet beyond. Sure, these sites are very close to the trail, but once you and the Sandman get reacquainted, it won't matter. These are the last campsites before the big hill that gains more than 2300 feet on the way to **Escondido Ridge**.

As for Escondido Ridge, hang on to your hat and prepare mentally for one of the most challenging up-and-overs you'll face in the Snoqualmie to Stevens PCT section. From Camp 9 to Waptus River is 12.9 miles, but it'll feel much farther thanks to the ascent, a lengthy stretch of subalpine terrain at the top, and then a forever-feeling descent that takes its time delivering you to the river valley far below. The saving grace is the spectacular scenery that keeps getting more and more beautiful as you go. Take your time, take breaks, and enjoy every drop of visual deliciousness.

Continue in the forest past Camp 9, as the PCT takes you toward a switchback near an impressive avalanche chute at the base of Lemah Mountain. Your climb begins! There are at least half a dozen seasonal water trickles and creeks coming off the peaks above, the last of them 0.6 mile beyond Camp 9. Fill up when you can, because your next water is a tarn at the top of the ridge, which in dry years can be less than desirable. Additionally, the effects of a past fire near the ridgeline make for exposed climbing, which can be overwhelmingly warm on sunny days. Stay hydrated and avoid heat headaches and muscle gripes.

The PCT switches back under hemlocks, vine maples, and western red cedars, giving you increasingly better views of Lemah Mountain, Chikamin Ridge, and Three Queens. These rocky fortresses wear snowy pockets deep in their ridge folds, inviting frequent photos. Trust me when I say the view gets better, so save your camera card and batteries, unless you have plenty of both. In 2.8 miles from Camp 9, arrive at a trailside camp (**Camp 10**) near a switchback, to the right (west), with room for two small tents. This camp gets a fair amount of use despite its being close to the trail and waterless. Use it in a pinch or if you want to get a few extra miles under your belt.

In another 1.1 miles, arrive at **Camp 11**, a small one-tent site to the left (west), located in healthy trees just before approaching the fire zone. This site is also close to the trail and waterless, but when desperate times call for desperate snoozing, stake it, claim it, and call it home. Immediately after this camp, enter the fire zone, which is bursting with seasonal fireweed. Thanks to the dead standing blackened trees, views here are incredible. The snowy granite mountain grandeur in the distance, coupled with fuchsia fireweed and white pearly everlasting in the foreground, is so inspiring you'll

Opposite: *A tarn reflects the splendor of the mountains as a backpacker cruises its edge.*

A hiker pauses to enjoy Delate Creek as it drops peacefully from lofty heights.

reach for pen and paper to channel your inner Robert Frost.

With each switchback, the visions are swoon-worthy. In 1 mile beyond Camp 11, an easy-to-miss spur trail shows up going seemingly straight ahead, as the PCT turns hard to the right (southwest). This short spur heads to a small alpine cirque and the first of the **Escondido Tarns** 💧—the first opportunity for water since the last trailside trickle 4.3 miles back. This is the best of the tarns for water due to its depth and natural-filtering rocky shoreline.

The camping rules here are confusing, so let me help sort them out. The Forest Service does not allow camping within 200 feet of the Escondido Tarns, including this one, and hikers are discouraged from camping along this section of the PCT because of the short growing season and because fire-recovery areas are environmentally sensitive. In another 0.5 mile along the PCT, camping is actually prohibited for a 2-mile stretch. If you want to camp, your best bet is to get water here at this first Escondido Tarn and carry it to the next scenic, and allowed, camping spot, which is 2.9 miles farther along the PCT. A trail sign shows up noting the fragile area and mentioning the 2-mile camping restriction.

This is high country and alpine beauty abounds! Roam gently up and down through rocky granite hillsides dotted with subalpine fir, juniper, heather, and wildflowers as your heart rate and legs recover from the climb. In 1.2 miles past the first tarn's spur trail, another spur trail shows up to the PCT's left (north). This one leads to the second tarn 💧, which sits tucked in a small basin surrounded by talus and subalpine vegetation—another water option, although a bit murky at times. The PCT continues wandering through parkland and in 0.5 mile crosses an outlet 💧 near the third Escondido Tarn. The tarn itself can be stagnant, so if the outlet is flowing, it's a better source. If you plan to stay at Escondido Camp or on the descent to Waptus River, this is your last opportunity for water before the valley.

Marmots stationed on nearby rocks sound alarms to warn their furry family and friends of your approach before diving into their burrows. Keep your eyes open for pine martens too, a rare and wonderful creature that frequents this area on its hunts for mice and voles. Beyond the last tarn, the PCT traverses a sparsely forested hillside loaded with seasonal huckleberries for nibbling. To the right (south), views into the valley below show off the sparkling emerald-colored Escondido Lake.

In 1.2 miles from the last tarn (12.4 miles from the Spectacle Lake spur), arrive at a sign that says "Camping" with an arrow pointing to a designated area (**Escondido Camp**) to the right (south), which has at least four flat tent sites and a parkland setting, but unfortunately no water. In some years, a dribble—and I mean dribble—of water trickles in a small ravine 0.1 mile south along the PCT, but don't count on it. Play it safe and carry water if you intend to camp here.

Next up, 0.2 mile from Escondido Camp, come to a junction with **Waptus Burn Trail #1329C** (#1329.3 on some maps). The PCT stays left (north) here and begins the forever-long descent into the valley below. Thankfully, the steep rocky walls and sharp ridgelines of Bears Breast Mountain offer a visual distraction.

In 0.7 mile from the Waptus Burn Trail junction, arrive at **Camp 12**, to the right (southeast). A fire pit and hang-out area are across the trail from the tent site. There's no water here, so be sure to carry it if this is your destination. As you continue onward, Waptus Lake shows up in the valley below, along with a handful of trailside viewpoints that let you stop and scope it out. The wide and winding Waptus River almost looks like a road from this vantage as it curves through the valley.

At 0.8 mile from Camp 12 (14.1 miles from the Spectacle Lake spur), locate **Camp 13**, another waterless camp, with tent sites to both the left (northwest) and right (southeast) of the PCT. A group with three small tents could probably fit here provided you don't mind hearing each other snore. Just shy of 0.5 mile farther is the final camp on the descent (**Camp 14**), located to the right (southeast). This small camp has room for only one tent and, again, there's no water.

The gradual switchbacks with rocky tread take their time guiding you down. If you have an altimeter, don't look at it—the slow descent will play head games. Eventually, the small firs and stony terrain give way to wet swales loaded with thimbleberry, goatsbeard, and devil's club, a landscape still in recovery from a 1929 fire. If there's been recent trail maintenance, do your happy dance and make a note to thank those involved—this stretch of trail is a beast when it doesn't get clipped!

The final switchback turns left (northwest) and you actually hear the Waptus River for the very first time. Oh happy day! Cruise along the mossy, cedar-rich valley floor for a short distance before arriving at a junction with **Dutch Miller Gap Trail #1362** to the left (northwest) and the well-used, forested **Waptus River Camp** on the PCT's right (southeast). The camp and trail junction are 17.4 miles from the Spectacle Lake spur. More campsites are on the other side of the river (0.2 mile from this junction), also well liked, well used, and ample. The PCT crosses Waptus River on a sturdy wooden bridge just 0.1 mile beyond the trail junction. The Waptus River area is a viable distance from other landmarks and is extremely popular, especially on summer and holiday weekends, when it can be tough to find a campsite if you arrive late in the day. If you end up site-less, keep on trucking, because another beautiful camp lies only 0.7 mile farther at Spade Creek (see Camp 15 in next leg).

CAMP-TO-CAMP MILEAGE

Spectacle Lake Camp spur to Camp 6	0.8
Camp 6 to Camp 7	2.7
Camp 7 to Camp 8	0.7
Camp 8 to Camp 9	0.4
Camp 9 to Camp 10	2.8
Camp 10 to Camp 11	1.1
Camp 11 to Escondido Camp	3.9
Escondido Camp to Camp 12	0.9
Camp 12 to Camp 13	0.8
Camp 13 to Camp 14	0.5
Camp 14 to Waptus River Camp	3.0

3 WAPTUS RIVER TO DECEPTION PASS

DISTANCE 15.3 miles

ELEVATION GAIN/LOSS
+3890/-2470 feet

HIGH POINT 5550 feet

CONNECTING TRAILS
Waptus River Trail #1310, Spade Lake Trail #1337, Spinola Creek Trail #1310.1, Cathedral Pass Trail #1345, Deception Pass Trail, #1376, Deception Creek Trail #1059

ON THE TRAIL

Just beyond the **Waptus River** bridge, the PCT wanders through small evergreens and an understory of mossy river rocks, where ample flat spots have shockingly not been converted into camps. Long live the vegetation! In 0.7 mile beyond Waptus River, arrive at a sturdy wooden bridge over rushing **Spade Creek** 🄾. Beyond the bridge, on the left (northeast), is picturesque campsite **Camp 15**, complete with makeshift benches, a fire pit, and room for a couple of small tents. Nearby Spade Creek has plenty of flow and several small downstream pools where you can splash yourself clean, if your metatarsals and phalanges don't fall off in the chill.

In 0.1 mile beyond Camp 15, arrive at a junction with **Waptus River Trail #1310**, which heads right (southeast) down toward Waptus Lake. In the next mile, cross two hardy water sources that flow across the trail, giving you plenty of options if the bottles run dry. The vegetation is very riparian in nature—bracken ferns, salmonberry, and vanilla leaf under the sparse trees. To your right (southwest), catch peekaboo views of Waptus Lake in the valley below, through the trees and brush.

At 2.1 miles past Waptus River, **Spade Lake Trail #1337** arrives on the PCT's right (south), coming up from Waptus Lake below. A few feet farther, the same Spade Lake Trail continues uphill to the left (north), heading to Spade Lake high above.

The PCT trail continues straight and in 0.2 mile from this trail junction (2.3 from Waptus River), crosses a creek and reaches an idyllic campsite (**Camp 16**), several yards downhill to the right (south). This camp is visible from the PCT but offers some privacy because it's away from the trail. It boasts a fire pit, room for a couple of tents, and flowing water within a few steps. The white noise of the creek is all you'll need to sleep like a log.

In approximately 0.5 mile from Camp 16, the PCT bends left, heads northeast up the Spinola Creek valley, and begins climbing toward Deep Lake. **Spinola Creek Trail #1310.1** heads to the right (south), 1 mile from Camp 16, as you continue making your way through the thick-at-times vegetation. Talus fields pop up now and again and give some visual interest to this stretch, as the pikas who call them home sound their *eeeepppp* alarms as you walk by.

Eventually, the way turns more forested. In 2 miles from the Spinola Creek Trail junction, reach a sign with an arrow pointing right (southeast), which says "Camping." If you follow it, you'll be disappointed. This so-called camping area gets so little use that it's almost impossible to follow the spur trail or find an actual site, let alone one that's not completely taken over by huckleberries. Onward to the campsites at Deep Lake, instead! It might take you a while to get there, because it's hard not to stop every five minutes to eat huckleberries. Loaded bushes are in every direction—up high, down low, to the side. Gobble till you wobble, but watch your intake to avoid uncomfortable bloated-berry belly.

In 1.4 miles from the camping sign (6.7 miles from Waptus River), pass the sign for **Lake Vicente Trail #1365**, which heads left (west). The signs here are a little confusing—just stay straight and you'll remain on the PCT. In 0.2 mile beyond the junction, an unsigned trail shows up near a creek, to the PCT's right (east). It leads to camps-o-dung. Again, stay straight and avoid the horseplay. Just 0.1 mile farther, rock hop across a creek and just afterward, find several campsites tucked in the trees. Keep going to Deep Lake,

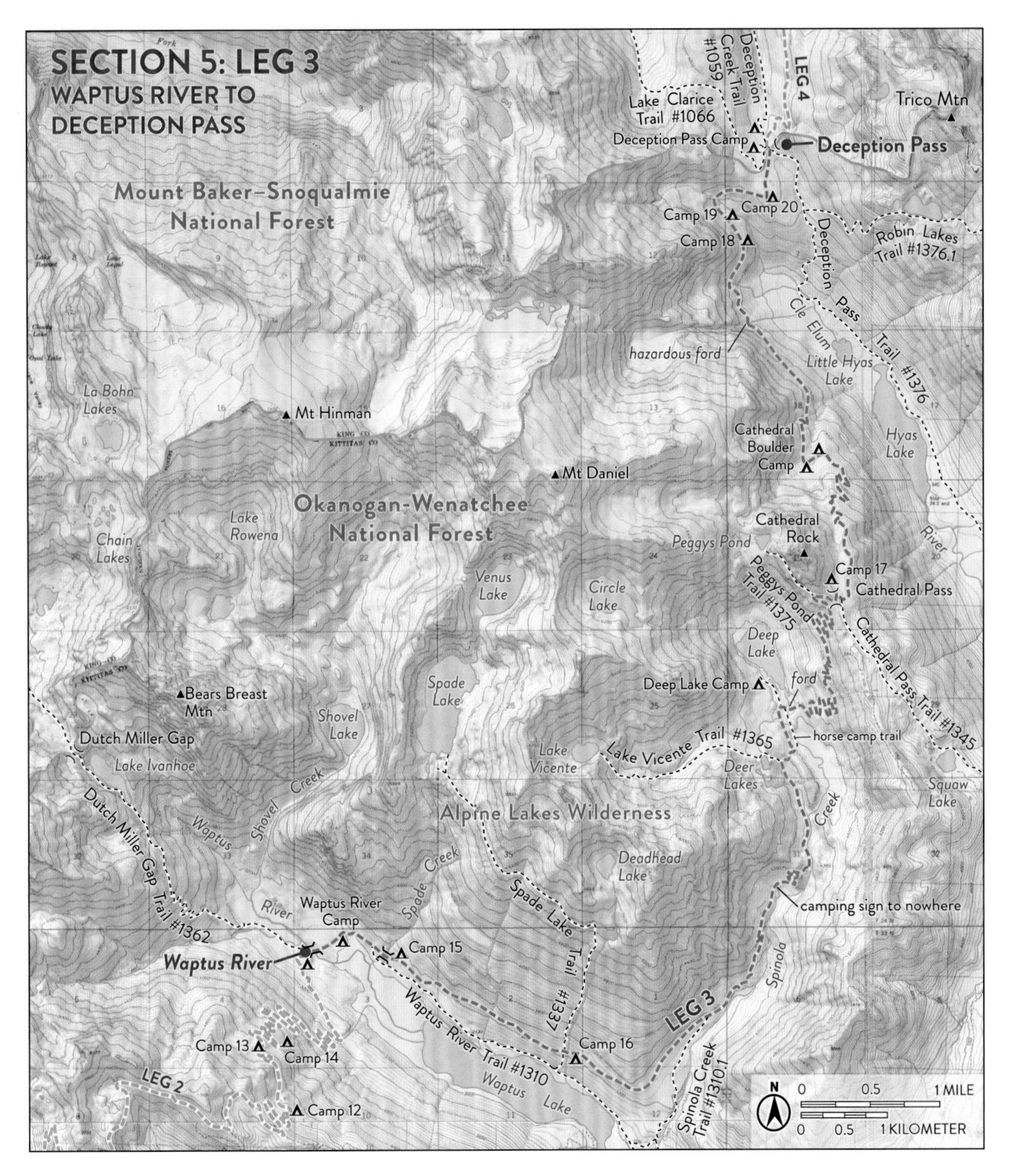

SECTION 5: LEG 3
WAPTUS RIVER TO DECEPTION PASS
Mount Baker–Snoqualmie National Forest
Okanogan-Wenatchee National Forest
Alpine Lakes Wilderness
Deception Pass
Deception Pass Camp
Deception Creek Trail #1059
Lake Clarice Trail #1066
LEG 4
Trico Mtn
Camp 20
Camp 19
Camp 18
Robin Lakes Trail #1376.1
Deception Pass Trail #1376
Cle Elum
hazardous ford
Little Hyas Lake
Hyas Lake
Mt Hinman
La Bohn Lakes
Cathedral Boulder Camp
Mt Daniel
Cathedral Rock
Peggys Pond
Peggys Pond Trail #1375
Camp 17
Cathedral Pass
Cathedral Pass Trail #1345
River
Lake Rowena
Chain Lakes
Venus Lake
Circle Lake
Deep Lake
Deep Lake Camp
ford
Bears Breast Mtn
Spade Lake
Shovel Lake
Dutch Miller Gap
Lake Ivanhoe
Lake Vicente
Lake Vicente Trail #1365
horse camp trail
Deer Lakes
Squaw Lake
Shovel Creek
Waptus
Spade Creek
Creek
Deadhead Lake
Dutch Miller Gap Trail #1362
Spade Lake Trail #1337
camping sign to nowhere
River
Waptus River Camp
Waptus River
Camp 15
Spinola
LEG 3
Camp 13
Camp 14
Camp 16
Waptus River Trail #1310
Waptus Lake
LEG 2
Camp 12
Spinola Creek Trail #1310.1
N
0 0.5 1 MILE
0 0.5 1 KILOMETER

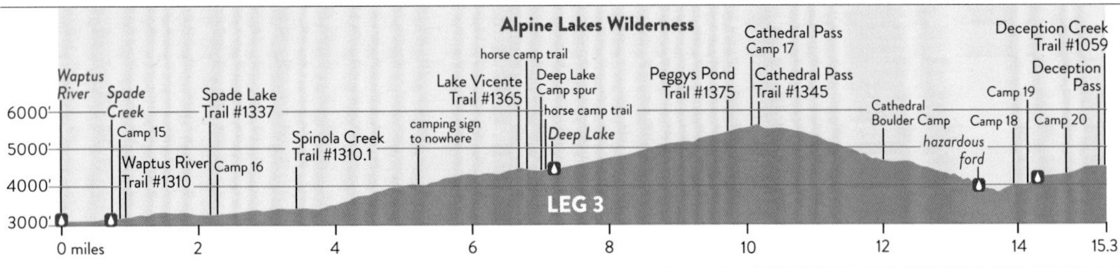

Alpine Lakes Wilderness
Waptus River
Spade Creek
Camp 15
Waptus River Trail #1310
Spade Lake Trail #1337
Camp 16
Spinola Creek Trail #1310.1
camping sign to nowhere
Lake Vicente Trail #1365
horse camp trail
Deep Lake Camp spur
horse camp trail
Deep Lake
Peggys Pond Trail #1375
Cathedral Pass Camp 17
Cathedral Pass Trail #1345
Cathedral Boulder Camp
hazardous ford
Camp 18
Camp 19
Camp 20
Deception Creek Trail #1059
Deception Pass
LEG 3
6000'
5000'
4000'
3000'
0 miles
2
4
6
8
10
12
14
15.3

PEGGYS POND

If time permits, or you want a scenic lunch or camp spot, follow Peggys Pond Trail #1375 for 0.7 mile (1.4 miles roundtrip) to the small turquoise lake tucked at the base of foreboding Cathedral Rock. Several campsites dot the lake's broad shoulders. Pack and saddle stock are not permitted in this area. Looking around, you're left to wonder, where is this namesake Peggy? She never bothers to show up when I visit, but plenty of other charming folks do, especially on weekends.

which has a plethora of camping options and is rarely full to capacity.

At 0.4 mile beyond the Lake Vicente Trail junction (7.1 miles from Waptus River), reach the 0.3-mile spur trail to **Deep Lake Camp**. Deep Lake is obviously deep but also crystal clear and framed by granite peaks on all sides, which makes for a camp with views—a worthy place to stay. A signpost in the meadow has an arrow pointing straight ahead with the word "Camp" and another arrow to the right with the word "PCT," written by some helpful person. To camp, follow the spur to several lakeside sites, complete with a primitive privy—you'll smell it before you see it. Oh the joys of backcountry think-n-stinks! **Campfires are prohibited within 0.5 mile of Deep Lake**. Sadly, most of the campsites have fire pits created by those who were unsure of the rules or who simply didn't care. Respect the rules and build karma points.

The PCT heads right (east) at the camp signpost and works its way around the southern end of Deep Lake before passing a signed horse camp trail to the right (south) and crossing the lake outlet and headwaters of Spinola Creek. There's no bridge over the creek, and during high water you may need to wade. Later in the summer, a balancing act of crossing small rocks can get graceful hikers across with dry feet. Get out your camera, though, because someone usually goes in the drink. **This is the last water for 6.3 miles**, so fill 'er up!

Say goodbye to the Deep Lake basin and start your climb toward Cathedral Rock on long, gentle switchbacks. Views across the valley become increasingly scenic as the granite, glacier-covered slopes of Mount Daniel, Mount Hinman, and a bevy of unnamed peaks show up to keep you company.

In 1.3 miles from the outlet creek near Deep Lake, a trail sign reminds you that campfires are prohibited above 5000 feet. You're now on the east side of the Cascade Crest—a drier climate, where the weather may be in your favor during wet spells. At 2.6 miles beyond Deep Lake, arrive at a trail junction to the left (west) with **Peggys Pond Trail #1375**.

If you're losing daylight, have sore feet, or feel a need for speed, continue on the PCT another 0.2 mile from the Peggys Pond Trail junction to a splendid viewpoint and Cathedral Pass. To the left (northwest) is waterless **Camp 17**, at the end of a short spur trail to the top of the hill. The campsite is on a durable surface and can fit one or two small tents.

CAMPING NEAR CATHEDRAL PASS

You might end up cursing my name if I didn't mention the issues with camping near Cathedral Pass. Aside from Camp 17, several flat areas exist; some even have prohibited fire pits. In this fragile area, however, most of the sites are on delicate grasses or vegetation not suitable for camping—pitching a tent in these spots is counter to wilderness ethics and will trouble your conscience. The need for an emergency campsite is understandable, but do your best to plan ahead so that you stay at suitable camps farther along. Give this area a rest and just enjoy the spectacular eye candy as you wander through the berries and flowers. With your help, the struggling vegetation, with its short growing season, will have a better chance of recovery and survival.

Cathedral Rock towers over tender meadows along the PCT.

In just 0.3 mile from the Peggys Pond Trail junction, arrive at the most confusing trail intersection on your adventure so far. You won't be the first to get lost here if you're not paying attention. A tree at this junction has grown limbs that seem to be pointing in every direction. **Cathedral Pass Trail #1345** is signed and located to the right (southeast); stock and pack travelers need to take this trail to avoid the ford just shy of 3 miles north on the PCT. But hikers turn left (north) to continue on the PCT and wander through gentle ups and downs at the base of Cathedral Rock.

Low-growing juniper and dwarf huckleberries, mixed with subalpine fir and gray rock slabs, make this a place to walk slowly, take pictures, and soak up the soul food. As you hike north, the spire of Cathedral Rock shows off its many faces, and you'll follow a series of forest switchbacks before leveling off in intermittent meadows and boulder gardens.

In 2.1 miles past the Cathedral Pass Trail junction arrive at a series of campsites (**Cathedral Boulder Camp**) and a dried-up creek. A couple of years ago, the creek at this location rerouted itself to flow underground and is difficult, if not impossible, to find. It seems to mock you—you can hear it, but the crazy dribble is nowhere to be found! Nature changes frequently, and it wouldn't surprise me if the creek eventually resurfaced, but carry water if you intend to camp here, to be on the safe side. The sites are ample and well established.

Beyond the camp, the PCT crosses a couple of talus fields and then begins to descend through wet swales and a really gnarly stretch of trail. Because of the steep hillside both above and below, trail crews have struggled year after year to maintain the tread as loose soil, roots, and foliage battle for dominance. Walk gingerly and watch your feet. When you do stop, check out Hyas Lake in the basin below and Mount Stuart to the east, the second-highest nonvolcanic peak in the state.

Keep your wits about you as the trail descends on loosey-goosey terrain to an unnamed creek draining the glacier-clad slopes of Mount Daniel, far above. The creek is 1.3 miles beyond Cathedral Boulder Camp (13.4 miles from Waptus River) and is one you'll likely hear about via the "trail telegraph" long before you arrive. This is a **precarious and potentially hazardous ford**—there's no bridge. Some years it's more challenging than others; the flow completely depends on snowmelt, weather, even time of day (with more meltwater on a hot afternoon). Some folks forgo shoes and socks and ford the various fingers, while others balance on spindly logs or rock hop and take their chances with the consequences of an unfortunate fall. Other hikers carry water shoes and throw them on here or simply give in and get their hiking shoes wet in an effort to keep their ankles and toes protected. One thing is certain—the water is cold, and I mean ffffffreeeezzzing. It'll leave you gasping for breath and dreaming of hot tubs. If you wade, move confidently and swiftly. Whatever you do, use extreme caution. This creek has put the hurt on dozens of hikers who didn't respect its power and ended up with twisted ankles and worse. Once across, breathe a sigh of relief and reward yourself with a tasty morsel from your pack—you earned it!

The PCT next traverses the hillside and meets up with yet another creek just 0.3 mile beyond the hazardous ford—this one is thankfully much easier to cross. In 0.6 mile from the hazardous ford, arrive at **Camp 18** to the right (east), tucked deep into the forest. This camp is very well established and has a fire pit and room for one big tent or two smaller ones. Water is 0.3 mile either north or south on the PCT. If this camp is taken, **Camp 19** is north another 0.2 mile, also in the forest to the right (east), with the same characteristics.

Just 0.1 mile beyond Camp 19, cross a small creek and continue in the conifer forest, now gently gaining elevation. If you intend to camp in the Deception Pass area, it's best to get water here. In 0.7 mile past Camp 19, find **Camp 20**, the last of the three popular camps on this hillside. This is the most desirable of the three, but it's usually taken so don't be too picky. Located off-trail about 20 yards, Camp 20 has a few log benches for furniture, room for at least two tents, an established fire ring, and a nearby pond for water. Some years, the pond is stagnant and you may want to carry water to be on the safe side.

The gentle climb continues in the evergreens and in 0.3 mile beyond Camp 20 arrives at a junction with **Deception Pass Trail #1376** to the right (southeast). Just a few yards later is a junction for **Lake Clarice Trail #1066** to the left, with a sign pointing toward Marmot Lake in the same direction. The campfire yo-yo continues, this time with a sign noting that fires are not permitted above 4000 feet. Another sign notes the PCT direction with arrows north and south. This is officially the forested and rather uneventful **Deception Pass**, 15.2 miles beyond Waptus River.

There are a few camping options here (**Deception Pass Camp**), although none are trailside. Two sites are 0.3 mile along the Lake Clarice Trail, and a couple more are along the Deception Creek Trail. To get to the latter, continue north on the PCT for 0.1 mile beyond the pass intersection and find **Deception Creek Trail #1059** to the left (northwest). Follow it for a short distance and find several established sites. Tarns, although stagnant at times, might be a water source, but your best bet is to carry water from the creek roughly 1 mile back. This area can be very buggy, so tangle with your bug goo before you hang out in camp, or the tiny biters may have you for dinner and possibly carry you away.

CAMP-TO-CAMP MILEAGE

Waptus River Camp to Camp 15 .... 0.7
Camp 15 to Camp 16 .... 1.6
Camp 16 to Deep Lake Camp 4.8
Deep Lake Camp to Camp 17 .... 2.8
Camp 17 to Cathedral Boulder Camp 2.1
Cathedral Boulder Camp to Camp 18 .... 2.0
Camp 18 to Camp 19 .... 0.2
Camp 19 to Camp 20 .... 0.7
Camp 20 to Deception Pass Camp 0.4

4 DECEPTION PASS TO HOPE LAKE

DISTANCE 13.2 miles

ELEVATION GAIN/LOSS
+3630/–3710 feet

HIGH POINT 5930 feet

CONNECTING TRAILS
Deception Pass Trail #1376,
Deception Lakes Trail #1059.2,
Deception Creek Trail #1059,
Surprise Creek Trail #1060,
Tunnel Creek Trail #1061

ON THE TRAIL

Beyond **Deception Pass** and **Deception Pass Trail #1376**, the PCT crosses a small cirque, which occasionally contains water, but it dries up in late season. No worries, more water is ahead. Duck into the forest, traversing the hillside, and be sure to note the views to the southwest of Mount Daniel, Mount Hinman, and the Lynch Glacier.

In 1.4 miles from Deception Pass, cross Deception Creek, with reliable water. The evergreen walk continues, with huckleberry shrubs landscaping the trail near your feet. At 1.8 miles from Deception Pass, reach another dependable creek and just beyond it **Camp 21**. Located off-trail to the left (west), this very well-established wooded camp is large enough for five or six small tents. It's a popular destination for groups, so if you're flying solo, you may want to offer to share or forgo the spot and leave it to the crowds.

Another creek shows up 0.5 mile from Camp 21, as the gentle trail steepens and starts opening up to more views. At 3.2 miles from Deception Pass, come to **Deception Lakes Trail #1059.2** on the left (west), along with a sign reminding you that campfires are prohibited

The jagged ridges of Pieper Pass make for a unique vista as the trail bobs and weaves through boulder gardens.

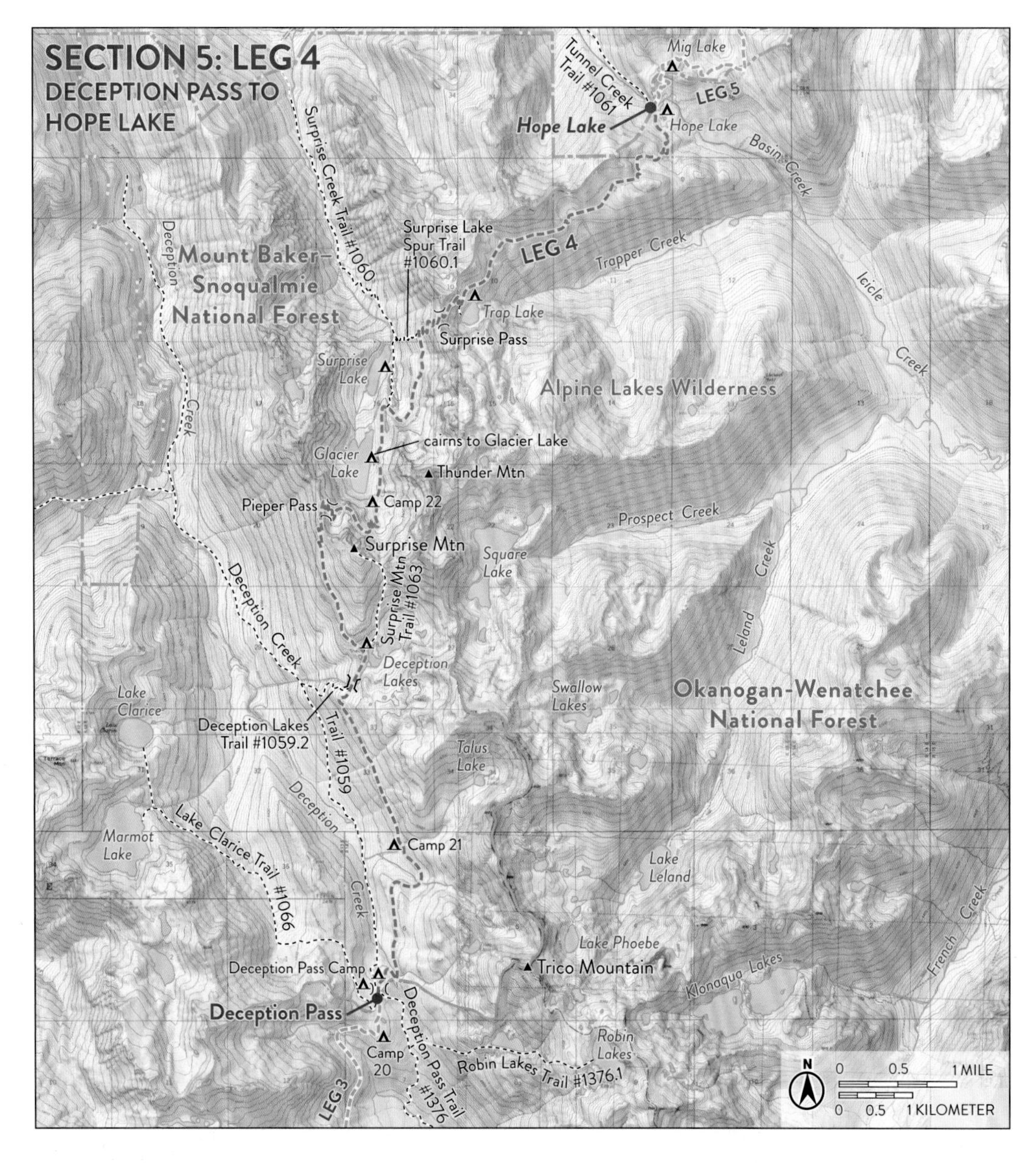
SECTION 5: LEG 4
DECEPTION PASS TO HOPE LAKE
Mig Lake
Tunnel Creek Trail #1061
LEG 5
Hope Lake
Hope Lake
Basin Creek
Surprise Creek Trail #1060
Surprise Lake Spur Trail #1060.1
LEG 4
Trapper Creek
Icicle Creek
Deception Creek
Mount Baker–Snoqualmie National Forest
Trap Lake
Surprise Pass
Surprise Lake
Alpine Lakes Wilderness
cairns to Glacier Lake
Glacier Lake
Thunder Mtn
Pieper Pass
Camp 22
Prospect Creek
Surprise Mtn
Square Lake
Surprise Mtn Trail #1063
Leland Creek
Deception Lakes
Swallow Lakes
Okanogan-Wenatchee National Forest
Lake Clarice
Deception Lakes Trail #1059.2
Trail #1059
Talus Lake
Deception Creek
Marmot Lake
Lake Clarice Trail #1066
Camp 21
Lake Leland
French Creek
Lake Phoebe
Deception Pass Camp
Trico Mountain
Klonaqua Lakes
Deception Pass
Camp 20
Deception Pass Trail #1376
Robin Lakes
Robin Lakes Trail #1376.1
LEG 3
0 0.5 1 MILE
0 0.5 1 KILOMETER

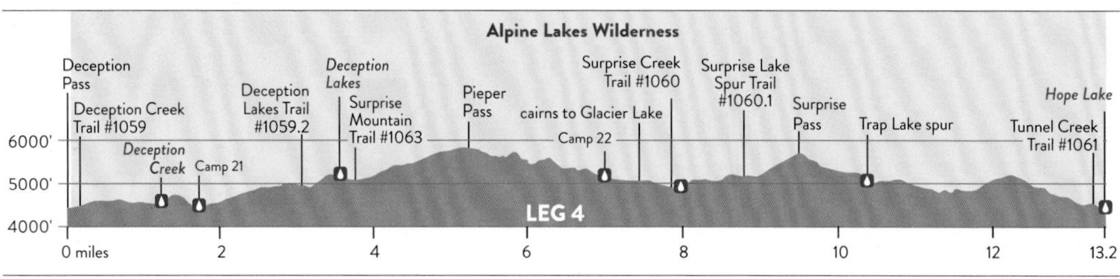
Alpine Lakes Wilderness
Deception Pass
Deception Creek Trail #1059
Deception Creek
Camp 21
Deception Lakes Trail #1059.2
Deception Lakes
Surprise Mountain Trail #1063
Pieper Pass
cairns to Glacier Lake
Camp 22
Surprise Creek Trail #1060
Surprise Lake Spur Trail #1060.1
Surprise Pass
Trap Lake spur
Hope Lake
Tunnel Creek Trail #1061
6000'
5000'
4000'
LEG 4
0 miles
2
4
6
8
10
12
13.2

beyond this point—you're nearing Deception Lakes, and the Forest Service frowns upon burning the place down.

In 0.1 mile beyond the trail junction, cross a sturdy bridge over an outlet creek that flows trailside all the way to **Deception Lakes** 💧, a short 0.2 mile farther. **Deception Lakes Camp** offers plenty of options, so wander around and find a spot to your liking. This area has a stock campsite as well, so if you find horse apples, you've likely stumbled on it and will want to keep looking. If you're just passing through, fill up on water before you trot up the trail, as the next reliable source is 3.6 miles north.

The trail levels off and walks along the first of the Deception Lakes before it turns hard to the left (west) at an intersection with **Surprise Mountain Trail #1063**. From there, cruise past a couple more solid campsites and the toilet spur trail, to the PCT's left (south) roughly 100 yards from the trail junction. For all the traffic this area receives, the privy is in decent shape.

From Deception Lakes, the PCT jogs right (northeast) for a short distance at a sign with an arrow noting "Stevens Pass" before it ascends north, crossing a narrow and at times very exposed hillside, giving way to views of Terrace Mountain, Mount Index, Three Fingers, and other granite spires of the Alpine Lakes Wilderness. The climb switches back rather steeply to **Pieper Pass**, just shy of 2 miles beyond Deception Lakes. Even though the climb is relatively short, it feels much longer, so stop, breathe, and take in the views at the top. The ridge shows off your next valley and the azure Glacier and Surprise lakes nestled below.

Heading down after Pieper Pass is a treat for the eyes but a challenge for the feet, as the rocky path winds through boulder fields mixed with sparse vegetation. Each corner is more interesting than the next, and you're left to wonder where the hobbits live. Pass a small brown seasonal tarn to the right before descending a scree- and talus-covered trail leading to a large rocky cirque. Above you, grand granite spires watch over this valley and make for interesting photos on clear days. A landslide, which hit this area during a rainstorm a few years back, almost obscured the trail signs, but the tops survived and are now choking in the silt. One of them, surrounded by debris, says "Trail abandoned." Um . . . no kidding! Another sign points uphill toward Snoqualmie Pass and Pieper Pass. Our path continues downhill and quickly ducks into a sparse evergreen forest dotted with boulders and heather.

At 1.7 miles from Pieper Pass, cross a small creek 💧 and find two well-established campsites (**Camp 22**), one to the left (west) and one to the right (east) of the PCT. Both are visible from the trail and have room for two small tents. Another creek is 0.2 mile beyond, as the PCT ducks deeper into a mix of talus fields and forest and comes upon **Glacier Lake**, slightly downhill

Mountain bistort, lupine, arnica, and more grace the meadows near Trap Lake in season.

A hiker takes in the sublime scenery from the shore of panoramic Trap Lake.

to the left (west). Trailside boulders around here are as big as cabins and worth a quick camera snap.

At 2.1 miles from Pieper Pass (4 miles from Deception Lakes), watch closely for a couple of easy-to-miss cairns to the left (west), hidden in a boulder field. If you find the cairns, you'll find the trail that leads down to **Glacier Lake Camp**. There are a couple of flat campsites around the shoreline, but Surprise Lake has more sites and is better suited for groups.

At 2.5 miles beyond Pieper Pass, arrive at a junction with **Surprise Creek Trail #1060**. To camp at Surprise Lake, go straight ahead (north) for roughly 0.5 mile to several well-established campsites (**Surprise Lake Camp**) and a backcountry toilet. The Forest Service requires all campers to use only designated sites, noted by a hiker symbol. If you camp at Surprise Lake, you can loop back to the PCT from the lake's north end via **Surprise Lake Spur Trail #1060.1** (#1060A on some maps). While this route is not well traveled and has plenty of blowdowns, it's doable and might save you some time.

If you aren't stopping at Surprise Lake, go right (east) at the Surprise Creek Trail junction and continue on the PCT. A well-marked sign helps you figure it out, but going right (east) instead of straight (north) doesn't feel correct even though it is, so be sure to pay attention. Just 0.1 mile from the Surprise Creek Trail junction, reach a reliable creek.

From there, the trail crosses a talus-filled cirque with plenty of rocky peaks for views before it ducks back in the woods and arrives at the spur trail from Surprise Lake, 1 mile past the Surprise Creek Trail junction. **Surprise Pass** is only 0.8 mile ahead, but the switchbacks ascend steeply and, like with so many hills around here, the distance seems longer than it really is. Just keep plodding, one foot in front of the other, and you'll get there . . . eventually.

From the pass, **Trap Lake** appears within yet another valley. The lake stays in focus as the PCT descends on switchbacks and traverses the hillside just above the lake basin. In 0.7 mile from Surprise Pass, note a curious unsigned side trail heading downhill to your right (east). This leads 0.2 mile to chilly Trap Lake, a pleasant lunch spot, and **Trap Lake Camp**, with several shoreline sites. Once you sit by the cerulean lake, surrounded by fresh alpine breezes, the beauty might, in fact, trap you. If you manage to break free, or if you choose not to stop, the PCT continues north and crosses two more reliable creeks within the next mile.

The subalpine country from Trap Lake to Hope Lake alternates between meadows and forest and shows off the best of both. Wildflowers and huckleberries dot the open spaces, while hemlock and Douglas-firs keep watch from above as you gently ascend toward Hope Lake. Keep your eyes open for pine martens—they've been known to dart around rocks and logs, often seeing you before you see them. This is a fragile subalpine zone, so please avoid camping here.

In 2.8 miles from Trap Lake, arrive at **Tunnel Creek Trail #1061**, coming in from the left (west), and the shores of **Hope Lake** **O** to the right (east). Hope Lake and Mig Lake, just to the north, get a fair amount of day hikers and campers arriving from Tunnel Creek and Stevens Pass. If you plan to stay, *hope* you get a campsite (**Hope Lake Camp**). There are quite a few sites, so your odds are very good. Next, *hope* it's quiet. One time, camping here with friends, we had the unfortunate experience of sharing the lake with a pack of teenage boys who enjoyed howling at the moon as we tried to sleep. Mig Lake is just 0.9 mile to the north—if Hope Lake Camp is full, or full of teen wolves.

CAMP-TO-CAMP MILEAGE

Deception Pass Camp to Camp 21 .... 1.8
Camp 21 to Deception Lakes Camp......... 1.7
Deception Lakes Camp to Camp 22 .... 3.6
Camp 22 to Glacier Lake Camp spur........ 0.4
Glacier Lake Camp spur to Surprise Lake Camp spur.......................... 0.4
Surprise Lake Camp spur to Trap Lake Camp spur.......................... 2.5
Trap Lake Camp spur to Hope Lake Camp ... 2.8

HUCKLEBERRY UTOPIA

Washington is a huckleberry lover's dream come true in late August and early September. Small countries could be fed from Mother Nature's massive bounty along the PCT alone. It's hard to wrap your head around the quantity and variety—dwarf huckleberry, Cascade huckleberry, mountain huckleberry, and oval-leaved bilberry are just a few. A serious party for the senses!

The dwarf variety produces a bright blue berry that tastes, to me, exactly like a sweet fresh apple, while others tend to have a tart or even sour flavor. Whatever hits your palate, know that you're doing your body a favor. One serving of wild huckleberries has more antioxidants than any other fruit or veggie except lingonberries. These small berries are associated with lowering cholesterol and preventing cancer, heart disease, diabetes, and macular degeneration. They are a tremendous source of vitamins C and B, supporting a faster metabolism and improving immune-system function.

There is a downside, however. The delicious little devils, if overconsumed, can cause some wicked GI discomfort, which I playfully call bloated-berry-belly-n-bad-news-bowels. If you succumb, you'll be sprinting to the woods with your trowel, shaking your fist at the brambles. So, be forewarned and pace yourself at the berry buffet—there are likely more up ahead!

5 HOPE LAKE TO STEVENS PASS

DISTANCE 8.3 miles

ELEVATION GAIN/LOSS +1930/–2270 feet

HIGH POINT 5250 feet

CONNECTING TRAILS Tunnel Creek Trail #1061, Icicle Creek Trail #1551

ON THE TRAIL

Leave **Hope Lake** and climb gently through huckleberry shrubs and small grassy meadows amid swaying conifers. At 0.8 mile from Hope Lake, arrive at **Mig Lake** and the first of two toilet trails heading left (west). I'm not sure why there are two privies here, except perhaps that the Forest Service saw the copious huckleberries and thought it best not to take chances. A couple of **Mig Lake Camp** sites are tucked in this area, away from the lake, and there are more ahead. The second toilet trail shows up to the left (north) as you arrive at the north end of the lake, 0.1 mile farther, with a couple more campsites to the right (south) near the shore. Mig Lake is rather shallow and in a flat meadow area, with evergreens for sparse shelter around the lake. If you need water, you won't find another good source for 3.2 more miles, so take what you need.

Heading north from Mig Lake, follow gentle ups and downs and pass a stagnant tarn to the left (west), 0.6 mile beyond the lake. Then, climb, climb, climb, first on a hillside traverse and then via huffy and puffy switchbacks to a saddle near 5200 feet, where the grade eases up. If you listen closely, you'll hear the buzz of vehicles from US Highway 2 in the distance. Civilization is just around the corner.

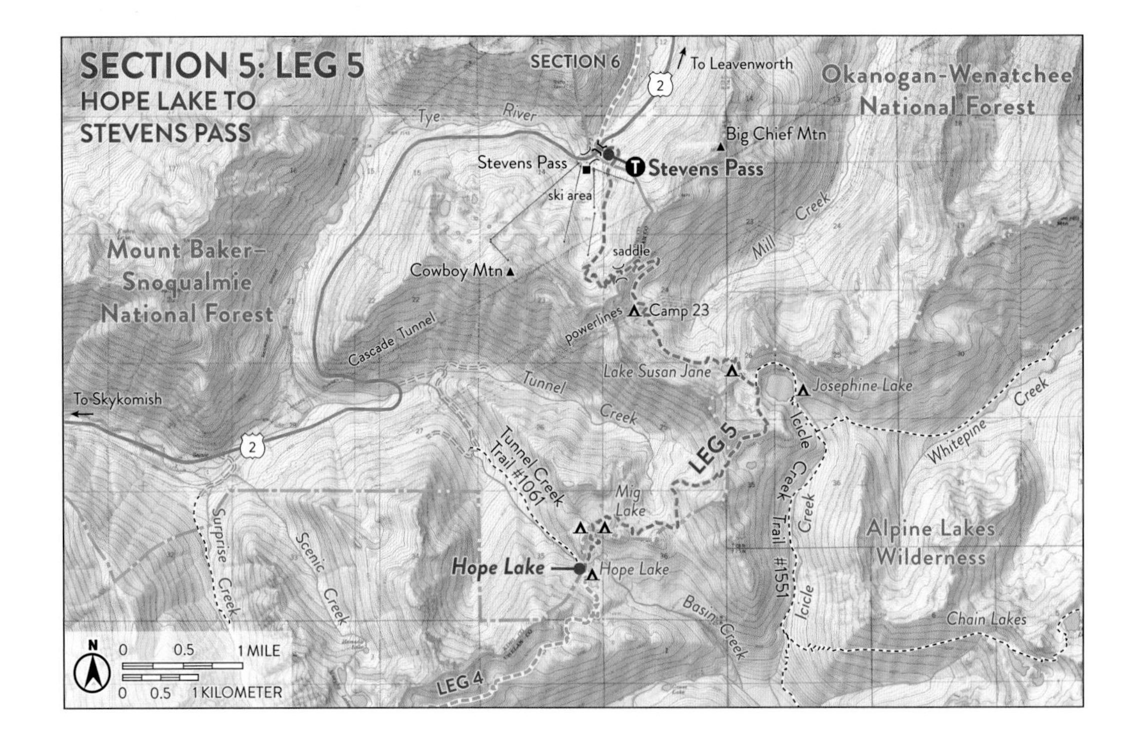

At 2.7 miles from Mig Lake, a viewpoint to the right (east) gives you a glimpse of Josephine Lake, accessed via **Icicle Creek Trail #1551**, located 0.1 mile beyond the viewpoint. If you're looking for a campsite, there are several desirable spots at Josephine Lake, but they are more than 1 mile and 320 feet of elevation loss away.

A better option, if you aren't interested in straying that far, is **Lake Susan Jane**, which is just 0.5 mile ahead (3.2 miles from Mig Lake). This quaint, small lake is to the PCT's left (south) and offers a variety of flat, well-established camps and evergreen trees for weather protection. If you aren't staying, give her a wave or photo snap as you cruise by and continue your quest for Stevens Pass. Powerlines and ski slopes are visible now across the valley and remind you that you're getting close.

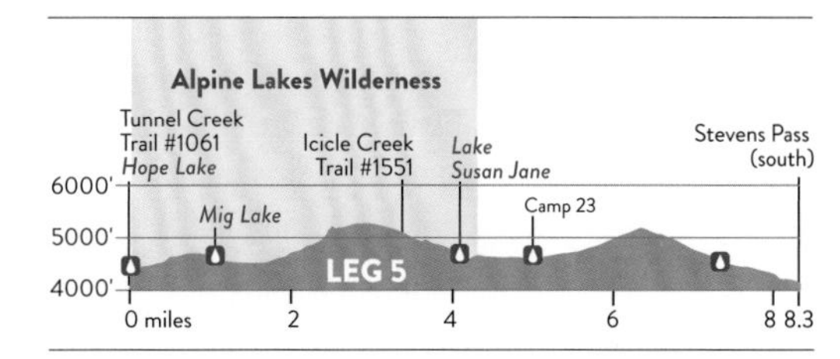

A WET AND CROAKY NIGHT

It seems that no hike of mine is complete without a story of an encounter with a creature, and the PCT is no different. One wet and foggy night, camped at Deception Lakes, my bladder would not let me sleep.

Despite the weather outside the tent, my body simply would not take no for an answer. I sat up, trying not to wake my sleeping husband, and began the lengthy process of putting on every stitch of raingear. First the pants, then the jacket, then hat, then Gore-Tex socks. Next was the very precarious task of opening the rainfly and avoiding a deluge onto our dry shoes and my hubby's head. I did my best to quietly escape and I disappeared into the mist with the beam of my headlamp barely illuminating the surrounding trees.

Beware of bewildered toads!

When I returned, I gingerly opened the rainfly again and immediately discovered a large toad that was startled to see a human predator hovering above. It hopped over shoes, getting its long legs tangled in our gear as I tried to shoo it away from the tent. My husband, deliriously tired, tried to help me get into the tent, completely oblivious to my toad-wrangling attempts. He unzipped the tent door and the toad saw a much better option: he jumped inside and in a choreographed dance, hopped on my husband's head and got wrapped in his hair. My husband sat up, frazzled, and went to work scooting the large amphibian out of the tent.

That night I learned that toads don't hop when you scoot them. Instead, they flip over, baring their white tummies and flailing their arms and legs like a beetle, helpless, until they're righted. The stunned toad finally did make it back out into the night and bounced off—a very hoppy ending for all.

WHAT'S THE DEAL WITH CAMPFIRES?

Let me do my best to speak candidly about the conflagration of campfire regulations. You'd think it would be fairly straightforward: yes I can build a campfire here, or no I can't. But that ain't the case. Here are the Forest Service rules.

1. Campfires are prohibited within 0.5 mile of lakes.
2. Campfires are prohibited above 4000 feet on the west side of the Cascade Crest and above 5000 feet on the east side.
3. Seasonal restrictions apply during years of drought and may be imposed at any time.

The second rule in particular is the confusing part. Who the heck knows whether they're traveling on the west side of the crest, the east side, or smack-dab in the middle? Occasionally, it's obvious. For example, when ponderosa pinecones are dense as fog and you're shedding layers to beat the heat, you're probably on the east side. When salal and ferns try to overtake the trail, and you're pulling out your raincoat every twenty minutes, you're probably on the west side. But there are no signs that say "crossing into the west" or "welcome back to the east." When I first read about this rule, my immediate thought was why didn't they make it simple and just keep one elevation for the whole thing?

The Forest Service has posted occasional signs along the PCT reminding you where fires are restricted, though the signs aren't consistent and can be confusing. For instance, what about the occasional "No campfires beyond this point" sign? Where does that point end? Are we to assume the restriction is all the way to Canada?

Confusion aside, let me get on my soapbox and give you some rules of thumb. When in doubt, don't build a fire. Generally, low river valleys are fair game, while high subalpine terrain is not. If you *do* decide to light up, keep trash out of the fires, clean up after yourself, don't build a fire pit if one is not already established, help out by destroying fire rings that flout wilderness ethics, and keep Smokey the Bear happy. While you're at it, keep yourself happy—good fire etiquette helps keep wildfires at bay, which means you can keep hiking. Hear that? It's the happy tap dance I'm doing as I wiggle off of this soapbox.

At 0.9 mile from Lake Susan Jane (5 miles from Hope Lake), drop into a valley and cross two small reliable creeks followed by a campsite (**Camp 23**), under the powerlines on the trail's left. While this is not the most scenic camp spot, it is flat and has a log for sitting. From the camp, walk under the powerlines and begin a series of switchbacks to reach a saddle near the top of the Tye Mill chairlift, 1.2 miles beyond Camp 23 (2.1 miles past Lake Susan Jane).

In recent years, summer construction at the ski area has included blasting along the trail on weekdays. If they're blasting, crews will honk a horn loudly three times to indicate it's about to happen. One horn honk gives the all clear. Signs remind hikers of the signals and warn of the activity. Arms and legs come in handy, so stay alert.

Once over the saddle, the PCT drops into trees and flirts with ski runs and chairlifts, building excitement as you approach civilization and US 2. At 1.2 miles from the saddle, a small creek provides water if you need it. Traverse a hillside above the ski lodges and US 2, which rumbles and echoes across the valley. At 2.1 miles beyond the saddle (8.3 miles from Hope

Visible from the trail, Stevens Pass Ski Area offers limited summertime services.

Lake), arrive at the **Stevens Pass Trailhead** for the PCT and a large parking lot, complete with a pit toilet.

The Stevens Pass ski resort recently opened a mountain-bike park, which means that restaurants and facilities are open in the summer during select hours. Even if the resort is closed, there are outdoor picnic tables and electric outlets, should you want a real chair for your bum as you charge your phone or GPS. If you're continuing north on the PCT, use the **pedestrian bridge** near the ski lodges to safely cross US 2. Otherwise, pat yourself on your grimy back and do your happy dance to celebrate your accomplishment!

CAMP-TO-CAMP MILEAGE

Hope Lake Camp to Mig Lake Camp 0.9
Mig Lake Camp to Lake Susan Jane Camp . . . 3.2
Lake Susan Jane Camp to Camp 23 . . . . 0.9
Camp 23 to Stevens Pass 3.3

SECTION 6

STEVENS PASS TO RAINY PASS

THIS SECTION OF THE PCT has a primitive feel, stunning scenery, and less traffic than Snoqualmie Pass to Stevens Pass, all reasons I'm such a huge fan. The trail crosses through the Henry M. Jackson Wilderness, complete with sparkling lakes like Valhalla, Janus, and Pear, before delivering you to some of Washington's most scenic high country, looping around the ever-changing faces of Glacier Peak and through its namesake wilderness area. Ups and downs are plentiful, and there's never a shortage of vistas, high alpine and subalpine terrain, and deep, forested valleys. One such valley, near the Suiattle River, is home to evergreen behemoths that will make you feel like an ant among their giant bases and massive limbs.

You'll also pass through Lake Chelan National Recreation Area and North Cascades National Park, where the PCT leads to the west end of the Stehekin Valley Road—a shuttle can pick you up and deliver you to the tiny historical village of Stehekin, a worthy final destination or side trip. The Stehekin Pastry Company has some of the best cinnamon rolls in the world, and biking, kayaking, touring historical sights, and fly-fishing are all possibilities. If your mission is to continue onward, the PCT next wanders east of the Cascade Crest and tours the drier-side climate, showing off ponderosa pines, sandy soil, and giant rock faces. Get out there and make some footprints!

DISTANCE 126.6 miles

STATE DISTANCE 315.8–442.4 miles

ELEVATION GAIN/LOSS +31,065/–31,040 feet

HIGH POINT 6580 feet

BEST TIME OF YEAR Aug–Sept

PCTA SECTION LETTER K

LAND MANAGERS

- Mount–Baker Snoqualmie National Forest (Skykomish Ranger District, Darrington Ranger District)
- North Cascades National Park Complex (Lake Chelan National Recreation Area; Golden West Visitor Center, Wilderness Information Center)
- Okanogan-Wenatchee National Forest (Methow Valley Ranger District, Henry M. Jackson Wilderness, Glacier Peak Wilderness)

PASSES AND PERMITS NW Forest Pass to park at Stevens Pass and Rainy Pass trailheads. Free North Cascades National Park backcountry permit at national park ranger stations. Free self-issue wilderness permits at wilderness area trailheads.

MAPS AND APPS

- Halfmile's WA Section K
- USFS PCT Map #10 Northern Washington
- Green Trails Stevens Pass #76, Benchmark Mtn #144, Glacier Peak #112, McGregor Mtn #81, Stehekin #82, Washington Pass #50
- Halfmile's PCT app, Guthook's overall PCT app and PCT WA app

ACCESS

Stevens Pass

From Seattle, head east across Lake Washington to Interstate 405 in Bellevue. Drive north on I-405, take exit 23 (for State Route 522 East), and continue to the exit for US Highway 2 (Stevens Pass Highway). Drive east on US 2 for 50 miles to Stevens Pass. Turn right (south) into the ski area and drive to the far left

Opposite: *The refreshing backcountry near White Pass soothes the soul.*

LEGS

1. Stevens Pass to Pear Lake
2. Pear Lake to White Pass
3. White Pass to Mica Lake
4. Mica Lake to Suiattle River
5. Suiattle River to Stehekin Valley Road
6. Stehekin Valley Road to Rainy Pass

(northeastern) corner of the huge parking area signed for the PCT. Finding the actual northbound trailhead can be challenging. Walk toward the ski area and locate a pedestrian walkway that crosses the highway. Once across it, head east. The PCT Trailhead sneaks into the backcountry next to a ski area maintenance shed and power substation. There's a small easy-to-miss trailhead sign.

Rainy Pass

From Marblemount, drive east on State Route 20 (North Cascades Highway) for a little more than 50 miles to Rainy Pass. Turn left (north) toward the Rainy Pass Trailhead and parking area. Parking is plentiful. Vault toilet available.

NOTES

Cities and Services

Near the southern trailhead, find gas, groceries, dining, and lodging in Skykomish and Leavenworth. Near the northern trailhead, find gas, groceries, dining, and lodging in Marblemount and Winthrop. Stehekin is a side trip along the route or an access point by boat or seaplane to Chelan, which offers services.

Camping and Campfire Restrictions

Camping is prohibited on the ridge around White Pass, and at Red Pass, and is limited to designated camping areas. **Campfires** are prohibited within 0.5 mile of Lake Sally Ann and Lake Valhalla. The **North Cascades National Park Complex** (which includes the park and the Lake Chelan National Recreation Area) allows camping in designated sites only, and permits for overnight stays are required along the PCT from 2 miles south of Stehekin Valley Road to 3.5 miles south of Rainy Pass. Permits are free and available the day of, or the day prior to, your intended stay from the Wilderness Information Center in Marblemount or the Golden West Visitor Center in Stehekin. No reservations are accepted, and permits are first come, first served. But camps are ample, so if your preferred camps are full (especially possible on weekends), you can still usually find a spot if you're flexible—you can always don your headlamp, give your feet a pep talk, and make a longer day of it. Most PCT hikers take the shuttle bus from the upper Stehekin Valley Road to Stehekin to get their permit.

While pets are not permitted on trails in national parks, they are allowed on leashes along the PCT through North Cascades National Park. Marijuana, while legal in Washington State, is prohibited on federal lands, including North Cascades National Park. Drones or unmanned aircraft may not be launched, landed, or operated on lands managed by the National Park Service. People who can legally possess firearms may do so provided they understand and comply with applicable laws. For more information, visit the North Cascades website listed in appendix 2.

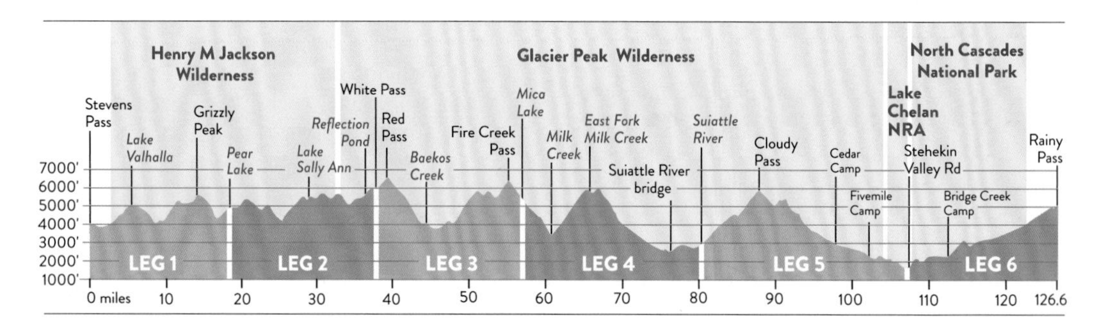

SECTION 6
STEVENS PASS TO RAINY PASS
North Cascades National Park
To Marblemount
SECTION 7
To Winthrop
20
Washington Pass
Rainy Pass
North Cascades Hwy
LEG 6
Bridge Creek
Stehekin Valley Road
Lake Chelan National Recreation Area
Agnes Creek
Stehekin River
Stehekin
Mount Baker–Snoqualmie National Forest
LEG 5
Suiattle River
Suiattle River
Suiattle Pass
Holden
Lucerne
Lake Chelan
Mica Lake
White Chuck River
LEG 4
LEG 3
Glacier Peak
Glacier Peak Wilderness
Trinity
Sauk River
Okanogan-Wenatchee National Forest
6200
White Pass
White River
Henry M Jackson Wilderness
LEG 2
Chiwawa River
Pear Lake
65
Little Wenatchee River
Lake Wenatchee
Lake Janus
Wild Sky Wilderness
LEG 1
Lake Valhalla
2
Stevens Pass
Nason Creek
To Monroe
Stevens Pass
2
SECTION 5
To Leavenworth
N
0 2 4 MILES
0 2 4 KILOMETERS

SUGGESTED ITINERARIES

Where noted, distances are to camp trail spurs; camp may be up to 0.2 mile from junction.

13 DAYS

		Miles
Day 1	Steven Pass to Lake Janus Camp	9.6
Day 2	Lake Janus Camp to Pear Lake Camp	8.7
Day 3	Pear Lake Camp to Lake Sally Ann Camp	10.8
Day 4	Lake Sally Ann Camp to White Pass Camp spur	8.5
Day 5	White Pass Camp spur to Sitkum Creek Camp	9.1
Day 6	Sitkum Creek Camp to Camp 19	9.9
Day 7	Camp 19 to Dolly Vista Camp	10.5
Day 8	Dolly Vista Camp to Suiattle Camp	12.9
Day 9	Suiattle Camp to Camp 30	8.0
Day 10	Camp 30 to Cedar Camp	9.8
Day 11	Cedar Camp to High Bridge Camp (permit required)	9.3
Day 12	High Bridge Camp to North Fork Camp (permit required)	8.0
Day 13	North Fork Camp to Rainy Pass	11.5
Alt Day 11	Cedar Camp to Stehekin Valley Road, town lodging (prearranged)	9.3

11 DAYS

		Miles
Day 1	Steven Pass to Lake Janus Camp	9.6
Day 2	Lake Janus Camp to Pass Creek Camp	15.2
Day 3	Pass Creek Camp to White Pass Camp spur	12.8
Day 4	White Pass Camp spur to Camp 16	12.2
Day 5	Camp 16 to Milk Creek Camp	11.5
Day 6	Milk Creek Camp to Vista Camp	9.7
Day 7	Vista Camp to Miners Creek Camp	13.8
Day 8	Miners Creek Camp to Cedar Camp	13.0
Day 9	Cedar Camp to High Bridge Camp (permit required)	9.3
Day 10	High Bridge Camp to Sixmile Camp spur (permit required)	11.4
Day 11	Sixmile Camp spur to Rainy Pass	8.1
Alt Day 9	Cedar Camp to Stehekin Valley Road, town lodging (prearranged)	9.3

8 DAYS

		Miles
Day 1	Stevens Pass to Pear Lake Camp	18.3
Day 2	Pear Lake Camp to Reflection Pond Camp	17.5
Day 3	Reflection Pond Camp to Camp 18	17.4
Day 4	Camp 18 to Vista Camp	17.8
Day 5	Vista Camp to Camp 30	17.0
Day 6	Camp 30 to Fivemile Camp	14.1
Day 7	Fivemile Camp to Bridge Creek Camp (permit required)	10.0
Day 8	Bridge Creek Camp to Rainy Pass	14.5
Alt 1 Day 7	Fivemile Camp to Sixmile Camp spur (permit required)	16.4
Day 8	Sixmile Camp spur to Rainy Pass	8.1
Alt 2 Day 7	Fivemile Camp to Stehekin Valley Road, town lodging (prearranged)	5.0
Day 8	Stehekin Valley Road to Bridge Creek Trailhead (SR 20)	17.8

Near Sitkum Creek, the deep emerald forest is enchanting as you wander amid protective conifers.

Water

On-trail water is scarce for nearly 9 miles north of Lake Janus.

Hazards

In years of heavy rains, this section is prone to bridge washouts and hazardous river crossings. In particular, the forested White Chuck River valley is a funnel for water coming off Glacier Peak. Be prepared for potentially treacherous crossings and possible glacial lahars. From Mica Lake to Milk Creek is also especially prone to washouts and landslides. Contact land managers or the PCTA prior to your departure for up-to-the-minute trail and bridge conditions. Black bears frequent the Stehekin Valley and are prolific in North Cascades National Park, especially during berry season. Practice good bear etiquette.

1 STEVENS PASS TO PEAR LAKE

DISTANCE 18.3 miles

ELEVATION GAIN/LOSS +4675/-3765 feet

HIGH POINT 5570 feet

CONNECTING TRAILS Smithbrook Trail #1590, Top Lake Trail #1506, Meadow Creek Trail #1057

ON THE TRAIL

Once you've successfully found the trailhead—onward! Spend the first mile or so walking on a gentle former railroad grade, where thimbleberry, grasses, and pearly everlasting are trying to reclaim the trail. A good swat with the trekking pole helps you make your way through. Just after the brush, the PCT traverses a lightly forested hillside with occasional views to the right (east) of A-frame cabin tops far below. Say goodbye to civilization and duck deeper into the woods, passing two water sources in less than 2 miles. At 2.3 miles, arrive at a creek crossing and two campsites, one on either side of the trail (**Camp 1**). In a pinch, they'd do, but their proximity to the trail might make you want to hold out for a site with more privacy.

Enter the Henry M. Jackson Wilderness at 3.2 miles and just 0.2 mile beyond, notice a spur trail heading left (southwest) to a desirable campsite (**Camp 2**) with an open meadow view and room for two tents. A seasonal spring trickles through the meadow, but you may want to carry water to this spot. The PCT next twists and turns through evergreens, crossing another stream—this one reliable—at 3.8 miles.

At 5.1 miles, Lake Valhalla appears to the right (east) and is a welcome sight in twinkling aqua. Footpaths in this area lead to a superfluity of dead-ends, so don't be tempted to wander too far from the main path. Instead, stay on the PCT just 0.5 mile beyond your first lake view to find the designated spur to the lake's southwestern shoreline, where a few campsites are tucked in the mix.

Lake Valhalla is nestled in a small rocky basin, quietly resting roughly 100 feet below the PCT. The towering Lichtenberg Mountain to the east gives a grand reflection on calm days. A Forest Service sign on the shoreline spur trail helps clarify the day-use versus camping areas and also helps you figure out exactly what the agency considers a designated campsite. **Lake Valhalla Camp** has six tent sites, each suitable for two to five small tents. The camp is tucked away from the lake, far enough to practice Leave No Trace camping but close enough to stroll down and grab water, making it the perfect place to call it a night. To the left (northwest), a spur trail directs pack animals away from water sources and the lakeshore. Two backcountry privies are in this vicinity, one just before the shoreline spur trail to the left (northwest) and one just after it to the right (southeast).

Beyond Lake Valhalla, the PCT enters the forest and continues to provide lake views as it ascends to a small ridge before gradually dropping to **Union Gap** and a junction with **Smithbrook Trail #1590**, 1.8 miles from Lake Valhalla (7.4 miles from Stevens Pass). Don't be surprised to see

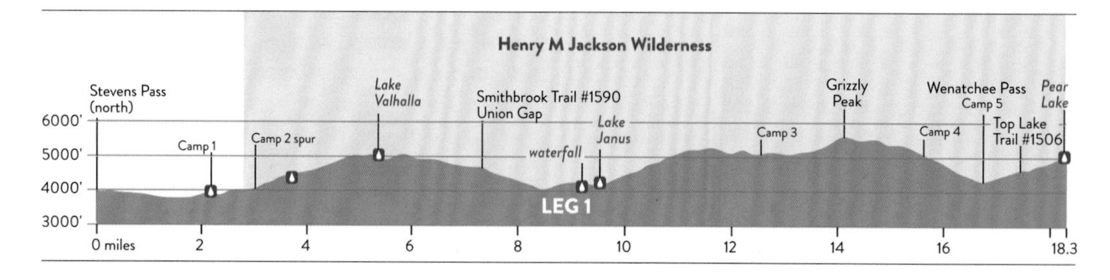

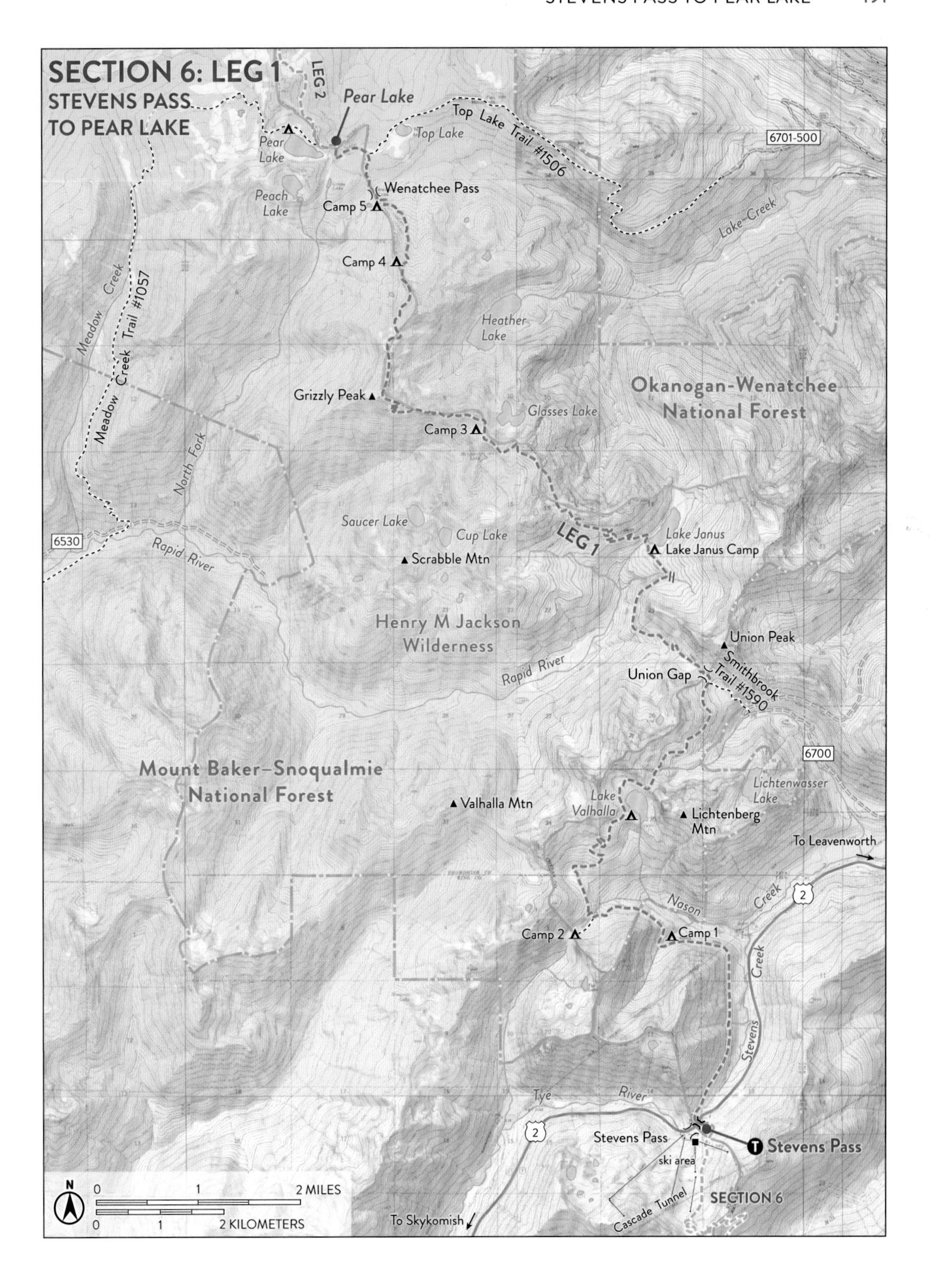

SECTION 6: LEG 1
STEVENS PASS TO PEAR LAKE
LEG 2
Pear Lake
Top Lake Trail #1506
Top Lake
6701-500
Pear Lake
Peach Lake
Wenatchee Pass
Camp 5
Camp 4
Lake Creek
Meadow Creek
Meadow Creek Trail #1057
Heather Lake
Okanogan-Wenatchee National Forest
Grizzly Peak
Glasses Lake
Camp 3
North Fork
Saucer Lake
Cup Lake
LEG 1
Lake Janus
Lake Janus Camp
6530
Rapid River
Scrabble Mtn
Henry M Jackson Wilderness
Union Peak
Rapid River
Smithbrook Trail #1590
Union Gap
6700
Mount Baker–Snoqualmie National Forest
Lichtenwasser Lake
Lake Valhalla
Valhalla Mtn
Lichtenberg Mtn
To Leavenworth
Nason Creek
2
Camp 2
Camp 1
Creek
Stevens
Tye River
2
Stevens Pass
Stevens Pass
ski area
SECTION 6
Cascade Tunnel
To Skykomish
N
0 1 2 MILES
0 1 2 KILOMETERS

Camping opportunities are plentiful near shallow Lake Janus.

HENRY M. JACKSON WILDERNESS

As you amble through the large Douglas-firs and scrubby huckleberries in the Henry M. Jackson Wilderness, you might wonder why this area bears this name. Senator "Scoop" Jackson represented Washington from 1941 until his death in 1983. Nicknamed by his sister for a comic strip character, he fought for causes such as civil rights and energy and natural resource issues. One of his most significant accomplishments was authoring the National Environmental Policy Act, which encouraged harmony between landscapes and the people who use them. Because of its success, the law has been emulated all over the world and is one of the most influential in history. Just after giving a news conference in 1983, at age seventy-one, the senator succumbed to an aortic aneurysm and passed away. The year after that, the Henry M. Jackson Wilderness was created and now protects more than 103,000 acres of federally designated wilderness land.

fresh and happy day hikers, who pour in along this trail from nearby FR 6700.

From Union Gap, the PCT drops into a forested wonderland complete with late-season mushrooms, which push up aggressively through the heavy duff. You may end up squandering some daylight hours on your back with your camera, trying to capture the perfect macro of mushroom gills. At 1.8 miles beyond Union Gap, arrive at a reliable creek complete with a waterfall and rocky dipping pool, perfect for gathering water. You'll want to stock up here or at Lake Janus, because **water is scarce until Pear Lake, more than 9 miles to the north**.

Lake Janus sits 0.4 mile beyond the waterfall. A toilet trail goes off to the left (southwest) and a spur to the lake and lake campsites (**Lake Janus Camp**) goes right (northeast). The largest site is the stock camp, clearly marked with a wooden sign so that you, as a backpacker, can avoid getting your tent too horsey. If the sites via the lake spur trail are full, stay on the PCT for a few yards to find more sites. Lake Janus is a shallow forested lake sprinkled with lily pads—less impressive than Lake Valhalla. All the same, if it's home for the night, you'll enjoy (or not) the frogs that seasonally break out into a chorus so loud that it might trouble the sleep of Skykomish residents, miles away.

From Lake Janus, rock hop across the outlet at the lake's western edge and follow the PCT back into the woods, where it begins periodic switchbacks toward Grizzly Peak. Through the trees to the north, Glacier Peak comes into view and beckons you closer. The forest gives way to talus fields and then crests a saddle, 1.6 miles from Lake Janus. A gentle descent leads to the edge of a marshy meadow complete with seasonal flowers, giving your eyes a break from so much green. At 3 miles from Lake Janus, a waterless, exposed trail-side camp (**Camp 3**) shows up on the left (west) via a small spur, with room for one tent.

GRIZZLY BEARS IN THE NORTH CASCADES

With a name like Grizzly Peak, you might expect the area to be teeming with bears, or more specifically, grizzly bears (*Ursus arctos horribilis*). However, grizzly bears are critically endangered in the North Cascades and extremely rare. In fact, since the mid-1950s biologists have struggled to prove that any of the great beasts still roam here. Each year, thirty to forty reports of grizzly bears are submitted; of those, only about 15 percent are credible enough to send biologists into the field to attempt to capture data. Hundreds of hair samples have been taken and hundreds of paw prints have been studied, but until recently the proof has been fleeting. In 1996, a biologist came upon a bear and her cub in the Glacier Peak Wilderness and created a cast of the adult bear's track, which substantiated the existence of the great bears. That was the first glimmer of hope that grizzlies were returning to the region since federal agencies, more than two decades ago, deemed the habitat exceptional and supportive of such a population.

More recently, in the fall of 2010, a hiker near the upper Cascade River drainage, out of the town of Marblemount, happened upon a large bear and snapped some photos with his point-and-shoot camera. It wasn't until the spring of 2011 that, at the urging of friends, he took his photos to park rangers, who shared them with biologists from all around the country. They concluded that the bear in the photos was, in fact, a grizzly bear. Because the bear was seen so far from the Canada border and so late in the year, biologists surmised that it was likely a nontransient resident of the area.

Unlike black bears, grizzly bears have very distinct humps near their shoulders, round short ears, and a concave dish-like facial profile. Black bears, on the other hand, have a straighter face profile, taller ears, and no shoulder hump. Black bears vary in color—they're not just black—and come in all sizes, so those characteristics are not enough to distinguish the bear's type. The North Cascades is one of six critical recovery areas for grizzlies in the United States, whose mission is to restore populations decimated in the late nineteenth and early twentieth centuries by hunting and trapping.

Researchers believe there are fewer than twenty grizzly bears in the North Cascades and could use your help if you think you've seen one. Start by noting the time of day and determine the characteristics you believe constitute the grizzly variety. Photos, if possible, are helpful, as is quick reporting. Likewise, if you find grizzly bear tracks, take photos and cover them with light branches or other material, ensuring that weather does not disturb them. Mark a GPS way-point, or take clear notes about the tracks' location. Contact the US Fish and Wildlife hotline (1-888-WOLF-BEAR) and report your observations as soon as you're able.

A narrow stretch of trail guides hikers through verdant meadows near Grizzly Peak.

JOHN FRANK STEVENS

Every good story should start "Once upon a time, there was a man named John with a thick chevron mustache." Okay, maybe not that last part, but in this case it does. You see, Mr. Stevens and his stache engineered many things back in the mid-1800s to early 1900s, including the Great Northern Railway and Panama Canal. He was clever, imaginative, and most of all, a brilliant engineer. In 1889, he was hired to design a rail route through the Cascade Mountains, a feat deemed extremely challenging if not impossible. But his technical skills proved equal to the task and he not only forged the railroad line but also created the original Cascade Tunnel, which was west of Stevens Pass. Sadly, the tunnel construction was fraught with difficulty, and on March 1, 1910, an avalanche near the tunnel killed ninety-six people and prompted reconstruction. Despite all that, Mr. Stevens's hard work is commemorated by the pass that bears his name. He died in June 1943, but he and his facial hair live happily ever after in our memory.

Wind through gentle ups and downs along rocky hillsides and amid small heather meadows before coming to the west shoulder of **Grizzly Peak**. While maps make this seem like a destination, it arrives without much fanfare—you might not even know you're here. The PCT follows a ridge and cruises round the edges of an unnamed peak before leading to a series of subalpine meadows that will make your soul smile—you may even want to pull out your lederhosen and start blowing your alpenhorn. Lupine, mountain bistort, and Sitka valerian scent the air with a sweet fragrance, while distant views of Glacier Peak light up the horizon. After all this glory, at 3.1 miles from Camp 3 (15.7 miles from Stevens Pass), reach another waterless camp (**Camp 4**) directly trailside to the left (west), with room for one tent.

The trail then begins a moderate descent, traversing open hillsides and winding through tree pockets to arrive at **Wenatchee Pass**, 1.1 miles beyond Camp 4. Once again, the fanfare is limited and you'll only know you're here by a few telltale signs. A weathered directional sign lying on the ground points hikers north and south on the PCT, while a slopey flat area nearby pretends it's a camp (**Camp 5**). Better camps are ahead at Pear Lake, but this spot would work in a pinch. A seasonal tarn is down a spur trail just behind the camp, but water might be iffy, so carry some if you plan to camp here. The site is large enough for two or three tents, though you'll have to rock-paper-scissors for who gets the flat spot. Then again, when it rains the flat spot becomes a swamp, so don't mind that tree root mackin' on your backside as you roll over at 2:00 a.m.

Climb moderately through intermittent meadows and trees and arrive at a junction with **Top Lake Trail #1506** in 0.8 mile. The ascent continues and delivers you to a junction with **Meadow Creek Trail #1057**, 0.7 mile beyond Top Lake Trail. The access to **Pear Lake** and its campsites (**Pear Lake Camp**) is via Meadow Creek Trail,

As nighttime closes in, Pear Lake looks serene.

A layer of threatening clouds hides the summit of Glacier Peak.

roughly 0.1 mile. Fair warning: The first camp you'll see to the trail's left is huge, lakeside, and tempting, but it's most frequently used by stock. Odds are that even if you don't see any droppings, you'll smell like a horse barn if you pitch your tent here. I speak from experience. Instead, continue past the big camp and follow Meadow Creek Trail toward the northwest side of Pear Lake, 0.2 mile farther, where several desirable camps are nestled under tree clusters.

CAMP-TO-CAMP MILEAGE

Stevens Pass to Camp 1	2.3
Camp 1 to Camp 2	1.1
Camp 2 to Lake Valhalla Camp	2.2
Lake Valhalla Camp to Lake Janus Camp	4.0
Lake Janus Camp to Camp 3	3.0
Camp 3 to Camp 4	3.1
Camp 4 to Camp 5	1.1
Camp 5 to Pear Lake Camp spur	1.5

2 PEAR LAKE TO WHITE PASS

DISTANCE 19.3 miles

ELEVATION GAIN/LOSS
+5000/–3940 feet

HIGH POINT 6010 feet

CONNECTING TRAILS
West Cady Ridge Trail #1054, Pass Creek Trail #1053, Cady Creek Trail #1501, Cady Ridge Trail #1532, North Fork Skykomish Trail #1051, Bald Eagle (Curry Gap) Trail #650, Little Wenatchee Trail #1525, Indian Creek Trail #1502, White River Trail #1507

ON THE TRAIL

From **Pear Lake**, the PCT meanders through berries, juniper, and evergreens before arriving in a rocky gully with giant, and I mean giant, boulders. Half the fun here is figuring out where the trail is taking you as you climb higher and higher and steeper and steeper among the house-sized boulders to crest a ridgeline, 1.6 miles beyond Pear Lake. The trail drops over to the western side of the ridge before it settles into a rolling pattern, keeping you ever so close to the crest. Juniper, heather, huckleberry, mountain ash, and more dance along the trail as the wind whips through these high hills.

The PCT briefly turns west before hair-pinning back to the east and crossing a meadow near the top of an unnamed ridge. Ahead of you, Glacier Peak's snowfields mixed with dark rocky spires will prompt dreams of cookies and cream. Visible, too, is a sneak preview of where you're headed: the meadowy high country, including Saddle Gap and Skykomish Peak beyond. Meadows and talus fields come and go, until you arrive at the first reliable water since Pear Lake, 4 miles back.

A similar landscape continues until you reach the flat grassy meadow known as **Saddle Gap**, 4.7 miles past Pear Lake. From the gap, begin a descent through subalpine hillsides and in 0.3 mile reach a junction with **West Cady Ridge Trail #1054**, arriving from the left (west). The word "Cady" is everywhere in these parts—Cady Ridge, Cady Creek, Cady Pass. Perhaps whoever did the naming was dreaming of having a "caddy" to help share the load. A strong back will have to do as you continue your descent toward Pass Creek, dropping on steep switchbacks into an evergreen forest.

In 1.5 miles beyond the West Cady Ridge Trail junction, the PCT reaches a couple of designated campsites complete with backcountry toilet (**Pass Creek Camp**). In its infancy, this camp was well cared for, but lack of maintenance and continual blowdowns tarnished the area's charm. It is, however, one of the few camps with the creature comforts of a privy and nearby creek. Just past the camp, roughly 200 feet to the left, is the lightly used **Pass Creek Trail #1053,** heading northwest toward Bald Eagle Mountain. And 0.1 mile beyond

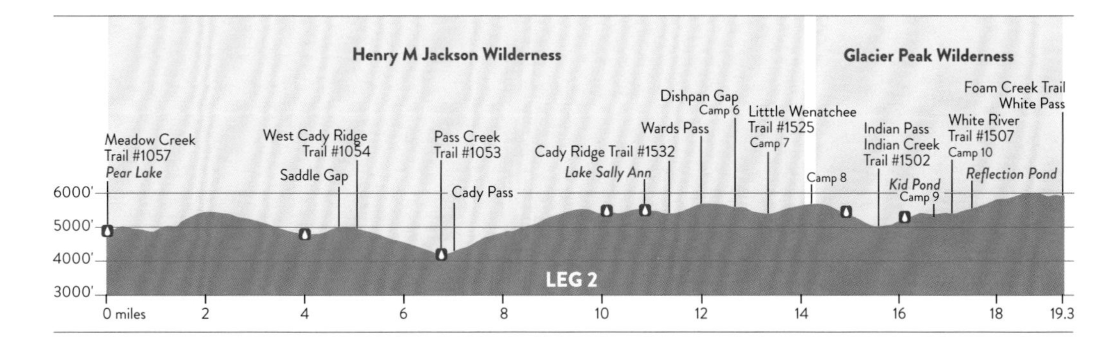

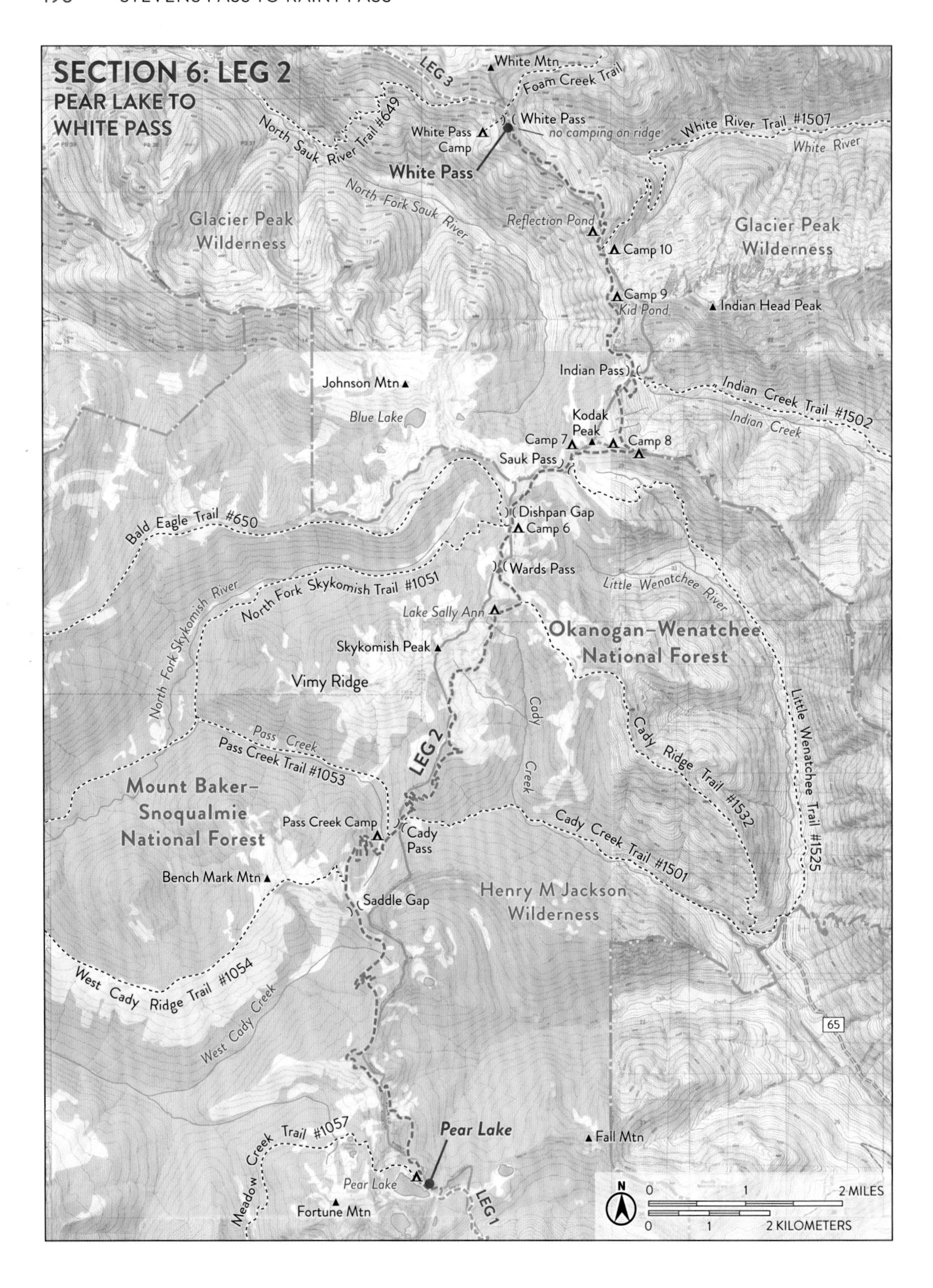
SECTION 6: LEG 2
PEAR LAKE TO WHITE PASS
LEG 3
White Mtn
Foam Creek Trail
North Sauk River Trail #649
White Pass Camp
White Pass
no camping on ridge
White River Trail #1507
White River
White Pass
North Fork Sauk River
Glacier Peak Wilderness
Reflection Pond
Camp 10
Glacier Peak Wilderness
Camp 9
Kid Pond
Indian Head Peak
Indian Pass
Johnson Mtn
Indian Creek Trail #1502
Indian Creek
Blue Lake
Kodak Peak
Camp 7
Camp 8
Sauk Pass
Dishpan Gap
Camp 6
Bald Eagle Trail #650
Wards Pass
North Fork Skykomish Trail #1051
Little Wenatchee River
North Fork Skykomish River
Lake Sally Ann
Okanogan–Wenatchee National Forest
Skykomish Peak
Vimy Ridge
Cady Creek
Little Wenatchee Trail #1525
Cady Ridge Trail #1532
Pass Creek
Pass Creek Trail #1053
LEG 2
Mount Baker–Snoqualmie National Forest
Pass Creek Camp
Cady Pass
Cady Creek Trail #1501
Bench Mark Mtn
Saddle Gap
Henry M Jackson Wilderness
West Cady Ridge Trail #1054
West Cady Creek
65
Meadow Creek Trail #1057
Pear Lake
Fall Mtn
Pear Lake
Fortune Mtn
LEG 1
N
0 1 2 MILES
0 1 2 KILOMETERS

Fragrant flower fields and pastoral hillsides greet hikers near White Pass (Glacier Peak Wilderness).

that is the reliable Pass Creek. This clear, cold stream is a tasty place to wet your whistle. The next reliable water is 3.6 miles farther, so take what you need.

What goes down must go up, so rock-hop across Pass Creek and begin gently ascending, now in the tunnel of green, for 0.5 mile to **Cady Pass** and **Cady Creek Trail #1501**, which leads right (east). A forested camp here has been used often but is not optimal—it's covered in forest debris and blowdowns. Knowing it's there is useful, if your aching feet are in dire need of a rest, but most folks find the gumption to continue on to the mind-blowingly gorgeous Lake Sally Ann. Switchbacks continue steeply as you huff and puff your way out of the evergreens to arrive back in meadowy terrain.

In roughly 2.3 miles from Cady Pass, the trail reaches an unnamed saddle and the grade gives your heart and calves a break. At this point, the PCT begins traversing the lower subalpine flanks of Skykomish Peak, with views to the east of Cady Ridge. Marmots and pikas whistle and squeak as you walk through their rocky, flowered homes. In 3.6 miles beyond Pass Creek, reach the first reliable creek, flowing through boulders that make fine places to sit. Lewis's monkeyflower brings pops of pink to the creek banks, while marmots crash out on nearby rocks, sleeping with one eye open and watching you as you get water or grab a bite.

In 0.6 mile beyond the creek, arrive at the exquisite **Lake Sally Ann** (10.8 miles from Pear Lake). Even if you're just passing through, you'll want to stop, dig out your camera, quietly watch

the jumping fish, and simply swoon. Those lucky enough to camp here (**Lake Sally Ann Camp**) will not be alone, since grandeur like this must be shared. It's popular but generally not overly so, because stock are prohibited. Nestled in a subalpine basin, surrounded by green meadows and low-growing trees, the lake brings a peace that seeps into your very bones. Established campsites are tucked away from the lake in tree pockets to the east, along with a backcountry privy. Campfires are prohibited and for good reason. If this place burned, we'd all have to join Smokey the Bear in a fit of tears. Get water here, as the next 3.7 miles are seasonally dry.

Continue past Lake Sally Ann, traversing more blissful and green open hills until you reach a junction in 0.5 mile with yet another Cady, this time **Cady Ridge Trail #1532**, heading right (east). From here all the way to White Pass and beyond, you'll be walking through divine subalpine meadows, which will entertain your eyes and capture your heart. Glacier Peak stands tall and proud from vista to vista, while wildflowers offer lively colors near your feet. The PCT turns gently northwest before several switchbacks lead you to **Wards Pass**. Because the landscape looks so similar, it's difficult to tell which pass is which as you continue traversing the ridgelines and one blends into the next.

In 0.6 mile from Wards Pass, arrive at **Dishpan Gap**, where a couple of trails converge. Directly to the left, **North Fork Skykomish Trail #1051** heads west, **Bald Eagle Trail #650** goes north, and the PCT angles slightly right to the northeast. Two campsites (**Camp 6**) are here, but the only water in sight is in murky seasonal tarns, which look sketchy at best. Filter if you're brave, or be on the safe side and carry water if you intend to camp here. The PCT continues in alluring high open country as you make your way to **Sauk Pass**. Without much fanfare, it comes and goes, and you're left scratching your head wondering if that was it.

At 1 mile past Dishpan Gap, reach a junction with **Little Wenatchee Trail #1525**, which drops southeast to the headwaters of the Little Wenatchee River. Roughly 300 feet beyond the junction, find waterless **Camp 7**, with a small site suitable for one tent. In 0.7 mile from the junction, two beautiful campsites (**Camp 8**) overlook the high country, accessed via spur trails to the left (northwest) and right (southeast) of the PCT. Just after, the **Glacier Peak Wilderness** welcomes you with a squatty sign on a cut-off log. The sign, placed in the open green mountain meadow, makes a fantastic photo souvenir.

The trail then begins its descent toward Indian Pass and in 0.2 mile from the wilderness sign crosses your first usually reliable water in a while, a small seasonal trickle amid the hillside vegetation. For those camped on the ridge, this is the closest water. Another seasonal creek dribbles along 0.2 mile from the last, so take your pick, but get water if it's flowing, because stagnant water is more prevalent as you move forward. The evergreens increase on your descent, although the short growing season limits their height and the subalpine feeling persists.

In 1.3 miles past the wilderness sign (15.6 miles from Pear Lake), the PCT reaches a flat bench known as **Indian Pass**, also a junction with the lightly used **Indian Creek Trail #1502**. Stop for a break if necessary, or keep 'er rollin'. The trail traverses a wildflower hillside and overlooks a valley with layers of gray mountain peaks, looking like fine art. In 0.7 mile beyond Indian Pass, arrive at a trickling creek, dribbling from the hillside above, which, even into late season, usually flows. Besides tarns and ponds, this is the last running water for at least 3 miles.

Just 0.3 mile beyond the creek, the muddy **Kid Pond** shows up to the right (east) and immediately past that, to the right (north), is a small campsite (**Camp 9**) suitable for one tent. Neither the camp nor Kid Pond inspire poetry; if possible, hang tight for better camping opportunities ahead. In 0.5 mile, reach an intersection with **White River Trail #1507**, where there's also a small mediocre campsite (**Camp 10**), located roughly 30 feet to

Opposite: *A hiker makes his way through the lush, iridescent hillsides in Glacier Peak Wilderness.*

Rising like a grandiose fortress, Glacier Peak is the most isolated of all the volcanoes in Washington State.

the east (right). Water is not available, so carry some if you plan to camp here.

From the junction, climb gradually for 0.4 mile and pass **Reflection Pond** to the left (west). Larger, clearer and deeper than Kid Pond, Reflection Pond has year-round, stagnant water and several campsites on its western perimeter (**Reflection Pond Camp**). Water should be treated all along the PCT, but it's even more important with standing water. Parasites passing through the paunch can be a serious buzzkill and might end your PCT party.

Gentler climbing takes you through mountain meadows and peaks so grand that you might get misty. Obtain a ridgeline and continue to wander, watch, and walk. Grasshoppers jump from leaf to leaf among colorful wildflowers, while marmots scramble up hillsides foraging for food and sound alarms alerting all to your presence. The White Chuck and Suiattle glaciers to the northeast draw your eyes, while behind you Indian Head Peak shows off its jagged summit. Rolling green hills tempt you to twirl, dance, or holler for echoes. This landscape will simply make you happy, so take it all in with deep, soul-cleansing breaths. This is why we hike!

The area around **White Pass** and farther north to Red Pass is some of the most magnificent terrain in Washington, and pictures don't do it justice. The subalpine wildflower meadows of the high ridgeline are so engaging you'll want to stay all summer, or for a night or two. The Forest Service prohibits camping on the ridgeline around White Pass, but in 1.8 miles from Reflection Pond, a well-signed spur to the left directs you downhill 200 yards to designated campsites (**White Pass Camp**), complete with a backcountry privy. Seasonal snowmelt provides the camp's water, a fickle source in late season. To be safe, BYOW (bring your own water) or just keep walking north on the PCT for 0.2 mile to a dribble coming off the hillside.

Roughly 150 feet beyond the camp spur trail is a trail leading right (northeast), signed for **Foam Creek**. Most maps don't show this trail, but it lives! If time permits, Foam Creek basin makes a fun side trip, introducing you to even more meadows and wildflowers at the base of White Mountain. This side trail eventually peters out into a climbers' approach to Glacier Peak. If you follow the trail to the top of the ridge, the views of Glacier Peak will knock your boots off, laces and all.

CAMP-TO-CAMP MILEAGE

Pear Lake Camp to Pass Creek Camp	6.5
Pass Creek Camp to Lake Sally Ann Camp	4.3
Lake Sally Ann Camp to Camp 6	1.8
Camp 6 to Camp 7	1.0
Camp 7 to Camp 8	0.7
Camp 8 to Camp 9	2.3
Camp 9 to Camp 10	0.5
Camp 10 to Reflection Pond Camp	0.4
Reflection Pond Camp to White Pass Camp	1.8

3 WHITE PASS TO MICA LAKE

DISTANCE 19 miles

ELEVATION GAIN/LOSS
+5480/–6060 feet

HIGH POINT 6580 feet

CONNECTING TRAILS
North Fork Sauk Trail #649

ON THE TRAIL

From **White Pass**, bear left (northwest) at the Foam Creek Trail junction and continue on the PCT as it traverses the now familiar open hillsides of wildflowers and buzzing insects. To the west, the summits of snowy Sloan and Bedal peaks grab your attention, as will any weather systems headed to the mountains from the coast. Three small seasonal creeks (all reliable even into late season), percolate down the hillsides before the next trail junction.

In 0.5 mile from White Pass, pass a junction with **North Fork Sauk Trail #649**, which goes left (southwest). This is the only maintained connecting trail in the area and is a reliable way to get to a forest road, should you need to bail or choose a different stopping or starting location on this stretch. Other connecting trails and forest roads have been washed out and obliterated by storms dating back to 2003. This trail and the forest road (FR 49) are well maintained and can deliver you to the closest town, Darrington, if you have arranged for transportation.

From the North Fork Sauk Trail junction, the PCT heads northwest and in roughly 1.2 miles reaches meadowy hillsides populated with gray granite talus, a more alpine landscape. Just beyond, the trail turns to the north and comes to **Camp 11** on the left (west), downhill approximately 75 feet. Getting there requires tricky footwork over boulders, but the site is well established and has great views. If the snow is gone, there won't likely be water, so bring your own.

Reach **Red Pass** 0.1 mile from the camp (1.8 miles from White Pass), as the PCT turns northeast and gives you a view toward White Mountain and the talus fields below. To the northeast, Glacier Peak stands proud and tall and you realize just how close you are! Even though the area is flat and open, camping at Red Pass proper is prohibited. From the pass, begin your descent in the glacial deposits, switching back through stone and using extra caution—pay attention to your feet, or you'll feel like you're on a skateboard. Everywhere you look is stunning! Glacier Peak is laden with glaciers at every angle, while White Mountain's snowfields send cascades of water down barren hillsides. To the left (northwest), the maroon shoulders of the White Chuck Cinder Cone are truly a vision.

At 1.6 miles beyond Red Pass, enter the edge of an evergreen forest and reach **Cinder Cone Camp**, located on a small rise to the right (northeast), with room for two small tents. From this point nearly all the way to Mica Lake, you'll have plenty of water thanks to creeks, tributaries, and rivers that surround the trail (see this leg's profile). Cinder Cone Camp is my personal favorite on clear days due to the sweeping views of Glacier Peak from your campsite's private "porch." A broken outhouse sign sits along the PCT nearby, but the outhouse has made itself scarce. I hunted high and low for the stinky little rascal and had no luck.

Camp 12, with room for two small tents, is in the trees 0.2 mile north of Cinder Cone Camp. It has some privacy, but views of the volcano are limited. During busy summer months, if the first camps you come to are full, keep descending—there are plenty.

Leave the high country and drop steeply at times to a green tunnel of old-growth evergreens and so many creek crossings and camping opportunities you'll lose count. Almost all the creeks have camps near them, so if you're sleepy, you're in luck. In a little less than 1 mile from Camp 12, three more campsites (**Camp 13**) show up next to a tributary creek. Continue your descent through so-green-it-hurts moss, scrub, and trees, rock hopping over a tributary before arriving at a crossing of the **White Chuck River**, roughly 1.1 miles past Camp 13.

On October 12, 2003, a raging storm obliterated the old bridge, knocking it in the river and twisting it sideways. A sturdy new bridge is downstream from where the old one was, safely shuttling you across the glacier-fed roar. The old bridge, wedged in the rocks at the waterfall upstream, is a sobering reminder of how powerful mountain storms can be.

More mossy forest and woody duff greet your feet on the other side as you carry onward for 1 mile to **Baekos Creek** (6.6 miles from White Pass) and two lovely forested campsites (**Baekos Camp**), one before and one after the creek. Baekos Creek is a moody, glacier-fed flow that originates from Glacier Peak and has been known to take out a bridge, like a bad driver mowing down safety cones. Thankfully, a new bridge built a few years ago has been sturdy and trustworthy thus far. Because the creek is silty, if you're staying at Baekos Camp, get water at one of the many fresh trickles beyond Red Pass before you arrive. Next up, 1.7 miles from Baekos Creek, is an unnamed tributary crossed via foot log, with several more campsites nearby (**Camp 14**). There are so many campsites along this leg that it's hard to decide which spot is best.

At 0.2 mile past Camp 14, reach a junction where a tree sign announces **White Chuck Road** and **White Chuck Trail #643**. Before 2003, this trail was a primary connector to the White Chuck Road and Kennedy Hot Springs. But that year's floods annihilated the trail, washed out the road, and wiped the hot springs off the map. This trail is now decommissioned, even though most maps still

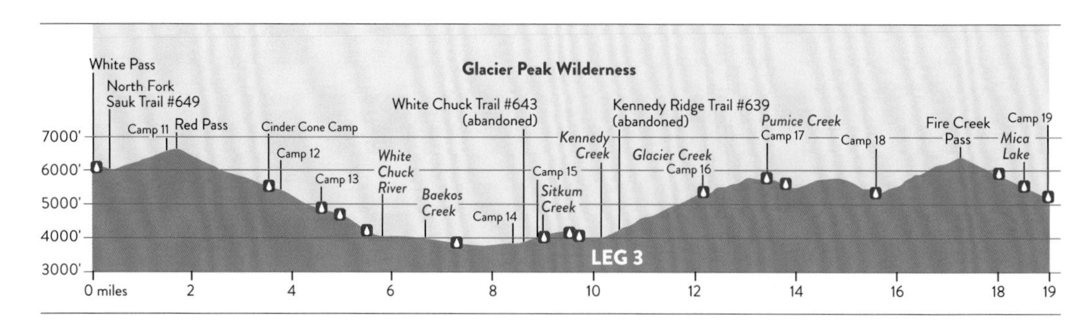

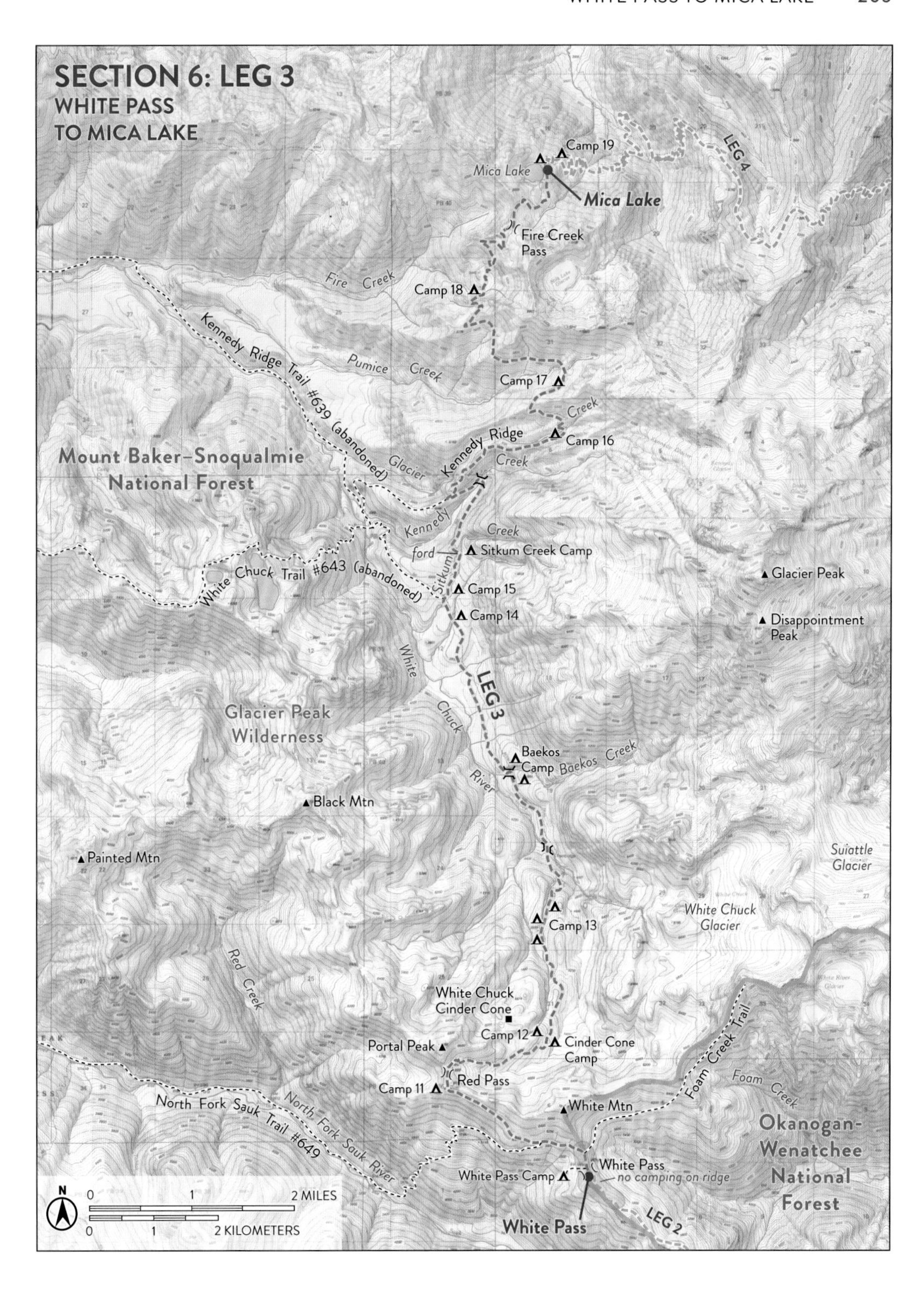
SECTION 6: LEG 3
WHITE PASS
TO MICA LAKE
Camp 19
Mica Lake
Mica Lake
LEG 4
Fire Creek
Pass
Fire Creek
Camp 18
Kennedy Ridge Trail #639 (abandoned)
Pumice Creek
Camp 17
Creek
Kennedy Ridge
Camp 16
Glacier Creek
Mount Baker–Snoqualmie
National Forest
Kennedy
Creek
ford
Sitkum Creek Camp
Sitkum
White Chuck Trail #643 (abandoned)
Camp 15
Camp 14
Glacier Peak
Disappointment
Peak
White
LEG 3
Chuck
Glacier Peak
Wilderness
Baekos
Camp
Baekos Creek
River
Black Mtn
Painted Mtn
Suiattle
Glacier
White Chuck
Glacier
Camp 13
Red Creek
White Chuck
Cinder Cone
Camp 12
Cinder Cone
Camp
Portal Peak
Foam Creek Trail
Foam Creek
Red Pass
Camp 11
North Fork Sauk Trail #649
North Fork Sauk River
White Mtn
Okanogan-
Wenatchee
National
Forest
White Pass
no camping on ridge
White Pass Camp
White Pass
LEG 2
N
0 1 2 MILES
0 1 2 KILOMETERS

Bridges, like this one over Kennedy Creek, are prone to washouts during floods or rapid snow melts. Use extra care when crossing bridges that look damaged.

show it. Due to hazardous conditions, this trail no longer serves as an entry to or exit from the PCT.

Reach **Camp 15**, nestled in the forest with room for one tent and not much else, 0.3 mile past the White Chuck Trail junction. There's no water nearby, so bring it with you or skip this spot and camp just a short distance farther.

In 0.5 mile past the trail junction, you'll find **Sitkum Creek** and several established campsites (**Sitkum Creek Camp**), along with a backcountry privy. Like nearly all camps in the White Chuck Valley, this one is in deep forest with a purring creek nearby. Crossing this particular creek in rainy weather can be as dangerous as trying to hug a rabid wolf; if possible, wait until the squalls have stopped. If the crossing is hazardous, walk downstream 20 yards to a huge log that provides a sketchy-but-doable crossing to the other side. Or simply wade—the odds of something going sideways stack up six one way, a half dozen the other. Just take your time, focus, breathe, self-talk words of confidence, have faith, and go for it. If the weather is decent, lucky you—rock hop your way across with few worries.

Cross several more creeks, including many that aren't glacier-fed, as the PCT continues northbound to the chocolate-milk-colored **Kennedy Creek** in 1 mile. This cantankerous creek has been the subject of a recent volcanic tantrum, including flows of mixed snow, glacial ice, and mud—known as lahars—that have eroded banks into high slopes of loose sand. If that big white snow cone you've been circumnavigating didn't give it away, you're in volcano country and this creek is an

Opposite: *North of Red Pass, Glacier Peak looks over abundant, luxurious meadows as the trail descends into the forest.*

The sun sets over Glacier Peak on a warm day.

in-your-face reminder. At present, the log bridge over the creek is broken in the very center, making a V shape. It's still anchored solidly on both sides and seems resolute in its mission to get you across with a bit of adventure in your step and "wow" in your photos.

Once across, the trail makes its way up to **Kennedy Ridge** on narrow hillside traverses that have little margin for error. If you plan to look around, stop first. In 0.4 mile beyond Kennedy Creek, arrive at a tree sign pointing toward Kennedy Hot Springs and White Chuck Road via **Kennedy Ridge Trail #639**. The trail still exists, but it hasn't been maintained for years, so getting in or out using this old path could be an interesting adventure to say the least. The hot springs and their outbuilding are completely gone, with no trace that they ever existed. In 2011, FR 23 (White Chuck Road) was reopened to a junction near FR 27, adding roughly 5 miles of road walking to reach car access. It's good to know this trail and outside access are here, but they're best used only in emergencies.

Continue climbing, steeply now up the ridgeline, and in 1.7 miles arrive at **Glacier Creek** and a picturesque small campsite with room for one tent (**Camp 16**) to the west, with clear water running nearby. You're in the high country now, surrounded by wildflower meadows, huckleberries, and views. You'll see the trail traverse you'll soon be crossing, visible between pockets of evergreens. In 1.2 miles from Glacier Creek (13.4 miles from White Pass), arrive at another small campsite (**Camp 17**), with high-country views and the flowing water of nearby Pumice Creek **O**. The creek can flow heavily, but is usually a rock hop in summer months.

The subalpine country is off-limits to campfires, so make your peace with the rules and if time and gumption allow, break down any verboten fire rings you find. Off to the PCT's east, Kennedy Peak on Glacier's northwest side is so magnificent that it hurts. Churning with rivers of ice and volcanic fury, the slopes of the mighty volcano are a treat for the eyes and a shampoo for the soul. Take it all in, and then continue your traverse in emerald meadows to a crossing of a Fire Creek tributary, 2.2 miles from Pumice Creek. Marmots whistle and peek at you from the tops of rocks and near dirt burrows as they flit around gathering wildflowers and leaves for snacks. Chartreuse moss on the rocks near the creek, mixed with bright magenta Lewis's monkeyflower wrapped in dark green mountain heather, make a colorful vision. **Camp 18** is to the left (west) just beyond the creek, with room for one tent.

The views just keep getting better as you switchback steeply up to the alpine zone of **Fire Creek Pass**, 1.7 miles beyond Camp 18. An emergency-only-style campsite is just before the pass but has no water and is very exposed. When you arrive at the pass, stop and take a long look. You're perched on one of the highest ridges from Stevens Pass to Rainy Pass, and the panoramic views stretch from mountain highs to valley grandeur. A giant arrow made of stones between two cairns points the way north as the PCT begins its interesting geological descent through layers of metamorphic rock marked by banded dikes, which are fascinating to investigate. I'm no geologist, but I'd be willing to guess that some of the mineral is mica. Listen for the clicking and clacking of mountain-goat hooves near the snow patches and amid the stone gardens all around you.

At 0.5 mile from the pass, cross a trickling brook of snowmelt. Marmots peek at you from their rocky burrows as you continue switchbacking down the exposed slopes. In the far distance, across the valley in front of you, a curious zigzag in an avalanche chute makes you stop to question its purpose. When you figure out that you're looking at the continuation of the PCT, making tight switchbacks

A foggy evening settles in at misty Mica Lake.

up from the very deep valley, it sends a jolt of fear to your quads. Thankfully, when you actually get there, it's not as bad as it looks from this vista.

In 1.2 miles from Fire Creek Pass, arrive at the peaceful, rock-strewn shores of teal-green **Mica Lake**. This alpine lake tucked high in a rocky cirque is a vision and a great place to stop for water, lunch, or photos. Don't even think of swimming unless you brought your wet suit, because even on hot sunny days, the water is so cold you might end up a shivering blob on the shoreline (which is actually kind of fun if you're into such things). One exposed campsite (**Mica Lake Camp**), with room for two small tents, is near the lake's outlet. If the spot is taken or you want a more protected spot, keep rolling past Mica Lake and in 0.5 mile, find a campsite with room for one or two small tents (**Camp 19**), located on a grassy bench before your descent to Milk Creek.

CAMP-TO-CAMP MILEAGE

White Pass to Camp 11	1.7
Camp 11 to Cinder Cone Camp	1.7
Cinder Cone Camp to Camp 12	0.2
Camp 12 to Camp 13	0.9
Camp 13 to Baekos Camp	2.1
Baekos Camp to Camp 14	1.7
Camp 14 to Camp 15	0.5
Camp 15 to Sitkum Creek Camp	0.3
Sitkum Creek Camp to Camp 16	3.1
Camp 16 to Camp 17	1.2
Camp 17 to Camp 18	2.2
Camp 18 to Mica Lake Camp	2.9
Mica Lake Camp to Camp 19	0.5

ERUPTIONS AND LAHARS: HARDY, HAR, HAR

Traveling through Glacier Peak's volcano country is no laughing matter. While less known than some of Washington's other volcanoes, Glacier Peak is an active volcano and has produced some of the state's largest historical eruptions. In layperson's terms, it could still throw down some hurt. That said, the odds of volcanic outbursts taking place while you're happily hiking the PCT are very slim, and you needn't hike with fear or trepidation. Awareness of the what-ifs, however, is a good idea.

Lahars: The biggest risk is an event known as a lahar, which would happen near a creek or river. Lahars occur when rainfall, volcanic activity, or warming temperatures cause glaciers or glacier dams to break and shake material loose. The energy and force of all that debris and water shoots downhill into the river valley below. As the flow moves along, boulders, soil, and other glacial remains may pick up hitchhiking trees, campsites, bridges, or even complete hillsides. Signs of lahars may include shaking ground, a strong gust of wind coming down the mountain, rapidly rising water, water coloration changes, a deep guttural roaring noise, or strong onset of the smell of earthy soil. If any of these warnings occur, get to higher ground immediately. Once you're at least 160 feet above a valley floor, you'll be in what is considered the safety zone.

Eruptions: Throughout history, Glacier Peak has been known for having tephra eruptions, the last of which was roughly three hundred years ago. During most of these eruptions, lava domes have extruded on the volcano's flanks or summit and then collapsed to produce ash clouds and pyroclastic flows (think Mount St. Helens). It's very unlikely that in our lifetime we'll see Glacier Peak blow her lid, but if she did, there would be signs of her getting grumpy long before it happened and, thankfully, scientists are paying attention. The University of Washington's geophysics program, in cooperation with the US Geological Survey, watches for increased earthquake activity that might indicate a future volcanic burp or explosion. With watchdogs keeping a close eye out for our safety, enjoy the romp through Glacier Peak's wilderness and admire the strength and power of her snowy flanks without worry.

An immense smoky cloud towers above Glacier Peak during wildfire season.

4 MICA LAKE TO SUIATTLE RIVER

DISTANCE 23.5 miles

ELEVATION GAIN/LOSS +5960/–8740 feet

HIGH POINT 5970 feet

CONNECTING TRAILS Suiattle River Trail #784

ON THE TRAIL

Just below **Mica Lake**, a flat bench has at least one campsite **(Camp 19)**, and a nearby year-round creek makes for a pleasant place to overnight. From here, the PCT takes you down, down, down, dropping like a rock into the Milk Creek valley far below. In 2.1 miles from Mica Lake, arrive at an avalanche swath complete with babbling brooks that serve up an icy beverage.

The trail precariously switchbacks along a somewhat unstable hillside. Blowdowns and detours are common due to washouts, landslides, and erosion. The remoteness of this stretch of the PCT also makes it challenging to maintain and so it's often brushy, adding to the possibility of doing an unexpected triple toe loop. Watch your footing carefully, especially in wet weather. The Milk Creek valley and the next valley over, the Suiattle River valley, have been subject to dramatic storm damage. In 2009, the Milk Creek bridge was rebuilt at a crossing 0.5 mile downstream from the former bridge site. The old trail is still visible heading up the hill on the opposite bank.

Continue descending very steeply and at 3.8 miles beyond Mica Lake, and just before the new Milk Creek bridge, note a small spur trail leading uphill to the right in a patch of evergreens, which delivers you to a small forested camp with room for one tent **(Camp 20)**. **Milk Creek** is just that, milk-colored, glacier-fed, roaring, and difficult to get down to. If you camp here, bring water or be prepared for a little grit in your drink.

Cross Milk Creek bridge and 0.1 mile afterward, arrive at a junction with unmaintained Milk Creek Trail #790. This trail, too, was a casualty of mountain storms and no longer provides access to or from the PCT. Next, a series of short switchbacks gives way to a southeastern traverse in brushy riparian flora. Glacier Peak shows off Vista and

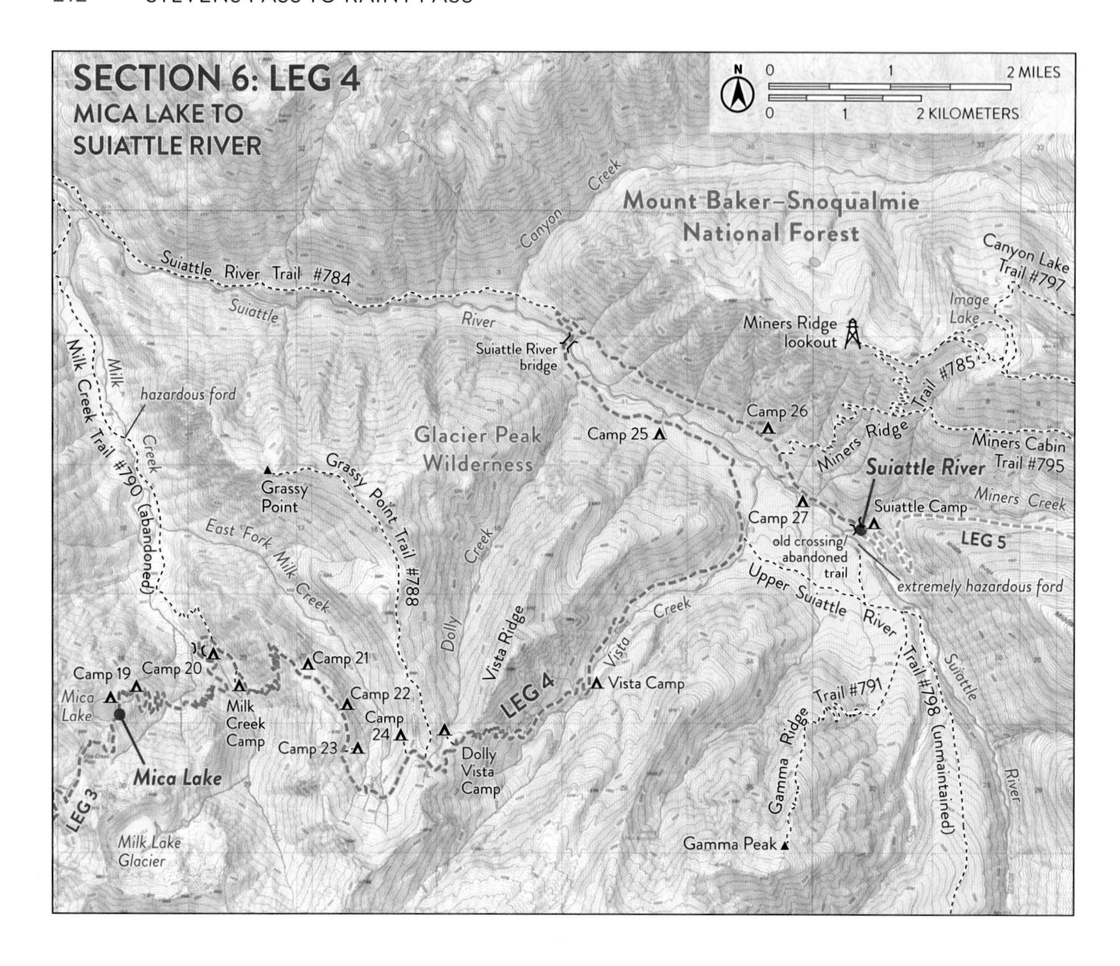

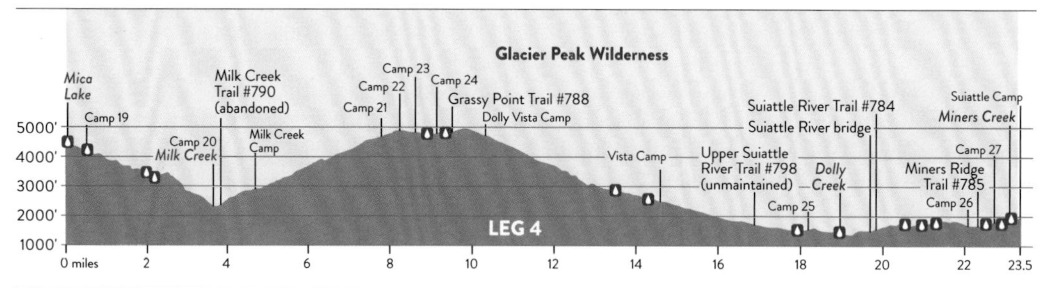

Ptarmigan glaciers nestled deep against her dark stone flanks—a spectacle to behold!

In 0.8 mile beyond the abandoned Milk Creek Trail junction, arrive at a very obvious, but unsigned, side trail heading downhill to the right (south), leading to four very desirable campsites (**Milk Creek Camp**) and a backcountry privy. You have the moody Milk Creek and the work of the Forest Service to thank for this little hillside camping gem; this was the old trail before it was rerouted. Bring water if you camp here, unless you don't mind the silt of Milk Creek.

Sweeping views make it hard not to stop every few steps and snap a picture near Grassy Point Trail.

Just before the PCT begins more switchbacks, a curious red sign is bolted to a tree to the right, reading "Together we took the paths that run west of the moon and east of the sun, dark warriors cache, 1966–1980, My Great Hart." There's some mystery shrouding this sign, since no one, including Forest Service personnel, knows who put it there or what it represents. Several theories exist, including its being a tribute to someone who has passed on, using a version of words from a song in the Tolkien *Lord of the Rings* films. Another theory suggests that perhaps Frodo himself decided to decorate. Whatever the case, it's curious and engaging—words to ponder as you climb the rocky switchbacks you saw from way back near Mica Lake. When you stop for a break, look back and see if you can find Fire Creek Pass and Mica Lake tucked into the alpine landscape to the southwest. Thankfully, the switchbacks don't feel as bad as they look.

Once at the top, marmots whistle to greet you as they waddle through juniper, lupine, and grasses in the subalpine terrain along the gentle ridge. In 4 miles from the Milk Creek bridge (7.8 miles from Mica Lake), find **Camp 21** to the left (northeast).

The camp is waterless, but it's flat and well used. If you camp here and nature calls, be sure to double check for ground bees that make their homes in downed logs and woody duff. I learned this lesson the hard way and came out from behind a tree flailing, hollering, and swatting until my nerves calmed down.

The trail climbs gently through subalpine meadows and boulder fields and begins crossing a series of grand alpine cirques. As you're planning your itinerary, **consider camping in this area**. The vastness of the high ridge, evening alpenglow on the stone peaks, and subalpine surroundings make this a desirable place to spend the night.

The next camp (**Camp 22**) is 0.6 mile past Camp 21, to the left (northeast) in a clump of trees. The camp is small and waterless, but it makes a good place to see stars, and I don't mean the kind you see if you stand up too quickly from staking your tent. Another small camp, with room for one small tent (**Camp 23**), is just 0.4 mile beyond, to the left (northeast) along a short spur. Water is 0.3 mile farther north along the PCT. Pink Lewis's monkey-flower flourishes near mossy rocks as you traverse a series of small babbling brooks, which delightfully giggle as they flow from the snowfields above.

In 0.4 mile from Camp 23, a spur trail to the left (north) leads to another camp (**Camp 24**) in the East Fork Milk Creek basin, where water abounds. This camp is a little larger than most, with room for two or three small tents, provided you don't mind listening to your hiking partners snore. More small creeks dribble off the high peaks as the PCT then turns north and arrives at an unsigned junction with **Grassy Point Trail #788** to the left (north). This unmaintained and lightly used trail rolls along a ridgeline to the north, eventually petering out near the north face of Grassy Point. A few camp spots are along this trail, but they're not used often.

The PCT keeps going on its hillside traverse, with plenty of high-country views as well as marmots that spy on you. The trail begins a long set of switchbacks and after a couple of zigzags, arrives at

TRYING TO WADDLE THE SUIATTLE

Before 2003, the PCT turned southeast just past the Upper Suiattle River Trail and worked its way down to the Suiattle River. Back then, the sturdy wooden crossing, known as the Skyline Bridge, was a work of art, meticulously crafted and well used. Then, on October 17, 2003, a devastating storm dropped 10 inches of rain in 24 hours, damaging 45 miles of the PCT and wiping out the bridge, leaving no evidence of its existence. In subsequent years, as a temporary fix, hikers detoured to the east side of Glacier Peak over some rough terrain and walked approximately 3 miles on a dirt road. Some hikers, determined to not detour, crossed the dangerous and swift Suiattle River on a precarious log.

During this time, plans were made to replace the bridge downstream approximately 0.5 mile from the original crossing at a site surveyors deemed fit. But in November 2006, another massive storm triggered a large flood that significantly widened the river, dashing any hope of a new bridge at the selected site—the builders were back to square one. A helicopter was summoned to fly over the area in hopes of locating a site that might meet all the requirements for a new crossing. Luckily, a spot was found, this time with bedrock on both ends to secure the crossing, hopefully permanently.

Completed in 2011, after nearly eight years of work, a new and beautiful 270-foot bridge now escorts hikers across the furious Suiattle River. The bad news is that the new route adds 4.8 miles to the PCT in this area. The good news is that it has opened up some breathtaking terrain, taking you through mammoth old growth conifers larger than almost any in Washington State. Trust me when I say these giants will make you feel like a speck of dust. Get out your wide-angle lens!

Opposite: *Primeval giants soar above the new stretch of trail near the Suiattle River, showing off some of the most colossal conifers in the entire state.*

Purple posies and a dancing creeklet near Milk Creek make for a picture-perfect scene.

the well-used **Dolly Vista Camp** to the left (northwest), 1.3 miles from Camp 24 (10.5 miles from Mica Lake). The camp has seasonal and somewhat unreliable water, room for three small tents, a pit toilet, and so many huckleberries surrounding it that you'll burst. For a couple of years in a row now, wasps have made their home near the toilet—give a close look before you reign upon the throne.

More switchbacks take you down out of the high country and into forest that alternates with brushy riparian hillsides. Because of steep pitches and the remoteness of the area, blowdowns make themselves at home on the trail, and most years you'll encounter an obstacle course of over-and-unders. This descent seems to take forever, so try to fall deep in thought to pass the time. In 2.9 miles from Dolly Vista Camp, a creek flows for your drinking pleasure. In another 0.8 mile, another creek crosses the trail. Water, water everywhere!

In 3.9 miles from Dolly Vista Camp, arrive at the heavily wooded **Vista Camp** to the trail's right. For nonsilted water, backtrack 0.2 mile to a brook across the PCT. Better yet, stop on your way to camp. Vista Camp is large enough for three small tents and is set to a river soundtrack of white noise, not a bad way to fall asleep. You're now in the beating heart of the Suiattle River valley and walking through a tunnel of giant evergreens. Someone took the time to count the rings on one fallen old tree and penned a faded "658 years old" near the top of the cut. Oh the years this tree has seen!

In 2.3 miles beyond Vista Camp (16.7 miles from Mica Lake), arrive at a junction with unmaintained **Upper Suiattle River Trail #798** to the right. This is the old PCT route. As you continue on the new trail, admire its construction. In 1.6 miles from the junction, cross a small bridge over a seasonal dribble and a small one-tent trailside camp (**Camp 25**) to the left (south).

After the camp, the **grove of giant trees** begins and you'll want to stop often to stare. Thanks to the temperate climate and little fire danger, these

SASQUATCH AND SPIRITS

Thump. Thump. Thump. "Did you hear that?" my husband calmly asked as I looked around wondering the same thing. We listened for breaking sticks, for rustling, for other indications of animals, but the forest was silent. The thumps repeated and sounded as if something large was repeatedly stomping. I'd heard this sound many times before when hiking, the result of an elk crashing through the forest. In those cases, more noise followed. What could the powerful stomping possibly be, we wondered?

We were on the new stretch of PCT near the ancient grove of trees by the Suiattle River. Suddenly, a pinecone hit me in the head. "Ouch!" I shouted. Then another one landed nearby. I looked up, trying to find the Douglas squirrel responsible, but there was no sign of one. Two more pinecones came flying before we decided to move on and get away from the eeriness of whatever was happening in the forest. The large trees and mossy undergrowth gave off an unearthly feeling, and we weren't interested in finding out what might be lurking nearby.

Let the record show that in all my miles of boots on trails, I've never seen a Sasquatch. When people talk about the beast's existence, I land somewhere in the middle, usually sliding back and forth between those who *know* Sasquatches exist and those who *know* they are mythical. But since my husband and I couldn't explain the unsettling feeling we'd had, or the pinecones-to-the-noggin', or the loud thumping, I went on a quest to resolve the incident after I returned home. The most logical explanation, I was told by local rangers, was a Douglas squirrel gathering fruit and nuts for the winter, just as I had suspected. During late summer, the squirrels store bounty for cold-weather nourishment and it's commonplace for them to drop many cones at once. Could the thumping have been from dropping pinecones? Perhaps, even likely. Although my husband and I both agreed that the thumping was very heavy and sounded bigger than a careening pinecone. The trees were tall, so it's possible we didn't see or hear the squirrels as they busily worked.

Part of me believed the Douglas squirrel answer, but another part wasn't convinced. Then, some months later, I happened to be talking to a fellow outdoorsman who had spent a great deal of time in the Darrington area. When I told him our story, without missing a beat he calmly said, "Oh, those were the spirits." I questioned him further and he told me that years ago, the ancestors of local tribes hunted and fished in that area and rumor had it that their souls still inhabited those forests and rivers. My husband and I were not, he explained, the first to hear strange rumblings in that area. As I listened to more stories he shared, about others who had encountered similar happenings along the Suiattle River, I began to shudder. To this day, I have no idea what my husband and I felt and heard as we walked along the river, and I suppose I'll never know. Whether the answer is logical or mythical, as you wander through the large trees and mossy green forest of the new stretch of PCT, keep your eyes peeled, your ears open, and your cameras ready.

MINERS RIDGE LOOKOUT

If time permits, the Miners Ridge lookout makes a wonderful diversion. The lookout was built in 1938 and still stands proudly, boasting a misty-eyed view of Glacier Peak and surrounding hills. If that isn't enough to fill your viewfinder, head over to Image Lake, where the reflection—hence the name—shows off a picture-perfect Glacier Peak. You can make a detour to the lookout and lake by following Miners Ridge Trail #785 and popping out farther north along the PCT. This detour is roughly a 10-mile trip, whereas staying on the PCT is about 9 miles, so I'd say the difference is nearly a wash.

Goliaths have stood the test of time and still grow happily in the acidic soil. In just shy of 1 mile beyond Camp 25, rock hop across the reliable Dolly Creek and continue on your way.

Find the new **Suiattle River bridge** 1.4 miles past Camp 25. As you start to cross, check out the large well-used campsite to the right in the trees, complete with log furniture and ideal flat spots for tents. One tired night, I tried several times to get there, but on each bushwhack attempt I found myself faced with a deep bramble-filled channel of slow-moving water. I finally gave up and the camp access remained a mystery until a forest ranger unraveled the stumper. This base camp was set up and used by trail crews who built the bridge during 2010–11. They used ladders to get up and down unless the riffle was dry, in which case they followed a lightly trod boot path. That path is now overgrown, and the water channel makes access after rains or during peak runoff impossible. Perhaps someday another camp will pop up near the bridge, but for now camps are some distance in either direction.

Once across the bridge, the trail ascends and in 0.3 mile arrives at a junction with the **Suiattle River Trail #784** to the left. This is an access point to the recently repaired Suiattle River Road approximately 7.7 miles away. If you need to get off the PCT and get to a forest road, this is the place.

Keep on the PCT, climbing gradually to a hillside traverse that hugs the 2800-foot contour under evergreens. A handful of reliable creeks provide water on the approach to **Camp 26**, 2.6 miles past the bridge. This large camp to the trail's left (northeast) can support at least three tents and has a well-used fire pit and logs for sitting.

Almost immediately after the camp, arrive at a junction with **Miners Ridge Trail #785**, where a sign points uphill toward **Image Lake**. Through the trees on a sunny day, Glacier Peak lights up the horizon. In 0.5 mile from the junction find another camp (**Camp 27**)—this one is small, with room for one tent. Immediately after the camp, along the PCT to the east, a clear trickling stream is perfect for filtering.

In 1 mile beyond the Miners Ridge Trail junction, cross a skinny log bridge with good handrails over **Miners Creek**, which flows clear and fresh. Just on the other side, up a small knoll straight ahead, find a well-used camp with room for at least three tents (**Suiattle Camp**). If this camp is full, there's room for a few more tents along an old trail to the right, toward the Suiattle River, although past storm damage has made this area less than aesthetically pleasing. In 0.1 mile beyond Suiattle Camp, arrive at the old PCT, completing the new reroute and beginning your ascent toward Suiattle Pass.

CAMP-TO-CAMP MILEAGE

Mica Lake to Camp 19 .... 0.5
Camp 19 to Camp 20 .... 3.3
Camp 20 to Milk Creek Camp 0.9
Milk Creek Camp to Camp 21 .... 3.1
Camp 21 to Camp 22 .... 0.6
Camp 22 to Camp 23 .... 0.4
Camp 23 to Camp 24 .... 0.4
Camp 24 to Dolly Vista Camp 1.3
Dolly Vista Camp to Vista Camp 3.9
Vista Camp to Camp 25 .... 3.9
Camp 25 to Camp 26 .... 4.0
Camp 26 to Camp 27 .... 0.6
Camp 27 to Suiattle Camp 0.5
Suiattle Camp to old PCT junction 0.1

5 SUIATTLE RIVER TO STEHEKIN VALLEY ROAD

DISTANCE 27 miles

ELEVATION GAIN/LOSS
+4710/–6625 feet

HIGH POINT 6010 feet

CONNECTING TRAILS AND ROADS
Buck Creek Pass Trail #789,
Stehekin Valley Road

ON THE TRAIL

Now on the north side of the **Suiattle River**, join the former PCT and climb through tall timbers in a healthy understory of twinflower, moss, seasonal mushrooms, and small saplings longing to be just like their big brothers. In 3.1 miles, arrive at the first of at least five small creeks in the next mile. Water is prevalent from here to Stehekin Valley Road, so save your feet and back and carry only what you need.

In 4.1 miles from the old PCT junction, arrive at **Buck Creek Pass** and an intersection with **Buck Creek Pass Trail #789**, to the right—but don't be surprised if you walk right by it. A tree sign is bolted to an evergreen, but man oh man, does it blend with the bark. To the left (north), just across from the junction, is the abandoned Miners Creek Camp, which is no longer maintained. It appears that some folks have been using it, but it's far from ideal, best suited for desperate times only. There are much better spots ahead in a short distance, including a very well-used camp near the flowing Miners Creek.

Don't be surprised if hikers start to thicken like hair on a dog's back from Buck Creek Pass all the way to Cloudy Pass. The loop from Spider Meadows to Buck Creek Pass is to blame. This spectacular hike is well known and documented, for good reason: it's a seriously impressive adventure complete with glaciers, flowered meadows, and high alpine peaks. Make a mental note of that trip for another day, and continue on the PCT for 0.6 mile to find the sparsely forested **Miners Creek Camp**, near a sturdy bridge over Miners Creek. The camp has a least three sites, some on the left (west), some on the right (east), all with suitable flat spots for tents. If Miners Creek is murky, as it can be after heavy rains, backtrack south 0.3 mile to a clear tributary. Or just plan on getting a little water before you arrive to play it safe.

From Miners Creek, the trail gently switchbacks in riparian brush of twisted stalk, dwarf dogwood, and vanilla leaf before arriving at the first of at least five playful creeklets as you make your way toward Suiattle Pass. The forest alternates between spindly trees and riparian foliage as it heads east for just shy of 1 mile, and then it switches north again. Your huffing and puffing begins to pay off in the form of views. Fortress Mountain shows off its rocky crest to the southeast, while to the southwest the top of Glacier Peak peers over the ridgelines.

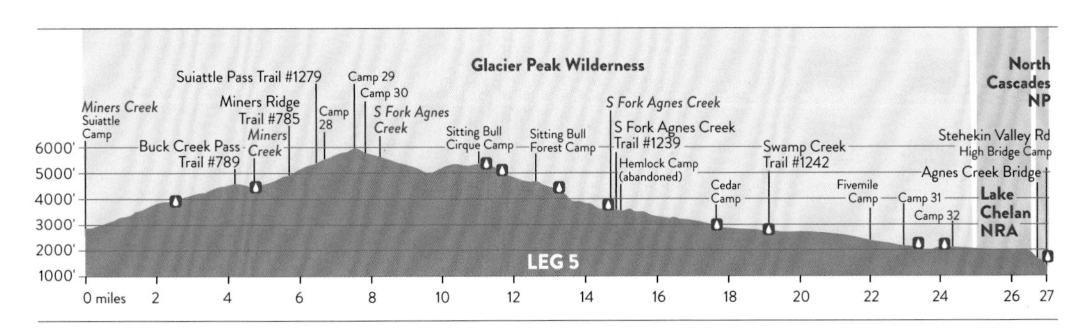

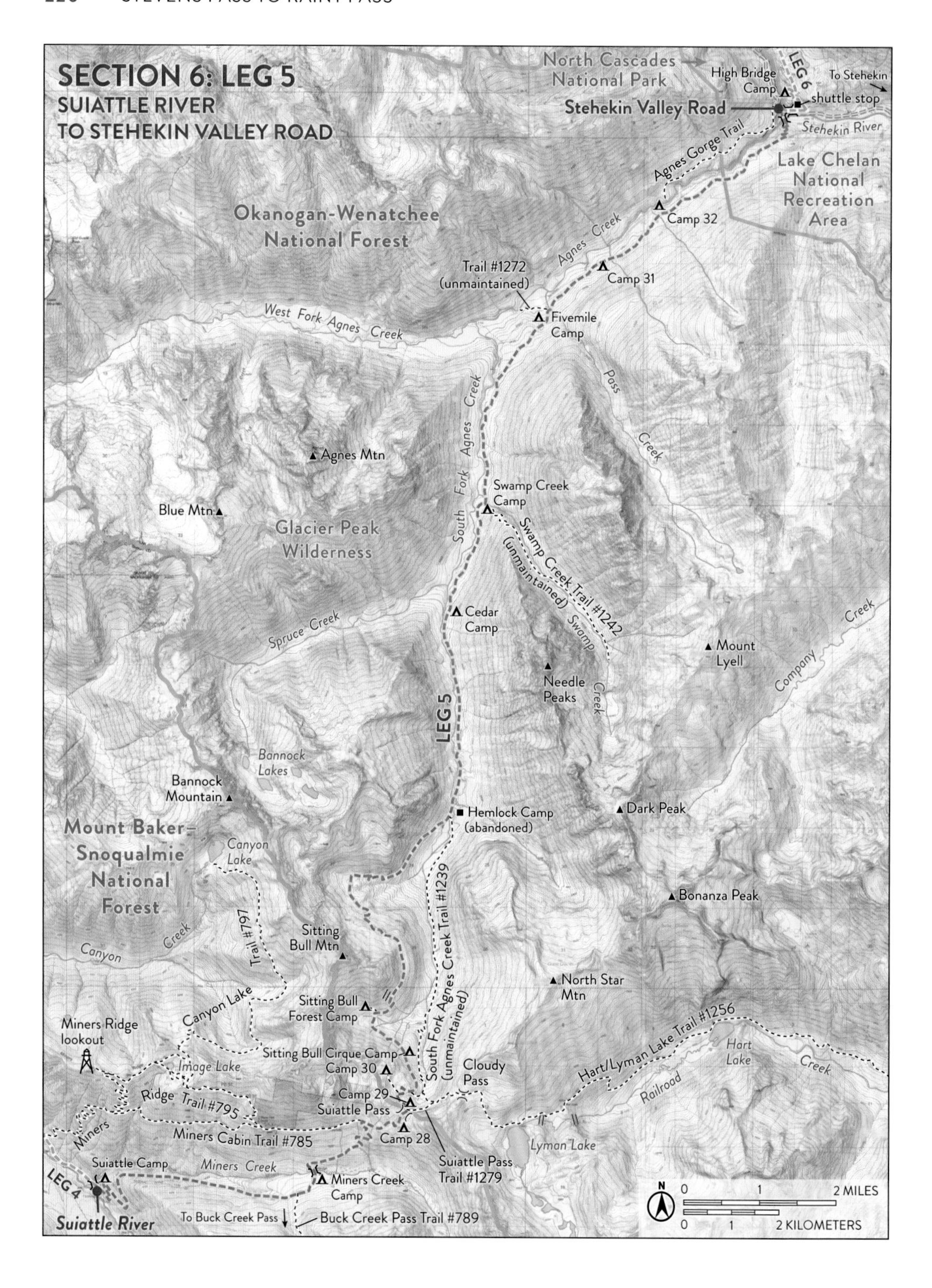
SECTION 6: LEG 5
SUIATTLE RIVER
TO STEHEKIN VALLEY ROAD
North Cascades National Park
High Bridge Camp
LEG 6
To Stehekin
shuttle stop
Stehekin Valley Road
Stehekin River
Agnes Gorge Trail
Lake Chelan National Recreation Area
Camp 32
Okanogan-Wenatchee National Forest
Agnes Creek
Camp 31
Trail #1272 (unmaintained)
Fivemile Camp
West Fork Agnes Creek
Pass Creek
South Fork Agnes Creek
Agnes Mtn
Swamp Creek Camp
Blue Mtn
Glacier Peak Wilderness
Swamp Creek Trail #1242 (unmaintained)
Cedar Camp
Spruce Creek
Swamp Creek
Mount Lyell
Company Creek
Needle Peaks
LEG 5
Bannock Lakes
Bannock Mountain
Hemlock Camp (abandoned)
Dark Peak
Mount Baker-Snoqualmie National Forest
Canyon Lake
Bonanza Peak
Canyon Creek
Trail #797
Sitting Bull Mtn
South Fork Agnes Creek Trail #1239 (unmaintained)
North Star Mtn
Sitting Bull Forest Camp
Canyon Lake
Hart/Lyman Lake Trail #1256
Miners Ridge lookout
Sitting Bull Cirque Camp
Camp 30
Cloudy Pass
Hart Lake
Creek
Image Lake
Railroad
Ridge Trail #795
Camp 29
Suiattle Pass
Miners
Miners Cabin Trail #785
Camp 28
Lyman Lake
Suiattle Camp
Miners Creek
Suiattle Pass Trail #1279
LEG 4
Miners Creek Camp
Suiattle River
To Buck Creek Pass
Buck Creek Pass Trail #789
N
0 1 2 MILES
0 1 2 KILOMETERS

Near Sitting Bull Mountain, a big cirque offers rocky terrain and scenic landscapes.

In 1.8 miles beyond Miners Creek (6.5 miles from Suiattle River), arrive at a junction with **Miners Ridge Trail #785**, which heads west. Just down this trail a few paces is Miners Creek, if your thirst needs quenching. Back on the PCT, the landscape changes to shorter fir trees, huckleberries, lupine, and juniper as you climb into the high country. Cloudy Peak shows up through the trees, as do two campsites (**Camp 28**), the first 0.7 mile from the Miners Creek Trail junction. The camps are 0.1 mile apart along the PCT, and both are accessed by spur trails heading right (east). Both have room for a couple of small tents, views, and a smattering of trees for privacy. Bring water if you intend to camp here, since none is accessible nearby. The second camp is a few hundred feet before a junction with **Suiattle Pass Trail #1279**, signed "**Cloudy Pass Hiker Trail**," leading right (east). This trail serves as a connector for hikers who want to access Cloudy Pass without dropping down into the Agnes Creek basin. This junction also marks the beginning of Suiattle Pass, which stretches northward.

In 0.2 mile beyond the Cloudy Pass connector trail, reach two more waterless campsites (**Camp 29**) down spur trails to the right (east). As the PCT descends from Suiattle Pass, it arrives at another camp (**Camp 30**), this one marked with a triangle-shaped tent sign pointing left (west), directing you down a spur trail. The sign is on a hairpin turn 0.6 mile from the Cloudy Pass connector trail and is easy to miss if you're exhausted.

A seasonal creek drips nearby but dries up in hot weather, so plan accordingly. At this camp you can snooze in a two-tent site with a fair amount of privacy.

In 0.3 mile from Camp 30, a second junction with a trail to Cloudy Pass arrives, confusing the whibbles out of you. This junction is signed "**Cloudy Pass, S Fork Agnes**," and the way leads to both Cloudy Pass via Hart/Lyman Lake Trail #1256 and South Fork Agnes Creek Trail #1239.

The PCT next makes its way north, teeter-tottering through gentle ups and downs before entering the first of two cirques on the shoulders of **Sitting Bull Mountain**. This subalpine country is full of house-sized boulders, whistling marmots, and a flurry of butterflies sucking on wildflowers—a vision for the eyes and a salve for the soul. The steep canyon walls and the lack of trees show how avalanche prone this area is and make you grateful

ALTERNATIVE ROUTE: SOUTH FORK AGNES CREEK TRAIL

If you've been walking through a lot of snow, you may want to drop into the Agnes Creek basin and follow South Fork Agnes Creek Trail #1239, the old PCT route. The newer, rerouted PCT stays higher and crosses some grand glacial cirques before meeting up with this detour near the abandoned Hemlock Camp. Of course, you'll miss that high-country scenery, and you'll have to fight some overgrown brush and rotten boardwalks, as the old trail is not maintained. Definitely avoid this alternative if you have stock. But it may be the lesser of two evils if your two feet have been slipping and sliding.

There's a fungus among us! Due to Washington's humidity and wet climate, a wide variety of seasonal mushrooms are found throughout the entire length of the PCT in the state.

The High Bridge Trailhead adjacent to the Stehekin Valley Road is both the shuttle pickup location as well as the continuation of the PCT to the north.

you're here in the summer. Stop to take pictures, have a bite if your belly grumbles, suck in the fresh air, and just enjoy feeling tiny next to these giant walls.

In 2.8 miles from the South Fork Agnes Creek Trail junction (11 miles from Suiattle River), arrive at a small triangle-shaped tent sign pointing downhill to a spur trail on the right, near the beginning of the second cirque. Roughly 50 yards down the spur, you'll find **Sitting Bull Cirque Camp**, with a couple of flat spots to rest for the night. For your camping and drinking pleasure, water abounds in this valley. The Forest Service has tried to limit camping in this fragile subalpine area, so please use designated sites.

The PCT next descends via switchbacks in an open landscape dotted with firs, contouring around this first cirque across water drainages on footbridges, one of them broken and squeaking—it sounds like the mischief of partying mice. Duck back into the forest just past the second cirque, 1.6 miles beyond Sitting Bull Cirque Camp, and find another camp (**Sitting Bull Forest Camp**) to the left (north), noted again with a triangular-tent sign. There are a couple of sites in this wooded area. Backtrack into the cirque for water, or carry some with you if you plan on busting out your gourmet surprise before bed.

In 0.4 mile from Sitting Bull Forest Camp, a small cascading waterfall with a shallow pool provides an excellent place to stop for a splash or refreshing refill. From here, the PCT passes in and out of conifers and brushy hillsides as it moderately descends toward the Agnes Creek basin. The warmer climate becomes increasingly indicative of the east side of the Cascade Crest, and the landscape begins to match. More grasses show up in the riparian brush, which seems to beg for water as you fight your way through it. Peekaboo views of North Star Mountain's jagged profile give your

On the other side of this large bridge, you officially enter North Cascades National Park.

eyes some entertainment as you whack back the thimbleberries.

In 2.3 miles past Sitting Bull Forest Camp, arrive at a couple of emergency campsites just before the **South Fork Agnes Creek** crossing. Years ago, flooding took out the bridge, so your options are to follow the red-taped detour 50 yards north to a downed log for an easy walk across, or wade if the water is low. I recommend the log unless it's a hot day or you smell like a goat and you could use a little splishin' and splashin'. Once across, arrive at a junction with **South Fork Agnes Creek Trail #1239**, which rejoins the PCT here from the south (see the "Alternative Route" sidebar).

Next, the PCT almost immediately arrives at the abandoned Hemlock Camp. As bad luck would have it, the mountain pine beetle has made its home here, causing the diseased trees to fall into the campsites. Shame on those catastrophic coleopterans! The Forest Service has closed the camp indefinitely because nothing says "bad day" like getting crowned by a beetle-infested hemlock. Instead, use Sitting Bull Forest Camp (south) or a small camp 1.9 miles south on the South Fork Agnes Creek Trail, or keep trucking on the PCT next to purring Agnes Creek to **Cedar Camp**, 2.8 miles north. Cedar Camp is in a grove of . . . wait for it . . . drapey western red cedars. A tree sign points the way to roughly five well-used sites with fire pits for warming your toes and logs for lounging. Agnes Creek is a mess of snarled logs near

HIGH BRIDGE CAMP

A short 85 yards up the road to the left (northwest) from where the PCT meets the Stehekin Valley Road is High Bridge Campground (**High Bridge Camp**). The camp has a shelter, built by the Civilian Conservation Corps in the 1930s, and a pit toilet, thankfully built more recently. There are two primitive campsites and your water source is the river below. Like all camps in the North Cascades, you must have a permit to stay here overnight.

STEHEKIN VALLEY ROAD

If you've never been to Stehekin, you should know that Stehekin Valley Road is the area's artery, a real lifeline. Built in 1897 by miners hunting for gold, this 12-foot-wide arterial connects the town of Stehekin to the High Bridge trails and camps, where the shuttle bus route ends. Before October 2003, the road was almost twice as long, allowing 10 more miles of vehicle access for hikers and campers. Unfortunately, an unprecedented flood, the kind that happens only once every 500 years or so, wiped out several parts of the dirt and gravel roadway, including one stretch near Shady Camp, where the road vanished into a now near vertical hillside. Thankfully, those on foot can still travel the road the old-fashioned way as it winds up the valley paralleling the PCT (otherwise known as the Old Wagon Road in these parts), until the road ends at the washout and diverges onto a side trail leading you to Bridge Creek Camp. Once there, the road serves as the makeshift PCT for several hundred yards until it meets a single-track path that turns off the road to the right (northwest). Or, just continue on the PCT—your call!

camp, but water is still accessible. From here, the PCT continues its northward trek amid signs of the drier east-side climate, including white pine and Engelmann spruce and sparse pops of green- and dried-grass understory.

In 1.4 miles from Cedar Camp (19.1 miles from Suiattle River), arrive at **Swamp Creek Camp**, slightly less desirable but pleasant all the same. Several dead trees have been cut up and are spread around, making the camp less than aesthetically pleasing, but at least three sites have flat spots for your snoozing pleasure. Swamp Creek itself is very close to camp and is poorly named, as it's clear and playfully trips along the boulders underneath. The unmaintained **Swamp Creek Trail #1242**, simply signed "Swamp Creek" with an arrow, heads right (east) here and leads through the beautiful Swamp Creek basin to some off-trail scrambling and technical climbing of Dark Peak.

A log footbridge guides you over Swamp Creek, while the horsey crowd fords to the west. The PCT then climbs high above Agnes Creek, with occasional views to the churning gorge below. Views of high Heather Ridge to the east also pop in and out. In 2.9 miles from Swamp Creek, arrive at **Fivemile Camp**, which has a very open feeling thanks, unfortunately, to trees thinned by beetle damage. Thankfully, most of the dead trees are on the outskirts of camp and the Forest Service has not deemed the camp hazardous. There are at least half a dozen sites here, complete with downed logs for parking your hiney while warming yourself up at the fire pit. You can also park your hiney on the handy backcountry privy. **This is the last major camp before Stehekin Valley Road**. Water is either from Pass Creek if it's flowing, or a short walk to Agnes Creek. If you're exhausted, it's not a bad idea to carry a little water with you to this camp.

Years ago, there was a junction around here for West Fork Agnes Creek Trail #1272, heading left (west). But the trail has been abandoned since the bridge over Agnes Creek washed out. If Fivemile Camp is full or "horsey," or you want to splash in or retrieve water from Agnes Creek, use your scouting skills to follow the old lightly used trail descending west from camp. A campsite still exists near the old bridge's concrete supports.

Back on the PCT, a waterless camp (**Camp 31**) is 1 mile north of Fivemile Camp to the right (east), complete with a fire pit. It lacks privacy but is an option if Fivemile is full or you want a longer day. Cross a creek on a footlog in 1.6 miles from Fivemile Camp and another with a small bridge 0.6 mile beyond that. Roughly 0.1 mile later, find a small one-tent site to the left, west (**Camp 32**). Because of its proximity to the trail, it's not ideal, but if you're too sleepy to make the final 2.7 miles to Stehekin Valley Road, it would serve you well.

Accessible only by boat, plane, foot, or hoof, the tiny town of Stehekin has a surprising amount of resources.

Blowdowns on this stretch can slow you down, and they seem to have their own strategy, falling just after the trail crews have left. Arrive at a sign 3 miles past Fivemile Camp announcing the **Lake Chelan National Recreation Area**. The Lake Chelan NRA encompasses 61,958 acres, including the northern end of Lake Chelan as well as the Stehekin River and its valley, and is managed by the National Park Service as part of the North Cascades Complex.

In about 1 mile from the sign, begin a set of ten switchbacks leading you down toward Agnes Creek, the signed boundary of **North Cascades National Park**, and a stunning up-to-date bridge over the rushing water. In the winter of 2006–7, a large tree squished its predecessor. The following summer, the Park Service went to work and on July 2, 2008, the new bridge was flown into place. Admire the skill of all those who put it there as you cross.

From the Lake Chelan NRA through the national park, until you cross back onto Forest Service land, some **new rules apply**. First, you must camp in designated sites. Second, you must have a free backcountry permit in your possession to use those designated campsites. In other words, you must now be organized, so wake up your "trail brain" and tell it to work again. Here's the tough part: permits are only issued on the day of or day before your requested overnight stay. So if you plan to camp from this point to 3.5 miles south of Rainy Pass, you must go to Stehekin and obtain a permit from Golden West Visitor Center.

THE RAGING METROPOLIS OF STEHEKIN

Say you found yourself in town for a day or two, while you waited for a ferry back to Chelan, or waited for the post office to open after a holiday, or heck, if you just wanted to spend some time off the trail. What luck! It's hard to be bored in Stehekin. The North Cascades Lodge rents kayaks by the hour, and you can explore the petroglyphs and little inlets of Lake Chelan. Bike rentals, available by the honor system, are also available near the town park. Or, take the shuttle up the road to explore Rainbow Falls, Buckner Orchard, or my favorite, the old schoolhouse. Lastly, if you fly-fish, you could take a guided trip on the Stehekin River with Stehekin Fishing Adventures. The fish are plentiful and the river scenery is spectacular. There's so much to do, you might wish that the post office stayed closed longer!

Golden West Visitor Center: Obtain your backcountry camping permits from this visitors center on the main road to the east of the North Cascades Lodge. The stunning historical building has interesting exhibits with facts about the flora and fauna of the North Cascades. It's a great place to get your bearings and get all squared away with your camps as you continue on your PCT journey toward Rainy Pass.

Stehekin wildlife: You are in the transition zone now, or as I like to call it, the land of **rattlesnakes** and black bears. In the upper valley, the slithering ones aren't very common, but along the trails and the road near Stehekin they are more prolific. Thankfully, these creatures are the ladies and gentlemen of the snake world and will give you a courtesy tail shake, asking you not to tread on them. They are on the menu of large birds of prey, so they do their best to slither out of the way, rarely aggressive unless provoked and generally not a problem.

While you might not see a snake, if you spend any time in the upper and lower Stehekin Valley, you'll likely see a **bear**. During late July, it's not uncommon to see bears hanging out under the apple trees in Buckner Orchard or walking on trails, including the PCT. During one stay we saw a bear a day! Thankfully, the bruins keep to themselves and are generally timid around people. As always, practice good bear etiquette and keep an eye out for prints on the dusty trails.

Lastly, pesky little nippers and stingers are also found around the Stehekin Valley. In spring and early summer, **ticks** may be found on valley trails and wait on plants and brush to find a host, otherwise known as an unsuspecting hiker or munching mammal. Thankfully, most of the valley ticks do not carry diseases, but they're annoying all the same. **Bees and hornets**, especially near the rivers, are plentiful and seem to make a beeline (wait, really?) for you as you filter water or splash around. Because I'm allergic, I tend to get a little paranoid about them, but the best course of action I found was to ignore them altogether. If they land on you, they often just tickle your skin and fly off. Some people pay good money for a massage, yet here it is for free! I'm just sayin'. Also biting and annoying are the likes of **horseflies and mosquitos**. Both can be a nuisance depending on the season and the temperature. Use plenty of bug spray, especially on hot summer days. Horseflies are little rascals and often disguise themselves as bees, so you'll be afraid to swat. But don't let them get away with it! Their eyes are large and fly-like and their bodies are much more round. The females are the biters of the battalions, using sharp serrated teeth to slice off layers of flesh as soon as they land on your bare skin. They are not your friends, so get in a few swats and keep score! If you do get bit, it hurts much like a bee sting. Thankfully, the sting goes away in a few hours, but wowza, it's no fun. As a side note, some people are allergic to horsefly bites and will show signs of a serious reaction within minutes. Keep an eye out and seek help immediately should that happen.

Horses and mules are common sites along the PCT near Stehekin.

Whether you're headed to town or just hiking to Rainy Pass, follow the PCT another 0.2 mile beyond the bridge until you arrive at **Stehekin Valley Road**. The town of **Stehekin** is 11 miles east down this mostly deserted road, and the only way there (unless you know a local resident who shipped a car to this cut-off town) is via the Park Service shuttle, which runs just four times a day in high season (see the "Shuttling to Stehekin" sidebar).

SHUTTLING TO STEHEKIN

If you need a lift into the tiny town of Stehekin, a large red Park Service shuttle bus runs between town and the High Bridge, 11 miles up the valley, near where the PCT meets the road. The shuttle fee is payable in cash and the service has three seasons—Early Season, Summer Season, and Late Season. The schedule varies. In the summer, the shuttle runs approximately four times a day. Check current fares and schedule at the North Cascades National Park website (www.nps.gov/noca/planyourvisit/stehekin-transportation.htm)—and bring the schedule with you. If you miss the last run, the only way to town is to walk 11 dusty miles.

Head right (east) down the road and cross the large car bridge spanning the **Stehekin River**. A picnic table to the left (north) is a good place to sit and wait for the shuttle if you're headed to town. As a side note, you're entering an area with a lot of human history that long predates the PCT. Former trail names have stuck, and the locals often refer to them instead of the PCT. To wit: Many a southbound hiker has been baffled by the sign where the PCT meets Stehekin Valley Road, which just says "Agnes Creek Trail."

CAMP-TO-CAMP MILEAGE

Old PCT junction to Miners Creek Camp	4.7
Miners Creek Camp to Camp 28	2.5
Camp 28 to Camp 29	0.3
Camp 29 to Camp 30	0.4
Camp 30 to Sitting Bull Cirque Camp	3.1
Sitting Bull Cirque Camp to Sitting Bull Forest Camp	1.6
Sitting Bull Forest Camp to Cedar Camp	5.1
Cedar Camp to Swamp Creek Camp	1.4
Swamp Creek Camp to Fivemile Camp	2.9
Fivemile Camp to Camp 31	1.0
Camp 31 to Camp 32	1.3
Camp 32 to Stehekin Valley Road	2.7

6 STEHEKIN VALLEY ROAD TO RAINY PASS

DISTANCE 19.5 miles

ELEVATION GAIN/LOSS
+5240/–1910 feet

HIGH POINT 4900 feet

CONNECTING TRAILS
Twisp Pass Trail

ON THE TRAIL

Getting back on the PCT on the north side of **Stehekin Valley Road** can be tricky and has stumped many a hiker before you. From where you popped off the PCT near Agnes Creek, walk the road to the right (east) across the car bridge over the Stehekin River. Look to your left (north) and find a faint trail between a private residence with a barn and a horse stable at the **High Bridge Trailhead**. Look for a small sign near your knees that says "High Bridge, Coon Lake, Bridge Creek." Even though it doesn't say it, voilà, this is the PCT! Please be very respectful of the private residence and maintain your distance. The occupants have little tolerance for folks who knock on their door asking for directions, water, or information.

The dusty trail ascends through evergreens and in 0.6 mile from where you met Stehekin Valley Road for the first time, it makes a T and arrives at an equestrian-trail junction. Follow the arrows to the left (north) toward Coon Lake, McGregor Mountain, and Bridge Creek, also known as northbound PCT, although it's not noted.

Play hopscotch to avoid ruining your shoes in a pile of horse dukey. The trail you're hiking *is* the PCT, but this particular stretch is referred to by several names: Coon Lake Trail, McGregor Mountain Access Trail, Detour Trail, the Old Wagon Road. In the 1890s, a long stretch of what became the PCT was built to accommodate primitive wagon travel. In the 1930s, the Civilian Conservation Corps (CCC) moved the main road down along the river, and the Old Wagon Road became a detour route. These days, there's little evidence of past wagon use, except the wider tread. Can you imagine hitting some of the big trail bumps on wooden wheels? I may rupture a disk just thinking about it.

In 0.7 mile from the horse-trail junction, arrive at water-lily-covered **Coon Lake**, a day-use-only area. The bottom of this shallow lake is weedy and muddy, so it's best to skip a dip. The warm water buzzes with dragon- and damselflies and, unfortunately, plenty of mosquitos. Look for beavers and western toads near the water's edge along with a wide assortment of birds, such as western tanagers, Barrow's goldeneyes, and harlequin ducks. Such a healthy ecosystem!

Just 0.1 mile beyond Coon Lake, arrive at a junction to the right (northeast) for the climb up **McGregor Mountain**. The 7-mile one-way summit bid gains roughly 6000 feet to a hands-and-feet talus scramble at the top—a long, difficult

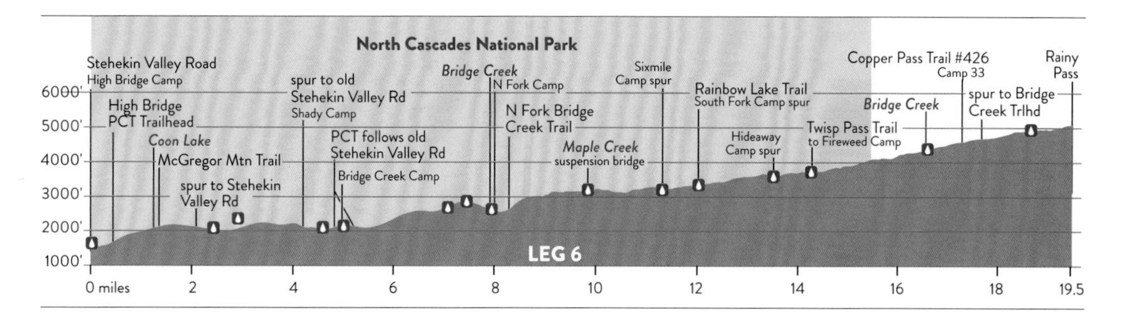

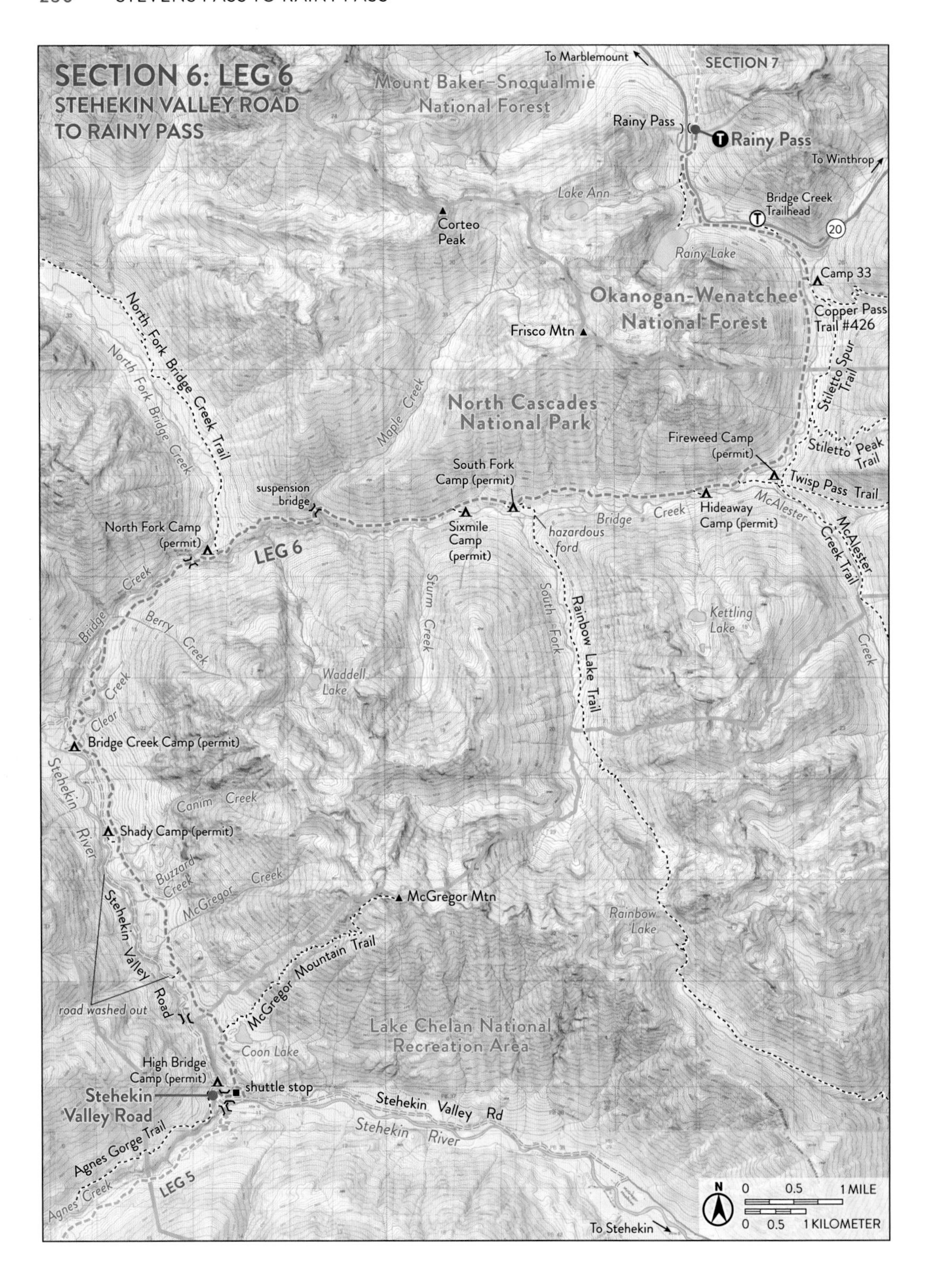

SECTION 6: LEG 6
STEHEKIN VALLEY ROAD
TO RAINY PASS
To Marblemount
SECTION 7
Mount Baker–Snoqualmie
National Forest
Rainy Pass
Rainy Pass
To Winthrop
Lake Ann
Corteo
Peak
Bridge Creek
Trailhead
20
Rainy Lake
Camp 33
Okanogan-Wenatchee
National Forest
Copper Pass
Trail #426
Frisco Mtn
North Fork Bridge Creek Trail
North Fork Bridge Creek
Stiletto Spur
Trail
Maple Creek
North Cascades
National Park
Fireweed Camp
(permit)
Stiletto Peak
Trail
South Fork
Camp (permit)
Twisp Pass Trail
suspension
bridge
Hideaway
Camp (permit)
McAlester
Sixmile
Camp
(permit)
Bridge
Creek
hazardous
ford
McAlester
Creek Trail
North Fork Camp
(permit)
LEG 6
Creek
Sturm Creek
South Fork
Rainbow Lake Trail
Kettling
Lake
Bridge
Berry
Creek
Creek
Waddell
Lake
Creek
Clear
Bridge Creek Camp (permit)
Stehekin
River
Canim Creek
Shady Camp (permit)
Buzzard
Creek
McGregor Creek
McGregor Mtn
Stehekin Valley
Road
Rainbow
Lake
McGregor Mountain Trail
road washed out
Lake Chelan National
Recreation Area
Coon Lake
High Bridge
Camp (permit)
Stehekin
Valley Road
shuttle stop
Stehekin Valley Rd
Stehekin River
Agnes Gorge Trail
Agnes Creek
LEG 5
To Stehekin
N
0 0.5 1 MILE
0 0.5 1 KILOMETER

Coon Lake, near the High Bridge Trailhead, is a popular destination for day hikers and equestrians.

albeit beautiful side trip if time and gumption permits. From the junction, the PCT gently drops 0.3 mile to a North Cascades National Park sign. After you crossed Stehekin Valley Road, you were technically back in the Lake Chelan National Recreation Area, but the boundaries here are confusing. Besides, who's counting? The Park Service manages the greater Stehekin area so all the same rules apply.

At 2.1 miles from Stehekin Valley Road (0.4 mile from the national park sign), the trail arrives at a junction to the left (west)—you could hop over to Stehekin Valley Road here. Signs point the way to help you along toward Bridge Creek and north along the PCT.

Pass through the drier east-of-the-crest landscape consisting of maples, ponderosa pines, and western red cedars until you arrive at the crossing of McGregor Creek, just 0.6 mile past the trail junction. Buzzard Creek follows in 0.4 mile, both decent water sources.

In 0.3 mile beyond Buzzard Creek, arrive at the site of the August 2005 Shady Fire, sporting charred trees that help open views to peaks above. Pine saplings attempt to restore the forest, growing sturdily in the well-lit acidic soil, while deer graze

Crossing Maple Creek is fun on a short, swinging suspension bridge.

on various plants in the rebounding meadows. Just past the burn zone, the ecosystem changes and presents an old-growth patch of towering western red cedars. Pass the lightly flowing Canim Creek. Then, just shy of 1 mile from the burn zone, reach an infrequently used trail on the left that leads to Stehekin Valley Road and Shady Camp.

In 0.4 mile from the trail junction, cross another creek on a small wooden bridge surrounded by more cedars and some shade, nice if you need to get out of the heat or just hug a tree. In another 0.4 mile (5 miles from Stehekin Valley Road), the PCT becomes the Stehekin Valley Road and continues to **Bridge Creek Camp** ⓿, with sites on both sides of the road-turned-trail. This camp has it all. Six sites (including a group site), picnic tables, toilets, a stock camp and corral, a CCC-built shelter, fresh water from Clear and Bridge creeks, great views of surrounding peaks—we're talking five-star luxury, if the stars align and a permit is available. As a side note, the cabin located here is private and not open to hikers.

A short 0.3-mile walk up the road-turned-trail leads to a junction where the PCT continues to the right (northeast) while the old road goes straight. A sign points the way along the narrower tread toward North Fork Trail, Fireweed, and Rainy Pass—that's where you're headed! Ponderosa pine needles and grasses litter the trail, along with periodic piles of bear scat teeming with huckleberry remnants. If you haven't noticed yet, you're now firmly planted on the drier, warmer side of the Cascade Crest, where the rock and pines feel made for a Stetson cologne commercial. Sadly, most of the hikers you pass will not smell as nice.

In 1.6 miles from where the PCT left the road, cross Berry Creek and then traverse a hillside, which grants views down to flowing Bridge Creek in the valley to the north. Water, for now, is plentiful, so don't fret if your bottle is a little low—there's more where that came from. The trail descends gently and 2.6 miles after leaving the road crosses a picturesque wooden bridge spanning **Bridge Creek** in the narrow valley.

Once across, in a short 0.1 mile arrive at **North Fork Camp**. The camp has reliable water access, a pit toilet, twelve campsites, fire pits, and a sturdy wire for hanging your food. Bears frequent this camp and have been known to trot off with unsecured meals. Don't let your gorp (or you) become a bruin-ruin. Next up, 0.3 mile from camp, is a junction with the **North Fork Bridge Creek Trail**. A thick knee-high post points directions and, judging by the worn top, has proved a convenient albeit splintery trail seat.

As you make your way northeast, the PCT affords views of rocky peaks, deep canyons, evergreen-dotted hillsides, and river valleys. In 1.6 miles past the North Fork Bridge Creek Trail junction, the PCT turns sharply north and then hairpins south in a scree- and talus-filled narrow canyon, guiding you over swift **Maple Creek** on a well-crafted **suspension bridge**. A sign points hikers up and over the talus field to the bridge, while stock users are directed straight ahead to the ford. Don't miss your turnoff—it's easy to do! The bridge sways back and forth and click-clacks as you make your way across the wooden slats using twisted steel rope for handrails. Channel your inner Indiana Jones and take your time enjoying the novelty.

Maple Creek flows reliably in the summer, so you can only imagine what it's like in the rainy fall and spring melt-off. In fact, so much water comes down this canyon that the Park Service removes the bridge in the off-season. From here to the northern end of the park in the dry season, you'll need to hike down spur trails into the camps to get water from Bridge Creek, which flows a couple hundred yards from the PCT but is accessible only at the camps. To make life easier, if you plan on hiking to Rainy Pass without camping, get water at Maple Creek.

Pressing on, the PCT maintains a gentle grade as it traverses sparse hillsides alternating between forest and thick brush. In 1.5 miles beyond Maple Creek, arrive at the spur for **Sixmile Camp**, which descends to the right (south). The camp boasts twelve sites, a pit toilet, water access, and a bear wire.

In another 0.7 mile, arrive at a junction with both **Rainbow Lake Trail** and the spur to **South Fork Camp**, both to the right (south). The hiker camp (there's a stock camp here too, like other camps on this stretch) has four sites, a pit toilet, fire pits, water access, and a bear wire. Make a mental note to come back and spend some time hiking around Rainbow Lake, where bears frolic in the evergreens and the rare wolverine was recently spotted. Several loops are possible and offer delicious backcountry visual treats. Because area trails have lost some bridges over rough water in the past several years, check with the Park Service before adventuring into the hinterlands beyond the PCT.

The PCT gently continues east through the now familiar landscape foliage and in 1.5 miles beyond the Rainbow Lake Trail junction, arrives at a spur for the most popular camp on this stretch, **Hideaway Camp**. This hiker camp has twelve sites, a pit toilet, water access, bear wire, and even seasonal butterflies. Green comma butterflies have been known to hang out in large numbers around camp, landing on you and your gear as you relax. One time, I was so covered in butterflies I felt like I was in a Disney cartoon. If I'd only had a bluebird on my shoulder the picture would have been complete. On hot days, also watch for mean-spirited wasps, which can ruin a good nap in a second.

In just shy of 1 mile, arrive at a junction with **Twisp Pass Trail**, which heads straight to shortly reach **Fireweed Camp**. The hiker camp has four sites, a pit toilet, water access, and fire pits. If you aren't camping at Fireweed, stay on the PCT, which makes a hard left (north) at this junction. Thankfully, a well-marked sign guides the way.

Signs point the way to the designated, permit-required camps in North Cascades National Park.

Disregard older trail maps, which show the PCT on the east side of Bridge Creek—that trail was abandoned long ago and the newer one, which you're now on, is the correct route. You're also about to step foot out of North Cascades National Park and into signed **Forest Service** land, just 1.5 miles from the Twisp Pass Trail junction. Beyond the boundary, cross a small tributary creek, the first one on the trail that reliably has water since you left Maple Creek, 6.2 miles back. The landscape then alternates between forest and brush before large evergreens win, leaving you to decide which side of the Cascade Crest you're on.

In 1 mile from the national forest boundary, arrive at a crossing of **Bridge Creek**. The thick wooden bridge that once safely spirited hikers across is severely damaged. Mother Nature's water chisel twisted the bridge sideways and made a mess of things. Until the damage is repaired, locate a small spur trail to the left (west), leading to a large downed log. The log has received so many footprints that the top is almost flat. Nevertheless, watch your footing carefully, especially if the log is wet, so you and your pack don't end up in the drink.

In another 0.1 mile, find yourself at a well-signed junction with **Copper Pass Trail #426**, which heads right (east). **Camp 33** is down this trail roughly 25 feet. It's a large site, and thankfully the cars buzzing along SR 20 aren't audible from camp. From the Copper Pass Trail junction, the PCT turns slightly to the left (northwest) and arrives at a trail that leads 0.7 mile to the **Bridge Creek Trailhead**. There are so many "Bridge Creek" names that your head is probably spinning. If you're ending your hike at SR 20, this trailhead is an option for your final destination. This trailhead does see its fair share of hikers, but it's primarily used by the horsey crowd. The **Rainy Pass Trailhead** and parking area are still 1.7 miles away.

The PCT stays in the forest and parallels the highway. Within 1 mile from the Bridge Creek Trailhead junction, cross two footlogs over tributary creeks, remaining remarkably camouflaged from the buzzing highway. At last, the trail spits you out at a gravel pullout on the south side of SR 20. To get to the parking lot, play chicken and cross the road, and then walk 0.2 mile to the large parking area and outhouse awaiting your arrival. You've made it!

CAMP-TO-CAMP MILEAGE

Stehekin Valley Road to Bridge Creek Camp	5.0
Bridge Creek Camp to North Fork Camp	3.0
North Fork Camp to Sixmile Camp spur	3.4
Sixmile Camp spur to South Fork Camp spur	0.7
South Fork Camp spur to Hideaway Camp spur	1.5
Hideaway Camp spur to Fireweed Camp spur	0.9
Fireweed Camp spur to Camp 33	2.6
Camp 33 to Rainy Pass	2.4

SECTION 7

RAINY PASS TO E. C. MANNING PROVINCIAL PARK

IF YOU ENJOY high craggy peaks, alpine and subalpine vistas, remote and rugged landscapes, and a transition-zone climate, the PCT section from Rainy Pass to E. C. Manning Provincial Park in British Columbia will fill your soul's cookie jar. Not only are the panoramas jaw dropping, but the fact that you can walk to Canada and pop out near lodging and a major highway is something no other section can claim. North of Harts Pass, the open, rolling, meadowed hillsides lead back into true alpine country. In fall, you may even glimpse the turning larch trees that add a brilliant yellowish-orange to the terrain. On the Canada side, you'll wind around the base of Windy Joe Mountain before heading down, down, down to civilization. Along the way, you'll pass the northern terminus of the PCT at the international boundary, at Monument 78—a mandatory picture. So why not do it, eh?

ACCESS

Rainy Pass

From Marblemount, drive east on State Route 20 (North Cascades Highway) for a little more than 50 miles to Rainy Pass. Turn left (north) toward the Rainy Pass Trailhead and parking area. Parking is plentiful.

Manning Park Lodge

From Hope, British Columbia, follow signs for eastbound BC Highway 3 (Crowsnest Highway). Drive east for roughly 39 miles and find Manning Park Lodge to the south of the highway. Parking is available at the lodge and at the PCT Trailhead. To get to the trailhead, continue 0.4 mile east from the lodge on BC 3. Turn right (southwest) at Gibson Pass Road and proceed another 0.8 mile, crossing a bridge over the Similkameen River just before you reach the PCT parking area on the left (south).

DISTANCE 69.4 miles

STATE DISTANCE 442.4–511.8 miles

ELEVATION GAIN/LOSS +13,890/–14,860 feet

HIGH POINT 7130 feet

BEST TIME OF YEAR late July–late Sept

PCTA SECTION LETTER L

LAND MANAGERS Mount Baker–Snoqualmie National Forest, Okanogan-Wenatchee National Forest (Methow Valley Ranger District, Pasayten Wilderness), E. C. Manning Provincial Park

PASSES AND PERMITS NW Forest Pass to park at Rainy Pass Trailhead. Free self-issue wilderness permits at US wilderness area trailheads. Backcountry camping permit required in Manning Park.

MAPS AND APPS

- Halfmile's WA Section L
- USFS PCT Map #10 Northern Washington
- Green Trails Washington Pass #50, Mt Logan #49, Pasayten Peak #18, Jack Mountain #17, Manning Park online maps
- Halfmile's PCT app, Guthook's overall PCT app and PCT WA app

LEGS

1. Rainy Pass to Methow River
2. Methow River to Harts Pass
3. Harts Pass to Woody Pass
4. Woody Pass to Monument 78
5. Monument 78 to Manning Park Lodge

Opposite: *Beauty is everywhere you look north of Cutthroat Pass.*

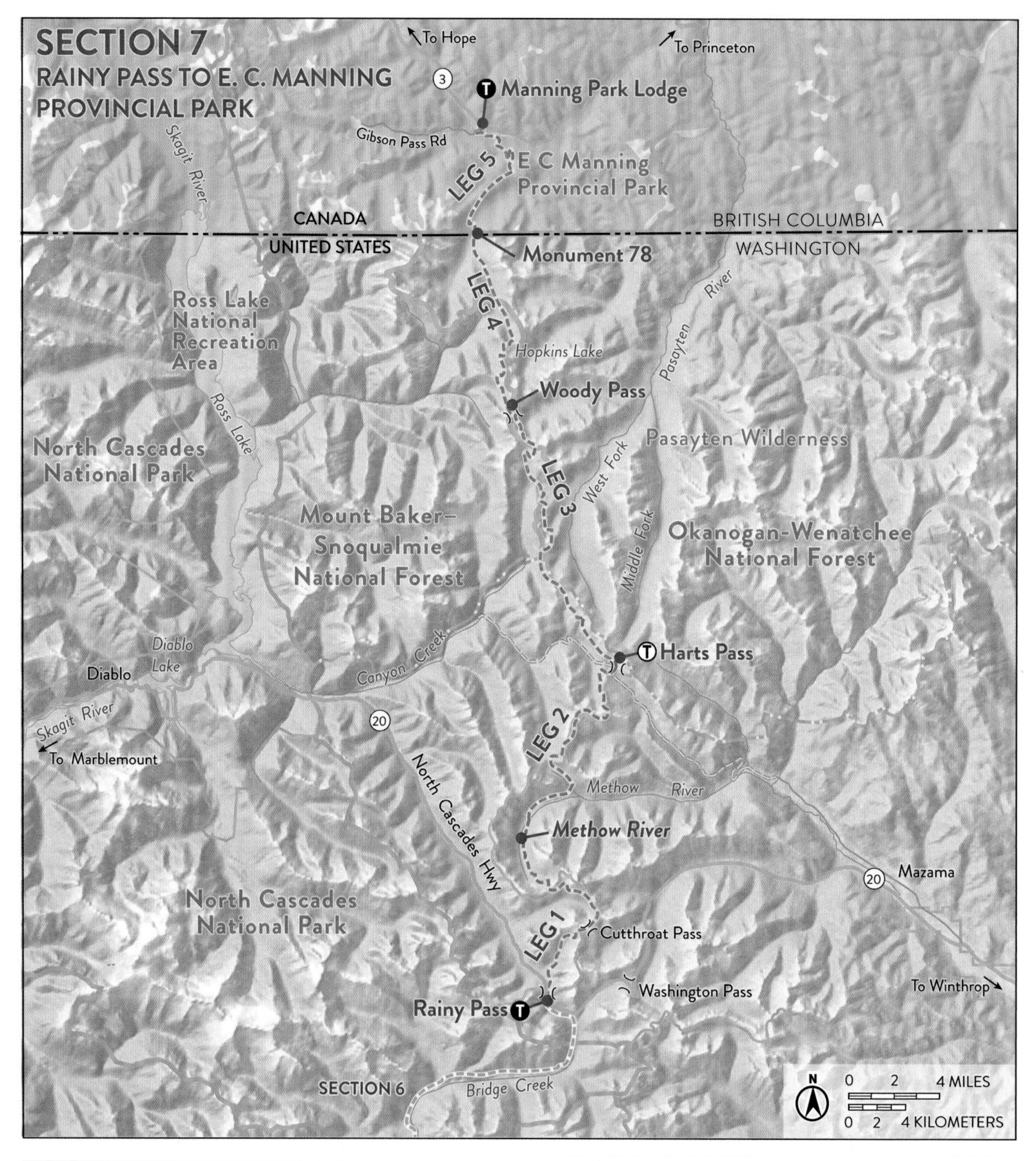

SECTION 7
RAINY PASS TO E. C. MANNING PROVINCIAL PARK
To Hope
To Princeton
3
Manning Park Lodge
Gibson Pass Rd
Skagit River
LEG 5
E C Manning Provincial Park
CANADA
UNITED STATES
BRITISH COLUMBIA
WASHINGTON
Monument 78
LEG 4
Ross Lake National Recreation Area
Pasayten River
Hopkins Lake
Woody Pass
Ross Lake
North Cascades National Park
Pasayten Wilderness
LEG 3
West Fork
Middle Fork
Mount Baker–Snoqualmie National Forest
Okanogan-Wenatchee National Forest
Diablo Lake
Diablo
Harts Pass
Canyon Creek
Skagit River
To Marblemount
20
LEG 2
North Cascades Hwy
Methow River
Methow River
Mazama
North Cascades National Park
LEG 1
Cutthroat Pass
Washington Pass
To Winthrop
Rainy Pass
SECTION 6
Bridge Creek
0 2 4 MILES
0 2 4 KILOMETERS

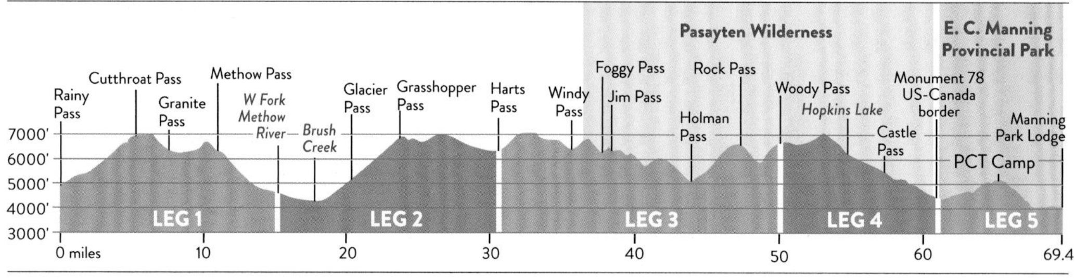

Pasayten Wilderness
E. C. Manning Provincial Park
Rainy Pass
Cutthroat Pass
Granite Pass
Methow Pass
W Fork Methow River
Brush Creek
Glacier Pass
Grasshopper Pass
Harts Pass
Windy Pass
Foggy Pass
Jim Pass
Holman Pass
Rock Pass
Woody Pass
Hopkins Lake
Castle Pass
Monument 78 US-Canada border
PCT Camp
Manning Park Lodge
7000'
6000'
5000'
4000'
3000'
LEG 1
LEG 2
LEG 3
LEG 4
LEG 5
0 miles
10
20
30
40
50
60
69.4

A large wooden sign announces the Rainy Pass Trailhead, the start of section 7.

NOTES

Cities and Services

Near the southern trailhead, find gas, groceries, dining, and lodging in Marblemount and Winthrop. At the northern trailhead, find gas, groceries, dining, and lodging at Manning Park Lodge.

Camping and Other Restrictions

Campfires are prohibited above 5000 feet north of Cutthroat Pass for 6 miles along the ridgeline. Due to the drier climate in this area, additional seasonal fire restrictions are often in place. Contact the land managers for current conditions. In Canada's **E. C. Manning Provincial Park**, you must use designated wilderness camps, which are first come, first served and charge a small fee (see "Passes, Permits, Regulations" in appendix 1). You can settle up when you get off the trail. Firearms are not permitted in Manning Park.

Water

North of Porcupine Creek, water is spotty for 7.7 miles until Snowy Lakes Trail. North of Brush Creek, water is scarce for 6.7 miles until a small spring, which in very hot summers may itself dry up, stretching the waterless miles to 12.8. From the small creek 0.3 mile north of Harts Pass, on-trail water is nonexistent for at least 5.3 miles. Water is limited from 2.2 miles north of Holman Pass for 8.5 miles. Lastly, just north of the border, Castle Creek is the last reliable water for 5 miles.

Hazards

The high country beyond Rainy Pass is very steep, treacherous, and potentially life-threatening if snowy. Do not attempt to cross during a sudden snowstorm or foggy conditions. Washouts are common between Rock Pass and Woody Pass and may be hazardous to cross. Washouts are also common north of Granite Pass before Snowy Lakes. Black bears (and the occasional grizzly bear) frequent the area near the US-Canada border. Use good bear etiquette and pay attention. In E. C. Manning Provincial Park, extreme avalanche hazards exist most years until July. Check with BC Parks for trail conditions if you intend to hike before that.

Border Crossings: For entrance into Canada, you'll need to secure paperwork in advance and carry it with you as you cross the border. Visit PCTA.org to download the "Application for Entry into Canada" form and mail it to the address listed. The application requires that you provide photocopied evidence of citizenship (see the form for details). Allow up to three months for the Canada Border Services Agency to approve your application and return it to you by mail.

When you reenter the United States at a designated border crossing, you'll need to show the required documents (see "Border Crossings" in appendix 1).

Entry into the United States from Canada on the PCT is prohibited. In other words, should your heart desire to head southbound from Canada, you'll need to start at Harts Pass and skip a section of trail. Or, if you insist on hiking the whole thing, hike from Harts Pass north to Monument 78, approximately 30 miles, and then backtrack south.

SUGGESTED ITINERARIES

7 DAYS

		Miles
Day 1	Rainy Pass to Snowy Lakes Meadow Camp	9.4
Day 2	Snowy Lakes Meadow Camp to Glacier Pass Camp	11.2
Day 3	Glacier Pass Camp to Camp 7	10.2
Day 4	Camp 7 to Shaw Creek Camp	10.6
Day 5	Shaw Creek Camp to Woody Pass Camp	8.4
Day 6	Woody Pass Camp to Castle Creek Camp (BC)	11.3
Day 7	Castle Creek Camp (BC) to Manning Park Lodge (BC)	8.3

6 DAYS

		Miles
Day 1	Rainy Pass to Snowy Lakes Meadow Camp	9.4
Day 2	Snowy Lakes Meadow Camp to Glacier Pass Camp	11.2
Day 3	Glacier Pass Camp to Camp 8	13.3
Day 4	Camp 8 to Spring Camp	12.3
Day 5	Spring Camp to Castle Pass Camp	11.0
Day 6	Castle Pass Camp to Manning Park Lodge (BC)	12.2

5 DAYS

		Miles
Day 1	Rainy Pass to Willis Camp	14.4
Day 2	Willis Camp to Spring Camp	10.2
Day 3	Spring Camp to Camp 10	15.1
Day 4	Camp 10 to Hopkins Lake Camp	14.9
Day 5	Hopkins Lake Camp to Manning Park Lodge (BC)	14.8

Cutthroat Pass is a vision in autumn, when the larch trees glow in brilliant shades of orange.

1 RAINY PASS TO METHOW RIVER

DISTANCE 15.1 miles

ELEVATION GAIN/LOSS +3200/–3690 feet

HIGH POINT 6840 feet

CONNECTING TRAILS Cutthroat Creek Trail #483

ON THE TRAIL

The PCT ascends from the Rainy Pass parking area in a forest of firs mixed with acid-loving plants like twinflower. In 0.7 mile, a reliable tributary flows over mossy lime-colored rocks, giving energy to the forest.

In 1.6 miles from the trailhead, arrive at the first of two branches of **Porcupine Creek** and a small one-tent campsite (**Camp 1**), to the left. Cross the second branch of Porcupine Creek just beyond the first, near a sign announcing its name. It should have been called Hornet Creek, given all the yellow jackets nesting in nearby dead trees and stumps. If you stop for water, use caution and do a double-take of where you intend to set down your pack—the little devils aren't fair fighters; they're aggressive and hold grudges if you tick them off. Hightail it out of there if you accidentally whack a hive.

In 2.1 miles from the trailhead, arrive at a wooded trailside camp (**Camp 2**) on a switchback to the trail's right (northeast). Two small tents could squish into the site, but one would be more comfortable. There's no water here, so pack it with you from Porcupine if you plan to spend the night. Over the next mile from Camp 2, several seasonal

It's hard to move quickly along the trail north of Rainy Pass when the views knock you off your feet.

creeks drip down from the hillside as the PCT turns east and begins climbing toward Cutthroat Pass.

At 1.4 miles from Camp 2 (3.5 miles from the trailhead), a sign with hiker and tent symbols points to a spur trail to the right, leading to a very large designated camp with room for at least five tents (**Cutthroat Camp**). This camp is very pleasant due to its location off the trail, in the middle of slow-growing larches and with views of surrounding monoliths. During warm spells, the seasonal creeks nearby may be dry, so plan on packing water with you unless the "trail telegraph"—a.k.a. hikers from the opposite direction—tells you otherwise.

From Cutthroat Camp, the PCT opens up to views of grand peaks such as Cutthroat Peak and Whistler Mountain to the south, making each step more exciting. The treeless exposure from here all the way to Methow Pass, 6.8 miles beyond, can cause a sunburned nose or windburned cheeks, lickety-split, so screen up! In late fall, this area becomes a vision in yellow, with larches adding even more drama to the jaw-dropping scenery. The high country takes on its own expressions as you switchback above tree line and into a true subalpine zone of silver boulders and basins filled with glacial-worn remnants. The trailside lawns are made of heather and dwarf huckleberries, which add a pop of color amid sheer cliffs of tan, gray, and snow. No man-made landscape could ever compare to this incredible natural mural! Could this be one of the most beautiful areas in Washington? Perhaps.

Camps, lots of them, are found in this subalpine environment (**Cutthroat Pass Camp**). The stunning beauty begs you to stay, but before you sleep under the stars, remember that this fragile

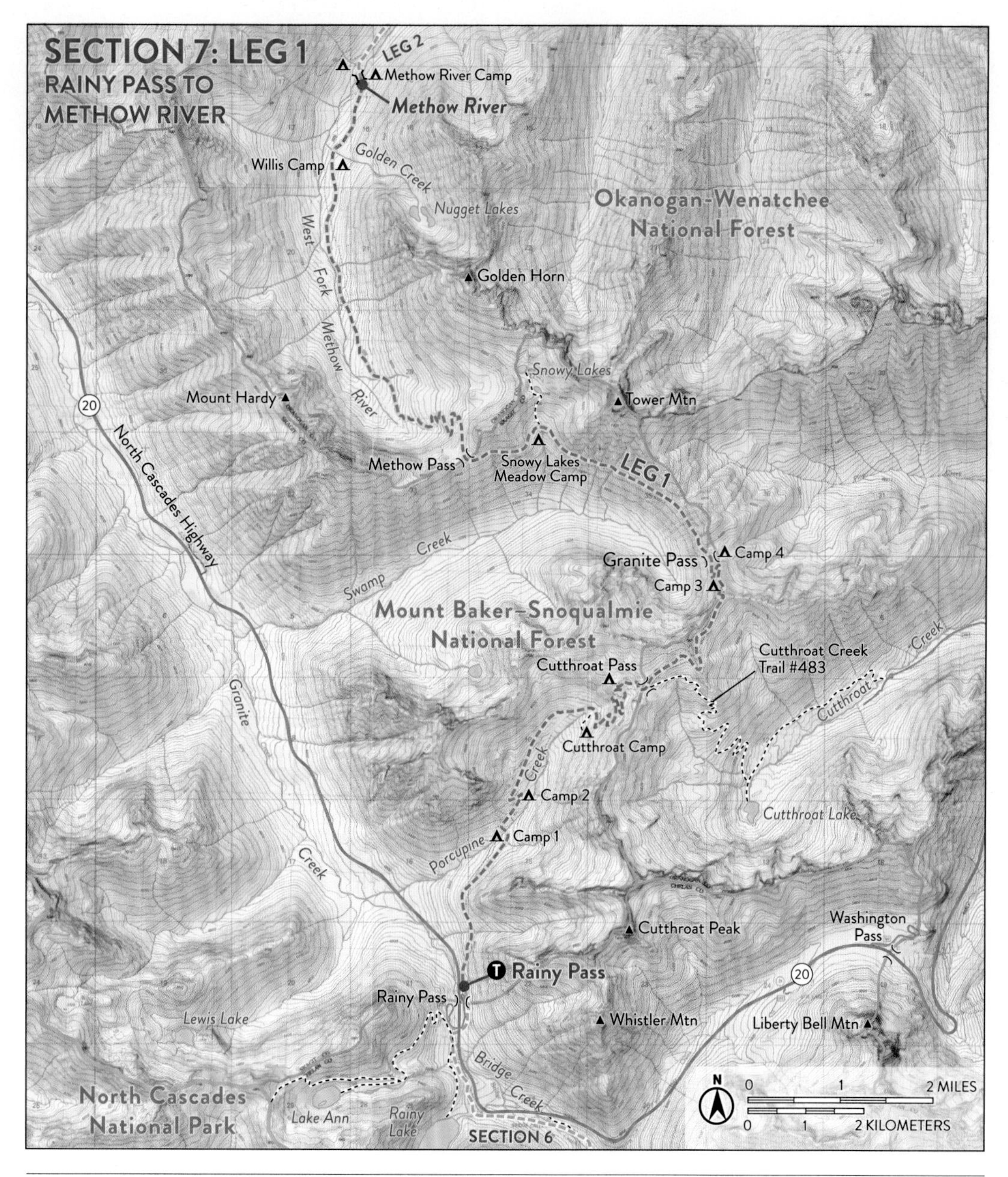
SECTION 7: LEG 1
RAINY PASS TO METHOW RIVER
LEG 2
Methow River Camp
Methow River
Willis Camp
Golden Creek
Nugget Lakes
Okanogan-Wenatchee National Forest
West Fork Methow River
Golden Horn
Snowy Lakes
Tower Mtn
Mount Hardy
20
North Cascades Highway
Methow Pass
Snowy Lakes Meadow Camp
LEG 1
Swamp Creek
Granite Pass
Camp 4
Camp 3
Mount Baker–Snoqualmie National Forest
Cutthroat Pass
Cutthroat Creek Trail #483
Creek
Granite
Cutthroat Camp
Cutthroat
Creek
Camp 2
Cutthroat Lake
Porcupine
Camp 1
Creek
Cutthroat Peak
Washington Pass
Rainy Pass
Rainy Pass
Whistler Mtn
Liberty Bell Mtn
Lewis Lake
Bridge Creek
North Cascades National Park
Lake Ann
Rainy Lake
SECTION 6
0 1 2 MILES
0 1 2 KILOMETERS

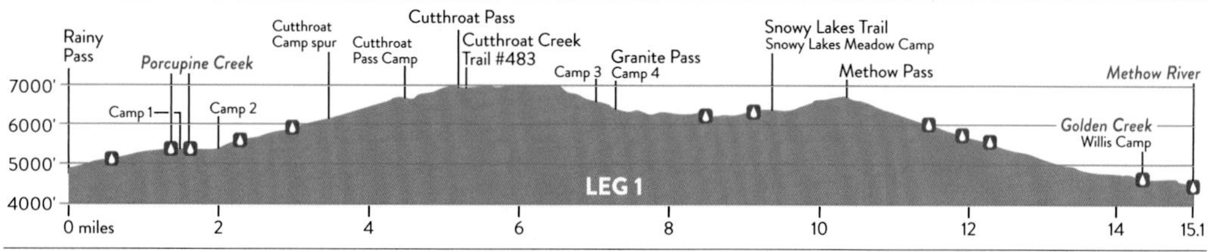
Rainy Pass
Porcupine Creek
Camp 1
Camp 2
Cutthroat Camp spur
Cutthroat Pass Camp
Cutthroat Pass
Cutthroat Creek Trail #483
Camp 3
Granite Pass
Camp 4
Snowy Lakes Trail
Snowy Lakes Meadow Camp
Methow Pass
Methow River
Golden Creek
Willis Camp
7000'
6000'
5000'
4000'
LEG 1
0 miles
2
4
6
8
10
12
14
15.1

South of Snowy Lakes, the trail gets somewhat dicey due to erosion and washouts. Stop with your feet planted firmly when you gawk at the impressive sights.

area deserves the utmost respect. Only camp in spots with no vegetation and place your tent on a durable surface. Campfires are prohibited along this ridgeline for roughly the next 6 miles, until the trail drops under 5000 feet, but unfortunately, many have not followed the rules. If time permits, help out the Forest Service and disassemble any fire pits you come upon, so others after you don't get the wrong idea. Water is scarce, so pack it with you if you're planning on staying up high.

In 1 mile from the Cutthroat Pass Camp spur, arrive at **Cutthroat Pass**, 5.0 miles from Rainy Pass. Once again, views knock your socks off, and will continue to for miles and miles. At the pass, **Cutthroat Creek Trail #483** heads right (southeast) and descends into Cutthroat Lake basin far below. The PCT stays nice and high, just below ridgeline, and continues wandering through the high country dotted with large boulders, heather-laden meadows, and deciduous, delicate larches. Giant stones, some as big as cabins, make you keep your eyes peeled for Fred and Wilma Flintstone. They could pop out at any minute! Then again, we hikers often look like Neanderthals, especially after a week or two on the trail, so your eyes might play tricks on you.

Wide-open sweeping views continue as you sway from one cirque to the next before moderately descending toward Granite Pass. A waterless one-tent site (**Camp 3**) is along a small spur trail to the left, 1.9 miles from Cutthroat Pass. Reach **Granite Pass**, a saddle on the ridgeline, in another 0.4 mile. There's a sloping one-tent camp (**Camp 4**) to the trail's right, buried in trees and again, no water. Stop at the pass for a minute and look around. Peaks in every direction resemble jagged molars gnawing high to the heavens, while the valleys below take on the familiar curve of ancient glacier-carved terrain. Mount Hardy, Golden Horn, and Tower Mountain show off their rocky summits and bid you to continue.

Just beyond Granite Pass, the PCT turns northwest and begins traversing a large scree- and talus-filled cirque on the flanks of Tower Mountain. Trail washouts are common and in places the steep hillside traverses are hazardous, so take your time. If you want to soak in the views, make sure your feet have stopped moving.

Over the next couple of miles, at least three creeklets drip and dance over the talus on their way to Swamp Creek in the valley far below. At 2.1 miles past Granite Pass (9.4 miles from Rainy Pass), arrive at a small meadow with a large well-used camp (**Snowy Lakes Meadow Camp**). The camp could easily accommodate four or five tents, has a nearby creeklet for water, and sports rocks and log benches for sitting. A cairn to the trail's right (north) marks the route to Snowy Lakes, a popular side trip.

After Snowy Lakes Meadow Camp, the PCT continues traversing open country and then switchbacks through boulder fields to **Methow Pass** in 0.9 mile, a level saddle with larches and fragile meadowlands. A couple of emergency camps are here, but they aren't great options due to the fragile alpine terrain. Instead, keep 'er rolling back down to tree line, where better camping awaits. Fleeting peekaboo views of both Mount Hardy and Golden Horn accompany you as you descend, as if the high country doesn't want to see you go. Admittedly, it is hard to leave, but the show isn't over till the fat marmot whistles. As you duck into the green tunnel and begin descending northwest, you'll pass at least three tumbling creeks and countless late-season mushrooms of every variety under the sun. If you decide to indulge, be sure you know that what you're eating isn't deadly or poisonous—nothing ruins a good trail day faster than needing a new kidney.

The woodsy landscape is like so many in the Cascades, complete with neon-green moss, a carpet of forest duff filled with conifer needles, and huckleberry bushes starved for fruit-producing light. In roughly 2.8 miles from Methow Pass, pass through an impressive landslide, which came sailing down the shoulder of Golden Horn, choking tree roots and blanketing the PCT with rocks and mud. The unstable hillside makes a perfect slide for winter avalanches, so new debris seems to show up each year. Thanks to the work of trail crews, the PCT has been rerouted over the top of the debris and several downed trees have been cleared. Navigating the short distance through the slide is very straightforward, but look for cairns if you get confused.

In 4.1 miles from Methow Pass, arrive at woodsy **Willis Camp** (whatchu talkin' 'bout, Willis?) and the chilly nearby waters of Golden Creek. The camp is well used, complete with a sign, and has ample room for several tents and the convenience of a running creek for rehydrating or taking a dip to wash off the essence of water buffalo.

SNOWY LAKES

One of the most popular trails in the North Cascades, the route to **Snowy Lakes**, is marked by a cairn just off the PCT, 2.1 miles past Granite Pass near Snowy Lakes Meadow Camp. Take the steep, ankle-twisty trail as it ascends roughly 0.5 mile to Lower Snowy Lake and then continue 0.3 mile to Upper Snowy. The panorama of the lakes with a backdrop of towering spires is mind-blowingly breathtaking any time of year, but especially so in the fall, when the larches begin turning gold. Camping up here is permitted, although due to the high number of visitors, restrictions may soon be in place. Until then, if you don't mind the extra mileage and huff and puff, haul your tent up to the alpine country, camp only on durable surfaces, don't build campfires, and practice Leave No Trace to the letter. For the best chance of solitude, avoid weekends and holidays. If you do happen upon theme-park-style crowds, give them your best trail-brained, scenery-drunk smile.

In 0.7 mile from Willis Camp, arrive at a sturdy wooden bridge across the babbling **West Fork Methow River** **O**, dipping and spinning in eddies as it rushes over downed trees and small rocks. There are two campsites here (**Methow River Camp**)—one to the south of the bridge and one to the north. The southern one is visible from the trail, well used, and one of the best campsites around. It has room for at least two tents, make-shift benches for sitting, and a fire pit for chilly nights, provided no burn bans are in effect. Just across the bridge, a "Methow River" sign hanging on a tree has been thoroughly sapped and looks like candle-wax-gone-bad. Dare you to touch it. Yes, I'm *that* friend.

Just a few steps away, another sign with tent and hiker symbols points to a spur trail and the northern campsite, approximately 75 feet off the PCT. This site is a tad smaller and has improvised sitting stumps, a fire pit, and a bit more privacy. Either site is a fine pick, so if this is goodnight, sweet dreams! Before you skedaddle out of this area, be sure to stop and fill up on water, since the river here is the last reliable water for 2.9 miles, until Brush Creek.

CAMP-TO-CAMP MILEAGE

Rainy Pass to Camp 1	1.6
Camp 1 to Camp 2	0.5
Camp 2 to Cutthroat Camp	1.4
Cutthroat Camp to Cutthroat Pass Camp	1.0
Cutthroat Pass Camp to Camp 3	2.4
Camp 3 to Camp 4	0.4
Camp 4 to Snowy Lakes Meadow Camp	2.1
Snowy Lakes Meadow Camp to Willis Camp	5.0
Willis Camp to Methow River Camp	0.7

2 METHOW RIVER TO HARTS PASS

DISTANCE 15.3 miles

ELEVATION GAIN/LOSS
+3670/–1870 feet

HIGH POINT 7000 feet

CONNECTING TRAILS
West Fork Methow Trail #480

ON THE TRAIL

From the **West Fork Methow River**, the PCT rolls gently on a fairly level grade through pockets of conifers and in 0.8 mile reaches a junction with the rarely traveled **East Creek Trail #756**. This trail, and the one following it, **Azurite Pass/Mill Creek Trail #755**, are unmaintained, as in don't explore them unless you can find your way out of a dark tunnel in a strange land, blindfolded atop a feral donkey. Years ago, the East Creek Trail was the part of the Cascade Crest Trail leading up to Meebee Pass and over to Gold Hill Mine, while Trail #755 led up Azurite Pass and toward Azurite Mine. Nowadays both trails are extinct bush-whacks, save for the wooden signs of yesteryear. In between the two trails, the dribbling, unreliable Jet Creek, if flowing, is the last water until Brush Creek in another 1.8 miles.

The PCT jumps between meadowy avalanche chute runouts, evergreen thickets, brushy foliage, and talus fields as it traverses the northwestern side of the valley between two slabby stone ridge-lines of unnamed summits. The dryness of the eastern Cascade Crest is evident, not only in the air you breathe, but also in the wildfire evidence on opposite hills and the rustling of dry grasses. The occasional quaking aspen clusters catch the wind just right and shimmy in a splendid dance choreographed to the wind gusts. The trail retains a very gentle grade, allowing your footsteps to find a faster cadence.

In 2.8 miles from the Methow River, arrive at **Brush Creek Camp**, a small one-tent site to the left (northwest) tucked into the hillside, surrounded by riparian foliage. The well-used site has log benches for lounging and a fire pit, and

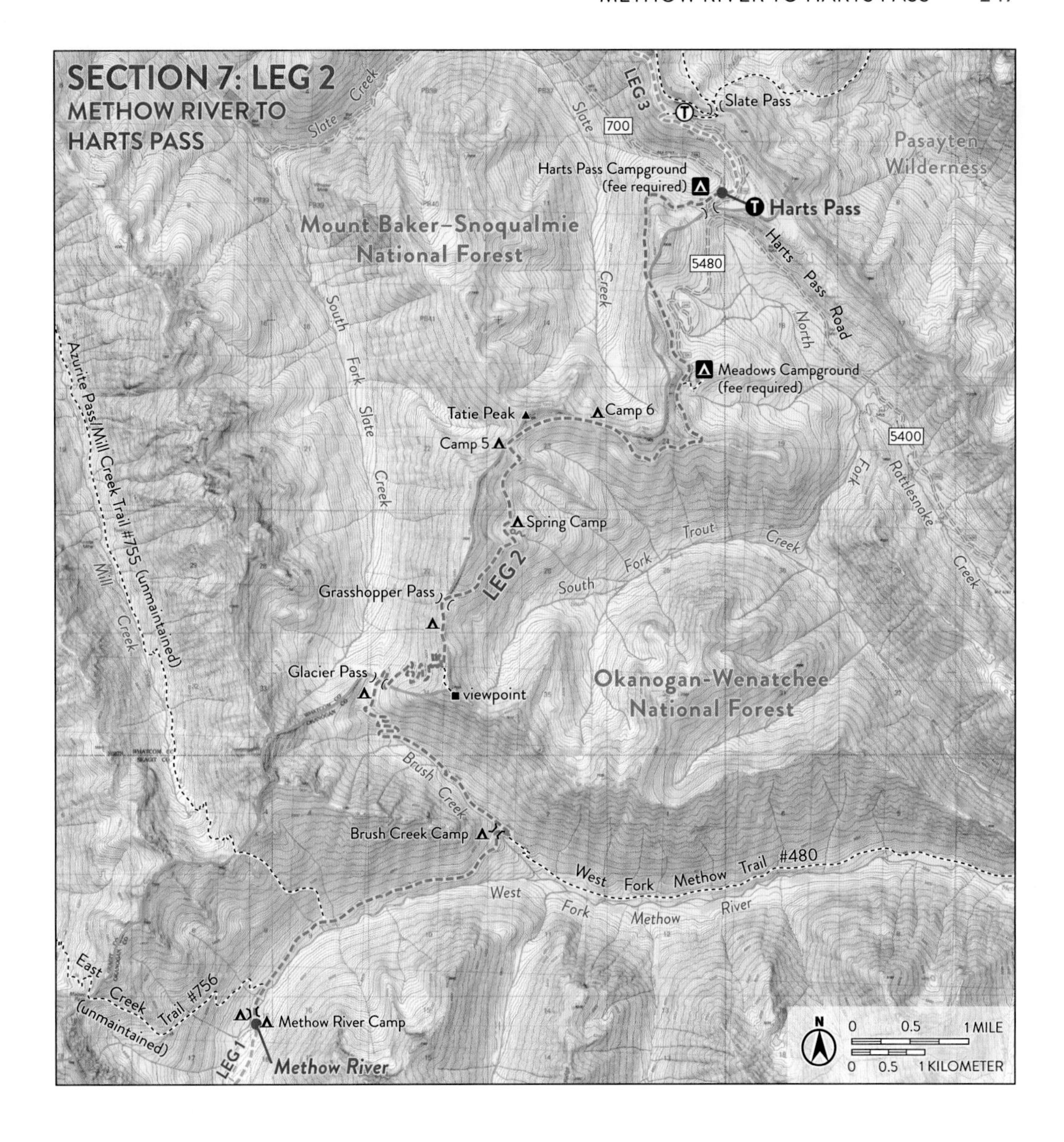
SECTION 7: LEG 2
METHOW RIVER TO HARTS PASS
Slate Pass
LEG 3
700
Harts Pass Campground (fee required)
Harts Pass
Pasayten Wilderness
Mount Baker–Snoqualmie National Forest
5480
Harts Pass Road
Meadows Campground (fee required)
Tatie Peak
Camp 6
Camp 5
5400
Spring Camp
LEG 2
Grasshopper Pass
Glacier Pass
viewpoint
Okanogan-Wenatchee National Forest
Azurite Pass/Mill Creek Trail #755 (unmaintained)
Brush Creek Camp
West Fork Methow Trail #480
West Fork Methow River
East Creek Trail #756 (unmaintained)
Methow River Camp
Methow River
LEG 1
0 0.5 1 MILE
0 0.5 1 KILOMETER

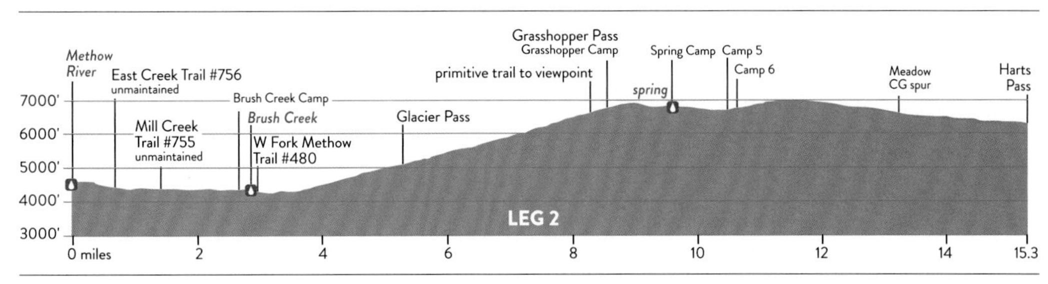
Methow River
East Creek Trail #756 unmaintained
Mill Creek Trail #755 unmaintained
Brush Creek Camp
Brush Creek
W Fork Methow Trail #480
Glacier Pass
primitive trail to viewpoint
Grasshopper Pass
Grasshopper Camp
spring
Spring Camp
Camp 5
Camp 6
Meadow CG spur
Harts Pass
7000'
6000'
5000'
4000'
3000'
LEG 2
0 miles
2
4
6
8
10
12
14
15.3

the reliable Brush Creek ◘ flows 0.1 mile beyond. Stop at Brush Creek and get water and plenty of it, because **you won't find easily accessible, reliable water for the next 6.7 miles**.

Cross Brush Creek on a durable wooden bridge and in 0.1 mile arrive at a junction with **West Fork Methow Trail #480**, going right (east) toward Rattlesnake Trailhead and River Bend Campground. The PCT turns left (northwest) and begins modestly ascending the Brush Creek valley in the shadow of lofty, granite Azurite Peak to the west. Cascade mountain ash, in late summer, exhibits a brilliant orange berry and gives an unexpected splash of trailside color as you climb higher and higher. Several chutes show evidence of avalanche debris where snow and ice has knocked down trees like bowling pins. Saplings in those chutes grow back despite their slim odds of a long life.

Cross several scree and talus fields lined with white pearly everlasting before switchbacking in evergreen groves and arriving at **Glacier Pass**, 2.6 miles from Brush Creek. The level, forested pass has no views but is protected from the elements, making **Glacier Pass Camp** a cozy choice. There's not a drop of water in sight, except for the occasional mud puddle, so be glad you schlepped it up from Brush Creek. Plenty of campsites line the trail, but the official one is via a spur trail left (west), midway along the pass. A separate horse camp is also located here, a fine place to lead a steed indeed!

After Glacier Pass, the PCT busts out above tree line and begins climbing to an unnamed ridge through grasses, wildflowers, dwarf huckleberries, subalpine fir, whistling hoary marmots, and squeaking Columbia ground squirrels. From here to beyond Harts Pass, you're traveling on somewhat exposed terrain. Keep your eyes open for afternoon thunderstorms and be sure to practice good lightning etiquette should you find yourself in an unexpected summer storm.

Near Grasshopper Pass, the trail traverses magical-looking terrain.

Layers and layers of brilliant mountain ridgelines create stunning panoramas as you head north toward Grasshopper Pass.

Back and forth you go, on what seems like a very long climb if not for the grand views getting better with each step. Reach the top of the ridge 2.7 miles beyond Glacier Pass and prepare to stop and suck in the sights. This is some of the most remote and rugged terrain in Washington, and the view from the ridge will rock your rucksack—majestic mountains everywhere! If you're sure-footed and want an even better view, drop your pack, grab your camera, and head south (right) to locate a steep, narrow trail that climbs the ridgeline roughly 0.2 mile to the tippy-top of an unnamed peak and one of the most breathtaking visions ever. One year, a photo of this mind-blowing panorama was my holiday card. Azurite Peak and Mount Ballard make up the western ridgeline, their rugged stone faces in shades of rust and gray softened by white glaciers. To the north, Tatie Peak shows an etching of the PCT across her shoulders. And to the south proudly stand Golden Horn, Holliway Mountain, Tower Mountain—and layers upon layers of more.

The PCT follows the ridge northbound to a magical playground of larches, firs, and ground-growing kinnikinnick, reaching **Grasshopper Pass** and several camp spots (**Grasshopper Camp**) 0.3 mile after gaining the ridge (8.6 miles from Methow Pass). Water is not available, and campfires are prohibited above 5000 feet, so let the stars be your sparks.

From Grasshopper Pass, a high-country traverse rolls you gradually along exposed slopes, with views of valleys sprinkled with boulders and conifers. In 1 mile from Grasshopper Pass, arrive at a very popular camping area (**Spring Camp**), to the right (east), with several desirable sites. Hooray!

With sparse larch trees and low-growing berries, the backcountry south of Harts Pass almost feels like a mythical playground.

This camp has reliable water from a spring, and it's the only source around, so stop and drink up. To access the spring, follow the trails from the camp southeast into the mossy valley below, where grateful PCT travelers bow down to the quiet dribble.

The PCT next heads to the shoulders of Tatie Peak, 0.9 mile past Spring Camp, alternating between barren hillsides and larch thickets and gently climbing toward a gap. Approximately 250 feet before the gap, reach a spur to a small one-tent camp (**Camp 5**) to the left (west). This camp is well used and has great views, but no water. Beyond the gap, the trail turns east and takes you around Tatie Peak's southern flank before popping up onto another ridgeline with a small camp (**Camp 6**), 1 mile from the gap. This waterless camp doesn't get much use due to its rocky soil and exposure.

Wildfires, and plenty of them, have burned many acres from here to Harts Pass. There is life after fire, and the burn zones showcase dwarf huckleberries, fir saplings, and grasses growing with reckless abandon in the acidic soil. Chipmunks dart around charred logs and woodpeckers find tasty morsels living in decaying trees. Beauty can be found in the most unexpected places.

After completing the traverse under Tatie's southern flank, the trail makes a sharp turn northbound and arrives at a large PCT sign, 3.5 miles from Spring Camp, noting various points and their mileages. Below you is **Meadows Campground**, a car campground with access via a spur trail to the right (east). This waterless Forest Service campground charges a small fee and has fourteen first-come, first-served sites, picnic tables, and vault toilets. Trailers are not permitted. In 2003, this campground was annihilated by the Needles Fire and has been rebuilt to be a very pleasant camping area, despite the blackened trees.

As you continue hiking north, you'll have better views of the basin and the resulting fire damage. The PCT pops in and out of the fire zone, traverses narrow hillsides, and occasionally opens up to views westward until it spits you out on a service road to Harts Pass, 2.2 miles from the Meadows Campground PCT sign.

If you're not stopping at Harts Pass, turn left and walk the road roughly 50 feet to find the PCT continuing to the road's right (northeast). **Harts Pass Campground** is to the road's right, a popular car-camping area and access point for those meeting friends or hopping off the trail. The waterless campground charges a small fee and has five first-come, first-served sites, picnic tables, and a vault toilet. Trailers are not permitted—and there's a reason for that. The road to Harts Pass from the town of Winthrop is considered one of the most treacherous in the state, complete with blind corners and narrow, winding, one-lane no-passing zones. Give your buddies a heads-up and wish them luck if they intend to meet you at the pass.

Trail Angels are often found lounging at Harts Pass Campground offering fruit, snacks, and water to fresh-food-deprived hikers. There's no trash service at Harts Pass, so pack it in and pack it out. There's no water either. But there is water up ahead, despite rumors to the contrary. One volunteer told me that the Forest Service has been struggling for years to debunk the myth that there's no water for 17 miles north of Harts Pass. Not so! **Just 0.4 mile beyond Harts Pass is a reliable creek** 🅾, flowing freely as it bounces down into the Slate Creek basin. Beyond that, seasonal water flows in 5.3 miles.

BOOM, ZAP, BLAZE!

Lightning. It's electric boogie-woogie-woogie! When lightning storms move in quickly in the high country, a little know-how just might keep your hair from standing on end and save you from charred cheeks. **Where there's thunder, there's lightning.** Pay attention and get ready to take precautions. **Get down, baby, get down!** Should you be on a ridgeline or exposed peak when the storm hits, head down a gully or into the forest. **Stay away from isolated or particularly tall trees and avoid water.** If shelter is not close by, put your feet together and **crouch low to the ground** on a foam pad if you have one. If not, don't sweat it, but avoid crouching on your pack. **Out of the tent, Kent!** When lightning strikes it seeks poles. Tents have poles. 'Nuf said. **Don't act like a rod.** Move metal objects, such as trekking poles, ice axes, or fishing poles away from you. **Quit texting about it!** Being on your phone could attract lightning. Save the OMG MSG for a time when you can POAHF (put on a happy face) about the experience. **Avoid being a barnacle to your hiking partner.** Keep at least 15 feet between you. Probably a good idea anyway—showers are scarce in these parts.

CAMP-TO-CAMP MILEAGE

Methow River Camp to Brush Creek Camp	2.8
Brush Creek Camp to Glacier Pass Camp	2.7
Glacier Pass Camp to Grasshopper Camp	3.0
Grasshopper Camp to Spring Camp	1.0
Spring Camp to Camp 5	0.9
Camp 5 to Camp 6	1.0
Camp 6 to Harts Pass	3.9

Dead standing remains of fir and larch trees bear evidence of the hot infernos that have ripped through the Harts Pass area in recent years.

HARTS PASS: WHAT WAS THIS PLACE?

It would be easy to enjoy the spectacular landscape around Harts Pass without giving much thought to the area's history, but it's fun to think about what was going on in these parts many years ago. In 1895, the Harts Pass area was a profitable gold-mining community. All told, more than thirty-five hundred people worked and lived near the mines, which were sprinkled throughout the surrounding hills. A small community boasted everything you'd expect from a functional old-fashioned town, including a saloon, sawmill, blacksmith shop, postal facility, theater, general store, and several hotels.

An entrepreneur named Thomas Hart commissioned Charles Ballard, a civil engineer, to chart a road through the steep peaks and valleys in order to transfer goods from town to the mining community and vice versa. Once the road bearing Hart's name was constructed, modified wagons and horse pack trains carried gold and supplies down the steep narrow route toward the Methow Valley. In a few years, as so often happened with gold rushes, word came of new strikes and more money to be made in other areas, such as British Columbia, Arizona, and parts of Alaska.

By the early 1900s, the gold rushers had completely deserted the Harts Pass area. They left in such a rush that those visiting in subsequent years found their belongings and personal effects, left behind perfectly in place as if the inhabitants had just up and vanished. Several mines in the area, harvesting various minerals such as copper, zinc, silver, lead, and whatever gold remained, were still in use after the gold rush folks left, but most mines were closed by the early 1930s. During that decade, Franklin D. Roosevelt's Green Army, the Civilian Conservation Corps (or CCC), widened the road to Harts Pass, allowing for car travel and easier access.

Today, Harts Pass is a premier recreation area and Mother Nature continues to take over evidence of yesteryear, although a few gold-mining claims are still active. Should you happen upon an abandoned mine, use your good wits and common sense. Of course they pose hazards and are unsafe to enter, so don't tempt fate.

3 HARTS PASS TO WOODY PASS

DISTANCE 19.4 miles

ELEVATION GAIN/LOSS
+4520/–4060 feet

HIGH POINT 6880 feet

CONNECTING TRAILS
Holman Creek Trail #472A,
Devils Ridge Trail #752

ON THE TRAIL

Follow the access road near **Harts Pass** approximately 50 yards to the left (northwest) and locate the continuation of the PCT. Duck into a sparse forest and arrive at a mediocre forested camp (**Camp 7**) to the left (northwest) in 0.3 mile. The lightly used site is best for one tent, although two friendly hikers could squish two tents here if they were determined. Water is just up ahead in a short 0.1 mile, in a reliable creek. Fill up here because **it's dry for at least 5.3 miles beyond this point** and possibly for almost 10 miles if you're traveling in a particularly hot summer.

In 0.2 mile beyond the creek, arrive at an unsigned spur trail to the right (northeast), which leads to the road above. Stay left (northwest) and continue on the PCT. In 0.8 mile from the spur, reach a spur to the **official trailhead** and wilderness-use permit box. Stop and fill out a permit, assuming you're going farther than Windy Pass, where you'll pass into the Pasayten Wilderness.

With the permit on your pack, climb through pockets of larch and fir and ascend a slope just under the **Slate Peak Lookout**, to the right (north), and gradually ascend open slopes through meadows of dancing flowers and far-reaching views. On a clear day, Mount Baker—an active glaciated stratovolcano—is visible to the north, along with a panorama of peaks, all visible from a high point on the trail just beyond the lookout. Descend gently to a sweeping westward trail curve and in 2.1 miles from the official trailhead find a mediocre two- or three-tent camp (**Camp 8**) to the left (southwest), near a cluster of trees and above the seasonal and unreliable Benson Creek. A lucky few will get water from Benson Creek; the rest of us, not so much. It's best to carry water through this section and let luck be a lady somewhere else.

This is probably a good time to mention that this open landscape lends itself to camping in many places and there are a few spots where folks have made it work, likely due to lack of daylight and/or desperation. I've done my best to list the most established spots that are within proximity of the trail, but you'll likely find more if you cruise around and follow spurs and connecting trails. Many of the camps in this area are simply mediocre and not optimal places to spend the night due to lack of water, odd slopes, or tree roots in your back. But when you're so tired that you start to stagger, and your eyes start playing tricks on you, those mediocre spots look like slappin' fine places to call home.

After the sweeping trail curve, the PCT straightens, turns northward, and with little fanfare arrives at level **Buffalo Pass**, 0.7 mile beyond Camp 8 (4.2 miles from Harts Pass). There are

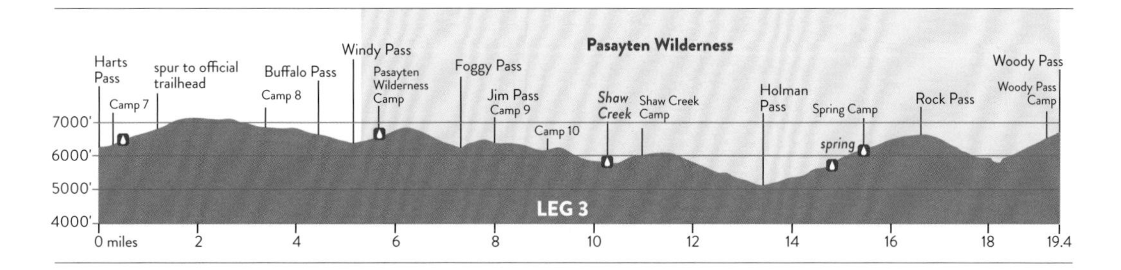

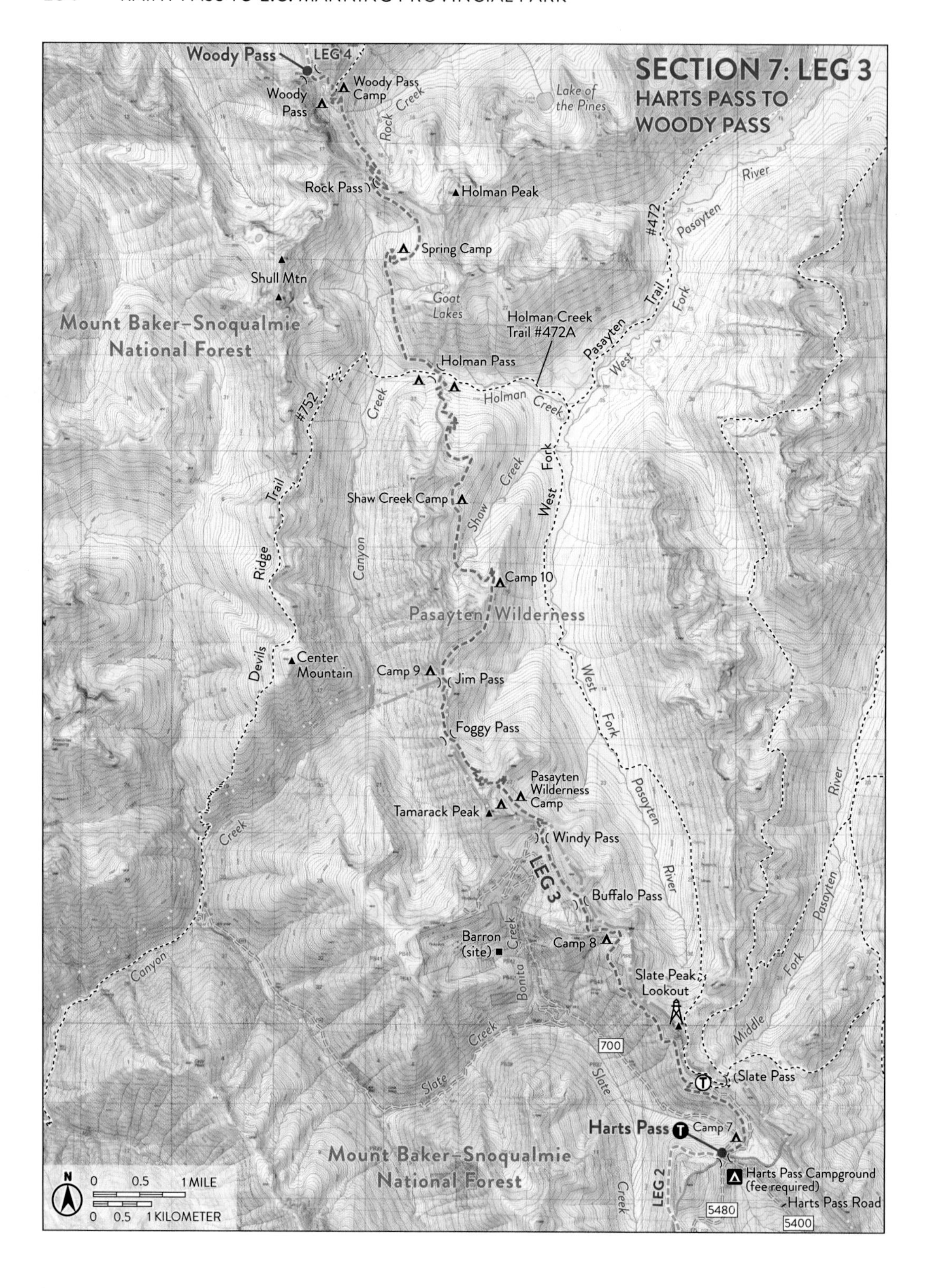
SECTION 7: LEG 3
HARTS PASS TO WOODY PASS
Woody Pass
LEG 4
Woody Pass Camp
Woody Pass
Rock Creek
Lake of the Pines
River
Rock Pass
Holman Peak
#472
Pasayten
Spring Camp
Shull Mtn
Trail
Fork
Goat Lakes
Holman Creek Trail #472A
Mount Baker–Snoqualmie National Forest
Pasayten
West
Holman Pass
Holman Creek
Creek
#752
Fork
Shaw Creek
Shaw Creek Camp
West
Trail
Canyon
Ridge
Camp 10
Pasayten Wilderness
Center Mountain
Devils
Camp 9
Jim Pass
West
Fork
Foggy Pass
Pasayten Wilderness Camp
Pasayten
River
Tamarack Peak
Windy Pass
Creek
LEG 3
River
Buffalo Pass
Pasayten
Barron (site)
Bonita Creek
Camp 8
Slate Peak Lookout
Fork
Canyon
Creek
Middle
700
Slate
Slate Creek
Slate Pass
Harts Pass
Camp 7
Mount Baker–Snoqualmie National Forest
N
0 0.5 1 MILE
0 0.5 1 KILOMETER
Creek
LEG 2
Harts Pass Campground (fee required)
Harts Pass Road
5480
5400

The Slate Peak Lookout tower stands proudly above the PCT north of Harts Pass.

SLATE PEAK LOOKOUT

This lofty spot has some interesting history. In 1924, just after the gold-mining boom in the area, a small gable-roof cupola cabin stood here, staffed by the Forest Service, which used it to protect the surrounding lands and watch for fires. During World War II, in the early 1940s, the lookout was staffed continuously by those searching for enemy aircraft as part of the military's Aircraft Warning Service. In 1954, the cabin was replaced by a classic L4 lookout tower, which was moved from nearby Leecher Mountain and dropped into place. Two years later, the US Air Force deemed the site a perfect location for a radar station and took over the land from the Forest Service.

With new construction underway, the L4 lookout was destroyed and 40 feet were bulldozed off the top of Slate Peak in an effort to make it flat for the new radar station. That was as far as the project went before it was abandoned—leaving Slate Peak flat-topped ever since. In 1956, the current tower was built high in the sky, close to the height of the original summit. Today, the tower belongs to the Forest Service and is one of few lookouts still occasionally in use. In recent history, when fires near Goat Peak and Elbow Basin broke out, the lofty lookout was used to monitor fire conditions and relay radio reports. The Slate Peak parking lot, at 7400 feet, is the highest elevation you can reach by car in Washington.

The views like this one near Woody Pass just keep coming.

several named passes in this area, and because the landscape is so similar it all begins to blur. You won't be the first to lose track of which pass is which or which pass you've passed. It's really more about the future than the "pass," so keep your eyes forward and don't sweat the map. Most passes around here are simply low divides, flat spots, or humps in the terrain and don't announce themselves with flashy trail signs. There's so much to see, that it won't matter much—just wander to your heart's content.

In 0.9 mile from Buffalo Pass, arrive at **Windy Pass** and a view across the ridge of Tamarack Peak and an area called the Glory Hole of mining. In 1894, men traveled from all over to mine this area, living in the small town of Barron, to the south, now a ghost town. Today, a teal-green yurt—called Barron Yurt—stands in Indiana Basin just below Windy Pass and functions, by special-use permit from the Forest Service, as a base camp for a local heli-ski outfitter.

In just another 0.2 mile, enter the **Pasayten Wilderness** at the north edge of Windy Pass, announced by a sign to the right (northeast). Larches grow with reckless abandon in thickets and greet you with bowing boughs. In 0.5 mile from the wilderness boundary, enter a small meadowed cirque with a scree-filled gully, a seasonal creek, and a few campsites (**Pasayten Wilderness Camp**). If water is flowing, which it often is, jackpot! If not, you'll be glad you muscled it in with you. The site to the right (northeast), via a spur trail, is the largest and most desirable of those in the immediate vicinity. The one to the left isn't frequently used but would do in a pinch. A few more wannabe sites are around this area and would work in the unlikely event that the inn is full. The PCT switchbacks out of the meadowed cirque and then immediately traverses another basin. To the right (east), in a cluster of trees, is a fine little two- or three-tent site visible from the trail and accessed via a spur trail. Water is from the creek near the other sites you just passed, or from the stash in your pack.

Next, switchback up a finger of Tamarack Peak, cross the ridge, and descend to a saddle called **Foggy Pass**, 2 miles from the Pasayten Wilderness boundary (7.2 miles from Harts Pass). True to its name, every time I've been here it's been foggy. Let's hope the clouds break for you and grant you some views! Previous travelers have made camps in meadows along the trail in this high country, and I've made a point to leave them out. Due to the short growing season and Leave No Trace ethics, these camps should be avoided.

A gentle, more wooded amble to **Jim Pass** takes you 0.9 mile beyond Foggy Pass. A one-tent waterless camp (**Camp 9**) is found just beyond the pass but isn't the best one in these parts. If you can wait, wait.

In 1.2 miles, a two-tent waterless camp (**Camp 10**) is just off the trail to the right (east), with a mountainside prow where you can perch and eat your oatmeal. Views to the PCT's right (east) show off a near valley thick with conifers and layer after layer of distant peaks and valleys, fit for a painter's canvas. Some trees show signs of insect damage, which is unfortunately becoming more and more common in the high country.

The trail crosses under a stony edge of Jim Peak, known as the Devils Backbone, before making a hairpin turn to the south and dropping into a small cirque with the reliable **Shaw Creek** and friends, the creeklets. *Stop for water if you need it, because the next trickle that crosses the trail is roughly 4.5 miles ahead.* The PCT next works its way west, then turns north, and drops into the forest. In 0.8 mile from Shaw Creek, arrive at a spur trail for **Shaw Creek Camp** on the right (east). Two well-established sites are visible from the PCT and have fire pits and logs for sitting.

The forest walk continues, twisting and turning in a series of short switchbacks through a dark spindly forest in a gradual descent. Deeper you go, with light dissipating and shadows looming on trunks and boughs. Even on the sunniest of days,

Look for mule deer grazing in grassy meadows as you head into the high country of the Pasayten Wilderness.

Landslides like this one between Rock Pass and Woody Pass, which occurred in 2013, may take place during periods of heavy rain. Use extra caution when crossing a slide—it may send you on a ride!

the Holman Pass area swallows brightness, obscuring views with ominous trees that might at any moment reach out for you. Thankfully, most hikers who have traveled this way have arrived safely at the valley bottom, **Holman Pass** proper, 3.3 miles past Shaw Creek. Here, a crossroads of trails meet under the thick canopy and several campsites await. To the left (west) is **Devils Ridge Trail #752**, to the right (east) is **Holman Creek Trail #472A**, and straight ahead (north) is the continuation of the PCT. Take either intersecting trail east or west to find camping options (**Holman Pass Camp**). Pack your water here, or visit Holman Creek, roughly 1 mile to the east.

Follow the signs toward Woody Pass—or just head north—climbing now and making your way up from the valley floor. To the east, Shull Mountain wears its stone face proudly and avalanche slides on lesser hills are evident. In 1.2 miles from Holman Pass, the first small brook since Shaw Creek crosses the trail, followed by another in 0.5 mile. While these flows aren't always heavy, they usually produce enough water to collect what you need.

A series of moderate switchbacks heading east help you gain some necessary elevation before the PCT turns north. At 2.2 miles beyond Holman Pass, the trail opens into a large meadow filled with seasonal lupine and various grasses on the shoulder of an unnamed ridge in the shadow of Holman Peak. As most trails through meadows do, this one breaks into two parallel tracks, leaving you to decide which tread is most comfortable on your tired soles.

The trail ascends through the vast open area and then swings northwest to a camp (**Spring Camp**) in a patch of trees to the left (west), roughly 0.1 mile into the meadow. There are at least four campsites in this area, making Spring Camp a good goal for those who are counting miles and making advance plans about where to crash each night. Thankfully, a reliable ground spring, hence the camp name, is also located here. **This is the last reliable water until Hopkins Lake roughly 8.5 miles farther.**

From Spring Camp, the PCT moderately ascends the meadowy ridge with views of Shull and Powder mountains, reaching the tippy-top crest known as Rock Pass at 1.1 miles from Spring Camp. You won't need a guidebook to tell you why this place is called **Rock Pass**! Giant stone faces on peaks in nearly every direction, not to mention the pebbles and scree under your feet, probably encouraged the obvious name.

From here, descend into the next valley to the north and then traverse the pastoral Rock Creek basin before climbing again, this time on the way to Woody Pass. An old trail high on the ridge looks tempting to follow, but it's a death wish—it literally falls off the mountain. Instead, be sure to follow a newly built stretch of PCT as it switchbacks down into the valley. In the summer of 2013, torrential rains sent a landslide crashing through this area, wiping out the former trail. The reroute was rebuilt slightly lower, adding more elevation gain and loss to this leg. Years before, a similar thing happened on the same hill. Trail remnants are scattered about, artifacts of Mother Nature's complete control of where the PCT ends up.

In approximately 2.5 miles from Rock Pass, the climbing eases and the landscape is filled with heather, juniper, dwarf evergreens, and gray boulders, a hillside fit for a gnome. The winding trail leads to four small campsites (**Woody Pass Camp**), two to the right (east and northeast), both accessible by spur trails, and two to the left (south and southwest), visible from the PCT, located roughly 0.1 to 0.2 mile apart along the trail. As always, use care not to camp on vegetation and pack out your toilet paper. Water can occasionally be found in a seasonal trickle to the PCT's left in a small grassy basin, but it's not reliable, so plan on packing water with you if you camp here. In 0.2 mile beyond the camp, 2.7 miles from Rock Pass, arrive at the rocky and somewhat deceptively named **Woody Pass**.

CAMP-TO-CAMP MILEAGE

Harts Pass to Camp 7	0.3
Camp 7 to Camp 8	3.2
Camp 8 to Pasayten Wilderness Camp	2.2
Pasayten Wilderness Camp to Camp 9	2.3
Camp 9 to Camp 10	1.2
Camp 10 to Shaw Creek Camp	1.7
Shaw Creek Camp to Holman Pass Camp	2.5
Holman Pass Camp to Spring Camp	2.2
Spring Camp to Woody Pass Camp	3.6
Woody Pass Camp to Woody Pass	0.2

Should you need to dispel any befuddlement, signs point in all directions at Castle Pass south of the border.

4 WOODY PASS TO MONUMENT 78

DISTANCE 10.9 miles

ELEVATION GAIN/LOSS
+930/–3320 feet

HIGH POINT 7130 feet

CONNECTING TRAILS
Boundary Trail #533,
Castle Pass Trail #749

ON THE TRAIL

Beyond **Woody Pass**, the PCT kicks up views to the northwest of countless unnamed peaks along with a handful of named ones, such as Joker and Freezeout mountains. What a view! The jagged spines recede in layer upon layer, almost making you dizzy.

Alternating between pockets of firs and meadows, the path traverses a hillside before arriving at a meadow-filled cirque with plenty of wildlife viewing if the critters don't hear you coming. Keep your eyes open for bear, fox, and coyote in the valley below. In 2.6 miles beyond Woody Pass, the trail gains a saddle and continues a moderate

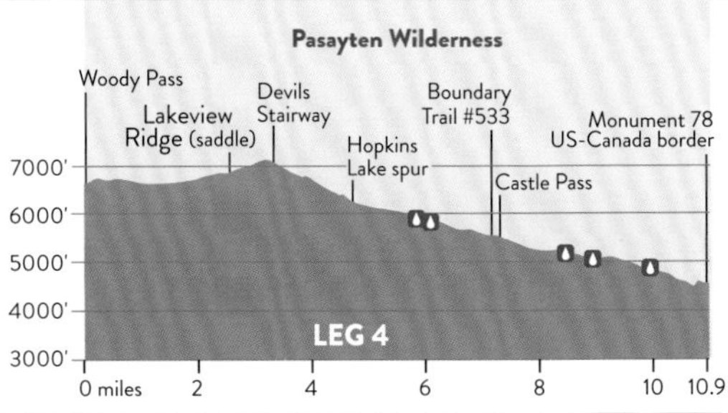

As seen from south of Devils Stairway, azure Hopkins Lake shines like a brilliant gemstone.

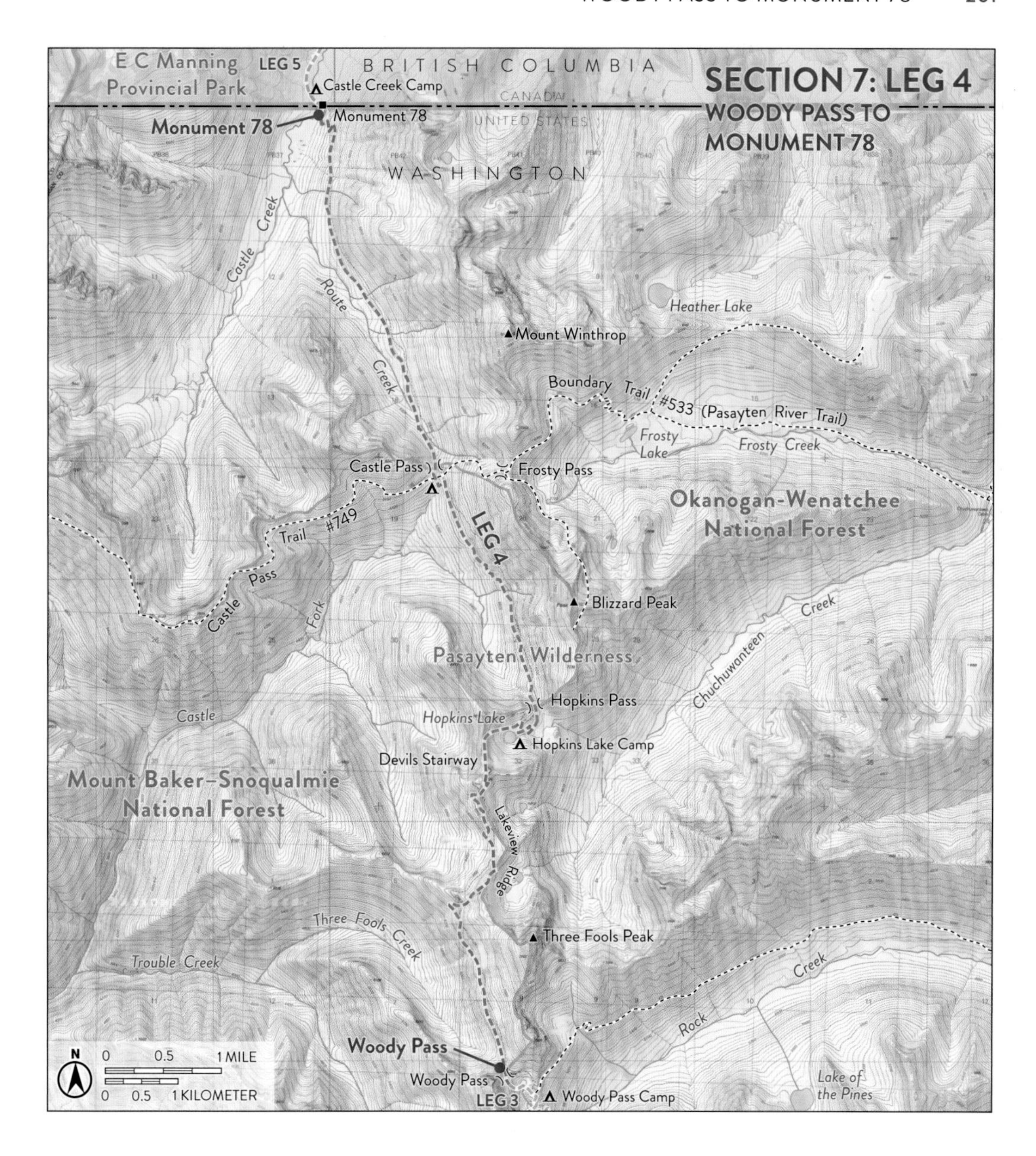

ascent toward Lakeview Ridge, the highest part of the PCT in Washington, with views to the east of craggy Three Fools Peak, Hopkins Lake to the north, and the Chuchuwanteen Creek valley to the east. This high country has an identity all its own. You're in the beating heart of the wilderness, and the haunting isolation with a twist of wonder and joyful solitude creates a soothing salve for the soul. These are feelings that only those who set foot in such remote country can comprehend, and it's one of the reasons we're called back time after addicting time.

The PCT descends along rocky, exposed switchbacks, heading down the ridgeline to the **Devils Stairway**, a series of tight, exposed switchbacks leading still farther down to **Hopkins Lake** and Hopkins Pass. "Devils Stairway" makes the route sound intimidating, but it's a snap provided it's not covered in snow or ice. The hazards are minimal compared to what you've already seen.

Roughly 2 miles from gaining the saddle and 1.4 miles from the top of the switchbacks, the trail ducks back into forest and arrives at a curious spur trail marked with a cairn to the right (southwest). Keep a keen eye out for it, especially if you need water or a place to camp. Several sites are at **Hopkins Lake Camp** around the secluded lake's perimeter.

In 0.2 mile beyond the camp spur cairn (4.8 miles from Woody Pass), attain the base of a talus field known as **Hopkins Pass**, marked with a sign on a post in the rocks. Here, the PCT angles left (north), although a spur trail also heads to the right (south), likely made from confused boots or those looking to explore the pass. The PCT descends on a gentle grade as you traverse a wooded hillside with peekaboo peaks out to the west.

After Hopkins Pass, cross two trickling creeks, at least one of which, 1.3 miles from the pass, is reliable in an average summer season. At 2.3 miles from Hopkins Pass, arrive at a junction with **Boundary Trail #533**, coming in from the right (east) and also known as the Pasayten River Trail—the junction is simply signed "Pasayten Riv. 16" with an arrow.

The PCT turns left (west) and then heads to the north for just 0.1 mile to meet with the **Castle Pass Trail #749**, coming in from the left (west) and a well-used camp (**Castle Pass Camp**). The camp has room for one average or two small tents, but it lacks water, so schlep it along if you plan to call this home. The wooden signs nailed to an evergreen announce the pass, pointing back toward Woody and forward to the US-Canada border—a must-have picture for your collection! Another sign points left toward Castle Pass Trail and simply says "Ross Lake." If you're feeling the magic of the nearing border, keep rolling north.

In 1.4 miles, arrive at the first creek beyond Castle Pass, followed by another in 0.4 mile and yet another in 1 mile beyond that. From Castle Pass to the border it is a gradual descent, and due to the remoteness of the area the trail often lacks maintenance. On wet mornings or rainy days, plan on getting a good soaking from the brushy avalanche swaths, which no amount of trekking-pole swats can quell. During dry spells, buzzing insects dive-bomb your ears and seek lunch on your vulnerable elbows. Thankfully, keeping your ears and eyes peeled for wildlife in the high brush distracts you from the somewhat unpleasant bushwhack. Keep putting one foot in front of the other and you'll get there! The excitement of Canada and a warm meal at the Manning Park Lodge almost consumes you, making the 3.7 miles from Castle Pass to the border the longest stretch of trail yet. Keep your senses aware for bears, especially during berry season in late summer—this is their playground and the very high brush can prevent you from seeing them.

BEAR BELLS

If you got lured into buying bear bells, perhaps what you really bought was a false sense of security. The US Geological Survey tested bear bells on Alaskan brown bears in Katmai National Park. First, an alder bush near a well-traveled bear trail was outfitted with bear bells, attached to fishing line. Next, a researcher concealed himself in a nearby blind.

When bears walked by, at first the researcher pulled the line gently and the bears ignored the sounds. Next, he yanked the line and still the bears weren't affected or interested. In fact, not one bear in fifteen groups that went by perked up a head or looked in the direction of the bells. The reason for the lack of response is unclear, although researchers guess that perhaps the bears tune out the jingling much like they would a babbling brook, singing birds, or other nonthreatening sounds.

Opposite: *Lakeview Ridge, the highest stretch of the PCT in Washington State, snakes through subalpine terrain toward Canada.*

The backcountry feels truly rugged and wild as you get farther and farther north of Harts Pass.

A brief forest respite comes roughly 1 mile from the border, giving you a change of scenery before the last brushy swale escorts you down four switchbacks and spits you out without much fanfare at the border, where you'll find **Monument 78**, the wooden **PCT northern terminus** pillars, and a large sign welcoming you to Canada and E. C. Manning Provincial Park. Where is the marching band and drill team? You've arrived! The clear-cut border boundary goes east to west, an eyesore if you didn't know its purpose.

Before you and your hungry belly hightail it past here, stop for a few things. First, the **metal monument** itself tips back and disassembles, which is key because underneath it, in this sneaky and excellent hiding spot, you'll find all sorts of treasures, including the trail register. Grab a snack from your pack and sit down with the register for some very entertaining reads. And don't forget to sign it! You might also find tea packets, magic soap bubbles, bits of string, small toys, playing cards, and other trinkets—it's fun to see who and what arrived at this isolated spot before you. Next, set up your camera to grab a shot of you with the pillars, a mandatory picture. If you climb them to stand or sit, be warned: they can be slippery when wet and your self-timer may capture you doing an unexpected twizzle to your coccyx.

Be sure to take a picture or two of the signs pointing both ways: back to Harts Pass and toward Manning Park, the very last stretch of your journey unless you plan to hike back to Harts Pass. If no one told you before now, you're still some 8 miles from Manning Park Lodge and civilization. The trail continues, albeit in a different country, and the final push is not a walk in the park—oh wait, actually it is. But it's challenging for a number of reasons. Because of your anticipation, excitement, and possible underestimation of the distance and terrain, the final stretch to Manning Park Lodge can feel excruciatingly long. One foot in front of the other gets you there, much as it put you here on the border. Celebrate, rejoice, laugh, and enjoy—you've reached Canada by the strength of your muscles, stamina, and gumption!

CAMP-TO-CAMP MILEAGE

Woody Pass to Hopkins Lake Camp spur..... 4.6
Hopkins Lake Camp spur to Castle Pass Camp 2.6
Castle Pass Camp to Monument 78......... 3.7

5 MONUMENT 78 TO MANNING PARK LODGE

DISTANCE 8.7 miles

ELEVATION GAIN/LOSS +1580/–1930 feet

HIGH POINT 5400 feet

ON THE TRAIL

The 8.2-mile stretch of trail and 0.5-mile road walk to Manning Park Lodge usually get little more than a passing mention in PCT accounts—except to complain about how long this short stretch feels. Knowing that you still have a ways to go after the US-Canada border is half the battle. The other half is knowing what to expect. Hikers are welcomed to Manning Park at **Monument 78** with a large wooden sign that has a small, confusing map. Ignore the map, because it will send your head spinning and you may end up in New York next January. Instead, simply continue northbound on the PCT and enter the park.

Funny how the landscape feels the same but your eyes and mind subconsciously scan for a difference. In a very short 0.2 mile from the border, you'll find one. Arrive at a spectacular wilderness campground (**Castle Creek Camp**), with sturdy logs for sitting, designated fire pits with metal frames, and the very clear, rushing **Castle Creek** for drinking water. The clearing in the conifers has an inviting feel, and after days or weeks of teetering on precarious downed trees or small rocks to eat your meals, you'll feel like you've arrived at a campground suited for a king!

There's a fee for camping in all Manning Park wilderness and front-country camps. But here's an interesting tidbit: the folks at Manning Park don't recognize Castle Creek Camp as a designated wilderness camp within the park. However, someone has kept it gorgeously maintained. This camp doesn't appear in any of the Manning Park literature and most park rangers will slyly shrug as if they know nothing about it—it's as if it doesn't exist. Despite that, BC Parks people tell me that wilderness camping fees apply here too.

After Castle Creek Camp, cross a sturdy, well-constructed wooden bridge over Castle Creek **O** and find the trail on the other side. In warm weather, **get water here**, since on-trail water can be seasonal for the next 5 miles.

Judging by what you've just seen—the well-used camp and solid bridge—you might think you are in for a well-maintained trail all the way to Manning Park Lodge. Unfortunately, that's not the case. About half of the trail is overgrown to the point of having to walk on slide-alder roots and bushwhack

This sign, in the Manning Park backcountry, is typical of what you should expect to see as you head toward civilization.

When you see this sign, you've made it to the northern terminus of the Pacific Crest Trail, Monument 78, the PCT wooden monument, and the US-Canada border!

CAMPING IN MANNING PARK

In E. C. Manning Provincial Park, you must use designated wilderness camps and can't practice dispersed camping. In other words, unlike most of the terrain you've just crossed, you can't park your tent wherever you choose. There's a small fee, and you can pay online up to two weeks in advance (see "Passes, Permits, Regulations" in appendix 1). Even if you pay in advance, the wilderness camps are first come, first served. I know, I know, what if you get there and they're all full? Well, keep walking or contact the park to see if you can sweet-talk them into a refund. For this reason, I highly recommend paying after you stay. Settle up at the front desk of the Manning Park Lodge or at the fee station at the Gibson Pass Road entrance. Major credit cards and Canadian coin currency are accepted at the fee station.

through brushy riparian foliage, although the trail is always obvious.

Wind northeast and play hopscotch between evergreens and brushy hillsides in a moderate climb traversing above the Castle Creek valley, gaining roughly 730 feet in under 1.5 miles. In 3.2 miles from Monument 78, on a bend in the trail, arrive at the first seasonal but usually reliable creeklet since Castle Creek.

From here, round two more trail bends and arrive at Manning Park's recognized **PCT Camp**, a designated park wilderness camp, 0.6 mile from the creeklet (3.8 miles from the border). You'll find a privy, a few campsites with room for approximately four tents, a seasonal stream, and a metal food storage box, which keeps what's left of your grub from going to the bruins. This is the last wilderness camp before the trail reaches civilization.

The signs from here to the PCT Trailhead in Canada can be confusing because they often

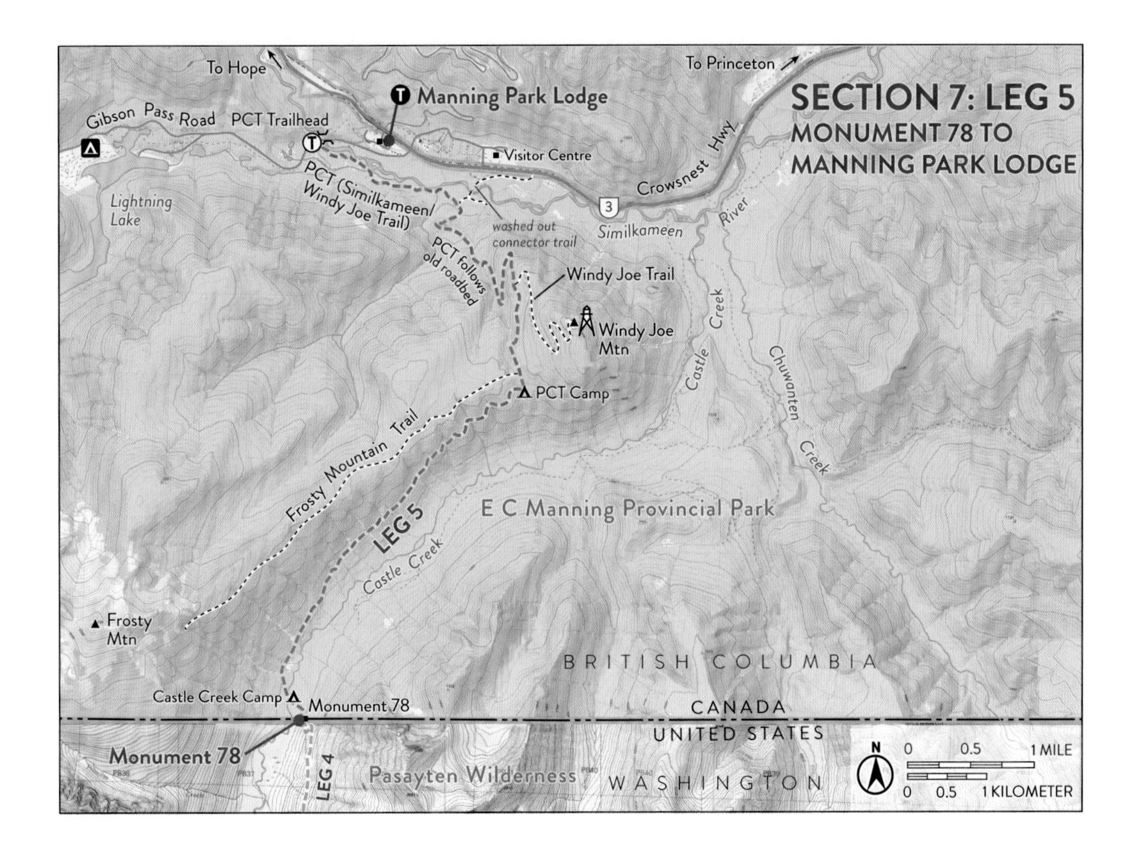

say "Pacific Crest Trail" with an arrow pointing back the way you came. If things start looking oddly familiar, stop immediately and consult your map! Ahead of you are junctions for the Frosty Mountain Trail and Windy Joe Trail, and signs often point ahead to those landmarks instead of to the PCT Trailhead. To make things even more confusing, you don't actually follow the PCT proper all the way to the Canada PCT Trailhead. Instead, you'll detour onto a section of the Windy Joe Trail, followed by the Similkameen Trail. Add to all this that you've likely succumbed to "trail-brain," a malady that leads to more focus on the sounds of babbling creeks and scolding squirrels than on where you should be going—the perfect burrito of discombobulation. Surprisingly, no signs along the way or at the trailhead point to Manning Park Lodge! One wrong turn could add some unfortunate additional steps to your plans, so stay sharp and focused at each intersection.

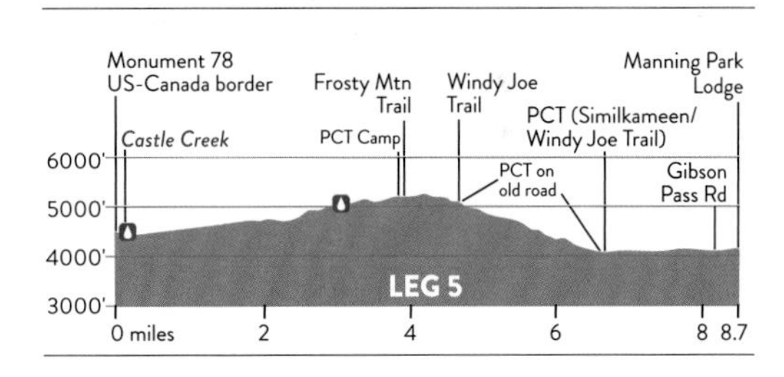

At the PCT Camp, the trail turns north and in 0.1 mile meets the **Frosty Mountain Trail**, which comes in from the left. Continue north, following the PCT across Windy Joe Mountain's western shoulders and in 0.8 mile beyond the Frosty Mountain Trail junction, arrive at the **Windy Joe Trail**. At this point, you'll leave the PCT and follow the Windy Joe Trail downhill on an old access road. To the right, the Windy Joe Trail heads toward the top of its namesake peak, where a fire lookout sits. To get to the trailhead and Manning

WINDY JOE MOUNTAIN

With a name like Windy Joe, you can be sure there's a history! Back in the day, a mountain man and longtime park employee named Joe Hilton theorized that the peak was so windy that snow couldn't stick to the top, hence the name Windy Joe Mountain. But there is much more to Joe Hilton than just a peak. In 1912, Joe's parents brought him to Canada from England at the tender age of two. His father had come to pursue a job in the coal mines on the eastern edge of what is now Manning Park.

As Joe grew up, his love for the mountains and the outdoors flourished. As a young man, he followed in his father's footsteps and briefly explored coal mining, but he was always driven by something greater deep down inside. When World War II erupted, he walked the entire 160 miles from Manning Park to Vancouver to enlist, only to be turned away upon hearing that his body was unfit for service. A mining accident years before had broken his hip and pelvis, and the military deemed him flawed. So, instead of pouting, he turned around and walked his "incompetent" body the 160 miles back to Manning Park.

With work in the mines becoming scarce, Joe began learning the art of trapping and spent his winters on snowshoes checking his traps and saving all the money he earned. Eventually he had enough to purchase the Gordon Brothers trapline, which encompassed the entirety of Manning Park and a bit beyond. Interestingly, the trapping rights to this day are still maintained by the Hilton family, namely Joe's grandchildren.

When 1945 rolled around, Manning Park superintendent Bob Boyd noted Joe's talents and hired him as his assistant, which suited Joe perfectly. His work consisted of four to five months of winter surveying in the mountains to gather data on snow depth. Clomping around on snowshoes in the backcountry was a dream come true. He continued his work for the Park Service for many years and branched out into building some of the first backcountry trails in the park.

In the spring of 1968, Joe began creating the north end of the Pacific Crest Trail when snow was still on the ground. Joe was a stickler about grading and wanted things perfect for hikers and horses alike. One of his famous rules was not to add any reverse grade unless absolutely necessary. He insisted that the trail avoid going down just to go up again if there was a flatter and more suitable alternative.

He was not only an accomplished trail builder but also a colorful character who stuck to very specific beliefs. He deduced that the backcountry tended to cause folks to slough off good graces and manners. So he required his backcountry trail crews to wash up before each meal and practice meticulous manners. At meal times, his crews became diligent about not reaching across the table, saying "please" and "thank you," and politely asking for various items to be passed. Thanks to Joe, the crew became renowned throughout the park for their kindly manners and gentle ways when they came back to the lodge after time on the trail. Additionally, it was rumored that Joe shaved with his Hudson Bay ice ax, which he kept razor sharp, arguing that an ax was only in proper working order if it could be used to shave your scruff.

Joe finally retired in 1975, several years after finishing the northern end of the PCT in Manning Park. His legacy lives on in the trails he built, which now deliver hikers like you and me to spectacular wilderness.

Castle Creek Camp in Canada serves as a perfect respite for hikers who need a break or a snooze.

Park Lodge, head left (downhill) for 2 seemingly endless miles, following the winding access road as it steeply descends while your calves and toes protest. Take heart: the traffic you hear in the distance is on BC Highway 3 (Crowsnest Highway), which means . . . you're almost there! Bikes are allowed on the Windy Joe and Similkameen trails, so yield to those on rubber wheels.

In 2 miles from the Windy Joe Trail junction, arrive at a junction to the left (west) with a sign pointing toward the PCT Trailhead, the final leg of your journey. Technically, this is the Similkameen Trail, but that's not noted anywhere except for a sign at the trail on Gibson Pass Road, which you haven't reached yet. In fact, some maps list this as the Similkameen/Windy Joe Trail, as if the two are inseparable. Who am I to question?

If you're following an older map, you might find yourself in a tizzy trying to find old trails with would-be shortcuts. Don't sweat your sweet face. Flooding over the years has wiped out many access points in this valley and now, the trail you're on is the only one that leads where you want to go. Your final stretch along the Similkameen/Windy Joe Trail is well maintained and wanders through a large coniferous forest in a wide corridor. The wooden bridges over creeks and swamps are slippery as skating rinks when they're wet, so tread gently in inclement weather. Bears are common in this forest, so get the camera ready just in case.

In 1.5 miles from the start of the Similkameen/Windy Joe Trail, arrive at Gibson Pass Road. There you'll stand, grubby but full of excitement, proud and happy yet reluctant to face the woes of everyday life. Were it not for the waiting warm

Lovely Manning Park Lodge offers everything a weary hiker might need, including a warm shower, soft bed, delicious food, and even guest laundry facilities.

meal, your long-absent friends and family, and the opportunity to wash twenty layers of scuzz off your body, you might just decide to turn back into the forest. But alas, Manning Park Lodge awaits!

If your feet aren't screaming too loudly, you may want to walk to the Canada PCT Trailhead sign to the left (west) for one final picture. However, if your body is begging you to go straight to Manning Park Lodge, head right (east) on the paved road and cross the bridge over the Similkameen River. In 0.4 mile from where you left the trail, notice a very wide, overgrown, gravel access road to the left (northeast). Save yourself a few steps and follow it as it shortcuts into the **Manning Park Lodge** parking lot in 0.1 mile. If you miss it, just stay on Gibson Pass Road and eventually you'll get there! Nearby, the cars and trucks fly by on the busy, bustling BC 3.

Let me be the first to say congratulations! Whether you made it across the whole state or put in double-digit miles, you deserve an exuberant celebration. Your feet have traveled the path of the fortunate few, powered only by the strength of your muscles and your sheer determination. You've seen countless miles of jaw-dropping peaks and quiet river valleys. You've witnessed small details such as raindrops on flower petals and the delicate wings of bumblebees. You've made friends with those in coats of fur and enjoyed the music of those wearing wind-worn feathers. You have postcard-quality pictures to share with folks you can't wait to see and memories to treasure when the winter days are dark and long. You are a backpacker and this is your moment. Enjoy every sweet drop!

CAMP-TO-CAMP MILEAGE

Monument 78 to Castle Creek Camp 0.2
Castle Creek Camp to PCT Camp 3.6
PCT Camp to Manning Park Lodge 4.9

APPENDIX 1

RESOURCES FOR WASHINGTON'S PCT

GENERAL

Pacific Crest Trail Association
www.pcta.org

MAPS

E. C. Manning Provincial Park maps
www.env.gov.bc.ca/bcparks/explore/parkpgs/ecmanning/#Location

Green Trails maps
https://greentrailsmaps.com

Guthook's apps
www.atlasguides.com

Halfmile's maps and apps
www.pctmap.net

US Forest Service maps
www.fs.usda.gov/main/pct/maps-publications

PASSES, PERMITS, REGULATIONS

E. C. Manning Provincial Park
backcountry camping
https://secure.camis.com/DiscoverCamping/Backcountry/E.C.Manning?Map

US Forest Service
Pacific Northwest Region
www.fs.usda.gov/detail/r6/passes-permits/recreation

Washington Department of Fish and Wildlife
wdfw.wa.gov/fishing/regulations (fishing)
wdfw.wa.gov/hunting (hunting)

A red-breasted sapsucker searches for a meal on an old deciduous tree.

BORDER CROSSINGS

Canada Border Services Agency
www.cbsa-asfc.gc.ca/menu-eng.html (general)
1-866-496-3987 (press "0" and ask for the Pacific Crest Trail Coordinator)

US Customs and Border Protection
www.getyouhome.gov (for accepted identification to enter the United States)

APPENDIX 2

LAND MANAGERS (SOUTH TO NORTH)

UNITED STATES

Columbia River Gorge National Scenic Area

www.fs.usda.gov/crgnsa

Headquarters
902 Wasco Street, Suite 200
Hood River, OR 97031
541-308-1700

Gifford Pinchot National Forest

www.fs.usda.gov/main/giffordpinchot

Mount Adams Ranger District
2455 Highway 141
Trout Lake, WA 98650
509-395-3402

Cowlitz Valley Ranger District
10024 US Highway 12
Randle, WA 98377
360-497-1100

Okanogan-Wenatchee National Forest

www.fs.usda.gov/okawen

Naches Ranger District
10237 US Highway 12
Naches, WA 98937
509-653-1401

Methow Valley Ranger District
24 West Chewuch Road
Winthrop, WA 98862
509-996-4003

Mount Rainier National Park

www.nps.gov/mora

Headquarters
55210 238th Avenue East
Ashford, WA 98304
360-569-2211

Longmire Wilderness Information Center
6.5 miles east of the Nisqually Entrance
360-569-6650

Mount Baker–Snoqualmie National Forest

www.fs.usda.gov/mbs

Snoqualmie Ranger District
902 SE North Bend Way, Bldg. 1
North Bend, WA 98045
425-888-1421

Skykomish Ranger District
74920 NE Stevens Pass Highway (US 2)
Skykomish, WA 98288
360-677-2414

Darrington Ranger District
Darrington, WA
360-426-1155

Green River Watershed

www.mytpu.org/tacomawater/water-source/green-river-watershed/

Tacoma Public Utilities
3628 South 35th Street
Tacoma, WA 98409
253-502-8600

Cedar River Watershed

www.seattle.gov/util/environmentconservation/education/cedarriverwatershed/

Seattle Public Utilities
P.O. Box 34018
Seattle, WA 98124
206-684-3000

North Cascades National Park Complex

www.nps.gov/noca

Golden West Visitor Center
Stehekin, WA
509-699-2080 ext. 14

Wilderness Information Center
7280 Ranger Station Road
Marblemount, WA 98267
360-854-7245

CANADA

E. C. Manning Provincial Park

www.env.gov.bc.ca/bcparks/explore/parkpgs/ecmanning

Manning Park Visitor Centre
7500 Highway 3
Manning Park, BC V0X 1R0
604-668-5953

Bull elk bugle from hilltops near White Pass as autumn caresses meadows near the PCT.

APPENDIX 3

SERVICES NEAR TRAILHEADS (SOUTH TO NORTH)

COLUMBIA RIVER AND ENVIRONS

Cascade Locks, Oregon, and Stevenson, Washington, are both near the southernmost PCT Trailhead in Washington, on the Columbia River. Both towns are small but have a handful of amenities, including a few lodging options, restaurants, and grocery stores (Stevenson has more restaurants than Cascade Locks). Cascade Locks is also home to the annual PCT Days festival in late August or early September, full of classes, vendors, and activities for PCTers (see PCTA.org for details).

Transportation

Gorge TransLink (www.gorgetranslink.com, 541-296-2266) is your source for getting to points along the Columbia River, with information on public transit and private companies. Skamania County Transit has a bus that runs from Vancouver, Washington, to Stevenson. Gorge Yellow Cab (gorgeyellowcab.com, 541-308-3383) is your taxi link between Hood River and Trout Lake.

Campgrounds

Oregon State Parks operates a campground at **Ainsworth State Park** (www.oregonstateparks.org, 1-800-452-5687). Private campgrounds include **Cascade Locks/Portland East KOA Campground** (koa.com/campgrounds/cascade-locks, 541-374-8668) and **Port of Cascade Locks (Cascade Locks)** (portofcascadelocks.org/campground, 541-374-8619).

Ranger Station

The closest ranger station is Gifford Pinchot National Forest's Mount Adams Ranger District, 0.5 mile west of Trout Lake on SR 141 (www.fs.usda.gov/main/giffordpinchot, 509-395-3402).

Package/Cache Mailing Addresses

Cascade Locks Post Office
Your Name Here
PCT Hiker, ETA: mm/dd/yy
c/o General Delivery
461 NW Wanapa Street
Cascade Locks, OR 97014

The Cascades Locks Post Office (541-374-5026) is open Monday–Friday, with a lunch break. Call ahead for current hours. There's no lobby service on Saturdays, but you can pick up packages if the postal attendant is there; knock on the back door or the wooden door in the lobby.

Port of Cascade Locks (USPS)
Your Name Here
PCT Hiker, ETA: mm/dd/yy
c/o Port of Cascade Locks
PO Box 307
Cascade Locks, OR 97014

Port of Cascade Locks (UPS/FedEx)
Your Name Here
PCT Hiker, ETA: mm/dd/yy
c/o Port of Cascade Locks
355 Wanapa Street
Cascade Locks, OR 97014

The Port of Cascade Locks (portofcascadelocks.org/campground, 541-374-8619) accepts hiker parcels, with no storage fee. Pick up packages at the administration office during business hours, Monday–Friday. Check ahead for current hours.

FOREST ROAD 23 AND ENVIRONS

Trout Lake is 14 miles south from the PCT parking area off FR 23. Although small, the town has a unique, welcoming charm, complete with town PCT information (troutlakewashington.com

/pacific-crest-trail-hiker-information) and resident Trail Angels.

Transportation

Amtrak (www.amtrak.com, 1-800-872-7245) runs from Portland, Oregon, to Bingen, Washington (near White Salmon). Greyhound (www.greyhound.com, 1-800-231-2222; or www.gorgetranslink.com/regional-greyhound.html, 1-877-875-4657) connects Portland to Hood River, Oregon. White Salmon and Hood River are roughly 25 miles south of Trout Lake.

In Trout Lake, PCT Trail Angel Doug Anderson (509-395-3611, dougdjr@gorge.net) maintains a list of folks who are happy to drive hikers to and from the PCT Trailhead. Some drivers ask for a small fee to cover gas, others appreciate a couple of bucks, some say nothing. All are cheerleaders for PCT hikers. Making arrangements in advance is appreciated but not necessary. Additionally, Andy and his staff at Andy's Valley Chevron Station (509-395-2211) are wonderful people who occasionally help out with rides from town to trailhead.

Lodging and Campgrounds

A private lodging and camping option in Oregon is **Elk Meadows RV Park and Cabins** (www.elkmeadowsrvparks.com, 509-395-2400; coin-op laundry, showers, flush toilets for guests). Klickitat County in Washington operates a campground at **Guler–Trout Lake County Park** (www.klickitat-county.org, 509-773-4616; showers, flush toilets). Gifford Pinchot National Forest (www.fs.usda.gov/activity/giffordpinchot/recreation/camping-cabins) has several campgrounds, including **Crest Campground** (small and primitive, just 4 sites, vault toilet), **Panther Creek Campground** (potable water, vault toilets), and **Trout Lake Creek Campground** (vault toilets, no water; rough access road, RVs and trailers not recommended).

Ranger Station

Gifford Pinchot National Forest's Mount Adams Ranger District office is 0.5 mile west of Trout Lake on SR 141 (www.fs.usda.gov/main/giffordpinchot, 509-395-3402).

Package/Cache Mailing Address

Trout Lake Post Office
Your Name Here
PCT Hiker, ETA: mm/dd/yy
c/o General Delivery
Trout Lake, WA 98650

For your convenience (because the post office is closed on weekends), PCT general-delivery packages are automatically routed to Trout Lake Grocery (2383 Highway 141, Trout Lake, WA 98650, 509-395-2777). This small store is happy to assist PCT hikers with a variety of needs, including offering motel rooms, package drop-offs and pickups, washers and dryers (free with room rental), Internet access, a food-exchange box, a PCT register, and information about Trout Lake's services in general.

WHITE PASS AND ENVIRONS

There's a ski area at White Pass, at the summit of US 12, located 0.5 mile west of the PCT Trailhead. It has a ghost-town feeling in the summer, but the Kracker Barrel convenience store (509-672-3105) goes out of its way to spoil PCT hikers: it has fuel for canister stoves, and the staff will even order you special items if you call in advance. More services are available in Packwood, roughly 20 miles west of the pass; and in Yakima, about 54 miles to the east.

Transportation

Lewis Mountain Highway Transit (www.transitunlimited.org/LEWIS_Mountain_Highway_Transit, 360-496-5405) offers bus service from Centralia to Packwood. Greyhound (www.greyhound.com, 1-800-231-2222) runs between Seattle and Yakima.

Lodging and Campgrounds

Find nearby lodging at **White Pass Village Inn** (www.whitepassvillageinn.com, 509-672-3131; full kitchens/kitchenettes, pool, Internet, coin-op laundry) and private camping at **Packwood RV Park** (www.packwoodrv.com, 360-494-5145; coin-op laundry). Gifford Pinchot National Forest operates **La Wis Wis Campground** (www.fs.usda.gov/activity/giffordpinchot/recreation/camping-cabins; potable water, flush toilets), and

Okanogan-Wenatchee National Forest operates **Dog Lake Campground** (www.fs.usda.gov/activity/okawen/recreation/camping-cabins; just 8 sites, vault toilets, no water).

Ranger Stations

Gifford Pinchot National Forest's Cowlitz Valley Ranger District office is in Randle, about 16 miles west of White Pass on US 12 (www.fs.usda.gov/main/giffordpinchot, 360-497-1100). Okanogan-Wenatchee National Forest's Naches Ranger District office is about 40 miles east of White Pass on US 12 (www.fs.usda.gov/okawen, 509-653-1401).

Package/Cache Mailing Addresses

White Pass Post Office
Your Name Here
PCT Hiker, ETA: mm/dd/yy
c/o White Pass Rural Branch Post Office
at the Kracker Barrel Store
48851 US Highway 12
Naches, WA 98937

The Kracker Barrel (509-672-3105) charges a small fee for package handling, and packages must be picked up during business hours, which are subject to change. Call ahead for current hours.

Packwood Post Office
Your Name Here
PCT Hiker, ETA: mm/dd/yy
c/o General Delivery
Packwood, WA 98361

The post office (360-494-6311) is open regular business hours Monday–Friday, with a lunch closure. Call ahead for current hours.

CHINOOK PASS AND ENVIRONS

While Chinook Pass itself is void of services save for vault toilets and trash cans, neighboring towns may meet your needs. In Greenwater, roughly 25.5 miles to the northwest, you'll find convenience stores, gas stations, dining, and lodging. Crystal Mountain ski area, 19.5 miles northwest from Chinook Pass, is open in the summer and offers dining, lodging, and recreational activities. East of Chinook Pass, Naches is the first decent-sized town, roughly 52 miles away. It has a couple of bed-and-breakfasts as well as dining, gas stations, and convenience stores.

Transportation

There are no public or private transportation services to the Chinook Pass area or Greenwater. The closest transportation is through King County Metro bus service (metro.kingcounty.gov), which offers routes to Enumclaw, roughly 45 miles to the northwest of the pass.

Lodging and Campgrounds

Nearby lodging options include **Alta Crystal Resort** (www.altacrystalresort.com, 1-800-277-6475), **Crystal Chalets** (www.crystalchalets.com, 360-284-7007), **Crystal Mountain Hotels** (www.crystalhotels.com, 1-888-754-6400), and **Silver Skis Chalet** (www.silverskischalet.com, 1-888-668-4368). Mount Baker–Snoqualmie National Forest (www.fs.usda.gov/activity/mbs/recreation/camping-cabins) operates **Dalles Campground** and **Silver Springs Campground** (both with potable water, vault toilets). Mount Rainier National Park (www.nps.gov/mora/planyourvisit/campgrounds.htm) operates **White River Campground** (potable water, flush toilets).

Ranger Station

Okanogan-Wenatchee National Forest's Naches Ranger District office is in Naches (www.fs.usda.gov/okawen, 509-653-1401).

SNOQUALMIE PASS AND ENVIRONS

There's a ski area at Snoqualmie Pass, about 53 miles east of Seattle on I-90, with summer activities that keep the area humming. You'll find a gas station, convenience stores (Lee's Summit Grocery stocks limited canister and white gas fuel), restaurants, and lodging at the pass. The closest town is North Bend, 24 miles to the west.

Transportation

There are no public or private transportation services between Seattle and Snoqualmie Pass. The closest transportation is through King County

Metro bus service (metro.kingcounty.gov), which offers routes to North Bend.

Lodging and Campgrounds

Just steps from the trail, try **Summit Inn at Snoqualmie Pass** (snoqualmiesummitinn.com, 425-434-6300; hot tub, sauna, Internet, in-room microwaves and fridges, coin-op laundry; ask for the PCT rate; rooms without air-conditioning cost less). Nearby campgrounds include Mount Baker–Snoqualmie National Forest's **Denny Creek Campground** (www.fs.usda.gov/activity/mbs/recreation/camping-cabins; potable water, flush toilets) and Okanogan-Wenatchee National Forest's **Kachess Campground** (www.fs.usda.gov/activity/okawen/recreation/camping-cabins; potable water, flush toilets).

Ranger Station

Mount Baker–Snoqualmie National Forest's Snoqualmie Ranger District office is in North Bend (www.fs.usda.gov/mbs, 425-888-1421).

Package/Cache Mailing Addresses

Snoqualmie Pass Post Office
Your Name Here
PCT Hiker, ETA: mm/dd/yy
HOLD AT CHEVRON STATION
c/o General Delivery
Snoqualmie Pass, WA 98068

Bob's Summit Deli and Chevron (425-434-6688) will hold packages for two weeks; there's no outgoing mail service. Packages left longer than two weeks will be returned to sender unless you make other arrangements. Call ahead for current hours.

Summit Inn at Snoqualmie Pass (USPS)
Your Name Here
PCT Hiker, ETA: mm/dd/yy
c/o Summit Lodge
PO Box 163
Snoqualmie Pass, WA 98068

Summit Inn at Snoqualmie Pass (UPS, FedEx)
Your Name Here
PCT Hiker, ETA: mm/dd/yy
c/o Summit Lodge
603 State Route 906
Snoqualmie Pass, WA 98068

If you stay at the Summit Inn (snoqualmiesummitinn.com, 425-434-6300), you can send packages to be held for the season, for free. If you don't stay at the inn, there's a package-holding fee. Pick up packages at the front desk; check ahead for current hours. Outgoing mail is only available using prepaid postage; flat-rate boxes are usually available at the inn, but you must have the prepaid postage labels with you.

STEVENS PASS AND ENVIRONS

There's a ski area at Stevens Pass, and the resort's recently opened mountain-bike park means that there's some food and lodging available during the summer. For more options, the historical railroad town of Skykomish is 15 miles west of Stevens Pass on US 2. And the charming Bavarian-themed tourist mecca of Leavenworth is 35 miles east, with even more services.

Transportation

Northwestern Trailways (www.northwesterntrailways.com, 1-800-366-3830) provides bus service to Stevens Pass from Seattle, Spokane, and several other Washington cities. A couple of other options can get you close: Community Transit buses (https://communitytransit.org, 1-800-562-1375) go from Seattle to Sultan, 43 miles west of the pass. And Amtrak (www.amtrak.com, 1-800-872-7245) has service from Seattle to Leavenworth.

Lodging and Campgrounds

In Baring (8 miles west of Skykomish), you'll find **Dinsmore's Hiker Haven** (www.dinsmoreshikerhaven.com, 360-677-1237; Internet). Mount Baker–Snoqualmie National Forest (www.fs.usda.gov/activity/mbs/recreation/camping-cabins) operates nearby **Beckler River Campground** and **Money Creek Campground** (both with potable water, vault toilets).

Ranger Station

Mount Baker–Snoqualmie National Forest's Skykomish Ranger District office is in Skykomish (www.fs.usda.gov/mbs, 360-677-2414).

Package/Cache Mailing Addresses

Skykomish Post Office
Your Name Here
PCT Hiker, ETA: mm/dd/yy
c/o General Delivery
Skykomish, WA 98288

The Skykomish Post Office (360-677-2230) is open for limited weekday hours (midday) and Saturday mornings. Call ahead for current open hours. Note: Beginning in 2017, Dinsmore's Hiker Haven will no longer accept resupply shipments.

Stevens Pass Ski Area (UPS, FedEx)
Your Name Here
c/o Stevens Pass
PCT Hiker, ETA: mm/dd/yy
93001 NE Stevens Pass Highway (US 2)
Skykomish, WA 98288

Pick up packages at the Granite Peak Lodge Coffee Bar, at the very center of the three ski lodges (www.stevenspass.com/site/summer/services/hiking, summer: 206-812-7844, winter: 206-812- 4510). Open hours vary with the season, so check ahead.

STEHEKIN

Stehekin is a small and friendly hamlet on the north end of Lake Chelan. It's accessible by boat, plane, horse hooves, and your own two feet, but not by car. The hundred or so year-round residents welcome the hustle and bustle of summer traffic, which is their livelihood. You won't find a cash machine, cell service, or Internet (most residents pay for limited satellite service). But the town does have options for lodging (most booked months in advance), delicious dining, and basic groceries, as well as—bonus!—a public shower and coin-op laundry.

Transportation

The *Lady of the Lake* (lady ofthelake.com, 509-682-4584) ferries passengers from the city of Chelan to Stehekin and other points along the lake. Chelan Seaplanes (www.chelanseaplanes.com, 509-682-5555) is another (more expensive) option. Whether you take a boat or plane, make arrangements as far in advance as you possibly can, because last-minute reservations can be challenging, especially in the popular summer months. If you find yourself stuck in Stehekin with no transportation, the North Cascades Lodge (www.lodgeatstehekin.com, 509-682-4494) is happy to assist you. Lastly, if you have connections or a little jingle in your pocket, the town also has public boat docks and a private landing strip.

For PCT Trailhead access, the Park Service oversees operation of a shuttle (www.nps.gov/noca/planyourvisit/stehekin-transportation.htm) from Stehekin along Stehekin Valley Road. Make sure to get a schedule from the website and bring it with you—it's a long and dusty 11-mile walk between town and trailhead if you miss the last bus.

Lodging and Campgrounds

You can't go wrong at either **Stehekin Valley Ranch** (stehekinvalleyranch.com, 509-682-4677) or **North Cascades Lodge at Stehekin** (www.lodgeatstehekin.com, 509-682-4494). There are also four small, free front-country campgrounds near town. Permits to camp are available first come, first served from the Golden West Visitor Center (www.nps.gov/noca, 509-699-2080 ext. 14) on the day of or day before your stay. The Park Service is considering designating Lakeview Campground as a PCT hiker-only campground. Call for the latest updates. From closest to the ferry landing, you'll find **Purple Point Campground** (0.3 mile from landing; 6 sites, potable water, flush toilets), **Lakeview Campground** (0.3 mile from landing; 8 sites, potable water, flush toilets), **Harlequin Campground** (4.4 miles from landing; 7 sites, vault toilets, no running water but close to the river), and **Rainbow Bridge Campground** (4.5 miles from landing; pit toilets, no running water).

Ranger Station

North Cascades National Park's Golden West Visitor Center is in Stehekin, open hours subject to change (www.nps.gov/noca, 509-699-2080 ext. 14).

Most PCT hikers stop here to get the park's required overnight backcountry permit, only necessary if you're planning to camp between Stehekin and Rainy Pass.

Package/Cache Mailing Addresses

Stehekin Post Office
Your Name Here
PCT Hiker, ETA: mm/dd/yy
c/o General Delivery
Stehekin, WA 98852

The Stehekin Post Office (509-699-2015) is tiny and hours vary. Call ahead for current open hours. I met one ingenious PCT hiker who missed getting his cache because of the Labor Day closure, so he abandoned his package and instead bought every cinnamon roll at the Stehekin Pastry Company—and then ate them all the way to Canada. Stehekin is your last resupply point if you're headed for the border, so make sure you have your Canada-entry paperwork and the accepted ID in your possession, or have those essentials mailed to you here.

RAINY PASS AND ENVIRONS

There are no services at Rainy Pass, but day hikers flock to the area in summer via SR 20 (North Cascades Highway). Marblemount is the closest town to the west, roughly 52.5 miles from the pass. Mazama is 23 miles to the east. And the western-themed town of Winthrop—the largest of the lot—is 35.5 miles to the east. All three towns offer dining, lodging, and gas stations. Mazama and Winthrop are in the Methow Valley, which has a subculture of recreationalists who enjoy the area's ample rock climbing and mountain biking. You'll also find organic grocery stores and local breweries in this outdoor tourism mecca. Sadly, this area has been in the national spotlight due to the searing-hot, wind-driven wildfires that have taken the lives of seven firefighters over the last fourteen years. Despite the hardships, the camaraderie of the salt-of-the-earth residents and the unique landscape they call home are so welcoming that you might find yourself wanting to stay longer than just one night.

Transportation

Transportation to Rainy Pass is very limited. Classic Mountain Cabby (jtd2014.wix.com/classicmountaincabby, 509-996-2894) offers rides between Rainy Pass and the Methow Valley area, and the company's service area is huge—they'll gladly take you all the way from Seattle to the pass, or even up the remote, twisty dirt road to Harts Pass Campground.

Campgrounds

Campgrounds are plentiful throughout the Methow Valley. Contact the Okanogan-Wenatchee National Forest's Methow Valley Ranger District for those listed here and more (www.fs.usda.gov/activity/okawen/recreation/camping-cabins, 509-996-4000): **Early Winters Campground** (potable water, vault toilets), **Harts Pass Campground** (just 5 sites, vault toilets, no water), **Lone Fir Campground** (potable water, vault toilets), **Klipchuck Campground** (potable water, vault toilets).

Ranger Station

North Cascades National Park's Wilderness Information Center is in Marblemount (www.nps.gov/noca, 360-854-7245).

MANNING PARK LODGE (BRITISH COLUMBIA)

If you're fortunate enough to hike the PCT all the way to E. C. Manning Provincial Park, there are plenty of camping options as well as the quaint, woodsy Manning Park Lodge to welcome you.

Transportation

Greyhound recently cancelled bus services that stopped at Manning Park Lodge. Hikers must arrange rides with friends, family, hitchhike at their own risk, or hire an expensive private shuttle (www.vancouvershuttlehire.com).

Lodging and Campgrounds

Manning Park Lodge treats PCT hikers very well (www.manningpark.com, 1-800-330-3321;

pool, hot tub, sauna, steam; reservable cabins and rooms or a less expensive first-come, first-served hostel; pool facilities, complete with hot showers, are available to nonguests for a small fee, waived for PCT hikers who have just come off the trail). BC Parks (www.discovercamping.ca, 1-800-689-9025) operates **Cold Spring Campground** (to the right/east of PCT Trailhead on Gibson Pass Road and then 1.3 miles left/west on BC Highway 3; pit toilets, no showers; half the sites are first come, first served) and **Lightning Lake Campground** (2 miles left/west of PCT Trailhead on Gibson Pass Road; hot showers, flush toilets; reservations required).

Ranger Station

Manning Park Visitor Centre, operated by Manning Park Lodge, is 0.6 mile east of the lodge (https://manningpark.com, 604-668-5953). You'll find bathrooms, picnic areas, maps, camping and trail information, and interpretive displays.

A brand-new northern terminus monument recently replaced this aging one that had marked the end of the trail to throngs of hikers throughout the years.

INDEX

T

ABOUT THE AUTHOR

TAMI ASARS is a writer focused on outdoor recreation and nature photographer, living in the Cascade foothills of Washington State with her husband, Vilnis, and her rough collie, Scout. She is the author of *Hiking the Wonderland Trail* and *Day Hiking Mount Adams and Goat Rocks* (both for Mountaineers Books) and a contributor and columnist for *Washington Trails* magazine, as well as a host of other outdoor publications and online hiking resources. She is almost as passionate about nature photography as she is about hiking, and her photos have appeared in a variety of periodicals, including *City Dog*, *Washington Trails*, and *Washington Magazine*, as well as for the City of North Bend's branding campaign.

As an employee of REI (Recreational Equipment, Inc.), she taught classes for nearly nine years about outdoor pursuits like the where-to's and how-to's of backpacking, hiking, and long-distance trails. She has also served as a professional guide, teaching and showing people of all skill levels the wonders of backpacking in the Pacific Northwest.

When she's not in her office tapping away on her keyboard, you can find her on one of the many trails in Washington State from the rugged coastline to the dense green forests of the Cascade Range, where she's explored almost every nook and cranny. For more information, or to drop her a line, please visit www.tamiasars.com.

ABOUT THE SERIES

The Pacific Crest National Scenic Trail meanders north from California's border with Mexico to the entrance of Manning Provincial Park in British Columbia, on the Washington State–Canada border. This rigorous trail has evolved since its earliest envisioning in 1926 to encompass approximately 2650 miles, traveling through some of the West Coast's most stunning country. Now with the new series **Hiking the Pacific Crest Trail** hikers and other adventurers can enjoy beautiful, full-color guides to section hiking the entire trail.

- All new guides, focused on section hiking the PCT
- Each volume researched and created by an experienced hiker and backpacker
- Inspirational full-color guides with more than 150 photographs
- Section-by-section routes for day hikers, backpackers, and thru-hikers
- Four volumes in series: Washington and Oregon available now; Northern California and Southern California available in Fall 2017